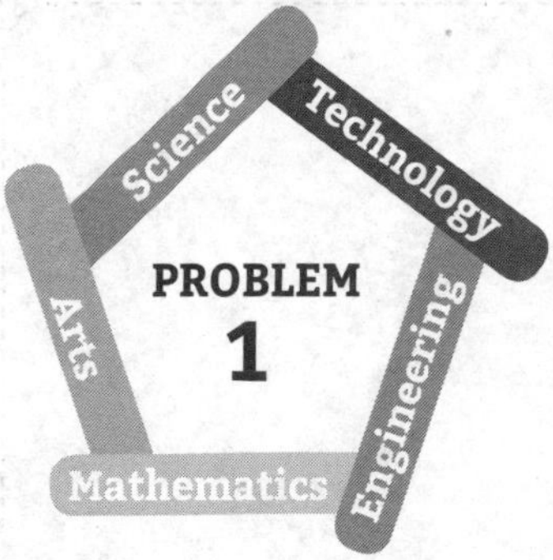

Ziad and his sister Tavleen visited a factory that manufactures metallic containers. They watched a crane pick up iron scrap from one place and drop it at another. They did some research on this and learned that such machines use electromagnets to move heavy pieces of scrap metal.

They want to learn more about electromagnets and create their own electromagnet. Help them collect some information on electromagnets and their properties. Also, help them create their own electromagnet.

Statement of the problem:

____

____

____

____

____

Research tips:

1. Solenoids
2. Electromagnets
3. Making a simple electromagnet
4. Strength of electromagnets
5. Polarity of electromagnets and direction of current

Gather information relevant for this problem.

1. ______________________________
   ____
2. ______________________________
   ____
3. ______________________________
   ____
4. ______________________________
   ____

Draw/Sketch your design.

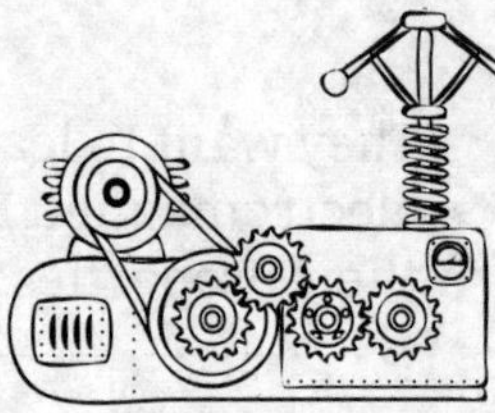

Materials required:

____

____

____

____

____

Construction (Write down the steps to construct your design):

1. ____
   ____
2. ____
   ____
3. ____
   ____
4. ____
   ____

Collins

National Curriculum Framework 2023
MIDDLE STAGE

SUPPLEMENTARY BOOKLET 7

Enhanced

Science Now

Revised Edition

Series Editor | Geetha Iyer

About the STEAM Activities

In the 21st century where the world is rapidly changing with sudden disruptions and unexpected real-world problems, being skilled in just one stream may not be enough. Many real-world problems can be solved only through interdisciplinary approach. Moreover, educationists have been emphasizing on the importance of subject integration and cross-curricular links. **Science**, **technology**, **engineering**, **arts** and **maths** (**STEAM**) education is one such approach where the integration of these five disciplines is utilized to solve real-world problems. Through this approach, a variety of skills such as critical thinking, creativity, innovation, communication, collaboration and entrepreneurship can be applied to make the students ready for the future, where these skills would be applicable in any field of study.

Students need to be introduced to STEAM education early on in life while their mind is still full of curiosity and imagination. STEAM education would not only help in producing tomorrow's designers and engineers, it would also help develop innovative mindsets and the ability to solve real-world problems. This would bring the students one step closer to becoming innovators or creators, not just passive consumers.

This supplementary booklet which comes along with the ***Enhanced Science Now, Revised Edition*** series, aims to introduce STEAM education to students from classes 1 to 8. There are two problems, based on ***real-world contexts***, in each booklet. The contexts have been carefully designed and mapped directly with the syllabus of each class. The students would be applying interdisciplinary concepts they have learnt in a class to find solution to the given problems. With each problem, research tips have been given to help in the initiation of idea. Clear directives have been given for students to identify the problem, research and record data, record their thinking, sketch their ideas, make observations and improve their designs or solutions as they work through creating the design or solving the problem.

This ***booklet*** is an attempt to give some form of exposure to STEAM education and its importance and benefits. We hope the students, while applying the concepts they have learnt to solve the real-world problems, would find their learning meaningful and thus be inspired to become future problem-solvers, critical thinkers, innovators or inventors.

Content Developed by Excelsoft Technologies Pvt Ltd.

Implementation of the prototype (Try out your model):

Step 1: ______________________________

Step 2: ______________________________

Step 3: ______________________________

Step 4: ______________________________

Observation (What worked? What did not work?):

____

____

____

____

____

Scope for improvement (How can you make it better?):

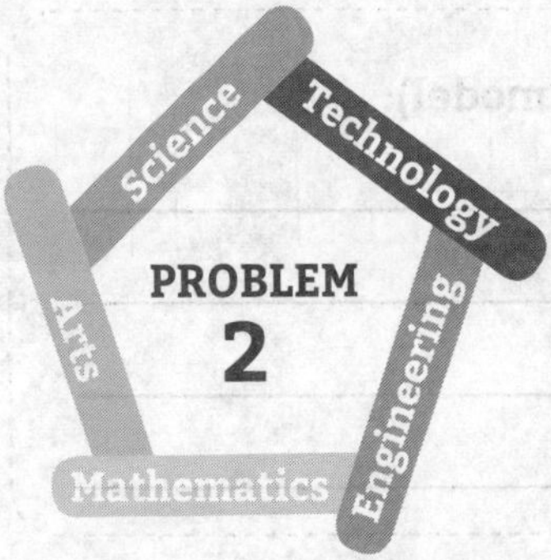

Ringsuwon and her classmates visited a weather station as part of an education trip from her school. There she observed various devices to measure the wind speed, humidity, temperature, rainfall, etc.

She wants to learn more about wind and measure wind speed using an anemometer. She wants to design a simple anemometer using materials available in her surroundings to measure the wind speed at the location of her house. Help Ringsuwon collect some information on an anemometer. Also, help her design and construct a simple anemometer. Use the same method to measure the speed of the wind.

Statement of the problem:

____

____

____

____

____

Research tips:

1. Wind speed
2. Measuring wind speed
3. Principle of an anemometer
4. Counting the number of rotations of a body about an axis in a given duration

Gather information relevant for this problem.

1. ______________________________

____

2. ______________________________

____

3. ______________________________

____

4. ______________________________

____

Draw/Sketch your design.

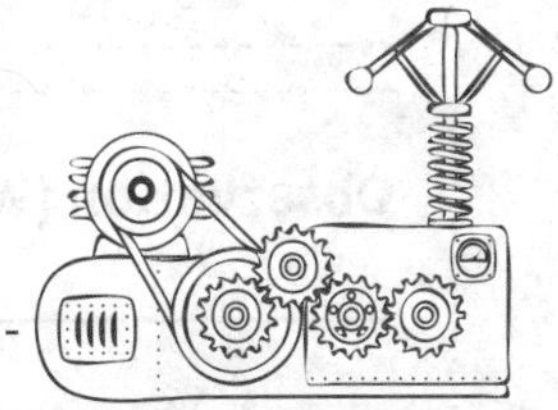

Materials required:

____

____

____

____

____

Construction (Write down the steps to construct your design):

1. ______________________________

____

2. ______________________________

____

3. ______________________________

____

4. ______________________________

____

Implementation of the prototype (Try out your model):

Step 1: ____________________

Step 2: ____________________

Step 3: ____________________

Step 4: ____________________

Observation (What worked? What did not work?):

____

____

____

____

____

Scope for improvement (How can you make it better?):

STEAM Vocabulary

Construction: The way in which a thing is built or put together

Implementation: Trying out/carrying out/experimenting

Prototype: A working model of a new product or a new version of an old product

Scope: Possibility

Assessment 1

CHAPTERS 1-5

(Maximum Marks = 10)

Choose the correct option. **(10 × 1 = 10)**

1. Insectivorous plants trap insects because they
   (a) do not contain chlorophyll.
   (b) do not perform photosynthesis.
   (c) grow in the soil that does not contain sufficient nitrogen.
   (d) have a different type of digestive system.

2. Which organ secretes salivary amylase, the digestive enzyme that breaks down carbohydrates into simple sugars?
   (a) Stomach (b) Liver (c) Pancreas (d) Salivary glands

3. What is the primary function of the abomasum in the digestive system?
   (a) Further breakdown of food into simpler compounds
   (b) Secretion of digestive juices
   (c) Absorption of nutrients
   (d) Excretion of undigested food

4. You are conducting an experiment to investigate the reaction between vinegar and baking soda. You observe gas bubbles being released when the two substances are mixed. To confirm the release of carbon dioxide, you decide to pass the gas through freshly prepared lime water. Which observation would confirm the release of carbon dioxide?
   (a) The lime water turns clear.
   (b) The lime water changes colour to yellow.
   (c) The lime water turns milky.
   (d) The lime water becomes fizzy.

5. Which statement best justifies why the process of crystallization is considered a physical change in context of separating salt from seawater?
   (a) Crystallization occurs when the boiled saltwater does not condense.
   (b) Crystallization is a result of the combination of salt and impurities.
   (c) Crystallization involves the formation of solid crystals through the rearrangement of salt molecules.
   (d) In crystallization, the salt molecules do not retain their chemical properties.

6. Which of the following is not a characteristic or behaviour of acids?
   (a) Acids are sour to taste.
   (b) Acids turn blue litmus red.
   (c) Acids can corrode metals.
   (d) Acids are insoluble in water.

7. Match the following.

i. Fungi	a. Autotroph
ii. Cuscuta	b. Insectivorous
iii. Pitcher	c. Parasite
iv. Touch-me-not	d. Saprophyte

(a) (i)-(d), (ii)-(c), (iii)-(b), (iv)-(a)
(b) (i)-(c), (ii)-(a), (iii)-(b), (iv)-(a)
(c) (i)-(a), (ii)-(d), (iii)-(c), (iv)-(b)
(d) (i)-(a), (ii)-(b), (iii)-(d), (iv)-(c)

8. What is the primary purpose of applying milk of magnesia on the affected area after an ant sting?
(a) To neutralize the acidic venom released by the ant sting
(b) To disinfect the affected area and prevent infection
(c) To increase the inflammation caused by the sting
(d) To prevent an allergic reaction to the ant sting

9. From which of the following breeds, a soft and lustrous wool fibre known as Mohair is obtained?
(a) Angora goat (b) Cashmere goat
(c) Merino sheep (d) Alpine goat

10. Which of the following processes is not a part of wool extraction?
(a) Shearing (b) Scouring
(c) Sorting (d) Reeling

How many questions did you answer correctly? Score yourself.

easy ☐ average ☐ advanced ☐ remembering ☐ understanding ☐ applying ☐
analysing ☐ evaluating ☐ creating ☐ justify ☐ associate ☐ analyse ☐
interpret/account for ☐ identification ☐ recognize ☐ select ☐ recall ☐

Assessment 2

CHAPTERS 6-9

(Maximum Marks = 10)

Choose the correct option. **(10 × 1 = 10)**

1. Which of the following liquids is filled in the bulb of thermometers?
   (a) Lead (b) Copper (c) Silver (d) Mercury
2. Which of these is an insulator of heat?
   (a) Steel (b) Copper (c) Rubber (d) Iron
3. How is heat loss through convection prevented in a thermos flask?
   (a) By the plastic or stainless-steel outer casing
   (b) By the shiny surface of the walls
   (c) By the vacuum between the two walls
   (d) All of these
4. **Assertion (A):** Respiration is also called the universal chemical process.
   Reason (R): Every living cell respires to survive.
   (a) A is true, but R is false.
   (b) Both A and R are true, but R is not the correct explanation of A.
   (c) Both A and R are true, and R is the correct explanation of A.
   (d) A is false, but R is true.
5. Which of the following statements is true regarding the switch from aerobic to anaerobic respiration in muscle cells during vigorous exercise?
   (a) Muscle cells produce alcohol during aerobic respiration.
   (b) Lactic acid is produced during anaerobic respiration.
   (c) Only carbon dioxide is produced during aerobic respiration.
   (d) Muscle cramps are caused by the accumulation of carbon dioxide in muscle cells.
6. Which of the following animals possesses blubber under its skin?
   (a) Elephant (b) Seal (c) Arctic fox (d) Red eyed frog
7. Which of the following completes the given analogy?
   Arctic fox : Polar region :: Fennec Fox : ____________
   (a) Temperate climate (b) Tropical climate
   (c) Deserts (d) Polar
8. **Assertion (A):** The polar bear has long curved and sharp claws.
   Reason (R): These help polar bear to walk on snow.
   (a) A is true, but R is false.
   (b) Both A and R are true, but R is not the correct explanation of A.
   (c) Both A and R are true, and R is the correct explanation of A.
   (d) A is false, but R is true.

9. What is the reason behind red soil developing a reddish colour?
   (a) Overgrazing
   (b) The presence of potash and magnesia
   (c) The presence of iron
   (d) The presence of copper

10. A dark organic matter that forms in soil when plant and animal matter decays is called ________________.
   (a) clay (b) humus (c) sand (d) silt

How many questions did you answer correctly? Score yourself.

easy	average	advanced	remembering	understanding	applying
analysing	evaluating	creating	justify	associate	analyse
interpret/account for	identification	recognize	select	recall	

Assessment 3

CHAPTERS 10–14

(Maximum Marks = 10)

Choose the correct option. **(10 × 1 = 10)**

1. Which of the following completes the given analogy?
   Red Blood Cells : Erythrocytes :: White Blood Cells : __________
   (a) Thrombocytes
   (b) Leucocytes
   (c) Lymphocytes
   (d) Monocytes

2. Which of the following is not needed to measure a patient's heart rate?
   (a) Palpating the patient's pulse
   (b) Using a heart rate monitor
   (c) Using an electrocardiogram
   (d) Measuring the temperature of the patient's body

3. Which of the following completes the given analogy?
   Rhizome : Water lily :: Corm : __________
   (a) Colocasia
   (b) Ginger
   (c) Tulip
   (d) Potato

4. **Assertion (A):** Fertilization occurs when the male gamete fuses with the female gamete inside the ovule.
   Reason (R): A zygote is formed as the first cell of the new organism.
   (a) A is true, but R is false.
   (b) Both A and R are true, but R is not the correct explanation of A.
   (c) Both A and R are true, and R is the correct explanation of A.
   (d) A is false, but R is true.

5. If the speed of an object along a straight line keeps changing, its motion is said to be __________.
   (a) uniform
   (b) non-uniform
   (c) circular
   (d) linear

6. The time required for a bus to cover a distance of 12 km at a speed of 40 m/s is __________.
   (a) 250 s
   (b) 480 s
   (c) 300 s
   (d) 174 s

7. When an electrical switch is in the OFF position, the electric circuit is said to be __________.
   (a) closed
   (b) open
   (c) complete
   (d) both 1 and 3

8. If the flow of an electric current produces heat in a conductor, it is called __________ effect of current.
   (a) magnetic
   (b) chemical
   (c) mechanical
   (d) heating

9. Choose the incorrect statement related to electromagnets.
   (a) An electromagnet works on the magnetic effect of current.
   (b) Only iron is used for making electromagnets.
   (c) An electromagnet can be made strong by increasing the number of turns in the coil.
   (d) Steel is used for making electromagnets.

10. Wind currents are generated due to __________ of the earth's surface.
   (a) cooling (b) uneven heating
   (c) uniform heating (d) none of the above

How many questions did you answer correctly? Score yourself.

easy	average	advanced	remembering	understanding	applying
analysing	evaluating	creating	justify	associate	analyse
interpret/account for	identification	recognize	select	recall	

Assessment 4

CHAPTERS 15-18

(Maximum Marks = 10)

Choose the correct option. **(10 × 1 = 10)**

1. The path of light is always __________.
   (a) a straight line
   (b) a curved line
   (c) a zigzag line
   (d) dependent on the medium
2. Which of the following mirrors is used as a shaving mirror?
   (a) Plane mirror
   (b) Convex mirror
   (c) Concave mirror
   (d) Spherical mirror
3. Newton's disc is a disc with seven colours. On rotating, it appears __________.
   (a) green
   (b) blue
   (c) black
   (d) white
4. Which of the following sources of water is not used for growing crops?
   (a) Lake
   (b) River
   (c) Ocean
   (d) Pond
5. **Assertion (A):** Conversion of a solid into a liquid on heating is known as melting.
   Reason (R): The process in which water changes into water vapour on heating is known as evaporation.
   (a) A is true, but R is false.
   (b) Both A and R are true, but R is not the correct explanation of A.
   (c) Both A and R are true, and R is the correct explanation of A.
   (d) A is false, but R is true.
6. Which of the following is not a source of wastewater?
   (a) Sewers
   (b) Homes
   (c) Industries
   (d) Hospitals
7. Sewage consists mainly of __________.
   (a) liquid waste
   (b) solid waste
   (c) gaseous waste
   (d) mixture of solid and gaseous waste
8. Canopy is the topmost layer consisting of __________.
   (a) leaves and branches of tall trees
   (b) shrubs and tall grasses
   (c) tall trees and tall grasses
   (d) decaying leaves, fruits and seeds

9. **Assertion (A):** Depletion of forests causes a lot of danger.
Reason (R): Forests are vital for the quality of life and environment.
(a) A is true, but R is false.
(b) Both A and R are true, but R is not the correct explanation of A.
(c) Both A and R are true, and R is the correct explanation of A.
(d) A is false, but R is true.

10. Which group of living organisms given below is a link in the food chain between green plants and hawk?
(a) Grasshopper, frog and snake
(b) Grains, rat and snake
(c) Millipedes, centipedes and sparrow
(d) Earthworm, hen and rat

How many questions did you answer correctly? Score yourself.

easy ☐ average ☐ advanced ☐ remembering ☐ understanding ☐ applying ☐

analysing ☐ evaluating ☐ creating ☐ justify ☐ associate ☐ analyse ☐

interpret/account for ☐ identification ☐ recognize ☐ select ☐ recall ☐

Global Citizenship Education

WEALTH AND POVERTY IN SOCIETY

Look at the given picture. This is Kanha with his mother and infant brother. They do not have any house to live in and hardly get enough food to eat. Do you think Kanha and his brother would have the same future as yours? Write your views.

Kanha's mother cannot afford food and shelter for her children. Would she be able to provide her children with good education?

Poverty is a complex term and may have a different meaning for different people. **Relative poverty** is when people can just afford basic necessities but are unable to meet the society's average living standards. **Extreme poverty** is when people cannot afford basic necessities such as adequate food, clean water, safe shelter and access to healthcare. **Subjective poverty** is when the actual income of people cannot meet their expectations and perceptions.

What are wealth and poverty according to you?

Give one example for each type of poverty.

GLOBAL DIGITAL CITIZENSHIP TO REDUCE POVERTY

What do you think of global digital citizenship?

How can global digital citizenship help reduce poverty in society? Complete the following chart.

Global Digital Citizenship Fighting Poverty

Online Education and Skill Development

Digital Inclusion

Collaboration and Knowledge Sharing

Job Opportunities and Entrepreneurship

Advocacy and Awareness

Financial Inclusion

My Global Actions!

My Thought Bubble!

Write the words that come to your mind when you think of the consequences of global poverty in the thought bubble given here.

My Thinking Circle!

Discuss with your classmates the ways you can contribute to reduce poverty in society. Write the major points in the given space.

My Action Plan!

How can you combine science with digital learning to reduce poverty in the society? Elaborate your action plan in the given space.

Skills You Need

FINANCIAL LITERACY

Finance is the money resources or the income of a nation, organization or person. Even your pocket money or allowances are finance. To be financially literate is to know how to manage your money. Managing your money is a personal skill that benefits you throughout your life. Thus, ***financial literacy** is the ability to use knowledge and skills to manage financial resources effectively.*

FINANCIAL LITERACY LEADS TO LONG-TERM FINANCIAL SUCCESS	Studies show that financial account experience at an early age can shape a young person's habits in a way that can last a lifetime.

WHY IS FINANCIAL LITERACY IMPORTANT?

Every stage of life can help us prepare for a more financially secure future. It provides us with in-depth knowledge on financial education and strategies that would help in achieving financial growth and success. This means learning the importance of paying our bills on time, how to borrow and save money responsibly. It is never too early to start. It is proven that people with appropriate financial education and knowledge make better financial plans. They make the most of the available financial resources to achieve maximum benefit.

Saving up

Budgeting

Setting goals

Spending wisely

Financial Literacy in Real Life

We can use the concepts of financial literacy in our day-to-day life and find opportunities for saving money in almost all walks of life.

- Compare the average prices of the items you purchase on a regular basis at different stores.
- Save on electricity, gas, air conditioning and water bills by being more mindful about how energy is used in our homes or apartments.
- Save on transportation expenses by riding a bicycle to nearby places.

Career Exploration

- Investment Banker
- Public Accounting
- Financial Planner
- Insurance Investigator
- Risk Manager

WHAT CAN YOU DO?

1. CREATE BUDGETS

Creating a budget will enable you to know how much you are spending and how much you can save.

2. SPEND WISELY

Spend your pocket money wisely. For example, a burger at a restaurant can cost five times more than the burger you make at home.

3. SAVE

Save at least 10–15% of your pocket money. You can even consider opening a savings account with the help of your parents.

4. SET GOALS

Set goals for yourself. Setting goals will help you save efficiently to afford the things you want the most.

FINANCE CLASS

Demonstration: Cost Savings Through Choice of Light Bulb

We need: Dry cell, incandescent bulb, CFL, wires, switch

Procedure: With the help of an adult, make two circuits using the cell and a switch. Use an incandescent bulb in one circuit, and a CFL bulb in the other circuit. Now turn on the switches of both circuits. Let both the bulbs glow.

Observation: The CFL lasts much longer than the incandescent bulb.

Conclusion: CFLs use one-third of the electricity and last longer than incandescent bulbs.

Replace all the incandescent bulbs with CFLs in your home. You will see a noticeable change in your electricity bill. By doing so, you can do your part in reducing carbon emissions.

Try It!

Find out other ways of reducing energy consumption. Think of its financial and environmental benefits.

Happiness Activity Sheets

LIVING IN AN INTERCONNECTED SOCIETY

All the physical objects that are in solid, liquid or gaseous state, either living or non-living, are collectively termed as nature. There exists a dynamic balance and self-regulation among all these physical objects or units. These units are categorized into four categories: materials, plants, animals and human beings.

Materials

The big land masses of the continents, gigantic water bodies (seas and oceans), metals and minerals, all fall into this category. This category provides water, fossil fuels, metals, non-metals, etc., to other categories.

Plants

Shrubs, herbs and trees constitute this category. They provide food for the other categories. Plants decay and turn into fossil fuels.

Human Beings

Human beings exhale carbon dioxide which is used by plants. Humans, like animals and plants, decay and turn into fossil fuels.

Animals

Animals, birds, insects, etc., form the third largest category. They help in pollination and help human beings carry out production and transportation activities.

We can see that all four categories are interconnected and coexist with each other. However, humans have not understood the harmony that exists between these categories. Humans exploit natural resources, animals and plants for their leisure and economic activities. Consequently, we have disturbed ourselves and also the balance among the other three categories.

Are you aware of your feelings?

How do you feel knowing that we are harming nature? Write 3–4 words that best describe your feelings in this thought bubble.

How mindful are you?

Do you know there are little habits we mindlessly practise every day without even realizing the negative effect they have on our planet? Reflect on and write down any such five habits.
How would you rectify these bad habits so as to help restore balance in our interconnected world?

What about a role play?

Arrange your class into groups. Let each group play a category of an interrelated society. What issues do you want to highlight in your play? Write your script in the post-it provided alongside. Start your role play!

Vernacular Names

Anteater • Assamese: *Bon-rou* • Bengali: *Ayantiyetara* • Hindi: *Chitikhor* • Kannada: *Chippu handi, Antitar* • Malayalam: *Urumputini* • Marathi: *khawlyaa manjar, Amtietara* • Tamil: *Alangu/ Azhungu, Antittar* • Telugu: *Eenampechi, pipilikabhaksini* • Urdu: *Anteater*

Arctic fox • Bengali: *Sumeru seyala* • Hindi: *Safed lomri* • Kannada: *Hima nari* • Meiteilon: *Angouba lamhui* • Marathi: *Artika kolha* • Malayalam: *Arttik kurukkan* • Mizo: *Safed lomdi* • Tamil: *Arktik nari* • Telugu: *Arktik nakka* • Urdu: *Patak shumali ki lomadi*

Cocklebur • Assamese: *Agora* • Bengali: *Cocklebur* • Hindi: *Chota dhatura* • Kannada: *Kaklebar* • Meiteilon: *Samnappi* • Marathi: *Koklebara* • Malayalam: *Keakkbur* • Tamil: *Ceval* • Telugu: *Cocklebur* • Urdu: *Gokhro*

Cotton plant • Assamese: *Kapaha* • Bengali: *Suti gacha* • Hindi: *Kapaas* • Kannada: *Hatti sasya* • Malayalam: *Keattan planr* • Meiteilon: *Lashing pambi* • Marathi: *Suit vanaspati* • Mizo: *La* • Tamil: *Paruthi alai* • Telugu: *Patti mokka* • Urdu: *Kapas ka Darakht*

Dandelion • Bengali: *Pitachumi* • Hindi: *Sinhaparnee* • Kannada: *Kadu shavanthi* • Meiteilon: *Tera paibi* • Marathi: *dudhll* • Malayalam: *Dugddhapheni* • Tamil: *Tenteliyan* • Telugu: *Patri* • Urdu: *Bathur*

Fern • Assamese: *Dhekia xak* • Bengali: *Pharnanga* • Hindi: *Farn* • Kannada: *Jarigida* • Meiteilon: *Lai-changkhrang* • Marathi: *Pharna* • Malayalam: *Phen* • Tamil: *Hpern* • Telugu: *Phern*

Frog • Assamese: *Bhikuli* • Bengali: Byana • Hindi: *Medhak* • Kannada: *Kappe* • Meiteilon: *Hang-ngoi* • Marathi: *Beduka* • Malayalam: *Tavala* • Mizo: *Leptolalax tamdil* • Tamil: *Tavali* • Telugu: *Kappa* • Urdu: *Meyndak*

Honeybee • Assamese: *Maumakhi* • Bengali: *Maumachi* • Hindi: *Madhumakkhee* • Kannada: *Jenu nona* • Meiteilon: *Khoi mapee* • Marathi: *Madhamasi* • Malayalam: *Tenicca* • Tamil: *Teni* • Telugu: *Tenetiga* • Urdu: *Shehed ki mukki*

Llama• Assamese: *Lama* • Bengali: *Lama* • Hindi: *Llama* • Kannada: *Lama* • Malayalam: *Lama* • Marathi: *Lama* • Tamil: *Lama* • Telugu: *Lama* • Urdu: Lama

Neem tree • Assamese: *Nima jad* • Bengali: *Neem gacha* • Hindi: *Neem ke ped* • Kannada: *Bevina mara* • Meiteilon: *Neem pambi* • Marathi: *Kadunimbachi Jadha* • Malayalam: *Maram etukuka* • Mizo: *Nim-thing* • Tamil: *Maram etuttuk kollunkal* • Telugu: *Vepa chettu* • Urdu: *Name ka darakht*

Sweet potato • Assamese: *Mitha alu* • Bengali: *Misti alu* • Hindi: *Shakarakand* • Kannada: *Sihi alugedde, sihi genasu* • Meiteilon: *Manggara angangba* • Marathi: *Ratale* • Malayalam: *Madhurakkilann* • Tamil: *Inipu urulaikkilanku* • Telugu: *Chilagadadumpa* • Urdu: *Methi shakarakandi*

Tamarind tree • Assamese: *Teteli* • Bengali: *Temtula gacha* • Hindi: *Imli ka ped* • Kannada: *Hunase mara* • Meiteilon: *Mang-ge* • Marathi: *Cincece jhada* • Malayalam: *Pulimaram* • Mizo: *Tengtere* • Tamil: *Puli maram* • Telugu: *Chintapandu chettu* • Urdu: *Imuli ka pedh*

What do you call these plants and animals in your language? Share the names with us at **schoolsupport@harpercollins.co.in.**

Collins

Enhanced

Science Now

Revised Edition

A Science Textbook based on Holistic Learning Theory

7

Name : ....

Grade : .... Section : ....

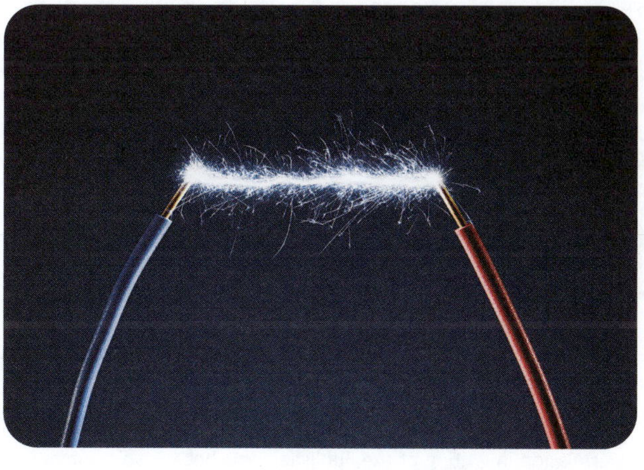

Picture me as a speedy traveler, racing through wires at almost the speed of light, powering your lights and devices instantly. My magical touch creates magnetic fields, bringing motors and MRI machines to life. With my shocking power and helpful applications, I illuminate your world with electrifying brilliance!

What am I? ....

Series Editor | Geetha Iyer

HarperCollins*Publishers*

Publishing operations in 17 countries and 120+ imprints globally

William Collins' dream of knowledge for all began with the publication of his first book in 1819. A self-educated mill worker, he not only enriched millions of lives, but also founded a flourishing publishing house. Today, staying true to this spirit, Collins books are packed with inspiration, innovation and practical expertise. They place you at the centre of a world of possibility and give you exactly what you need to explore it.

Published by Collins Learning
An imprint of HarperCollins*Publishers* India
Building No. 10, Tower A, 4th Floor, DLF Cyber City, Gurugram, Haryana 122002, India

First edition: 2024
Reprint edition: 2024
ISBN: 978-93-6213-241-3

Content developed by **Excelsoft Technologies Pvt Ltd.**
Artwork, typesetting and layout by **AptaraCorp Ltd., Mammoth Studioz Ltd, iBook Services**
Printed and bound in India by Thomson Press India Ltd

ACKNOWLEDGEMENTS

Title Page: Jorg Greuel

Inside: Page **5:** grafikazpazurem, Enis Aksoy, bsd studio; **6:** Qvasimodo, Qvasimodo; **9:** dominique landau; **11:** work by Lisa Kling; **12:** Julia Pivovarova; **13:** TwilightArtPictures, Gio.tto, dabjola; **14:** Max Sudakov, Raimundas; **20:** Douglas Sacha; **22:** wrangel, BarnabyChambers, 802290022, Backiris, towlake, BirdHunter591; **24:** JackF; **34:** ROHAN RAVINDRAN, slavadubrovin, Riza Azhari; **35:** Giordano Cipriani, Eniko Balogh, vichie81; **36:** John Carnemolla, saiva, snow_wons; **37:** aleksandr hunta, Milosz_G, andreanord, Jarry, Eric Isselee, kamalrana; **41:** neil hardwick; Sofi aworld, Eric Isselee; **43:** f9photos; **48:** andreanord, John Carnemolla, Eric Isselee; **49:** Victoria Bee Photography; **50:** Krasowit, Coprid, Humannet; **53:** Georgios Kollidas; **61:** talseN, Alexander Kazantsev; **62:** Dchauy, Nick_Nick; **64:** T.W. van Urk; **68:** talseN, Dchauy; **69:** Weiquan Lin, Evgenyi, **70:** apiguide, anurakss, joloei, Alina Cardiae Photography, FocalPoint, **71:** Eko Saputro / 500px, Sea Wave, ultimathule; **74:** oksana2010, Diana Taliun; **76:** Raimundas; **77:** Jasni; **78:** Georgios Kollidas; **79:** Aryo Hadi; **86:** Sjo, Photo by Tanvir Ibna Shafi; **87:** M. Unal Ozmen, gresei, Ase, gadag; **89:** Tatiana; **90:** Popova, Science Photo Library; **91:** Lipskiy; **93:** John Kasawa, igor.stevanovic; **97:** ttsz; **101:** Easy_Asa, John Kasawa, Darryl Vest; **102:** by Marc Guitard, Alvaro Espinoza Fotografía, dan tarradellas; **103:** Vaclav Volrab, Vadym Zaitsev, Skreidzeleu; **105:** Darren Pullman, maximult, Steve Heap; **111:** Alexander W Helin, Mark Newman; **112:** neelsky, Christopher Wood; Nicram Sabod, airn; **113:** hagit berkovich, Bernhard Richter Gillian Holliday; **117:** Nicram Sabod, airn, neelsky, Christopher Wood; **118:** Paul Souders; **120:** Guenter Fischer, Boy_Anupong, Hannares; **124:** Carlos Neto, PrairieArtProject, Tom Grundy; **135:** pixelfusion3d; **138:** Miles Boyer; **151:** iShootPhotosLLC, Prasert Krainukul, Martin Harvey; **152:** blueringmedia; **158:** GlobalStock; **162:** Kudryavtsev Pavel; **171:** Ed Reschke; **175:** Macrovector; **176:** Brian A Jackson, dimitris_k; **177:** FancyTapis, blueringmedia; **178:** Przemek Klos, Ethan Daniels, chinahbzyg, Oksana Alekseeva; **183:** Robbie Goodall; **185:** Alex Hubenov; **187:** Judy Crawford; **188:** ttsz; **190:** Yulia Glam; **196:** ADA_photo; **197:** messenjah, martin-dm, HstrongART; **198:** Papacool, Smileus, Zeljko Radojko; **201:** imagedb.com, LoopAll; **209:** adventtr, Fahroni, ImageMediaGroup; **210:** Marafona, Harvepino, Sergey Nivens; **211:** Marcel Jancovic, Cynthia Farmer; **218:** Harvepino; **219:** Sergey Nivens; **224:** natasaadzic; **225:** jesadaphorn, Boris Sosnovyy; **227:** HHakim; **232:** Kochneva Tetyana, Georgios Kollidas; **237:** Mats Silvan, roman makhmutov, jamesbenet; **238:** Lee Torrens, Janis Smits, Paisarn Praha; **245:** Alain Lauga, Ajay Bhaskar; **247:** Nagendra Yadav, Max Lindenthaler; **252:** Max Lindenthaler; **253:** Francesco Bergamaschi, filo; **254:** nadisja; Chukcha, seeyou, Grigoriev Ruslan; **255:** Denys Kurylow, Jakkrit Orrasri, Lightcraft Studio, **256:** Pi-Lens, Dr. Morley Read; **257:** Mopic, Eric Isselee, Chros, Eric Isselee; **260:** Sensvector; **270:** mylisa, Abramov Timur; **279:** mylisa, Abramov Timur; **280:** Boaz Rottem, lacer, VanWyckExpress

Supplementary Booklet: Pia Kolle, Icon_Craft_Studio, Olesia Kononenko, Julia_Sudnitskaya, colematt, lemono, mona, leosapiens, AlionaManakova, EllenM, AlionaManakova, Qvasimodo, AlionaManakova, sarunyu_foto, eliflamra, Mike Hill, retales botijero, vasiliki, PIER

Browse the complete Collins catalogue at www.collins.in.
For any queries/feedback, please write to us at SCHOOLSUPPORT@harpercollins.co.in.

Preface

Enhanced Science Now, Revised Edition is a transformative three-book series designed for Classes 6 to 8, aiming to provide students with a holistic and forward-looking learning experience. Embracing the principles of the **National Education Policy (NEP) 2020** and **National Curriculum Framework (NCF) 2023**, this series goes beyond traditional learning approaches to prepare students for the multifaceted challenges of the 21st century.

In this dynamic era, our students face both unprecedented challenges and opportunities that demand a deeper understanding of their role in shaping the world. As educators, we recognize the need to equip them with essential skills, knowledge and a growth mindset to navigate the complexities of modern life successfully.

Our series is founded on the principles of **Holistic Learning Theory**, guiding students to explore their identities, purpose and connection with the community and the environment. Through a strong core content in science, we foster intellectual, emotional, social, artistic, moral and spiritual development, nurturing well-rounded individuals who contribute positively to society.

Innovative features in the series encourage interdisciplinary projects, instill a scientific temper, promote vocational skills and cultivate regional and cultural sensitivities. The series prioritizes **Global Citizenship Education (GCED)** and emphasizes the value of **India's diverse knowledge systems**.

We extend our heartfelt gratitude to all the teachers and educationists who passionately reviewed our books and offered their invaluable feedback. Their contributions have elevated the quality of our content, which will enhance the overall learning experience for students.

Feedback, comments and suggestions from users are always welcome as we continue to strive for excellence in education and better serve the needs of our young learners. Together, let's shape a brighter future for education.

Authors

About the Series Editor

Dr Geetha Iyer is the Former Head of Sahyadri School KFI, Pune. She is an author, a naturalist and consultant in the twin fields of education and environment. She is a curriculum specialist with many years of experience in concept development and regularly conducts workshops on all aspects of teaching science.

Key Features

Enhanced Science Now Revised Edition aligns with the **National Education Policy (NEP) 2020** and the **National Curriculum Framework (NCF) 2023**, promoting holistic education. It focuses on developing intellectual, physical, cognitive, emotional and social skills. With features such as Cognitive Corner, Life Skills, Worksheets and a Supplementary Booklet that contains STEAM Activities, Skills You Need, Happiness Activity Sheets, Vernacular Names, GCED and Assessments, it fosters experiential learning, innovative thinking and creativity. Additionally, the series raises awareness of the Sustainable Development Goals (SDGs) to address global challenges.

Learn more about SDGs at https://www.un.org/sustainabledevelopment/.

The Holistic Learning Theory

Physical

- Gross motor skills
- Psychomotor skills

- Projects
- STEAM Activities

Intellectual

Bloom's Taxonomy

- Remembering
- Understanding
- Applying
- Analysing
- Evaluating
- Creating

- Summary
- Exercise

- Cognitive Corner
- Worksheet
- Skills You Need
- STEAM Activities

Social

- Coordination
- Working in a team
- Interaction with others
- Social competencies
- Communication with others

- Worksheets
- Vernacular Names
- Life Skills
- STEAM Activities

Emotional

- Empathy
- Self-regulation
- Interpersonal (others)
- Intra-personal (self)

- Life Skills
- Happiness Activity Sheets
- GCED

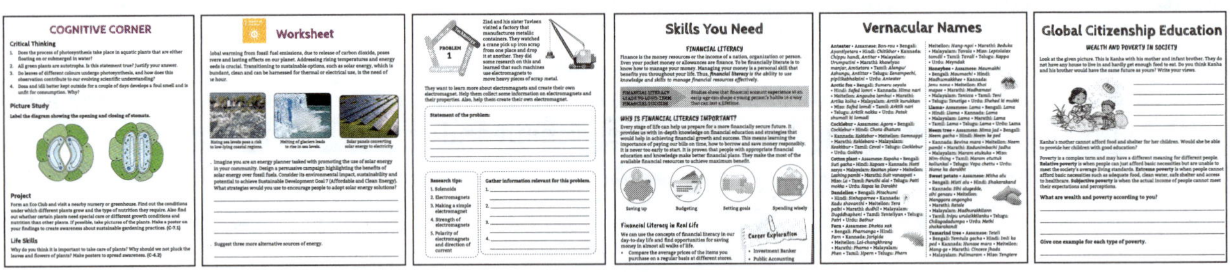

Collins | SUSTAINABLE DEVELOPMENT GOALS

Collins Learning supports the Sustainable Development Goals

Comprehensive Assessment

The assessment papers employ MCQs tagged with icons to indicate competencies such as Difficulty Levels, Bloom's Taxonomy and Science Learning Skills. Each assessment comes along with a scorecard for self-assessment.

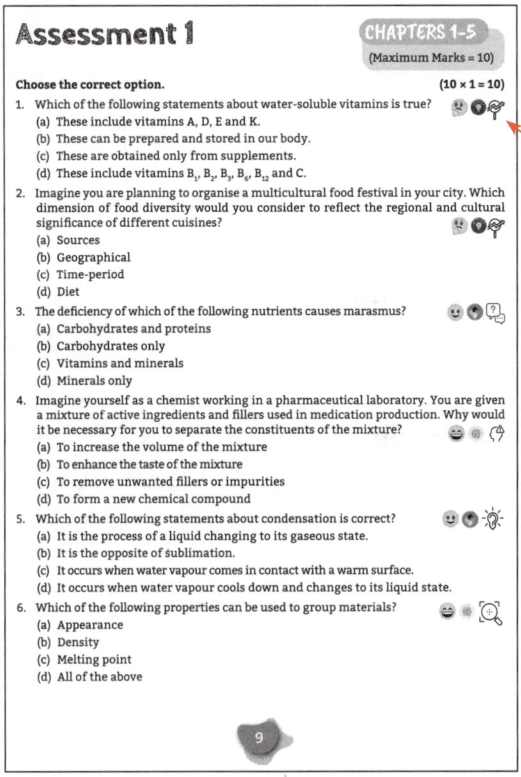

Assessment 1

CHAPTERS 1-5

(Maximum Marks = 10)

Choose the correct option. **(10 × 1 = 10)**

1. Which of the following statements about water-soluble vitamins is true?
   (a) These include vitamins A, D, E and K.
   (b) These can be prepared and stored in our body.
   (c) These are obtained only from supplements.
   (d) These include vitamins B_1, B_2, B_3, B_6, B_{12} and C.
2. Imagine you are planning to organise a multicultural food festival in your city. Which dimension of food diversity would you consider to reflect the regional and cultural significance of different cuisines?
   (a) Sources
   (b) Geographical
   (c) Time-period
   (d) Diet
3. The deficiency of which of the following nutrients causes marasmus?
   (a) Carbohydrates and proteins
   (b) Carbohydrates only
   (c) Vitamins and minerals
   (d) Minerals only
4. Imagine yourself as a chemist working in a pharmaceutical laboratory. You are given a mixture of active ingredients and fillers used in medication production. Why would it be necessary for you to separate the constituents of the mixture?
   (a) To increase the volume of the mixture
   (b) To enhance the taste of the mixture
   (c) To remove unwanted fillers or impurities
   (d) To form a new chemical compound
5. Which of the following statements about condensation is correct?
   (a) It is the process of a liquid changing to its gaseous state.
   (b) It is the opposite of sublimation.
   (c) It occurs when water vapour comes in contact with a warm surface.
   (d) It occurs when water vapour cools down and changes to its liquid state.
6. Which of the following properties can be used to group materials?
   (a) Appearance
   (b) Density
   (c) Melting point
   (d) All of the above

9

Icons

Scorecard

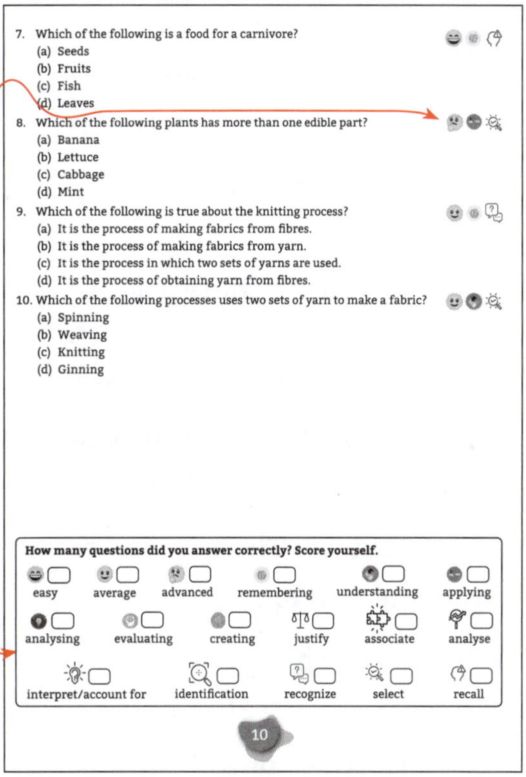

7. Which of the following is a food for a carnivore?
   (a) Seeds
   (b) Fruits
   (c) Fish
   (d) Leaves
8. Which of the following plants has more than one edible part?
   (a) Banana
   (b) Lettuce
   (c) Cabbage
   (d) Mint
9. Which of the following is true about the knitting process?
   (a) It is the process of making fabrics from fibres.
   (b) It is the process of making fabrics from yarn.
   (c) It is the process in which two sets of yarns are used.
   (d) It is the process of obtaining yarn from fibres.
10. Which of the following processes uses two sets of yarn to make a fabric?
   (a) Spinning
   (b) Weaving
   (c) Knitting
   (d) Ginning

How many questions did you answer correctly? Score yourself.

easy | average | advanced | remembering | understanding | applying
analysing | evaluating | creating | justify | associate | analyse
interpret/account for | identification | recognize | select | recall

10

Competencies and Icons in Assessment Papers

Difficulty levels

easy

average

advanced

Bloom's Taxonomy

remembering

understanding

applying

analysing

evaluating

creating

Science Learning Skills

justify

identification

associate

recognize

analyse

select

interpret/ account for

recall

Contents

Unit 1 Food

1. Nutrition in Plants 7
2. Nutrition in Animals 21

Unit 2 Materials

3. Fibre to Fabric 35
4. Physical and Chemical Changes 50
5. Acids, Bases and Salts 70
6. Heat and Temperature 87

Unit 3 The World of the Living

7. Weather, Climate and Adaptations of Animals to Climate 103
8. Soil 119
9. Respiration in Organisms 136
10. Transportation of Substances in Plants and Animals 152
11. Reproduction in Plants 169

Unit 4 Moving Things, People and Ideas

12. Time and Motion 184

Unit 5 How Things Work

13. Electric Current and its Effects 198

Unit 6 Natural Phenomena

14. Winds, Storms and Cyclones 210
15. Light 225

Unit 7 Natural Resources

16. Water 238
17. Forests: Our Lifeline 254
18. Wastewater Management 268

1 Nutrition in Plants

Curricular Goals

- Explore the living world in scientific terms **(CG-3)**
- Explore the nature and processes of science through engaging with the evolution of scientific knowledge and conducting scientific inquiry **(CG-6)**

Competencies

- Analyse patterns of relationships between living organisms and their environments in terms of dependence on and response to each other **(C-3.3)**
- Explain the conditions suitable for sustaining life on Earth **(C-3.4)**
- Formulate questions using scientific terminology and collect data as evidence **(C-6.2)**

Let's Get Started

A plant has different parts that function together to keep it alive: the root, the stem, the leaves, flowers, fruits and seeds.

The following are pictures of the various stages of plant growth. Number the stages in the correct order.

All living organisms need food in order to stay alive, grow, repair worn-out cells and reproduce. *The process by which living organisms obtain nutrients for their growth and development is called* ***nutrition***. Food is the source of nutrients. Just like animals and human beings, plants also need nutrients to grow and survive.

NUTRITION IN PLANTS

Nutrition in plants can be of two types: autotrophic nutrition and heterotrophic nutrition.

Autotrophic Nutrition

Most plants have green leaves. The green colour is due to the presence of a pigment called **chlorophyll** in them. Leaves that have chlorophyll trap the energy from the sun and make their own food. Such mode of nutrition wherein the food is made by the organism itself is called **autotrophic nutrition** (*auto:* self; *troph:* nourishment). *The organisms capable of making their own food are called* ***autotrophs***.

All green plants are autotrophs. They make their own food by a process called **photosynthesis**.

Photosynthesis

a

The word *photo* means 'light' and *synthesis* means 'putting together'. Photosynthesis, therefore, involves putting together carbon dioxide, water and minerals to make food in the presence of sunlight and chlorophyll. The essential ingredients are collected by the plant from its surroundings. These ingredients are discussed below.

Water and minerals: The root system in plants helps in absorption of water and minerals from the soil. These are carried to the other parts of the plant through tubular structures (tissues) called **xylem**.

Carbon dioxide: The leaves of plants absorb carbon dioxide from the atmosphere. Carbon dioxide is absorbed through minute openings on the underside of the leaves called **stomata**. Stomata (singular: stoma) are surrounded on either side by bean-shaped guard cells (Fig. 1.1). When water is taken up into the leaves, it enters the guard cells and causes them to swell. The guard cells expand and are pulled apart, creating the gap or an opening, which is called a stoma. When water is lost from the guard cells, they shrink and the gap is closed. Gases such as carbon dioxide and oxygen are exchanged via stomata.

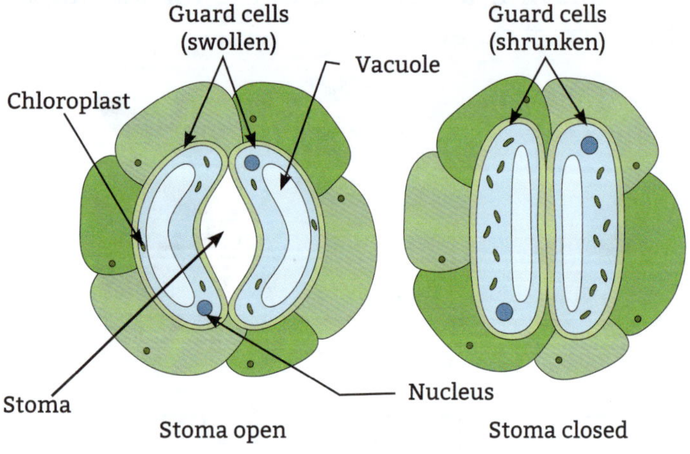

Fig. 1.1: The opening and closing of stomata

Light: Chlorophyll, the green pigment present in the leaves, helps in the absorption of sunlight. Cells of the leaves have special chlorophyll-containing structures called **chloroplasts** (Fig. 1.2). Chlorophyll absorbs sunlight and converts it into chemical energy, which is then used to prepare the food.

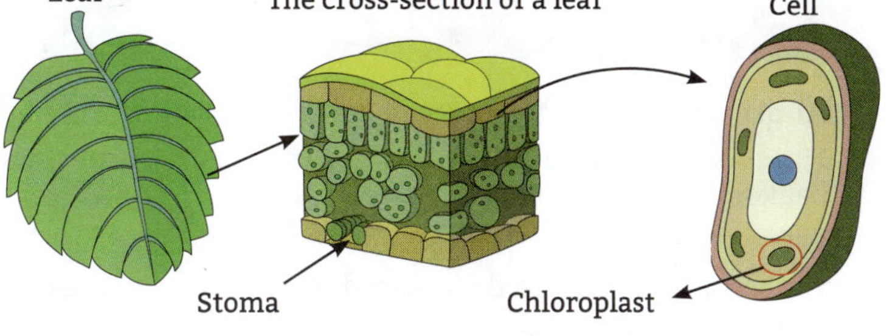

Fig. 1.2: Chloroplasts in the plant cell

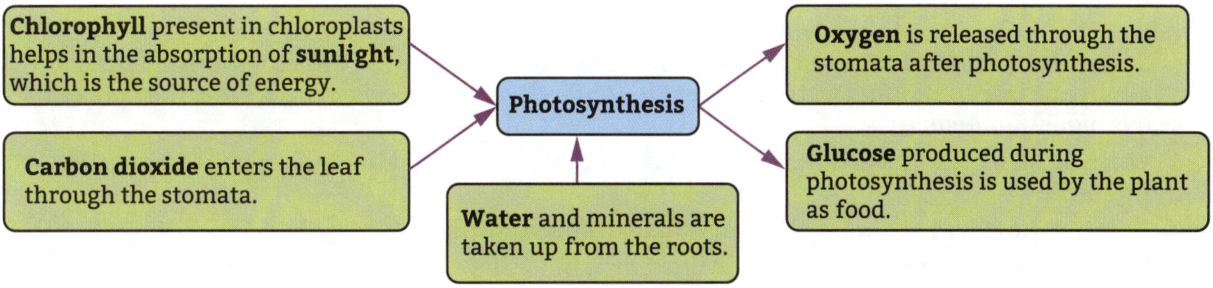

Fig. 1.3: Photosynthesis

Chemical Equation:

$$6CO_2 + 6H_2O \longrightarrow C_6H_{12}O_6 + 6O_2$$

$$\text{Carbon dioxide} + \text{Water} \xrightarrow[\text{Chlorophyll}]{\text{Light}} \text{Glucose} + \text{Oxygen}$$

During photosynthesis, the synthesized glucose is primarily utilized by plants for immediate energy needs and various metabolic processes. However, excess glucose can be converted into starch and stored in various plant parts such as roots, tubers and seeds. Oxygen and water are produced as by-products. The food synthesized in the leaves is transported to all parts of the plant through a network of pipe-like structures (tissues) called the **phloem**.

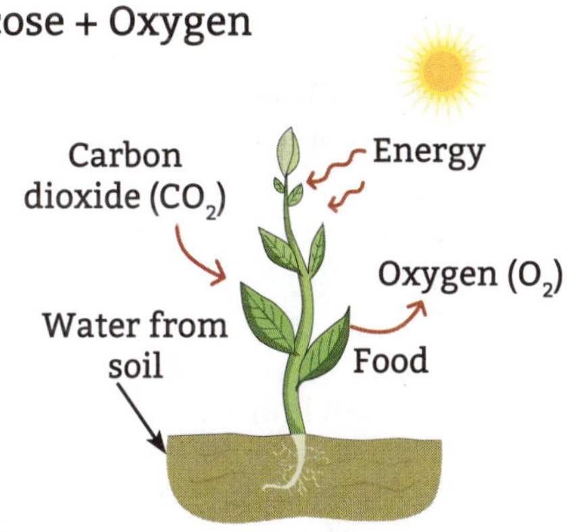

Fig. 1.4: The process of photosynthesis

Science in Context

Besides green plants, there are other organisms also that perform photosynthesis to make their food. These organisms have chlorophyll and are called **algae**. Non-flowering plants such as **ferns** and **mosses** also perform photosynthesis.

Activity 1

Boiling a leaf in alcohol

Aim: To test for the presence of starch in a leaf after photosynthesis

Materials required: Iodine, a dropper, Bunsen burner, test tube, beaker, alcohol, white tray, potted plant

Procedure:

1. Keep a healthy potted plant in darkness for about 24–48 hours to destarch it.
2. Pluck out a leaf of this plant before you keep it out in sunlight. This is Leaf A.
3. Now pluck another leaf from the plant after it has been in sunlight for at least one to two hours. This is Leaf B, which is your experimental leaf.
4. Place both leaves in a beaker containing hot water for a few minutes. Take them out of the beaker. Pour alcohol into a test tube and immerse the two leaves in it. Keep the test tube inside a 1 litre beaker containing water and heat it. (***Note:*** *Never heat alcohol directly over the flame as it is highly flammable.*)
5. When alcohol boils, the green colour comes out of the leaves and the chlorophyll dissolves in the alcohol.
6. Take out the leaves and wash them in water to remove alcohol.
7. Place the leaves on the white tray and put a drop of iodine on them with a dropper.

Observation: Iodine in Leaf A does not change its colour, whereas iodine in Leaf B changes to a blue-black colour, which indicates the presence of starch in it.

Activity 2

Experimental set-up

Aim: To demonstrate the requirement of carbon dioxide for photosynthesis

Materials required: A potted plant, a round-bottom flask, split cork, clamp stand, water, potassium hydroxide, iodine solution, dropper, test tube, tripod stand, beaker, ethyl alcohol and watch glass or plate

Procedure: Keep the potted plant in darkness/indoors for 24–48 hours to destarch it.

1. Take a round-bottom flask and fill it with potassium hydroxide solution.
2. Insert a leaf of the potted plant into the flask through the split cork without immersing it in the liquid as shown in the picture. Arrange the set-up as shown in the figure. Apply vaseline around the mouth of the flask and cork to make the set-up airtight.
3. Leave the experimental set-up near a window or in sunlight for a few hours.
4. Pluck out the leaf that was kept inside the flask as well as another leaf from the plant. Test for starch in both leaves.

Observation: When tested with iodine solution for the presence of starch, the leaf kept inside the flask did not show any change in the colour of the iodine. In contrast, the other leaf changed the colour of iodine to blue-black.

Conclusion: Potassium hydroxide in the flask absorbs carbon dioxide. Thus, due to the absence of carbon dioxide, photosynthesis does not take place in the leaf and starch is not produced. This is confirmed by the negative result for the starch test. The other leaves were untreated, and carbon dioxide was available. Starch was formed as confirmed by a positive result for the starch test. This proves that carbon dioxide is necessary for photosynthesis.

Activity 3

Aim: To prove that chlorophyll is required for photosynthesis

Materials required: Iodine solution, plant with variegated leaves, such as coleus and croton, and materials for starch test

A plant with variegated leaves

Procedure:

1. Take a large healthy leaf from a variegated plant that has been exposed to sunlight for 4–6 hours.
2. Draw the leaf in your notebook, carefully marking the areas on the leaf where chlorophyll is not present (or vice versa).
3. Perform the starch test as given in Activity 1.
4. Compare the colour of iodine seen on the leaf with your diagram. Where do you see the blue-black portions on the leaf?

Observation: Only those parts of a leaf that are green in colour due to the presence of chlorophyll will show the colour change for the starch test.

Conclusion: The above experiment shows that chlorophyll is required for plants to make their food.

Activity 4

Aim: To prove that light is required for the process of photosynthesis

Materials required: A potted plant, black paper and materials for the starch test

A potted plant kept in a dark room

Procedure:

1. Keep a potted plant in a dark room for 24–48 hours.
2. Before keeping it out in sunlight, cover one of the leaves with a piece of black paper.
3. Leave the experimental set-up in the sunlight for 6–8 hours.
4. Pluck two leaves, the one that was covered with black paper and any other healthy leaf from the plant.
5. Now test the leaves for starch as described in Activity 1.

A leaf in the plant covered with a piece of black paper

Observation: The leaf covered with black paper shows a negative result for the starch test, whereas the other healthy leaf tests positive for starch.

Conclusion: The above experiment shows that sunlight is required for the process of photosynthesis.

Science in Context

During photosynthesis, carbon dioxide is absorbed by the leaves to produce food and oxygen is released in the atmosphere. This does not mean that plants do not require oxygen for respiration. Both respiration and photosynthesis take place during daytime. But during night-time, only respiration takes place in plants because of the absence of sunlight.

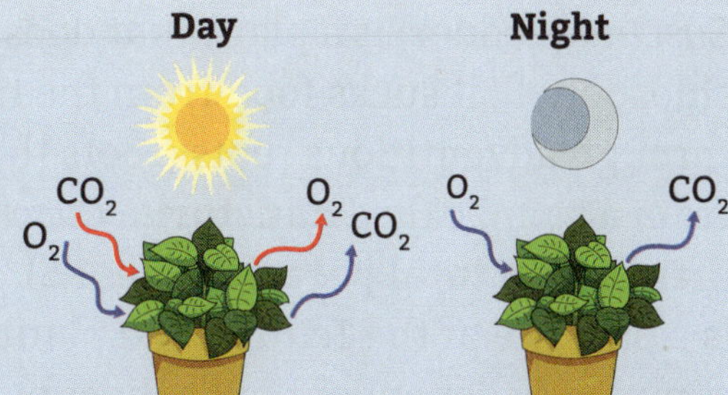

Photosynthesis and respiration are occurring at the same time.

Only respiration is occurring.

Revise and Recall

Fill in the blanks.

1. The pipe-like structures that transport the food in plants are called ______________. (xylem/phloem)
2. Carbon dioxide is absorbed by the plants through openings called ______________. (stomata/stroma)
3. Chlorophyll helps in the absorption of ______________. (light/water)
4. The water taken up into the leaves makes the guard cells ______________. (swell/shrink)
5. Organisms that make their own food are called ______________. (autotrophs/heterotrophs)

Heterotrophic Nutrition in Plants

Some plants lack chlorophyll, or grow in areas where they do not get enough sunlight. Likewise, certain plants obtain their nutrients by feeding on dead and decaying bodies or by residing within or on the bodies of other living organisms. This type of nutrition in which the nutrients are obtained from other organisms is called **heterotrophic nutrition** (*hetero* means other; *troph* means nourishment). Organisms that follow the heterotrophic mode of nutrition are called **heterotrophs**. Here are the four methods of heterotrophic nutrition in plants.

- **Parasitic nutrition:** Parasitic nutrition in plants is a type of nutrition in which certain plants, called **parasitic plants**, obtain their nutrition completely or partially from other plants. Plants that provide nutrition to parasites are called **hosts**. A parasitic plant slows down the host plant's growth, so it is harmful to its host.

  Cuscuta (dodder) is a plant that does not have chlorophyll; it sucks food from the host plant through adventitious roots (roots that grow from a stem) called **haustoria**. *Cuscuta* is, therefore, a **total parasite** (Fig. 1.5). *Rafflesia* is a parasite of the *Tetrastigma* plant. It is completely dependent on its host plant for food.

Fig. 1.5: *Cuscuta* on a host tree

Mistletoe plant has green leaves, and so, can carry out photosynthesis. This plant mainly absorbs water and minerals from the host plant. Therefore, mistletoe is called a **partial parasite** (Fig. 1.6).

Fig. 1.6: Mistletoe

- **Saprotrophic nutrition**: *Organisms that obtain nutrition from dead and decaying plants and animals are called **saprotrophs or saprophytes**. This kind of nutrition is called **saprotrophic nutrition**.* Organisms such as fungi produce enzymes that can break down plant and animal matter into liquids, which can be absorbed by their root-like structures called **mycelium**. Plants such as Indian pipe, coralroot and bird's nest orchid absorb nutrients from the mycelium of these fungi (Fig. 1.7).

  (***Note:*** *Fungi were earlier thought to be plants, but now they have been categorized into a separate group of their own.*)

Fig. 1.7: Bird's-nest orchid or *Neottia nidus-avis*

- **Insectivorous plants**: Some plants grow in harsh soil conditions where the soil is deficient in nitrogen compounds. Such plants, therefore, depend upon animal sources to meet their nitrogen requirement. These plants attract insects with the help of their attractive colour, scent and nectar and lure them into traps. *The plants that trap and consume insects to obtain nutrition are called **insectivorous plants.***

  These traps are activated by the movements or touch of insects. Some examples of insectivorous plants are the Venus flytrap, the pitcher plant, bladderwort and sundew.

  The leaves of the Venus flytrap have stiff hair-like projections on their edges and the entire leaf is divided into two parts, with the midrib acting as a hinge. When an insect sits on the leaf, it shuts tightly, trapping the insect inside it (Fig. 1.8).

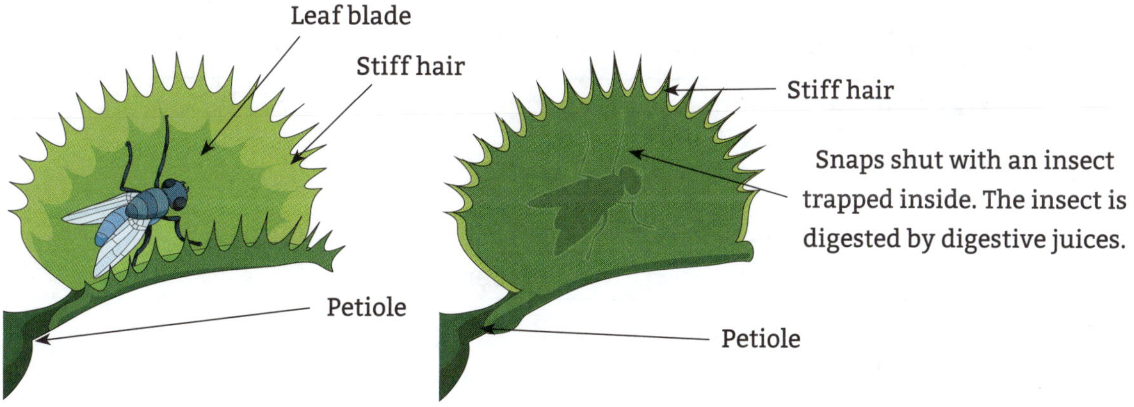

Fig. 1.8: The mechanism of trapping insects in Venus flytrap

The pitcher plant has a pitcher-shaped structure filled with a digestive liquid. It has a flap-like structure on its mouth. The edge of the opening of the pitcher is slippery. When an insect sits on its leaf, the lid closes and the insect gets trapped inside the pitcher (Fig. 1.9).

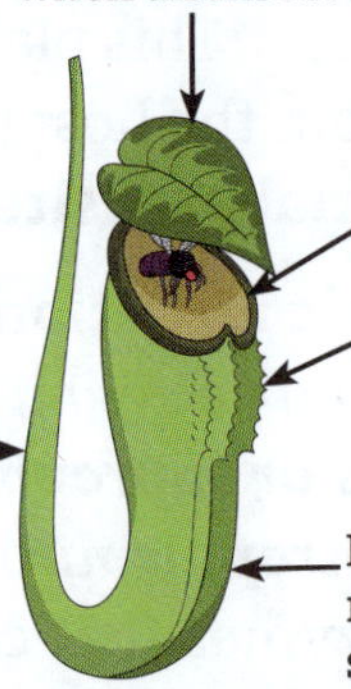

Fig. 1.9: The mechanism of trapping insects in pitcher plant

The sundew plant has long needle-like structures called tentacles covered with a sticky substance called mucous. Once an insect sits on it, it gets caught in the mucous and the tentacles fold inward, trapping the insect (Fig. 1.10).

- **Symbiosis: *Symbiosis*** *is a mutually beneficial relation between two or more organisms in which food and shelter are shared by both the organisms*. It is a unique relationship unlike what is seen between a parasite and its host plant. In a parasitic relationship, the parasite harms the host in the process of obtaining food from it. In symbiosis, however, both the organisms coexist and are benefitted without any harm done to either of them.

Fig. 1.10: Sundew

Plants that show a symbiotic relationship are called ***symbiotic plants***. Lichens are a good example, where microscopic chlorophyll-containing organisms called algae and fungi are involved (Fig. 1.11). Algae have chlorophyll and produce food through photosynthesis, while the fungi provide shelter to the algae and help it to survive in harsh weather conditions. Fungi also absorb water and nutrients from the soil to help the algae in photosynthesis.

Fig. 1.11: Lichens on a rock

Table 1.1: Differences between a parasitic and a symbiotic relationship

Parasitic Relationship	Symbiotic Relationship
1. The organisms involved are called hosts and parasites.	1. The organisms involved are called symbionts.
2. The parasite is benefitted; the host is harmed.	2. The organisms involved are mutually benefitted.
3. Parasites have modified roots called the haustoria to suck the nutrients from the host plant.	3. No special structures are used.

Science in Context

Ants guard the trees!

Acacia trees are guarded by ants. Ants depend on the secretions from the tree and the hard bark provides shelter to the ants. In return, the ants protect the trees from the herbivores, especially elephants, and other invading insects by stinging them.

Revise and Recall

Sort and list the following organisms as autotrophs or heterotrophs: coconut tree, lichens, lotus plant, sundew, bird's-nest orchid, pitcher plant, *Cuscuta*

Autotrophs	Heterotrophs

Science in Context

Plants with variegated leaves also have chlorophyll for photosynthesis. The only difference is they have lesser amounts of chlorophyll and higher amounts of other coloured pigments such as anthocyanins (red, purple or blue pigments) and carotenoids (yellow, red or orange pigments) in their leaves which mask the green colour and make the plant leaves appear coloured.

REVIVAL OF SOIL NUTRIENTS

Plants absorb nutrients such as nitrogen, potassium and phosphorus from the soil for their survival. But if the soil is not rich in these nutrients, it will result in lesser yield of the crop. As a result, the farmers will suffer a huge loss. Since the same land is used for repeated cultivation of crops, farmers use fertlizers to replenish the soil to ensure a good yield.

Leguminous crops do not need as much nitrogenous fertilizers as cereal crops. This is because the roots of leguminous plants contain legumes or nodules within which reside bacteria called *Rhizobium*. These bacteria convert the atmospheric nitrogen into nitrates, a soluble form that can be absorbed by roots. The plants provide nutrients to these bacteria. Peas, beans and pulses are examples of leguminous plants.

Go Green

Fertilizers are used to improve the nutrient content of the soil. However, excessive use of chemical fertilizers can pollute the ground water, change the soil profile and so affect human health. So, bio-fertlizers and bio-control measures are some of the ways that can be employed to keep the plants healthy.

Keywords

Nutrition: The process through which plants and animals obtain nutrients from their food

Autotrophs: Green plants/organisms that can make their own food using raw materials from nature

Heterotrophs: The organisms that depend on other organisms for their nutrition

Photosynthesis: The process through which plants produce their own food by using carbon dioxide and water in the presence of sunlight and chlorophyll

Parasites: The organisms that depend on other living organisms for their nutrition

Host: An organism from which a parasite derives its nutrition

Saprotrophs: The organisms that depend on the dead and decaying plant and animal matter for nutrition

Symbiotic relationship: A relationship where two organisms mutually depend on each other and are benefitted from it

Summary

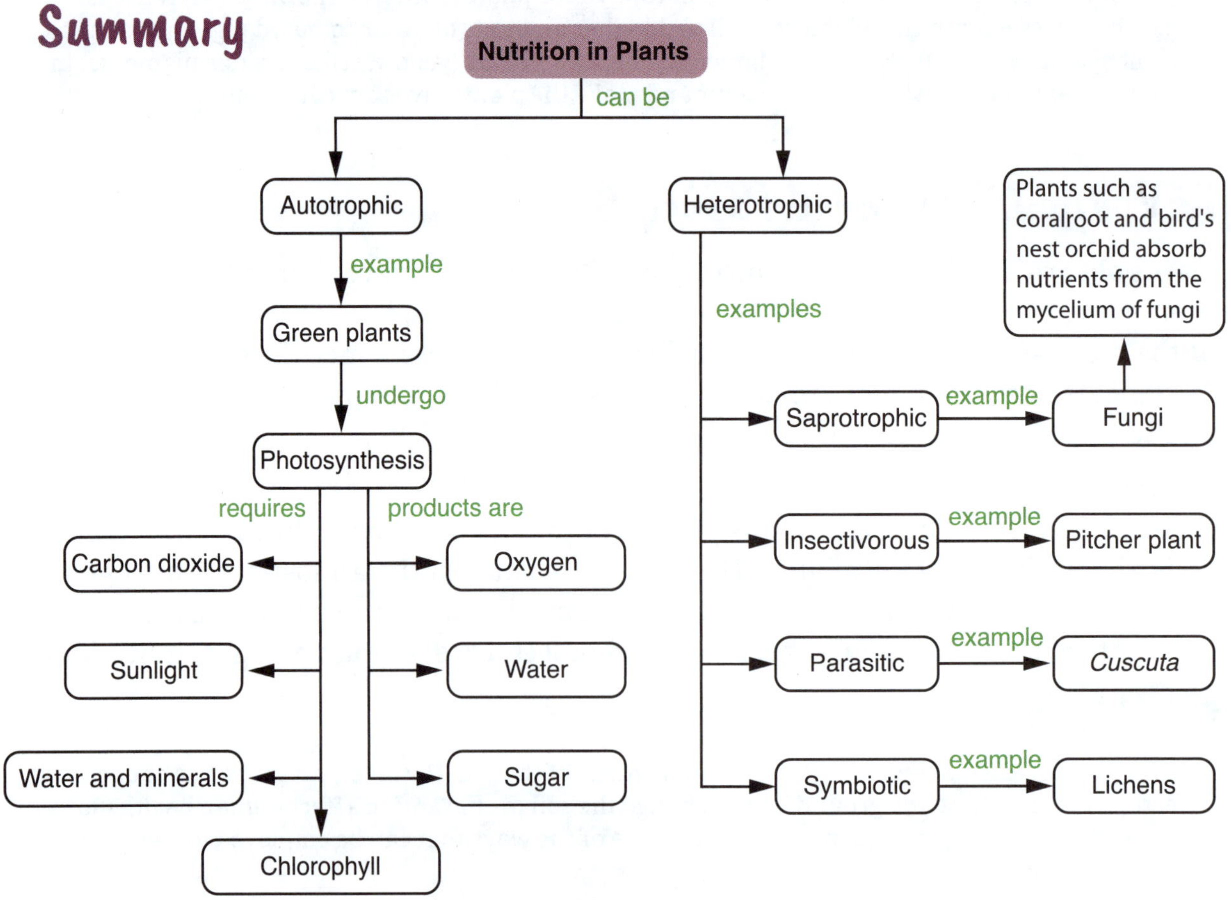

EXERCISE

W

ia

A. Choose the correct option.

1. __________ are chlorophyll-containing structures in a plant cell.
   (a) Stomata
   (b) Guard cells
   (c) Chloroplast
   (d) Xylem
2. During photosynthesis, the stomata help in the intake of __________.
   (a) carbon dioxide
   (b) oxygen
   (c) water
   (d) nitrogen
3. Which of the following is an insectivorous plant?
   (a) *Cuscuta* (b) Sundew (c) Coralroot (d) Mistletoe
4. *Rhizobium* is __________.
   (a) a parasitic and nitrogen-fixing bacterium
   (b) a non-symbiotic bacterium
   (c) a symbiotic and nitrogen-fixing bacterium
   (d) a saprophyte
5. Chlorophyll helps plants to __________.
   (a) exchange gases
   (b) absorb water from the stem
   (c) transport food from leaves to other parts
   (d) absorb sunlight

B. Fill in the blanks.

ia

1. Plants that produce their own food are called __________ . (autotrophs/heterotrophs)
2. Mistletoe is an example of a __________ . (saprophyte/parasite)
3. Insectivorous plants are __________ . (heterotrophs/autotrophs)
4. The food factories of the autotrophic plants are their __________ . (leaves/roots)
5. The food synthesized by the plants is stored as __________ . (starch/glucose)

C. State whether the following statements are true (T) or false (F).

1. A pitcher plant consumes insects as part of its nutrition. ☐
2. Photosynthesis can take place without the presence of chlorophyll. ☐
3. Saprotrophs obtain nutrients from dead and decaying matter. ☐
4. Parasitic nutrition is not a mode of heterotrophic nutrition in plants. ☐
5. The quantity of mineral nutrients in the soil remains the same even though they are continuously used up by the plants. ☐

D. Give two examples for each of the following.

1. Parasites ____________ ____________
2. Autotrophs ____________ ____________
3. Saprophytes ____________ ____________
4. Insectivorous plants ____________ ____________
5. Symbiotic plants ____________ ____________
6. Leguminous plants ____________ ____________

E. Give reasons for the following.

1. Leguminous plants are generally called nitrogen fixers.
2. Venus flytrap shows heterotrophic mode of nutrition.
3. *Cuscuta* is categorized as a parasite.
4. Farmers use fertilizers to ensure good yield.
5. Dodder plant has special roots called haustoria.

F. Answer the following questions briefly.

1. Which organisms have a symbiotic relationship to form lichens?
2. What is the role of stomata in photosynthesis?
3. How do leguminous plants replenish the soil?
4. Differentiate between parasitic and saprophytic plants.
5. What is the difference between a total parasite and a partial parasite? Give examples of each.

G. Answer the following questions in detail.

1. Describe the process of photosynthesis in detail with the help of a diagram.
2. Explain the experiment to test a leaf for the presence of starch.
3. How can you prove that the process of photosynthesis requires sunlight?
4. Explain the mechanism of trapping insects in Venus flytrap.
5. What are the different types of heterotrophic nutrition in plants? Give two examples of each.

COGNITIVE CORNER

Critical Thinking

1. Does the process of photosynthesis take place in aquatic plants that are either floating on or submerged in water?
2. All green plants are autotrophs. Is this statement true? Justify your answer.
3. Do leaves of different colours undergo photosynthesis, and how does this observation contribute to our evolving scientific understanding?
4. Dosa and idli batter kept outside for a couple of days develops a foul smell and is unfit for consumption. Why?

Picture Study

Label the diagram showing the opening and closing of stomata.

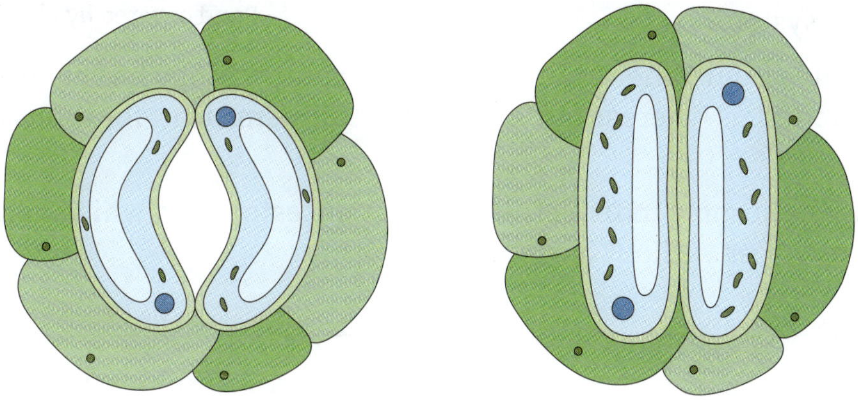

Project

Form an Eco Club and visit a nearby nursery or greenhouse. Find out the conditions under which different plants grow and the type of nutrition they require. Also find out whether certain plants need special care or different growth conditions and nutrition than other plants. If possible, take pictures of the plants. Make a poster on your findings to create awareness about sustainable gardening practices. **(C-7.1)**

Life Skills

Why do you think it is important to take care of plants? Why should we not pluck the leaves and flowers of plants? Make posters to spread awareness. **(C-6.2)**

Worksheet

Ponds and lakes have a rich ecosystem. That is, they host a variety of species of plants and animals. These species co-exist with each other in a balanced manner. However, in some places, certain human activities, such as excess use of fertilizers and detergents, have affected this balance.

The process by which water is enriched by nutrient salts causing structural changes to the ecosystem is called **eutrophication**. These structural changes lead to increased production of algae and aquatic plants, depletion of fish species and deterioration of water quality. Eutrophication is induced by the discharge of nitrogen or phosphorus containing detergents, fertilizers, or sewage into the aquatic system.

Pond covered by algae

Do you ever wonder, our generation with advanced technology has polluted almost all water bodies around us whereas our ancestors kept them clean for thousands of years?

A. Can you highlight some Indian ethos that our ancestors had which helped them use water resources without harming aquatic life?

B. Make a poster with catchy slogans to create awareness among people about saving water resources and aquatic life.

2 Nutrition in Animals

Curricular Goals

- Explore the living world in scientific terms **(CG-3)**
- Explore the nature and processes of science through engaging with the evolution of scientific knowledge and conducting scientific inquiry **(CG-6)**

Competencies

- Describe the diversity of living things observed in the natural surroundings, including at a smaller scale **(C-3.1)**
- Analyse patterns of relationships between living organisms and their environments in terms of dependence on and response to each other **(C-3.3)**
- Formulate questions using scientific terminology and collect data as evidence **(C-6.2)**

Let's Get Started

In the first chapter, you learned about the types of nutrition in plants. As animals cannot synthesize their own food, they depend on plants or other animals for food. Different types of animals have different food habits and ways of eating food. Look at the pictures given below and write the way in which each organism eats its food.

Uses tongue to capture food | Chews the cud | Drinks food | Chews food using teeth

Butterfly

____

Frog

____

Cow

____

Human being

____

All animals including human beings need food for their growth and survival. The food that animals eat contains complex substances that cannot be used by the body to get energy. Thus, it has to be broken down into simpler substances so that the body can absorb the nutrients in it. Not all of the food we eat is digested and absorbed; some part of it is excreted from the body as waste. Let us learn how different animals take in and digest food.

INGESTION OF FOOD IN DIFFERENT ORGANISMS

The process by which food is taken into the body of an organism is called **ingestion**. Different organisms have developed different ways of ingestion of food. Here are a few examples of ingestion of food in different organisms.

Fig: 2.1: Octopus

Octopus (Fig. 2.1), a multicellular organism, employs its **tentacles** to facilitate the ingestion of food.

Cockroaches (Fig. 2.2) take in food using their **specialized mouth parts**, which are designed for the purposes of biting and chewing.

Fig: 2.2: Ingestion in a cockroach

Frogs catch their prey by quickly extending their **long, sticky tongue** and retracting it into their mouth (Fig. 2.3). They swallow the prey by opening their mouth wide and gulp it.

Bolas spider, a member of the orb-weaver spiders, do not spin the typical orb web. Instead they spin a single silk line with one or more sticky droplet at its end, which are called **bolas**. They drop the silk line and swing it at moths or other insects to capture their prey.

Fig: 2.3: Ingestion in a frog

The female mosquitoes (Fig. 2.4) feed on the blood of animals and obtain it by sucking through their specialized **feeding tube**, known as a **proboscis**. The male mosquitoes feed on nectar from plants by the same method.

Fig: 2.4: Mosquito

The housefly survives by using its saliva to dissolve its liquid food and forms a solution. It then uses its **feeding tube** to **suck** and consume the solution.

A butterfly uses its specialized **proboscis** to **suck** nectar from flowers. The proboscis is kept coiled inside its mouth when not in use.

Fig: 2.5: Starfish ingesting a fish

Starfish have a unique mode of taking in food. They have a specialized structure called the **oral disc** located on the underside of their body which is surrounded by numerous **tube feet**. Starfish capture their prey (such as molluscs or small fish) by extending their stomach out of their body and wrapping it around the prey (Fig. 2.5). They release digestive enzymes to break down the food into a semi-liquid form, which is then absorbed into the stomach. Once digestion is complete, the stomach is retracted back into the body. This unique feeding method allows starfish to consume larger prey and extract nutrients effectively.

Birds have **beaks** to locate, capture and consume their food (Fig. 2.6).

Fig: 2.6: Kingfisher with an insect captured in its beak

NUTRITION IN AMOEBA

Amoeba is a single-celled aquatic organism. It feeds on microscopic organisms found in water. When *Amoeba* senses food in its surroundings, it starts moving in that direction with the help of finger-like projections of its cytoplasm called **pseudopodia**. The word *pseudo* means false and the word *podia* means feet. The false feet surround the food particles and engulf it with a drop of water. The food with a drop of water forms the **food vacuole**. The vacuole stores the food taken in. Some digestive juices are secreted by the cytoplasm of the cell into the food vacuole where the food is digested. The digested food is absorbed from the vacuole back into the cell. The vacuole with the undigested food then moves towards the edge of the body and bursts open to throw out the waste. This process of removing undigested waste from the body is called **egestion** (Fig. 2.7).

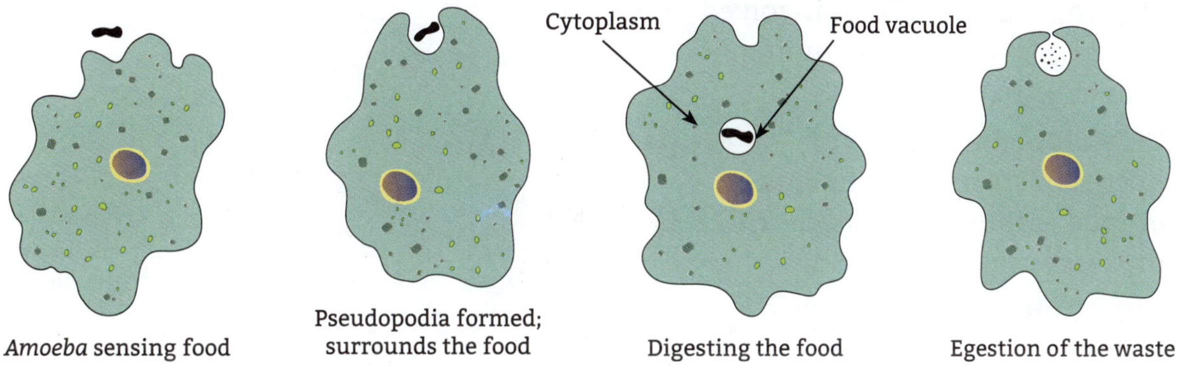

Fig. 2.7: Nutrition in *Amoeba*

NUTRITION IN HYDRA

Hydra lives in freshwater habitats. It has long flexible **tentacles** present around its mouth. These tentacles have special cells called stinging cells.

The tentacles encircle the prey, which are usually small aquatic organisms, and release the stinging cells. These cells secrete (produce) poisonous chemicals that paralyse the prey, which is then swallowed through the mouth.

The food is digested inside the central body cavity with the help of digestive juices secreted by the cells lining the walls of the cavity.

The undigested food is thrown out via the mouth. The digested food is absorbed into the cells that surround the central body cavity (Fig. 2.8).

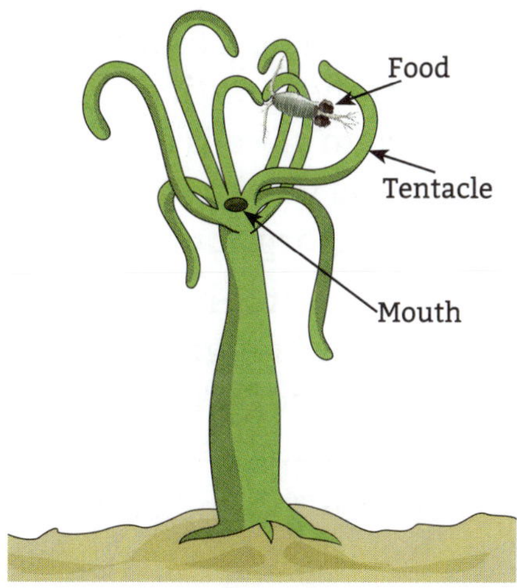

Fig. 2.8: *Hydra* capturing food using tentacles

Science in Context

An anteater feeds on ants, termites and other insects. Its tongue can reach 2 ft (61 cm) in length, but has a width of only half an inch (13 mm). The anteater can cover its tongue in sticky saliva, allowing it to trap ants. It can extend and withdraw it up to 150 times per minute. It uses its tongue to collect the eggs, larvae and adult insects. Using the long, sharp claws on its forelimbs, it opens up insect colonies in tree trunks.

NUTRITION IN HUMAN BEINGS

Briefly, there are five steps involved in nutrition in animals including human beings (Fig. 2.9):

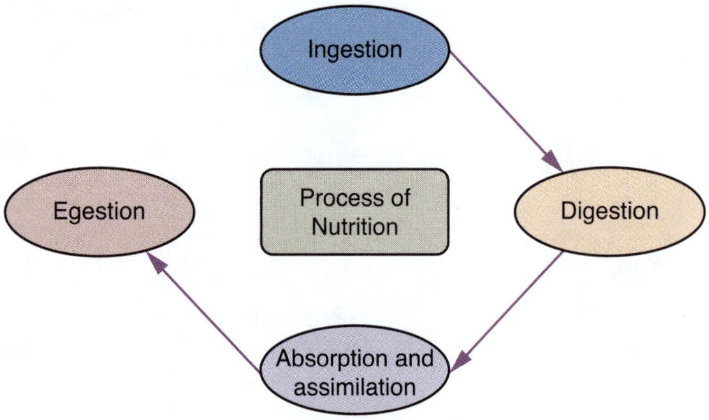

Fig. 2.9: Nutrition cycle in human beings

1. **Ingestion:** The process of nutrition starts with the intake of food through the mouth. This process is called **ingestion**.
2. **Digestion**: The ingested food is swallowed and enters the alimentary canal[1]. **Digestion** is the mechanical and chemical breakdown of complex food into simple substances in an easy to absorb form.
3. **Absorption**: The digested food is then taken up (absorbed) by the cells of the intestinal wall to be carried to all cells of the body via the blood vessels. This process is called **absorption**.
4. **Assimilation**: The absorbed food is either stored or used by the body to generate energy and for growth. This energy is used to carry out various metabolic activities inside the body. The stored materials and energy are also used to repair or replace worn-out tissues.
5. **Egestion**: The undigested food is a waste product, and it is removed from the body in the last stage by a process called **egestion**.

Word Web

[1]**Alimentary canal:** The tubular passage extending from the mouth to the anus

Nutrition in human beings is a complex process that involves the working together of different organs and organ systems. Let us study about the steps of nutrition in detail.

Ingestion

Ingestion of food occurs through the mouth. Teeth and tongue help in ingesting food.

Teeth

a

Food is chewed with the help of teeth. Teeth break down the food into smaller particles to make it easier to digest. This process is called the mechanical digestion of the food.

All teeth have a white crown and a strong root embedded in the jaw. There are four types of teeth:

> **Wonder!**
>
> Teeth are covered by a white substance called enamel. It is the hardest substance in the human body.

Incisors: These teeth are found in front of the mouth and are shaped like a chisel for cutting and biting food (Fig. 2.10). There are a total of eight incisors.

Canines: They are sharp teeth found next to the incisors. Canines are sharp and have pointed ends, which help to tear and pierce the food (Fig. 2.11). There are a total of four canines, one on either side of the incisors.

Premolars: These are broad, flat-structured teeth used for crushing food particles (Fig. 2.12). There are a total of eight premolars.

Molars: These are found at the back of the jaw. They have broad and flat surface, and strong roots (Fig. 2.12). Molars are used for grinding and chewing food particles. There are a total of 12 molars.

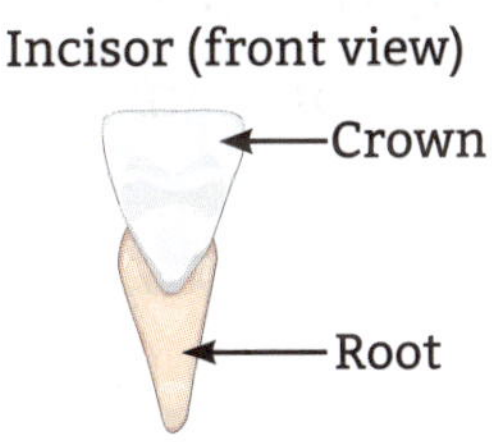

Fig. 2.10: Incisor

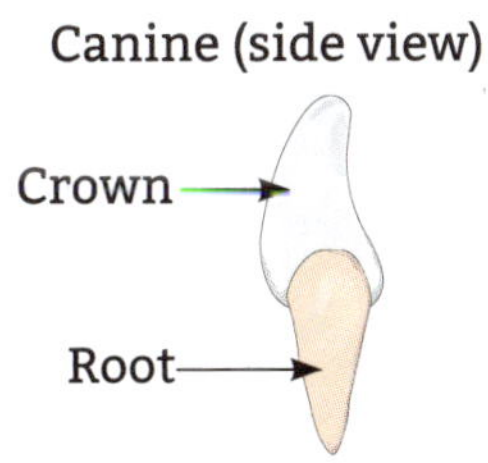

Fig. 2.11: Canine

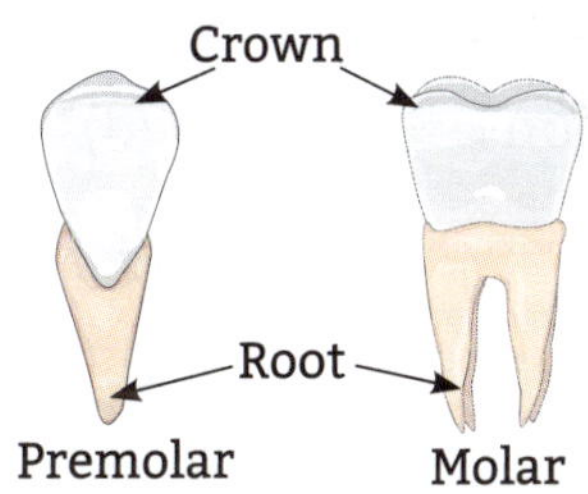

Fig. 2.12: Premolar and molar

The appearance of the first tooth in infants is called **teething**. Infants start teething when they are about 4–7 months old.

The first set of 20 teeth formed is called temporary teeth or **milk teeth**. At 6 years of age, the temporary teeth start falling off gradually, making way for the permanent set of teeth.

An adult human being has a set of 32 permanent teeth. The upper and lower jaws in the mouth have 16 teeth each. There are 4 incisors, 2 canines, 4 premolars and 6 molars in each jaw (Fig. 2.13). The last pair of molars are called **wisdom teeth** which appear at 17 to 18 years of age.

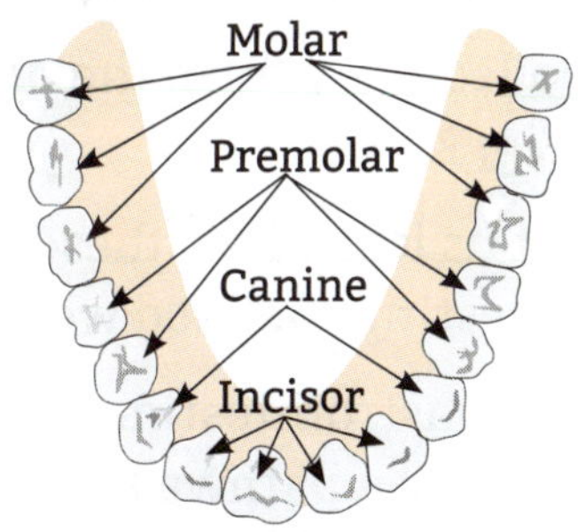

Fig. 2.13: Arrangement of teeth in the lower jaw of the mouth

Science in Context

The yellowing of teeth commonly observed in many people is due to the formation of **dental plaque**. Dental plaque is formed when the food particles stuck in the teeth mix with bacteria. Sugar from the sweets, chocolates and other food is used up by the bacteria present in our mouth to form acids, which affect the teeth. This causes tooth decay and leads to the formation of a hole called **tooth cavity**. The only way to avoid a tooth cavity is to brush your teeth twice a day and floss regularly.

Tongue

The tongue is a muscular organ. It helps in mixing the chewed food with saliva and then swallowing it. It has taste buds that detect different tastes present in the food.

Taste buds are located around small structures on the upper surface of the tongue called **papillae**. These structures are responsible for detecting different tastes such as salty, sour, bitter and sweet.

Revise and Recall

Match the following.

1. Ingestion	(a) Digested food is taken up by the cells of the intestinal wall and sent to the circulatory stream
2. Digestion	(b) Intake of food
3. Absorption	(c) Undigested food components are removed
4. Egestion	(d) Food is broken down into simple components

Digestion

The process of digestion of food in human beings involves various organs, which collectively form the **digestive system** (Fig. 2.14).

Let us learn how these organs help in digesting the food we eat.

The gastrointestinal tract or alimentary canal is a pathway by which food enters the body and solid wastes are removed.

a

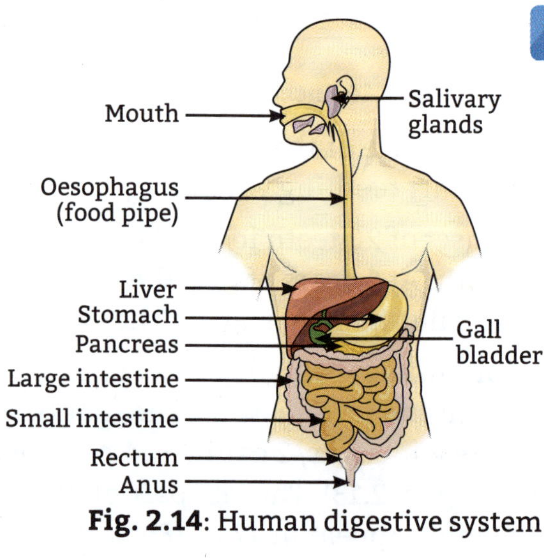

Fig. 2.14: Human digestive system

The pathway takes the following route:

Buccal cavity: The process of digestion starts in the mouth or the buccal cavity. The food is chewed with the help of teeth. The process of chewing the food is called **mastication**.

Saliva is secreted by the salivary glands located inside the mouth. The tongue mixes the food with saliva. The salivary glands secrete digestive enzyme called salivary amylase that breaks down carbohydrates into simple sugars. Once the food is chewed, it forms a bolus[1] which can be easily swallowed.

Word Web

[1]**Bolus:** A small, soft round mass of chewed food

The saliva helps in the easy passage of food through the oesophagus into the stomach. Starch is a carbohydrate present in food in high quantities. We can understand the effect of saliva on food by performing the following activity.

Activity

Aim: To study the effect of saliva on food

Materials required: Boiled rice, test tubes, dropper, Benedict's reagent

Procedure: Take two test tubes and label them as 'A' and 'B'. Put one teaspoonful of boiled rice in test tube 'A' and one teaspoonful of boiled rice after chewing (for 3–5 minutes) in test tube 'B'. Add 3–4 mℓ of water to each of the test tubes. Use a dropper to add 3–4 drops of Benedict's reagent into both the test tubes. Heat the test tubes for 10 minutes in a water bath.

A Boiled rice with water	B Chewed rice with water	Boiled rice, water and Benedict's reagent after heating	Chewed rice with water and Benedict's reagent after heating

Observation: In test tube A, there is no colour change in the solution. In test tube B, the colour of the solution changes to brick red.

Conclusion: Benedict's reagent turns brick red if sugar is present in a solution. As saliva breaks down the starch present in food into simple sugars, the test for sugar is positive in test tube B.

Oesophagus: It is a long muscular tube-like structure. When the muscles in its wall contract, they produce a wave-like motion. This movement is called **peristalsis** (Fig. 2.15). It helps to push down the food into the stomach. The food is transported from the buccal cavity through the oesophagus into the stomach. The movement of food through different parts of the alimentary canal happens as a result of the peristaltic movement.

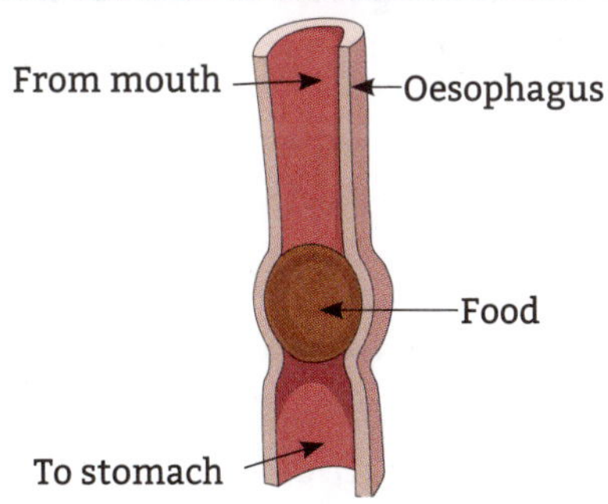

Fig. 2.15: Peristalsis

Science in Context

A small flap-like organ, epiglottis, prevents food from entering the trachea and channels it into the oesophagus. That is why when you try to talk with your mouth full, you often choke.

Stomach: Stomach is a muscular, sac-like organ. The inner lining wall of the stomach produces dilute hydrochloric acid, gastric mucosa[1] and digestive juices.

Dilute hydrochloric acid kills microbes that enter with food. The digestive juices help in the digestion of proteins. The gastric mucosa keeps the inner wall of the stomach safe from the harmful effects of the acids.

The food that is partially digested in the stomach is called **chyme**. This passes into the small intestine.

Word Web

[1]**Gastric mucosa:** A sticky and slimy layer of semi-solid secretion that helps in the easy movement of the food

Liver: It is the largest gland in the body. It produces bile juice that helps in the digestion of fats. *Bile juice is stored in a small sac-like organ below the liver called **gall bladder***. The bile juice from the gall bladder is secreted into the small intestine.

Pancreas: It is a glandular organ located in the abdomen (across the back of the belly, behind the stomach). It secretes pancreatic juices that contain enzymes that aid in digestion.

Small intestine: Bile juice helps in the breakdown of fat in the food present in the small intestine. The pancreatic juice contains digestive enzymes such as trypsin, amylase and lipase, which convert starch, proteins and fats into smaller molecules such as glucose, amino acids and fatty acids, respectively.

Here, the food being acted upon by the digestive juices is in the liquid form. Most of the food is digested in the small intestine.

Absorption

There are finger-like projections called **villi** (singular: villus) present on the inner walls of the small intestine (Fig. 2.16). These villi increase the surface area of inner walls for absorption of digested food. Each villus has a network of blood vessels to absorb the nutrients in the digested food.

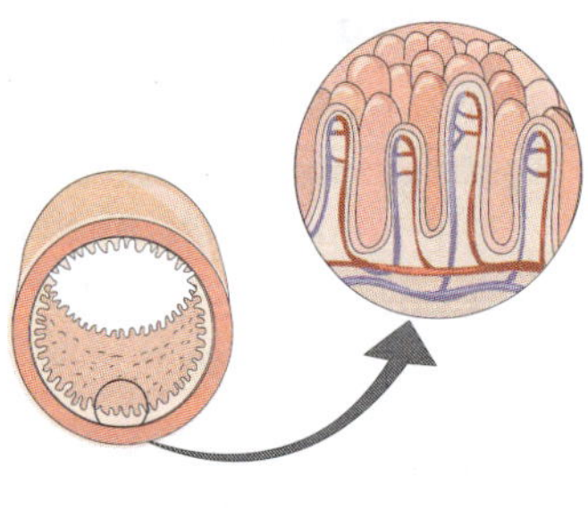

Fig. 2.16: Villi on the inner walls of small intestine

Assimilation

This happens in all the cells of our body including the cells of the alimentary canal. Assimilation is a process by which digested food reaching the cells through the blood is either converted into products necessary for them or is utilized for their activities. Glucose, which is the final product of carbohydrate digestion, is broken down with the help of oxygen into carbon dioxide and water to release energy.

Excess glucose (or glucose that is not used immediately) is converted into glycogen and stored in the liver for use when needed. Amino acids are used for the growth and repair of the worn-out cells. Fatty acids and glycerol are stored below the skin as energy reserves.

Egestion

The undigested and unabsorbed food moves into the large intestine to a part called **colon** where some amount of water and salts are reabsorbed from the undigested food. The remaining undigested food then moves to the second part called **rectum**. Here, it is stored and removed from the body through the anus. This process is called **egestion**.

DIGESTION IN RUMINANTS (GRASS-EATING ANIMALS)

You might have seen cows, buffaloes, sheep and goat chewing continuously. Plant-eating animals quickly swallow their food after chewing it once. The swallowed food goes to a chamber called rumen. They bring back the food later into the mouth and chew it again. These animals are called **ruminants** and the process is called **rumination**.

The stomach of ruminants consists of four compartments: rumen, reticulum, omasum and abomasum (Fig. 2.17).

The swallowed food first enters the rumen. The rumen has microorganisms that can break down cellulose, a complex carbohydrate present in plants. In the first two chambers, the rumen and the reticulum, the food is mixed with saliva and separated into layers of solid and liquid material. Solids clump together to form the **cud** or **bolus**.

The cud is brought back from the rumen to the mouth where it is chewed slowly by completely mixing it with saliva and is further broken down. This is called **chewing the cud** or **rumination**.

When the cud is chewed and swallowed again, it enters the omasum, where the food is broken down further into simpler compounds. The simpler compounds then enter the abomasum. Digestive juices are secreted in this chamber and the food is now fully digested. It is then sent to the small intestine for absorption and the leftover undigested food is passed to the large intestine from where it is excreted.

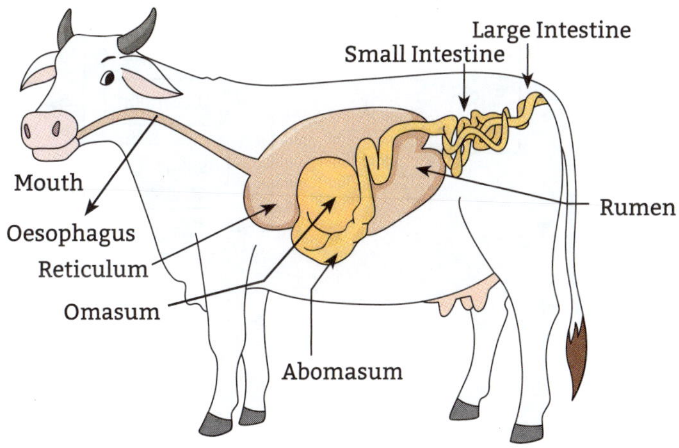

Fig. 2.17: Digestion in ruminants

Keywords

Pseudopodia: Finger-like projections in the body of *Amoeba*

Food vacuoles: Tiny pockets of water in a cell to store food, formed as a result of the pseudopodia closing in around the food

Ingestion: The process of intake or procurement of food

Digestion: The breakdown of food into simpler soluble substances

Absorption: The process in which the digested food is taken up by the cells of the intestinal wall and sent to the circulatory system

Assimilation: The use of the absorbed food for growth or the generation of energy

Ruminants: Plant-eating animals that bring back swallowed food into the mouth and chew it again

Rumen: The first chamber in a ruminant's stomach which has microorganisms that can break down cellulose

Summary

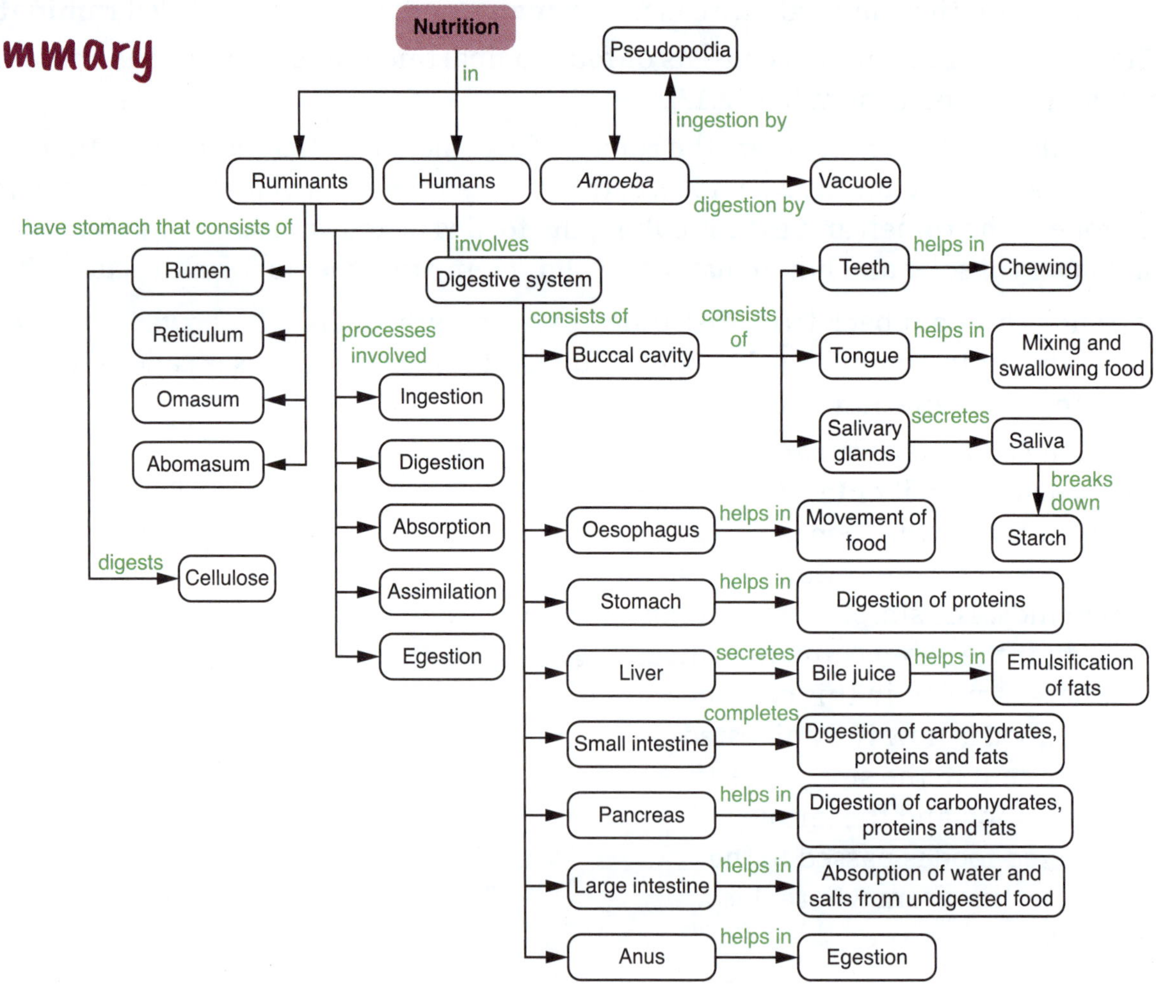

EXERCISE

W

A. Choose the correct option.

ia

1. During the process of digestion, carbohydrates are broken down into ____________.
   (a) glucose (b) minerals (c) proteins (d) vitamins
2. Which of the following organs stores bile?
   (a) Stomach (b) Liver (c) Pancreas (d) Gall bladder
3. In human beings, most of the nutrients are absorbed by the ____________.
   (a) liver (b) pancreas
   (c) stomach (d) small intestine
4. After chewing an apple, the crushed apple is swallowed and passed from the ____________ to ____________.
   (a) mouth, oesophagus (b) oesophagus, small intestine
   (c) oesophagus, stomach (d) mouth, stomach
5. The bile helps in the breakdown of ____________.
   (a) carbohydrates (b) proteins (c) fats (d) glucose

B. Fill in the blanks.

ia

1. *Amoeba* takes in food using ________________. (pseudopodia/tentacles)
2. The engulfed food in *Amoeba* is trapped in the ________________. (food vacuole/cytoplasm)
3. The digested food moves from the stomach to the ________________. (large intestine/small intestine)
4. Pancreas is located just below the ________________. (stomach/liver)
5. Excess water in the food is absorbed in the ________________. (large intestine/small intestine)
6. Grass is rich in a carbohydrate called ________________. (cellulose/glucose)

C. State whether the following statements are true (T) or false (F).

1. The teeth that stay for the whole life are called the milk teeth. ☐
2. Saliva helps in the breakdown of starch into simple proteins. ☐
3. The process of digestion in human beings starts in the stomach. ☐
4. The wall of the stomach is protected from hydrochloric acid by the mucous secretion. ☐
5. The waste matter from the large intestine is stored in anus which is later removed from the body. ☐

D. Match the following.

1.	*Amoeba*	(a)	Tentacles
2.	*Hydra*	(b)	Bile juice
3.	Stomach	(c)	Four-chambered stomach
4.	Gall bladder	(d)	Gastric mucosa
5.	Ruminant	(e)	Pseudopodia

E. Answer the following in one word each.

1. The female mosquitoes feed on the blood of animals and obtain it by sucking through this specialized feeding tube
2. Organ that helps in providing nutrition in *Hydra*
3. Glands that produce saliva
4. Organ commonly called the food pipe
5. Example of a ruminant

F. Give reasons for the following.

1. The water we drink enters into our stomach and not any other part of the body.
2. Villi are essential for complete absorption of nutrients from the food.
3. Food does not enter the windpipe.
4. We cannot digest cellulose like the cattle do.
5. Chewed rice when treated with Benedict's reagent and heated changes its colour.

G. Answer the following questions briefly.

1. Write the functions of the tongue.
2. What is peristalsis?
3. What are villi?
4. How does the liver help in the digestion of food?
5. What is rumination?

H. Answer the following questions in detail.

1. Explain the nutrition in *Amoeba* with the help of a diagram.
2. Explain about the different kinds of teeth and their functions in human beings.
3. Draw a well-labelled diagram of human digestive system. Write the functions of the following organs in the digestive system: mouth, stomach, liver, small intestine and pancreas.
4. Explain the process of digestion in ruminants, and the role of a four-chambered stomach with the help of a diagram.

COGNITIVE CORNER

Critical Thinking

1. Why does your stomach grumble when you are hungry?
2. If we eat raw leafy vegetables, would we be able to digest them? What about raw meat? Give reason for your answer.
3. What would be the fate of the glucose inside the cells of a person:
   (a) who is starting to jog?
   (b) who is always inactive, sitting and watching television?

Picture Study

Rearrange the steps of nutrition in *Amoeba*.

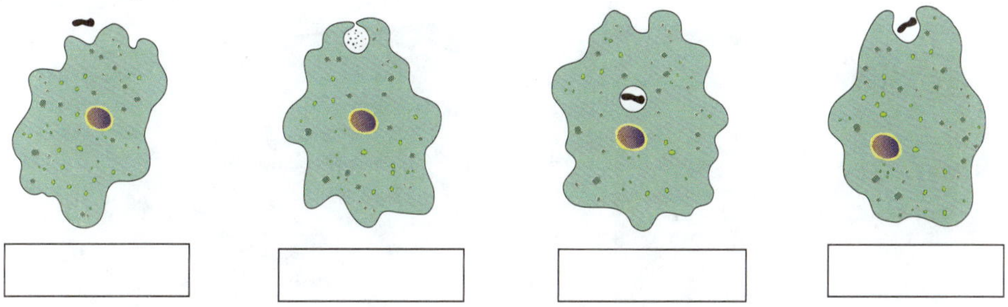

Project

Form a Health and Wellness Club with your classmates and using the Internet and the books in your school library, collect information on the importance of oral hygiene. Read about various items available in your kitchen that can be used to maintain a good hygiene. Make a colourful spread showing your findings and display it in your class. **(C-7.1)**

In the Library

Food products like probiotic yoghurt have become popular nowadays. Using reference materials, research and find out what the term 'probiotic' means and how such products are beneficial for our digestive system. Design and build simple models that effectively demonstrate the concept of probiotics and their positive impact on digestive health. **(C-7.2)**

Life Skills

Problems related to the digestive system, such as acidity and constipation, affect many people. Often, these problems can be avoided by following healthy eating practices such as taking meals at regular intervals and including enough roughage in the diet. List five healthy eating practices you would follow to keep your digestive system healthy. Furthermore, create diagrams to illustrate the relationship between these healthy eating practices and maintaining a healthy digestive system. **(C-7.3)**

Worksheet

Indian ethos has a long history of reverence and compassion for animals. It is deeply rooted in various religious, cultural, and philosophical traditions that emphasize the interconnectedness and value of all living beings. Additionally, Indian culture emphasizes cleanliness and discourages littering. However, today we have lost these values. Either willingly or unwillingly, our practices harm the environment and other life forms.

People sometimes throw food wrapped in plastic on the streets. Animals smell the food and eat plastic with the food. This causes upset stomach or choking which results in instant death.

A cow feeding on plastic

A sea turtle eating plastic

Dead whale washed up on the beach

The oceans too have become a big garbage pool. Large fishes, dolphins and whales simply mistake plastic for familiar food items. Dead bodies of these animals can be found on beaches all over the world. Plastic remains have been found inside their stomachs.

Write a slogan to be displayed on a banner in your neighbourhood, promoting Indian ethos on cleanliness and love and compassion towards other organisms. Mention the impact of littering on the innocent animals who suffer because of human activities.

3 Fibre to Fabric

Curricular Goals

- Explore the living world in scientific terms **(CG-3)**
- Understand the interface of science, technology and society **(CG-5)**

Competencies

- Describe the diversity of living things observed in the natural surroundings, including at a smaller scale **(C-3.1)**
- Distinguish the characteristics of living organisms from non-living things **(C-3.2)**
- Share views on news and articles related to the impact science and technology, and society have on each other **(C-5.2)**

Let's Get Started

Clothes are one of the basic needs of human beings apart from food and shelter. Clothes not only cover our body but also protect us from the harsh weather conditions, dust and insect bites. We wear different clothes on different occasions and according to the climate of the place we live.

You have studied that the materials used to make clothes are called **fabrics**. Look at the pictures given below. Name the type of fabrics that you would use to make clothes suitable to the given occasion or places.

Underwater diving

____

____

On a trip to desert

____

____

On a trip to cold region

____

____

Fabrics are made from yarns that are woven or knitted from hair-like strands called **fibres**. Fibres can be natural or artificial. Natural fibres are obtained from plants and animals. Artificial fibres are made by humans.

In this chapter, we will study in detail about the fibres obtained from animals and how these fibres are made into fabrics.

WOOL

Wool is an animal fibre obtained mainly from the fleece[1] of some animals. Wool fibres trap air in the spaces between them. As air is a bad conductor of heat, this prevents the loss of heat from the body, which helps in keeping the body of these animals warm.

Characteristics of the wool fibre

- It appears mostly creamy white in colour.
- It does not wrinkle easily.
- It is durable and elastic.
- It is a bad conductor of heat.
- It absorbs moisture to a great extent.

Word Web

[1]**Fleece**: The coat of soft, fine hair that covers the body of a sheep or a similar animal

Animals That Yield Wool

Sheep: They are the main wool-yielding animals. Two types of fibres are obtained from the fleece of a sheep:

- The coarse[2] beard hair.
- The soft and fine underhair that usually grows close to the skin.

Fig. 3.1: Merino sheep

The fibres for making wool are obtained from the fine underhair. There are many breeds of sheep that yield wool. Depending on the breed and the general condition of the sheep, the characteristics of wool fibres differ. The best and finest wool is obtained from the Merino sheep (Fig. 3.1).

Word Web

[2]**Coarse:** Rough

Goat: Wool is also obtained from the underfur of some goats. The Angora and Cashmere breeds are the ones that yield wool.

Angora goats are mostly found in the Ankara (Angora) region of Turkey (Fig. 3.2). A very fine, soft and lustrous wool fibre called 'Mohair' is obtained from Angora goats.

Fig. 3.2: Angora goat

Fig. 3.3: Cashmere goat

Cashmere goats are mostly found in the mountains of Tibet and China (Fig. 3.3). They produce a very soft and warm fibre called 'Cashmere'. It is a rare and expensive fibre as cashmere goats produce only a small amount of hair in a year.

Camel: The fleece of camel gives soft, warm and lightweight wool. Annually, 12–15 kg of wool is obtained from a male camel and about 6–8 kg of wool is obtained from a female camel.

Fig. 3.4: Bactrian camel

The best quality camel wool is obtained from Bactrian camels of Siberia, Mongolia and China (Fig. 3.4). Alpaca (Fig. 3.5), Vicuna (Fig. 3.6) and Llama (Fig. 3.7) are the animals that belong to the camel family and are mostly found in South America. A very fine, lustrous and lightweight wool is obtained from these animals.

Fig. 3.5: Alpaca

Fig. 3.6: Vicuna

Fig. 3.7: Llama

Science in Context

Alpacas are bred exclusively for their fibre and meat. The wool obtained from alpacas is water-repellent and is used to make coats, sweaters and blankets.

Rabbit and yak: A very fine, soft, fluffy and silky wool called Angora wool is obtained from the Angora rabbit (Fig. 3.8). Wool is also obtained from the hair on the body of yak, which is a cow species mostly found in Ladakh and Tibet (Fig. 3.9).

Fig. 3.8: Angora rabbit

Fig. 3.9: Yak

Rearing and Breeding of Sheep

Sheep live and move in groups called **flocks** and a big group of sheep is called a **herd**. *The process of domestication and raising of sheep is called* **rearing**. In India, sheep are reared mostly in Jammu and Kashmir, Himachal Pradesh and Uttarakhand. They are also reared in the plains of Haryana, Punjab, Rajasthan and Gujarat.

Sheep are herbivores and preferably feed on grass and weeds. Jowar, oil cakes (material left after extracting oil from seeds) and a mixture of pulses and minerals are also fed to them. Sheds with gunny bags and thatched roof are preferred as the shelter for sheep. Their shelters should be kept dry and well ventilated.

To improve the production and quality of wool, some sheep are selectively bred with other sheep. The desirable characters that can be taken into consideration while selecting the breeds are resistance to diseases, tolerance to environmental conditions, appearance of wool fibre and wool type.

The process of selecting parents for obtaining desirable characters in their offsprings is called **selective breeding.** *The bred animals are called* **breeds.**

Table 3.1: Some Indian breeds of sheep

Name of breed	Quality of wool	Name of the state where the sheep is mainly found
Lohi	Good quality wool	Rajasthan, Punjab
Rampur bushair	Brown fleece	Uttar Pradesh, Himachal Pradesh
Nali	Carpet wool	Rajasthan, Haryana, Punjab
Marwari	Coarse wool	Gujarat
Patanwadi	For hosiery	Gujarat

Table 3.2: Popular breeds of sheep around the world

Name of breed	Quality of wool	Name of the place where the sheep is mainly found
Merino	Fine wool	Spain
Barbado	Short, coarse wool	Texas, United States
Damara	Short wool	Angola, Namibia
Katahdin	Thick and coarse wool	United States
Targhee	Fine and long wool	United States

PROCESSING OF FLEECE TO FABRIC (WOOL PRODUCTION)

The process of obtaining woollen fabric from the sheared fleece involves the following steps (Fig. 3.10):

- **Shearing:** The process of the removal of fleece from the body of animals such as sheep is called **shearing**. It is done with the help of clippers, a pair of scissors or a shearing machine. The person who removes the wool is called a **shearer**.

The uppermost layer of the skin of sheep is usually dead. Thus, the process of sheering does not hurt the skin. In fact, the removal of fleece during the summer months helps the sheep to keep its body cooler. Hence, shearing is done mainly in the summer months.

- **Scouring:** Sheep's wool contains lanolin secreted by the sebaceous glands present in its skin. Lanolin makes the wool greasy and oily which is removed by washing the raw sheered fleece with detergent and alkali. The process in which the shorn hair is treated to remove grease and dirt is called **scouring**. Nowadays, scouring is done using machines.
- **Carding:** During this step, the dried wool is carefully removed, and the fibres are passed through the rollers with a series of metal teeth that straighten and blend into slivers. This process arranges the wool into a flat sheet called a web. During carding, the residual dirt and other matter left in the fibres are also removed.
- **Sorting:** The process of removal of any damaged and stained wool from the fleece is called **sorting**.
- **Grading:** The process of grouping the wool according to their length, colour, texture and ease of dyeing is called **grading**.
- **Dyeing:** The natural colour of the fleece of sheep and goats is white, brown or black. So, the sheared wool is dyed in various colours, depending on the requirements.
- **Drying:** After the dyeing of the wool, it is dried. The dyed wool is made to pass through machines that squeeze out the excess water. It is then packed into bales and then transported to the mill.
- **Spinning:** The fibres after drying are oiled, straightened, combed, washed, twisted and spun into yarns. The fibres are straightened by keeping them under rollers to stretch them and twisted into yarns.
- **Weaving and knitting:** The larger fibres are spun into yarns and knitted for making sweaters, whereas the shorter fibres are spun and woven into other woollen clothes.

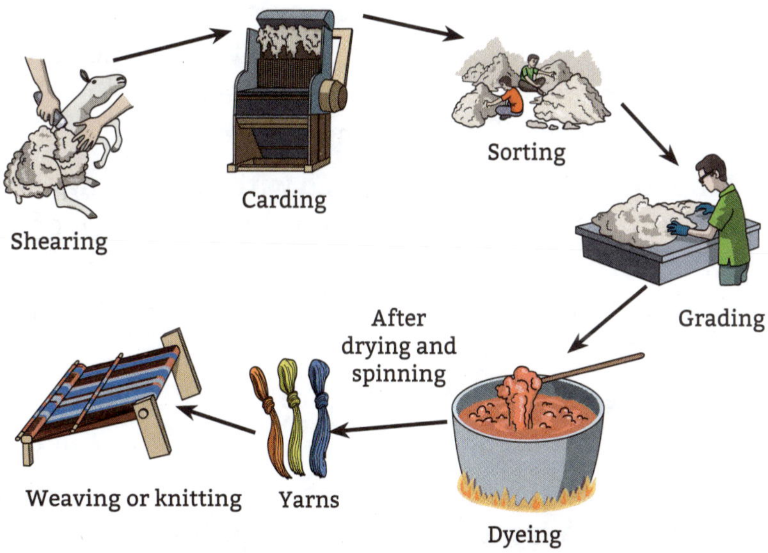

Fig. 3.10: Steps involved in the processing of wool

Health Hazards in Wool Industry

- The major health hazard faced by people working in the wool industry is an infection called **anthrax**. It is a common bacterial disease of goats and sheep and might affect the workers involved in the shearing and sorting processes. It is called 'sorter's disease'. This disease leads to skin, lung and intestinal disorders and also results in lesions in arms, neck and lungs.
- The usage of chemical dyes may result in the irritation of eyes, infection of skin and lungs and breathing problems.
- Inappropriate ventilation, high temperatures and humidity at the workplace can harm the general health of the workers.
- Hearing loss is another health hazard faced by the workers of the wool industry due to the loud noise made by machines during the processing of wool.

Revise and Recall

Fill in the blanks.

1. __________ are the major wool-yielding animals. (Goats/Sheep)
2. __________ goats are mostly found in the mountains of China and Tibet. (Cashmere/Angora)
3. Shearing is done mainly in the __________ months. (summer/winter)
4. The use of chemical dyes in the wool industry can lead to irritation of __________. (eyes/mouth)

SILK

The discovery of silk is believed to have originated in ancient China around 2698–2598 BCE. According to a legend, Empress Xi Ling-Shi discovered silk when a cocoon fell into her tea cup. As she tried to remove it, she noticed the delicate, shimmering threads unraveling from the cocoon. Intrigued by their beauty and strength, she began to explore the possibilities of these threads.

Empress Xi Ling-Shi is credited with developing the art of sericulture, which is the cultivation of silkworms for the production of silk. She discovered that the silkmoth caterpillars, or silkworms, spun cocoons made of fine threads of silk before transforming into moths. These cocoons were harvested and carefully unraveled to obtain the silk fibres.

Characteristics of the silk fibre

- It is lustrous and soft.
- It is a bad conductor of heat.
- It is very elastic, thus, resists creasing.
- It is as strong as a steel wire of the same diameter.
- It has a peculiar natural shine and dyes well.
- It is resistant to dust.

Life Cycle of a Silk Moth

a

The various stages involved in the life cycle of a silk moth (Fig. 3.13) are given below.

- **Laying of eggs:** After mating, the female silk moth lays hundreds of eggs on the mulberry leaves.
- **Hatching into larvae or caterpillars**: The eggs hatch and form larvae that develop into caterpillars (Fig. 3.11). We call them silkworms. The caterpillars feed on mulberry leaves for 3–4 weeks. They shed their 'skin' at least four times during this feeding stage. This process of shedding their skin is called **moulting** and with each moult the caterpillar grows in size.

Fig. 3.11: Caterpillar

- **Formation of cocoon**: After the final moult when the caterpillars have sufficiently grown in size, they cease to feed and begin to grow into a pupa. The pupating caterpillars start secreting a thin, filament-like substance from the salivary glands located on either side of their head. This secretion is made of a protein called fibroin. The secretion also contains a protein called sericin that adheres two filaments together. Caterpillars swing their heads from side to side in the form of the figure eight (8). The secretion hardens when it comes in contact with air and makes the filaments stick together to form fibres. The pupa completely covers itself with these silk fibres. This covering with the pupa inside is called the cocoon (Fig. 3.12).

Fig. 3.12: Cocoons

- **Emergence of a silk moth**: Inside the cocoon, the pupa develops into an adult moth (Fig. 3.14).

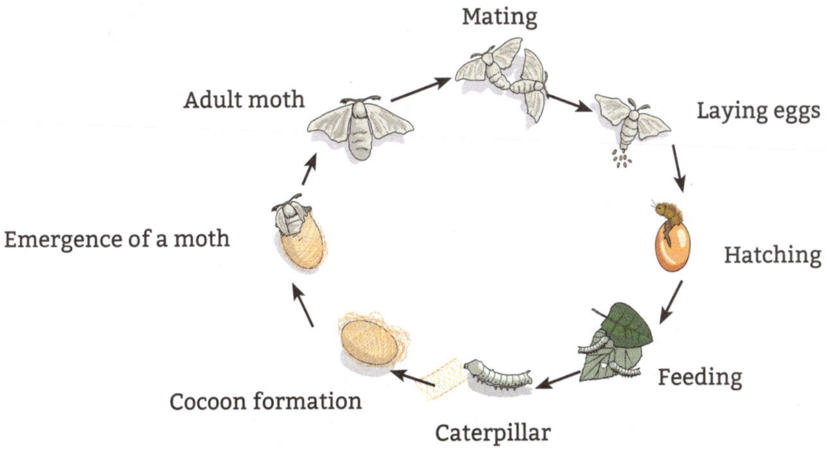

Fig. 3.13: Life cycle of a silk moth

Fig. 3.14: Silk moth

SERICULTURE

The process of rearing of silkworms for the production of silk is called ***sericulture***. This process includes both rearing and reeling of silkworms.

The rearing of silkworms includes the following steps:

- A female silk moth lays hundreds of eggs that are collected and placed on strips of cloth or paper.
- The eggs are stored under optimal conditions of humidity and temperature to facilitate hatching. As the eggs hatch, larvae or silkworms come out. These silkworms are placed in clean trays made of bamboo containing freshly chopped mulberry leaves (Fig. 3.15).

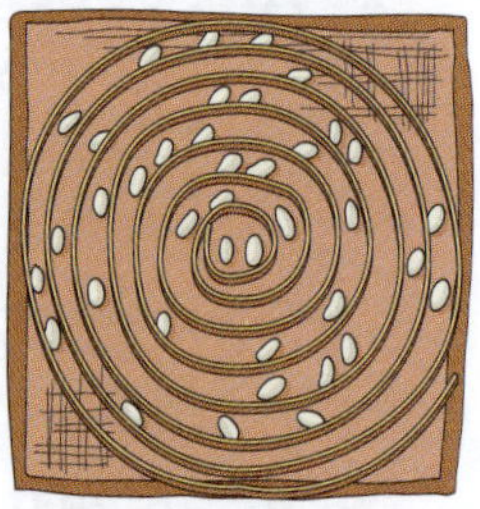

Fig. 3.15: Cocoons attached to the trays

- Newspapers are spread over the trays to absorb excess moisture from the leaves. The trays should be cleaned regularly after every few days. The silkworms are fed on mulberry leaves for about 20–35 days.
- The silkworms are then moved to small chambers of bamboo trays to spin cocoons after they stop eating and begin to pupate.
- These trays are provided with small racks or frames where the silkworms spin the cocoons. Spinning of cocoons takes about 3–7 days.

The processing of silk from the cocoons involves the following steps:

Fig. 3.16: Boiling of cocoons

- **Boiling of cocoons**: For obtaining silk fibres, a pile of cocoons is used. They are kept under the sun or immersed in hot boiling water to kill the pupae inside (Fig. 3.16). On boiling, the silk fibres separate out from the cocoons because the sericin that adheres the silk filaments together gets dissolved. This process is also called **degumming**.
- **Process of reeling**: The process of taking out the silk fibres or threads from the cocoons is called **reeling**. Reeling is done by using special machines to unwind the threads or fibres of silk from the cocoons (Fig. 3.17).

  Then, the fibres from a few cocoons are joined and twisted together to make a strong thread that is wound around a reel (Fig. 3.18). The fibre that is obtained by the process of reeling is called **raw silk** (Fig. 3.19).

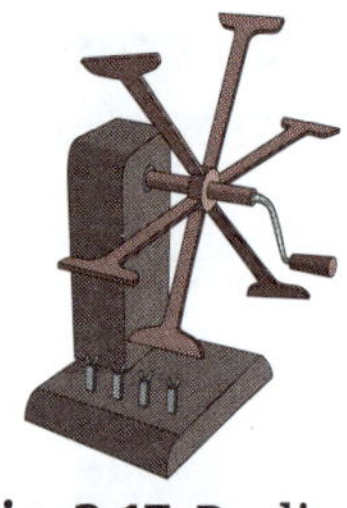

Fig. 3.17: Reeling machine

Fig. 3.18: Process of reeling

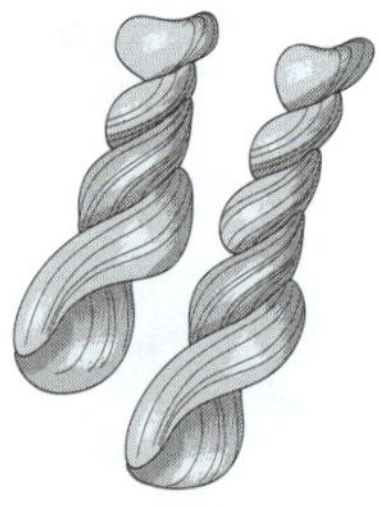

Fig. 3.19: Raw silk fibres

- **Dyeing of raw silk**: Depending on the requirement, the raw silk fibres can be dyed in various colours and then spun into silk threads.

  The silk threads are woven into silk cloth by weavers (Fig. 3.20).

  India is the second largest producer of silk in the world after China. Mulberry silk is the main variety of silk produced in India. About 90% of mulberry silk comes from Karnataka, Andhra Pradesh, Tamil Nadu and Uttar Pradesh. Assam, Madhya Pradesh and Odisha are other states in India that produce a major amount of silk.

Fig. 3.20: Woven silk cloth

Wonder!

To produce one kilogram of silk fibres, nearly 5000 silkworms are used.

Types of Silk Fibres

- **Mulberry silk:** It comes from the silkworm *Bombyx mori,* which feeds on the leaves of the mulberry trees. The commercial silk that is produced in the world mostly comes from this variety. The silk fibre obtained from this silkworm is soft, shiny, elastic and strong.
- **Tassar silk:** It is obtained from the silkworm *Antheraea paphia,* which mainly grows on plants such as Arjun and Asan (*Termanalia arjuna* and *T. tomentosa*). Tassar is rough in texture and generally appears light brown in colour. It is mostly used for furnishing and interior decoration items. It is usually less shiny than the mulberry silk.
- **Oak tassar:** It is a finer variety of tassar obtained from the silkworm *Antheraea proyeli,* which feeds on oak plants.
- **Kosa silk:** It is a kind of tassar silk from Central India. It is obtained from silkworms that feed particularly on Sal or Saja or Arjun trees. This silk is popular because of its soft and shiny texture. It is widely used in producing traditional Indian sarees.
- **Mooga (or Muga) silk:** This golden yellow coloured silk is obtained from the silkworm *Antheraea assamensis*. These silkworms mostly eat the leaves of the Soalu and Som plants. Like tassar, they are cultivated on trees.

Health Hazards in Sericulture

- Manual handling of the cocoons may lead to blisters, peeled-off skins or minor skin infections sometimes.
- The usage of chemicals to dye the silk may result in the irritation of eyes, infections of skin and lungs and breathing problems.
- Inappropriate ventilation, high temperatures and humidity in the factories can harm the general health of workers.

Activity 1

Aim: To distinguish a pure silk thread from a synthetic (artificial) silk thread

Note: To be performed in the presence and with the assistance of a teacher. Be careful while handling fire.

Procedure:

1. Collect pure silk threads and synthetic silk threads.
2. Light the candle/spirit lamp.
3. Using a tong or a forcep, bring each fibre to the flame. Do they burn?
4. Note the difference in smell while burning the pure silk thread and the synthetic silk thread, and observe the way each thread burns.

Observation table:

S. No.	Type of fibre	Burning	Smell
1.	Pure silk thread		
2.	Synthetic (artificial) silk thread		

Conclusion: If the thread burns slowly and curls away from the flame and ash is produced after burning with a bad smell, it indicates that the thread is pure silk. If the thread burns with a flame and melts with a burning smell of plastic resulting in the formation of a hard bead at the end of the thread, it indicates that the thread is an artificial silk.

Activity 2

Aim: To identify the type of fibre based on its structure

Procedure:

1. Collect the samples of the following fabrics: cotton, nylon, wool, polyester and silk.
2. Place each of the fabric samples under a dissection microscope and observe the texture of each of them carefully.
3. Record your observations as shiny, dull, silky, rough and smooth.

Observation: Fill the table based on your observations.

S. No.	Type of fabric	Texture
1.	Cotton	
2.	Nylon	
3.	Wool	
4.	Silk	

Keywords

Rearing: The process of domestication and rearing of animals

Selective breeding: The process of selecting a set of parents for obtaining desirable characters in their offspring

Shearing: The process of the removal of fleece from the body of animals

Sericulture: The process of rearing of silkworms for the production of silk

Reeling: The process of taking out the threads from cocoons

Raw silk: The fibres that are obtained through the reeling process

Summary

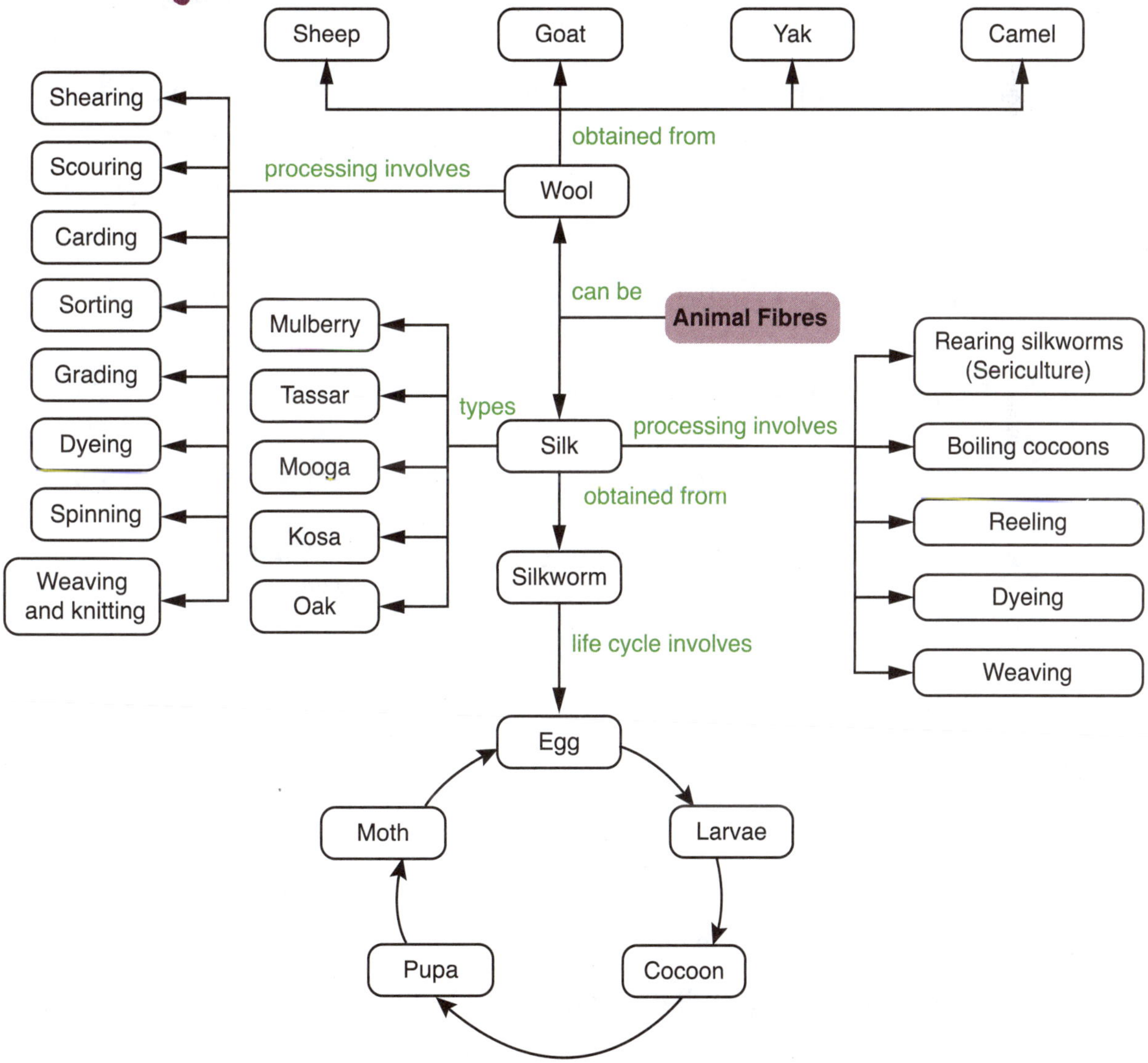

EXERCISE

W

ia

A. Choose the correct option.

1. Which of the following is the correct order of the processes involved in the processing of silk from cocoons?

   (a) Spinning, Reeling, Dyeing (b) Reeling, Dyeing, Weaving
   (c) Dyeing, Spinning, Weaving (d) Degumming, Reeling, Dyeing

2. Which animal is the main source of wool?

   (a) Alpaca (b) Sheep (c) Yak (d) Llama

3. Which of the following stages of a silk moth is also called a caterpillar?

   (a) Pupa (b) Larva (c) Adult moth (d) Egg

4. Alpaca is a species of ________________.

   (a) sheep (b) camel (c) cow (d) goat

5. Which of the following traps more air?

   (a) Cotton (b) Wool (c) Silk (d) Polyester

B. Fill in the blanks.

ia

1. A silkworm that feeds on mulberry leaves gives ________________. (mulberry silk/tassar silk)
2. Silkworms spin their cocoons during the ________________. (larva stage/pupa stage)
3. The finest wool is obtained from the ________________. (Merino sheep/Angora goat)
4. Mohair is a source of ________________. (Angora goat/camel)
5. The term 'scouring' related to obtaining wool from fibre means ________________. (washing/dyeing)

C. State whether the following statements are true (T) or false (F).

1. Silkworms are fed on grasses and pulses. ☐
2. Moulting is the process of shedding skin. ☐
3. The coarse beard hair of sheep provide the fibre for making wool. ☐
4. The pupa feeds on mulberry leaves for two months. ☐
5. Kosa silk is the main variety of silk produced in India. ☐

D. Name the following methods.

1. Removing fleece from the body of animals
2. Washing fleece to free it from grease, dirt and dust
3. Grouping of wool as per length, colour and texture
4. Colouring of the fibres
5. Twisting of fibres into yarns

E. Give reasons for the following.

1. Selective breeding is important in animal husbandry.
2. Shearing is done mainly in the summer months.
3. Cocoons should not be collected with bare hands.
4. Caterpillars shed their skin when they grow bigger.
5. The secretions of pupating caterpillars are important.

F. Answer the following questions briefly.

1. Mention the place and the type of the wool obtained from the following breeds of sheep.
   (a) Targhee
   (b) Nali
   (c) Lohi
   (d) Barbado
2. What is sericulture?
3. What are the characteristics of silk fibres?
4. What is selective breeding? State its advantages.
5. Distinguish between silk and wool fibres.

G. Answer the following questions in detail.

1. Describe the stages involved in the life cycle of a silkworm with a neat and labelled diagram.
2. Briefly explain the steps involved in the production of wool.
3. Explain about the rearing and breeding of sheep.
4. Briefly explain the steps involved in the processing of silk.
5. Describe different types of silk fibres.

COGNITIVE CORNER

Critical Thinking

What are the ethical implications of sericulture, particularly regarding the treatment of silkworms during the silk harvesting process?

Picture Study

Identify the animals shown in the pictures given below and name the fibre obtained from them.

Project

1. Make a scrapbook by collecting images of various wool-yielding animals and add a brief note on their origin. **(C-7.3)**
2. Collect information about the kind of silk varieties produced in India and name the leading producers of silk in India. Find out other uses of silk besides as a garment. Make a presentation based on your findings. **(C-7.1)**
3. Form an Eco Club with your classmates. Collect silk cloth pieces and paste them into your scrapbook. You can find them in a tailor's shop among the heaps of waste cut pieces. Identify silk types such as mulberry silk, tassar silk, eri silk and mooga silk with the help of your teacher. Compare the texture of these silk pieces with that of artificial silk pieces, which contain synthetic fibres. Try and collect pictures of different moths whose caterpillars produce the various types of silk. **(C-6.2)**

In the Library

Collect information about '*Ahimsa* silk' (the silk fibre obtained after the moth has emerged out of the cocoon, without killing it) from your library books and write a short article on it. **(C-7.1)**

Life Skills

A forensic person wants to identify the texture of a sample fabric that he collected. Does observing the fabric under microscope help him? If so, how? **(C-5.2)**

Worksheet

Ancient India had a rich history and knowledge of the cotton industry, traced back thousands of years. You will be surprised to know that the cotton industry played a significant role in India's economic growth and international trade, and was one of the factors that enabled India to gain the title of **Golden Bird** in ancient times. Some of the key features of cotton cultivation and textile in ancient India are discussed here.

Cotton bolls

- Use of plant-based compost or animal manure
- Crop rotation approach that maintained the health and productivity of the land
- Employing efficient water management techniques such as canal irrigation and rainwater harvesting to conserve water resources
- Use of natural dyes that minimized pollution of water bodies and had a lower ecological footprint
- Manual handloom weaving that does not require the use of electricity or other non-renewable energy sources

However, the modern methods used to produce cotton clothes are often harmful to the environment. There are three main areas of concern.

- The production and processing of cotton require a large quantity of water. It is estimated that about 20,000 litres of water is needed to produce one T-shirt and a pair of jeans!
- Cotton crop, over a period of time, depletes nutrients from the soil.
- A substantial amount of fertilizers and pesticides are used in cotton fields.

Do you think applying ancient Indian knowledge of cotton cultivation and textiles can help deal with environmental issues posed by the modern cotton industry? Explain.

____

____

____

____

____

4 Physical and Chemical Changes

Curricular Goals

- Explore the world of matter and its constituents, properties and behaviour **(CG-1)**
- Explore the nature and processes of science through engaging with the evolution of scientific knowledge and conducting scientific inquiry **(CG-6)**
- Communicate questions, observations and conclusions related to science **(CG-7)**

Competencies

- Classify matter based on observable physical and chemical characteristics **(C-1.1)**
- Describe changes in matter and use particulate nature to represent the properties of matter and the changes **(C-1.2)**
- Formulate questions using scientific terminology and collect data as evidence **(C-6.2)**
- Use scientific vocabulary to communicate science accurately in oral and written form, and through visual representation **(C-7.1)**
- Design and build simple models to demonstrate scientific concepts **(C-7.2)**

Let's Get Started

Look at the following images and name the substance that each of these objects is made up of.

Coins

____

Foil paper

____

Pencils

____

Substances undergo changes, altering their state without composition change or resulting in a new substance formation. These changes can be broadly categorized into physical and chemical changes based on their characteristics and how they occur.

PHYSICAL CHANGES

Some changes in nature do not produce any new substance but only bring about a change in the shape, state, colour, size, etc., of substances. Such changes are called ***physical changes***. For example, the process of dissolving sugar in water is an example of a physical change.

Characteristics of a Physical Change

- It is a temporary change that is sometimes irreversible. For example, melting of an ice cube can be reversed by freezing the water again. However, after cutting a sheet of paper into small pieces, it cannot be restored to its original form.
- Chemical composition and properties of the substance remain unchanged in a physical change. For example, when sugar is dissolved in water, the sugar molecules disperse throughout the water but remain chemically the same.
- There may be a change in shape, size, state or colour of a substance undergoing a physical change. Examples: crushing a can [Fig. 4.1 (a)], stretching a rubber band [Fig. 4.1 (b)], boiling water [Fig. 4.1 (c)] or melting an ice cube [Fig. 4.1 (d)].
- No new substance is formed in a physical change. For example, cutting a sheet of paper into small pieces does not form any new substances; it remains paper.
- There may or may not be any exchange of energy during a physical change. For example, melting ice requires the absorption of energy as heat, while condensing water vapour into liquid releases energy. However, some physical changes such as changing the shape of an object or dissolving a solid in a liquid may not involve a significant exchange of energy.

(a) Crushing of can (b) Stretching a rubber band (c) Boiling of water (d) Melting of ice

Fig. 4.1: Some examples of physical changes

CHEMICAL CHANGES

A ***chemical change*** *occurs when two or more chemical substances react to form new products that have an entirely different set of properties.* As you have learned in your previous classes, chemical changes are irreversible changes.

Characteristics of a Chemical Change

- A chemical change is a permanent change that cannot be reversed by applying simple physical methods. For example, burning a piece of paper. Once the paper undergoes combustion, it turns into ash and cannot be converted back into its original form.
- One or more new substances are formed in a chemical change. For example, the reaction between hydrogen and oxygen gases forms water.
- The composition and properties of the original substance change during a chemical change. For example, rusting of iron, where iron reacts with oxygen in the presence of moisture to form iron oxide (Fig. 4.2).

Fig. 4.2: Rusting of iron

- Large amount of energy is either absorbed or released in the form of heat or light. For example, combustion of a fuel such as burning wood releases energy in the form of heat and light.
- During chemical changes, the total mass before and after the reaction remains the same. Example: The reaction between vinegar and baking soda to produce carbon dioxide gas, water and a salt; although the appearance and properties of the substances change, the total mass before and after the reaction remains the same.

Activity 1

Aim: To identify the changes that take place during a physical change

Materials required: A sheet of paper, water, test tube, balloon, aluminium foil and a piece of copper wire

Note: *To be performed in the presence of a teacher.*

Procedure: Perform the following activities and record your observations in the observation table.

1. Take a sheet of paper and crumple it with your hands.
2. Boil water in a test tube until vapours begin to rise.
3. Inflate a balloon.
4. Tear an aluminium foil.
5. Hammer a piece of copper wire.

Observation: Write your observations in the table given alongside.

Activity	Changes observed			
	Change in shape	Change in colour	Change in state	Change in size
Crumpling a sheet of paper				
Boiling water				
Inflating a balloon				
Tearing an aluminium foil				
Hammering a piece of copper wire				

Conclusion: ______________________________

All these changes involve one or more substances. Each substance has a unique composition. So, in order to understand these changes in a better way, let us learn about the composition of these substances.

CHEMICAL SUBSTANCES

All substances are made up of matter. *Anything that has weight and occupies space is called* ***matter***. Chemical substances are made up of atoms and molecules. ***Atom*** *is the smallest unit of matter*. The word atom is derived from the Greek word *atomos* that means indivisible.

Atom can also be defined as the smallest particle of an element or a compound that exhibits all the properties of that substance and may or may not exist independently. *Two or more atoms that are chemically bound together form a* ***molecule***.

Generally, substances can be pure or impure. Pure substances consist of only one type of atoms or molecules, whereas impure substances are a mixture of different types of atoms or molecules. Elements and compounds are pure substances.

Elements: *Substances that consist of only one type of atoms and cannot be broken down into simpler substances physically or chemically are called* ***elements***. Each element has its own individual properties. Hence, the atoms of an element have all the properties similar to that specific element. Elements can be classified into three broad groups: metals, non-metals and metalloids. Some examples of elements are iron, copper, oxygen and carbon.

Compounds: *Substances in which two or more elements are combined together chemically in definite proportions are called* ***compounds***. When two elements combine to form a compound, they lose their characteristic properties. Hence, the new compound formed has properties of its own. For example, two atoms of hydrogen gas and one atom of oxygen gas combine in a definite proportion to form a molecule of water in liquid form. Iron is magnetic in nature, but when it combines with sulphur, it forms iron sulphide which is non-magnetic in nature.

Mixtures: *Substances in which two or more substances are mixed together physically in no definite proportion are called* ***mixtures***. Some examples of mixtures are sugar solution (a mixture of sugar and water) and air (a mixture of gases such as oxygen, nitrogen and carbon dioxide).

CHEMICAL SYMBOLS

There are about 118 known elements. Of these 118 elements, 94 have been found naturally on the Earth and the remaining 24 have been synthesized in laboratories.

Know the Scientist

The first scientist to use 'symbols' for elements was John Dalton.

To make it easier for us to remember them, elements have been designated with letters or abbreviations. *The representation of an element using the short form or abbreviation of its name is called its* ***chemical symbol***. All the names and symbols of the elements are approved by the International Union of Pure and Applied Chemistry.

In earlier times, pictorial representations of the elements were used. Later, elements were named after the name of the place where they were first found. For example, the name 'copper' and its symbol 'Cu' came from the Latin word *cuprum*, which means 'from the island of Cyprus'.

In the modern method of representation of elements, letters representing the names of the elements are used as symbols. Features of this method are as follows:

- For some elements, the first letter of their names is used as the symbol, which is written in capital letter. For example, C for carbon, O for oxygen and N for nitrogen.
- If two or more elements have their English names starting with the same letter, then a two-letter symbol is used. To represent such elements, the first letter of the name is used as the first letter of the symbol, which is written in capital letter. Then the next non-repeating letter of the name is used as the second letter of the symbol, which is written in small letter. For example, C for carbon, Ca for calcium, Cd for cadmium, Cl for chlorine and Co for cobalt.
- For some elements, the symbols are derived from their Latin names. For example, the Latin name of gold is *Aurum* and its symbol is Au.

Thus, each element has a unique name and chemical symbol (Table 4.1).

Table 4.1: Symbols of some elements

Element (Latin name)	Symbol	Element (Latin name)	Symbol	Element (Latin name)	Symbol
Hydrogen	H	Aluminium	Al	Zinc	Zn
Carbon	C	Nitrogen	N	Phosphorus	P
Boron	B	Argon	Ar	Sulphur	S
Iodine	I	Fluorine	F	Lead (*Plumbum*)	Pb
Lithium	Li	Oxygen	O	Silver (*Argentum*)	Ag
Beryllium	Be	Barium	Ba	Copper (*Cuprum*)	Cu
Silicon	Si	Bromine	Br	Gold (*Aurum*)	Au
Magnesium	Mg	Calcium	Ca	Helium	He
Manganese	Mn	Iron (*Ferrum*)	Fe	Neon	Ne
Chlorine	Cl	Sulphur	S	Potassium (*Kalium*)	K
Mercury (*Hydrargyrum*)	Hg	Sodium (*Natrium*)	Na	Cobalt	Co

Atomicity

*The number of atoms that make up a molecule of an element is called its **atomicity**.*

The atomicity of an element is written on the right-hand side of its symbol as a subscript. Based on the number of atoms present, elements can be classified as monatomic, diatomic, triatomic and tetratomic (Table 4.2).

Table 4.2: Atomicity of some elements

Element	Atomicity	Molecules	Element	Atomicity	Molecules
Helium	1 (Monatomic)	He	Chlorine	2 (Diatomic)	Cl_2
Argon	1 (Monatomic)	Ar	Oxygen	2 (Diatomic)	O_2
Hydrogen	2 (Diatomic)	H_2	Ozone	3 (Triatomic)	O_3
Nitrogen	2 (Diatomic)	N_2	Phosphorus	4 (Tetratomic)	P_4

CHEMICAL FORMULAE

*The symbolic representation of the composition of a chemical compound is called its **chemical formula**.*

A chemical formula shows the different elements present in a molecule of a compound and the number of atoms of each combining or constituent element in the compound (Table 4.3).

For example, the chemical formula of sodium chloride (common salt) is NaCl. The formula conveys that a molecule of salt contains one atom of sodium and one atom of chlorine.

Table 4.3: Formulae of some compounds

Compound	Formula	Compound	Formula	Compound	Formula
Water	H_2O	Potassium chloride	KCl	Hydrogen sulphide	H_2S
Ammonia gas	NH_3	Carbon dioxide	CO_2	Methane	CH_4
Sodium chloride (Salt)	NaCl	Magnesium chloride	$MgCl_2$	Hydrochloric acid	HCl

Atomic Model

The structure of an atom can be described as follows.

- An atom is composed of three fundamental particles: protons, neutrons and electrons.
- The central part of an atom is called the **nucleus,** which is small and dense in nature.
- The **protons** (positively charged particles) and the **neutrons** (no charge/neutral particles) are present within the nucleus of an atom.
- Outside the nucleus, the **electrons** (negatively charged particles) revolve around the nucleus in various fixed paths called **orbits** or **shells**.
- The shells or orbits are represented by the numbers n = 1, 2, 3, 4 or by the letters K, L, M, N. These orbits or shells are also known as '**energy levels**' or '**energy shells**'.
- Each shell can accommodate only a fixed number of electrons. K-shell can hold 2 electrons, L-shell can hold 8 electrons, M-shell can hold 18 electrons and so on.
- The outermost shell of an atom is called its **valence shell**. The electrons in the valence shell determine the chemical reactivity of an atom and are called **valence electrons**. These valence electrons are lost, gained or shared when compounds are formed. So, the **valency** of an element is its ability to gain, lose or share electrons to form a compound.

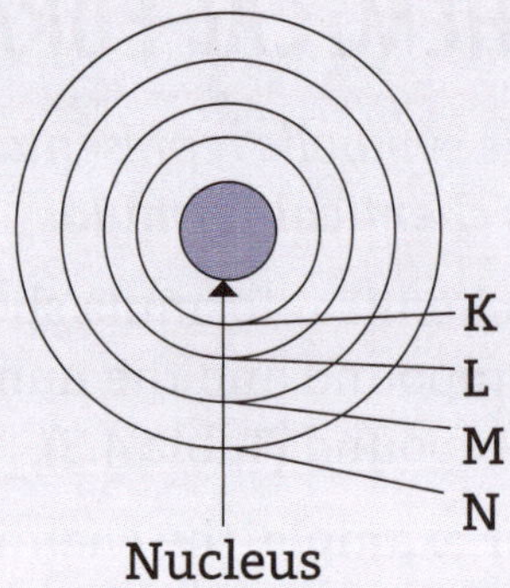

Valency

We know that compounds have elements in definite proportions. This definite proportion refers to the maximum quantity (expressed in number of atoms) of one element that can combine with the maximum quantity (i.e. number of atoms) of another element.

*The combining capacity of the atom of an element with the atoms of other elements is called its **valency**.*

The electrons present in the outermost shell of an atom are called **valence electrons**. Valence electrons in an element have more energy than the inner electrons, hence they take part in a chemical reaction.

The valency of an element is always a whole number. We can determine the valency of an element by looking at the chemical formula of its compounds (Table 4.4).

For example, $MgCl_2$ is the chemical formula of magnesium chloride. From the formula, we know that one atom of magnesium combines with two atoms of chlorine. So, the valency of Mg is two and that of chlorine is one.

Consider another example of hydrogen chloride (HCl). One atom of hydrogen combines with one atom of chlorine. So, the valency of hydrogen and chlorine is one each.

In order to write the chemical formula of a compound, it is important to know the valency of the elements.

Table 4.4: Valencies of some elements

Element	Valency	Element	Valency	Element	Valency
Sodium	1	Magnesium	2	Chlorine	1
Potassium	1	Calcium	2	Carbon	4
Silver	1	Aluminium	3	Oxygen	2
Zinc	2	Hydrogen	1	Iodine	1

Writing a Chemical Formula

By following the steps given below, we can write the chemical formula of a compound.

1. Write the symbols of the elements that form the compound.
2. Write their valencies on top of their symbols as superscripts.
3. If the valencies are identical, cancel the valencies. If the valencies are different, then interchange the valencies with respect to the symbols by making arrows and write them as subscripts.
4. Simplify the formula by dividing the valencies by a common number, if divisible.
5. The valency of 1 need not be written in the final formula.

Keeping these steps in mind, let us write the chemical formula of the compounds 'magnesium chloride' and 'magnesium oxide'.

	Magnesium	Chlorine	
Step 1:	Mg	Cl	(Write the symbols of the constituent elements, here magnesium and chlorine)
Step 2:	Mg^2	Cl^1	(Write the valency of each element as superscript)
Step 3:	Mg^2 ↘ ↙	Cl^1	(Interchange the valencies and write them as subscripts)
	Mg_1	Cl_2	
Step 4:	$MgCl_2$ (Magnesium chloride)		(Divide the valencies by a common factor, if divisible)

	Magnesium	Oxygen	
Step 1:	Mg	O	(Write the symbols of the constituent elements, here magnesium and oxygen)
Step 2:	Mg^2	O^2	(Write the valency of each element as superscript)
Step 3:	Mg^2 ↘ ↙	O^2	(Interchange the valencies and write them as subscripts)
	Mg_2	O_2	
Step 4:	$Mg_2O_2 \longrightarrow MgO$ (Magnesium oxide)		(Divide the valencies by a common factor, here 2)

CHEMICAL EQUATIONS

A chemical change resulting in the formation of one or more new substances is called a ***chemical reaction.***

The representation of a chemical reaction using symbols and formulae of the elements or compounds involved in the reaction is called a ***chemical equation.***

A chemical reaction can also be expressed in words, that is, by writing only the names of the elements or compounds involved in the reaction. The equation is then called a **word equation**.

Writing a Chemical Equation

The chemical substances that participate in a chemical reaction are called ***reactants.*** *The new substances formed due to a chemical reaction are called* ***products.***

To write the chemical equation of a reaction, the reactants are written on the left-hand side (LHS) and the combination is shown with a plus sign (+) between them. The products are written on the right-hand side (RHS). If there is more than one product, then a plus sign is given between the products. The change of reactants to products is indicated by placing an arrow between them. The head of the arrow points towards the products, which conveys the direction of the reaction.

For example, consider the reaction of magnesium with oxygen. Magnesium reacts with oxygen to form magnesium oxide. The word equation of the chemical reaction would be:

$$\text{Magnesium} + \text{Oxygen} \longrightarrow \text{Magnesium oxide}$$

To write a chemical equation, the names of the reactants and the products are replaced with their symbols and formulae.

$$Mg + O_2 \longrightarrow MgO$$

$$\underset{\text{(Reactants)}}{\text{Magnesium (Mg)} + \text{Oxygen } (O_2)} \longrightarrow \underset{\text{(Product)}}{\text{Magnesium oxide (MgO)}}$$

The Law of Conservation of Mass states that mass can neither be created nor destroyed. In a chemical change, the total mass of the reactants always equals the total mass of the products. Hence, the number of atoms of each element on both sides of a chemical equation should be equal, that is, the equation should be balanced. Let us now learn how to balance an equation.

Balancing a Chemical Equation

Consider the chemical reaction of magnesium with oxygen.

$$Mg + O_2 \longrightarrow MgO$$

1. Count the number of atoms of each element in the reactants and products of the chemical equation.

Element	Number of atoms in reactants (LHS)	Number of atoms in products (RHS)
Mg	1	1
O	2	1

From the above table, we can see that one atom of magnesium and two atoms of oxygen take part in the reaction to form one molecule of magnesium oxide. But one oxygen atom is enough to react with magnesium to form one molecule of magnesium oxide.

Oxygen cannot be destroyed; so, if there are two oxygen atoms participating in a reaction, each will need a magnesium atom. So, we balance the equation to show the correct number of atoms participating in the reaction. How do we do that?

2. To balance oxygen atoms on both sides of the equation, multiply the product (RHS) by 2.

Element	Number of atoms in reactants (LHS)	Number of atoms in products (RHS)
Mg	1	$1 \times 2 = 2$
O	2	$1 \times 2 = 2$

$$Mg \text{ (Magnesium)} + O_2 \text{ (Oxygen)} \longrightarrow 2MgO \text{ (Magnesium oxide)}$$

Now in the equation, the number of oxygen atoms is balanced but the number of magnesium atoms on both sides is not balanced.

3. To balance magnesium atoms on both sides of the equation, multiply the magnesium atom in the reactants (LHS) by 2.

Element	Number of atoms in reactants (LHS)	Number of atoms in products (RHS)
Mg	$1 \times 2 = 2$	$1 \times 2 = 2$
O	2	$1 \times 2 = 2$

$$2Mg \text{ (Magnesium)} + O_2 \text{ (Oxygen)} \longrightarrow 2MgO \text{ (Magnesium oxide)}$$

Now, the above chemical equation is said to be balanced.

Revise and Recall

Write balanced equations for the given chemical reactions.

1. ________ Hg + ________ $O_2 \longrightarrow$ ________ HgO
2. ________ Al + ________ $Cl_2 \longrightarrow$ ________ $AlCl_3$
3. ________ Zn + ________ HCl $\longrightarrow$ ________ $ZnCl_2$ + ________ H_2
4. ________ $K_2O \longrightarrow$ ________ K + ________ O_2
5. ________ Na + ________ $O_2 \longrightarrow$ ________ Na_2O

CHEMICAL REACTIONS

*A **chemical reaction** is a type of chemical change that occurs when two or more chemical substances react to form new products that have an entirely different set of properties.* As you have learned in your previous classes, chemical changes are irreversible changes.

Let us learn about some of the properties of a chemical reaction.

- **Change in energy**: Some chemical reactions may give out heat, while some may absorb heat from their surroundings. *A change or reaction where heat is released is called an **exothermic reaction**.*

For example, in a reaction between carbon and oxygen, carbon dioxide is formed with the generation of heat.

Carbon + Oxygen $\longrightarrow$ Carbon dioxide + Heat

A change or reaction in which heat is absorbed from the surroundings is called an ***endothermic reaction****.*

For example, in a reaction between carbon and sulphur, carbon disulphide is formed with the absorption of heat.

Carbon + Sulphur + Heat $\longrightarrow$ Carbon disulphide

- **Change in colour**: The colour of the product may differ from that of the reactants. For example, copper sulphate is blue in colour, but after reacting with iron, the product formed (iron sulphide) is green in colour.
- **Evolution of gas**: Some chemical reactions also produce gases. These gases are actually the products formed in the gaseous state. Generally, the gases produced can be carbon dioxide, hydrogen and ammonia. The presence of carbon dioxide can be confirmed as it turns lime water milky, and the presence of hydrogen can be confirmed as it burns with a pop sound when a burning splint is brought near it.
- **Formation of precipitate**: In some chemical reactions, the product formed may be an insoluble solid. It separates from the solution and forms a different mass or layer. This insoluble solid is called a precipitate. For example, in a reaction between copper sulphate and hydrogen sulphide, copper sulphide and sulphuric acid are formed. The copper sulphide formed is given out as a precipitate.

  $CuSO_4 + H_2S \longrightarrow CuS + H_2SO_4$

Let us learn about some everyday examples of chemical reactions.

- **Rusting**

  Look at the images given alongside (Fig. 4.3). You might have seen these objects covered with a reddish-brown substance when their surface gets exposed to air and moisture (water) for a long time. *The process of formation of a reddish-brown flaky substance on the surface of iron objects in the presence of moisture and air is called* ***rusting****.* The reddish-brown deposit formed on the iron objects is called **rust**.

Fig. 4.3: Rusted articles

  The chemical reaction of rusting can be represented by the following chemical equation:

Iron (Fe) + Oxygen (O_2) + Water (H_2O) $\longrightarrow$ Rust (Iron oxide, Fe_2O_3)

The presence of moisture and oxygen (air) is necessary for the process of rusting.

Rusting may lead to the damage of bridges and ships as these are made of iron. The process of rusting can be prevented by painting and oiling iron objects regularly.

The process of coating iron objects with a thin layer of zinc is called ***galvanization***. For example, the iron pipes used for supplying water at our homes are galvanized to prevent rusting.

Science in Context

Salt water expedites the process of rusting, which results in huge monetary loss to the shipping industry.

- **Browning of cut fruits and vegetables**

  Look at the images given alongside (Fig. 4.4). You might have noticed that some of the cut pieces of vegetables and fruits such as brinjal, potato, pear and apple turn brown when exposed to air, if they are not consumed immediately. Have you ever thought what kind of a change it is?

(a) Pear (b) Brinjal

Fig. 4.4: Browning of cut fruits and vegetables

  It is an example of a chemical change or reaction in which some compounds present in these fruits and vegetables react with oxygen present in the air to form a brown-coloured pigment called 'melanin'. *The process in which the surface of cut fruits and vegetables turns brown when exposed to air is called* ***browning***.

- **Reaction between vinegar and baking soda**

  Take vinegar (acetic acid) in a glass beaker and add a pinch of baking soda (sodium hydrogen carbonate) to it. You will see gas bubbles coming out of the beaker (Fig. 4.5). This reaction is an example of a chemical change as gas bubbles are formed due to the release of carbon dioxide. This can be confirmed by making the produced gas pass through freshly prepared lime water (Fig. 4.6). The lime water turns milky when carbon dioxide is passed through it due to the formation of calcium carbonate.

  Vinegar + Baking soda ⟶ Carbon dioxide + Water + Other compounds

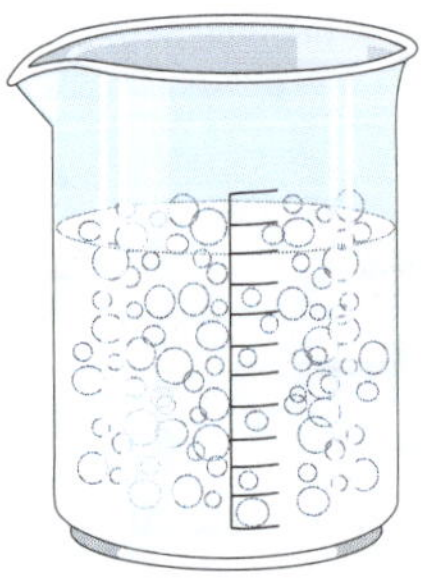

Fig. 4.5: Reaction between vinegar and baking soda

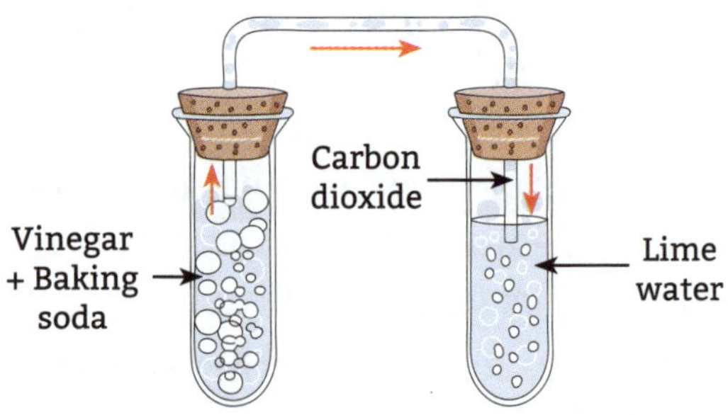

Fig. 4.6: Set-up showing the passage of carbon dioxide to lime water

The chemical reaction can be represented by the following equation:

Carbon dioxide (CO_2) + Lime water [$Ca(OH)_2$] ⟶ Calcium carbonate ($CaCO_3$) + Water (H_2O)

- **Reaction between copper sulphate solution and iron filings**

Take some water in a glass beaker and add a pinch of copper sulphate to it to form copper sulphate solution. Add a few drops of dilute sulphuric acid to the solution till it turns blue. Drop an iron nail into the copper sulphate solution. After some time, you will notice that the blue colour of the copper sulphate solution turns green due to the formation of a new substance called iron sulphate (Fig. 4.7). The brown-coloured deposit formed on the iron nail is of copper. As there is formation of new substances in this reaction, it is an example of a chemical change.

The chemical reaction can be represented by the following equation:

$$\underset{\text{(blue)}}{\text{Iron + Copper sulphate}} \longrightarrow \underset{\text{(green)}}{\text{Iron sulphate + Copper}}$$

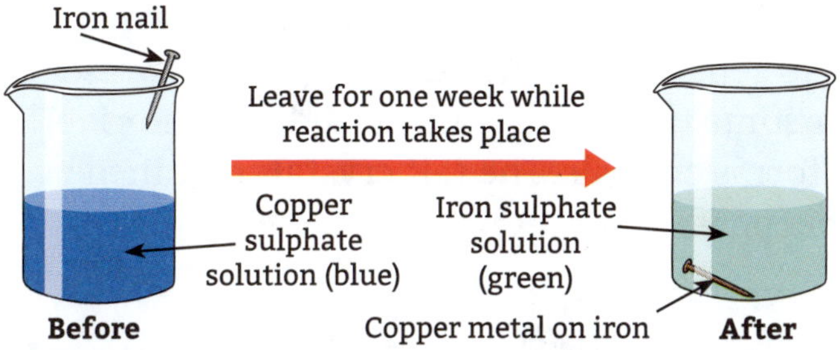

Fig. 4.7: Reaction between copper sulphate and iron

Science in Context

A burning candle is an example of both physical and chemical changes. The melting of wax is a physical change. Burning of candle wick and wax vapour are chemical changes.

Activity 2

Aim: To identify the changes that take place during a chemical change

Materials required: Test tubes, paper, table salt solution, potato slices, chemical reagents such as hydrogen peroxide, dilute hydrochloric acid, silver nitrate and magnesium ribbon

Note: *To be performed in the presence and with the assistance of a teacher.*

Procedure: Perform the following activities and record your observations in the observation table.

1. Burn a piece of paper.
2. Take a few drops of table salt solution in a test tube and add a few drops of silver nitrate into it.
3. Take hydrogen peroxide in a test tube and put a slice of potato in it.
4. Place a small piece of magnesium ribbon in a test tube. Add a few drops of dilute hydrochloric acid into the test tube. Carefully touch the lower surface of the test tube and feel the difference.

Activity	Changes observed			
	Change in colour	Formation of gas	Formation of precipitate	Release of heat
Burning the paper				
Reaction between sodium chloride (table salt solution) and silver nitrate				

Conclusion: ____________________

Crystallization

a

The process of formation of crystals is called ***crystallization***. The process of crystallization is an example of a physical change.

Separation of salt by crystallization process: The process of evaporation is used to obtain common salt (sodium chloride) from sea water, which has a large amount of salt dissolved in it. The salt obtained by this process consists of many impurities such as sand and magnesium chloride. This impure salt can be purified by the crystallization process (Fig. 4.8).

Fig. 4.8: Separation of salt from sea water

Thus, for crystallization, a large amount of salt is dissolved in water and allowed to boil. The boiled solution is then filtered to separate the insoluble impurities present in it. The filtrate is kept undisturbed for some time until the salt (sodium chloride) present in the solution aggregates and forms crystals. The salt crystals obtained by this process are then used for various purposes.

Activity 3

a

Aim: To find out whether crystallization is a physical or a chemical change

Materials required: Beaker, Bunsen burner, water, copper sulphate salt, dilute hydrochloric acid, watch glass, conical flask and glass container

Note: *To be performed in the presence of a teacher. Be careful while boiling the water.*

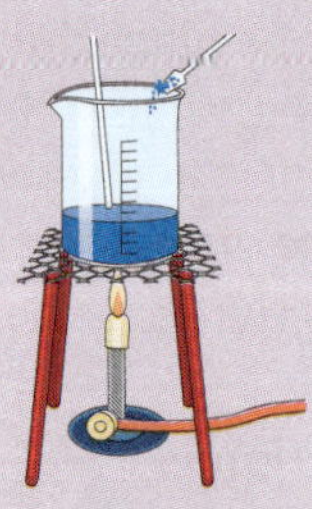

Dissolving $CuSO_4$ solution

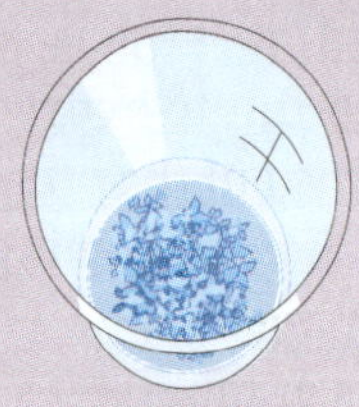

Filtrate of $CuSO_4$ solution

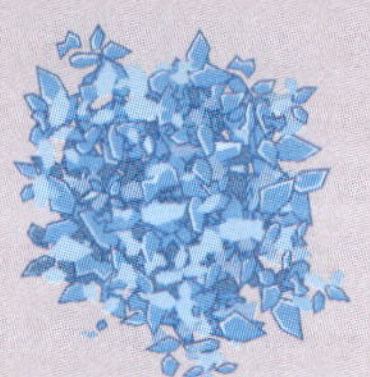

Crystals of $CuSO_4$

Procedure: Take 100 mℓ of water in a 250 mℓ beaker. Boil the water using a Bunsen burner/spirit lamp. Gradually, add copper sulphate ($CuSO_4$) salt to the water and stir the mixture until it has completely dissolved. Continue adding copper sulphate into the solution until it no longer dissolves. Add a small quantity of dilute H_2SO_4 to make the solution clear. This prevents the hydrolysis of copper sulphate. Allow the solution to cool. Take the watch glass and stick a label 'copper sulphate' on it. Filter the mixture into a conical flask and put a few drops of filtrate on the watch glass too. Label the container with filtrate and cover it with a piece of paper. Place the container and the watch glass undisturbed for two days. Observe what happens.

Observation: After two days, you can see crystals of copper sulphate formed on the watch glass and in the container too.

Conclusion: We can conclude that the process of crystallization is an example of a physical change.

Keywords

Atom: The smallest unit of matter

Molecule: Two or more atoms that are chemically bound together

Elements: Substances that consist of only one type of atoms

Compounds: Substances in which two or more elements are combined together chemically in definite proportions

Mixtures: Substances in which two or more substances are mixed together physically in no definite proportion

Atomicity: The number of atoms that make up a molecule of an element

Chemical reaction: A chemical change resulting in the formation of one or more new substances

Reactants: The chemical substances that participate in a chemical reaction

Products: The new substances formed due to a chemical reaction

Chemical change: The reactions in which two or more substances react to form new products that have an entirely different set of properties

Summary

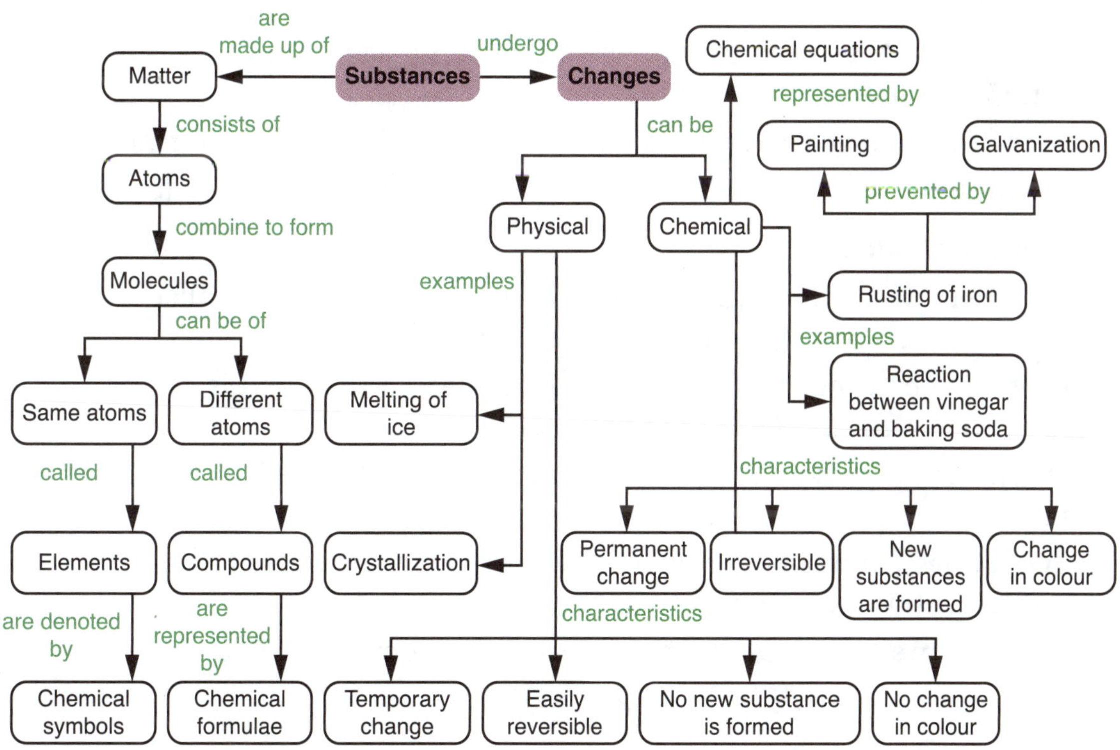

EXERCISE

W

A. Choose the correct option.

1. Manu dropped a horseshoe made of iron into a copper sulphate solution. After some time, he found that the horseshoe had a brown deposit on it. This was due to the formation of ____________.
   (a) iron sulphate (b) iron (c) copper (d) copper sulphate
2. Browning of fruits is an example of ____________.
   (a) physical change (b) chemical change (c) Both (a) and (b) (d) None of these
3. Which of the following is not a chemical change?
   (a) Inflating a balloon (b) Burning candle
   (c) Heating sugar (d) Rusting of iron
4. Iron forms rust when it reacts with ____________.
   (a) hydrogen and oxygen (b) oxygen and moisture (water)
   (c) carbon dioxide and hydrogen (d) water and carbon dioxide
5. The steps involved in writing the chemical formula of a substance are given below:
   i. Write the symbols of the elements.
   ii. If the valencies are identical, cancel the valencies.
   iii. Write the valency of the elements.
   iv. If the valencies are different, criss-cross and place them with reference to their symbol.

   Which of these is the correct sequence of writing the chemical formula?
   (a) i. ii. iii. iv. (b) i. iii. ii. iv. (c) i. iv. ii. iii. (d) i. iii. iv. ii.

B. Fill in the blanks.

ia

1. A change in which the composition of a substance changes is called ________________. (physical change/chemical change)
2. The number of atoms that make up a molecule of an element is called ________________. (atomicity/valency)
3. The symbolic representation of the composition of a chemical compound is called its ________________. (chemical formula/atomicity)
4. Salt obtained from sea water can be purified by the process of ________________. (crystallization/galvanization)
5. The chemical substances that participate in a chemical reaction are called ________________. (reactants/products)

C. State whether the following statements are true (T) or false (F).

1. The atoms of most of the elements exist independently. ☐
2. Elements are made up of different types of atoms. ☐
3. Each element has a name and a unique chemical symbol. ☐
4. Products of a chemical reaction are written on the left-hand side of the chemical equation. ☐
5. Rust is another form of iron. ☐

D. Define the following terms.

1. Valency
2. Chemical equation
3. Galvanization
4. Rusting
5. Crystallization
6. Reactants

E. Give reasons for the following.

1. The representation for the element oxygen and its molecule is different.
2. He, Ne and Ar do not have any valency.
3. It is important to know the valency to write a chemical formula.
4. CO_2 is a compound and not a mixture.
5. Each element has a unique chemical symbol.

F. Answer the following questions briefly.

1. Write the characteristics of a chemical change.
2. What are the differences between atoms and molecules?
3. The process of freezing is an example of a physical change even though water and ice have different properties. Why?
4. How are compounds different from mixtures?
5. How does the soaking of cut pieces of vegetables and fruits in water reduce the level of browning?

G. Answer the following questions in detail.

1. Distinguish between chemical and physical changes.
2. What are the steps involved in balancing a chemical equation? Explain with an example.
3. What is a chemical symbol? What are the features of the modern method of representing elements?
4. Distinguish between symbols, chemical formulae and chemical equations.

COGNITIVE CORNER

Critical Thinking

1. In an LPG cylinder, the contents are in the liquid form. When it comes out of the cylinder, it becomes a gas. What kind of change is it? Explain.
2. Why is the process of rusting more frequent in coastal areas?
3. Why is freshly prepared lime water used in experiments to test the evolution of carbon dioxide?

Picture Study

Look at the pictures given alongside and identify the phenomena.

____

____

Project

Collect information about the 'preparation of alum crystals and their uses'. Prepare a chart on it and display the same on your class noticeboard as a part of chemistry club. **(C-7.1)**

In the Laboratory

Aim: To study the conditions necessary for the process of rusting **(C-7.2)**

Materials required: Boiling tubes, iron nails, distilled water, water, coconut oil, grease, anhydrous calcium chloride, rubber corks and test tube stand

Procedure:

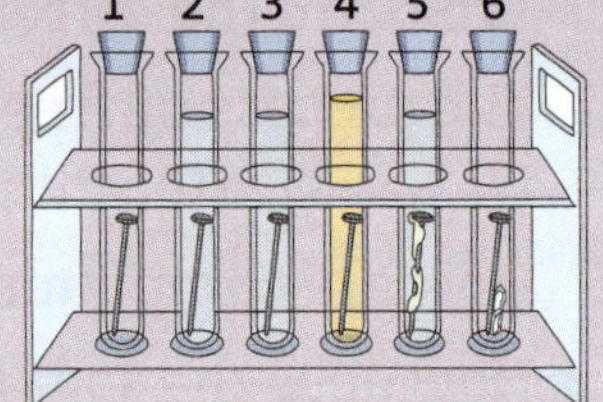

1. Take six clean 50 m*l* glass boiling tubes and label them as Set-up 1, 2, 3, 4, 5 and 6, respectively.
2. Place one iron nail in the boiling tube labelled as Set-up 1.
3. Take about 30 m*l* of boiled water (distilled water), water, coconut oil and water in Set-up 2, 3, 4 and 5, respectively.
4. Put one iron nail in Set-up 2, 3 and 4 and put an iron nail pre-coated with grease in Set-up 5.
5. Take 2–3 pinches of anhydrous calcium chloride in the boiling tube labelled as Set-up 6 and put one iron nail.
6. Seal the mouth of all the boiling tubes tightly with rubber corks and keep them in a test tube stand. Record your observations for each set-up in your notebook.

What do you conclude from the activity?

Life Skills

During Diwali, people burst firecrackers with their friends and family members. But in the recent times, we have been asked not to burst firecrackers. What is present inside a firecracker? Why should we completely avoid using fireworks? How it is harmful to the atmosphere? **(C-6.2)**

Worksheet

The railway network in India is one of the largest in the world. The Indian sub-continent is also criss-crossed by numerous rivers and their tributaries and distributaries.
To maintain seamless travel, the railways have built a large number of bridges which cross over these rivers while supporting railway tracks. These bridges are mainly built of iron. They are exposed to sun, wind, humidity, rain and in some states, snow throughout the year. In case they are weakened, disasters can take place. In history, quite a few bridges over rivers have collapsed due to old age and lack of maintenance.

Bridge across a river

Collapsed bridge

The main culprit for the wear and tear of iron is rust. Iron reacts chemically with oxygen and water vapour in the air to form a reddish, flaky compound called rust which eats away the iron and makes it weak.

Suggest 5 ways in which the railways can take care of these bridges so that no further accidents take place.

____

____

____

____

____

____

5 Acids, Bases and Salts

Curricular Goals

- Explore the world of matter and its constituents, properties and behaviour **(CG-1)**
- Explore the nature and processes of science through engaging with the evolution of scientific knowledge and conducting scientific inquiry **(CG-6)**

Competencies

- Classify matter based on observable physical and chemical characteristics **(C-1.1)**
- Formulate questions using scientific terminology and collect data as evidence **(C-6.2)**

Let's Get Started

Group the following things into salty, sour and bitter food items.

Tamarind

Neem

Sea water

Bitter gourd

Mango

Salty: ______________________________

Sour: ______________________________

Bitter: ______________________________

We all have tasted food that is salty, sweet, sour or bitter. Have you ever wondered why different food items have different tastes? Do all food items that have the similar taste possess the same properties? Do you know some fruits that are both sweet and sour in taste?

The taste of the food varies because each item has a unique chemical composition. These chemical composition can be categorized in different ways. One way is to classify them as acids, bases and salts.

Let us now learn about some of the properties and the uses of acids, bases and salts.

ACIDS

Some substances such as lemon, curd and tamarind have a sour taste (Fig. 5.1). This is due to the presence of a substance called 'acid' in them. Substances that contain acids are called **acidic substances.** The word acid comes from the Latin word *'acere'* meaning sour.

(a) Lemon (b) Curd (c) Tamarind

Fig. 5.1: Some acidic substances

Organic and Mineral Acids

Based on the sources they are obtained from, acids are categorized as organic acids and mineral acids.

Organic acids: *Acids that are naturally found in plants and animals (organisms) are called* ***organic acids.*** Table 5.1 lists some examples of organic acids.

Science in Context

Citric acid is a major industrial chemical, with over 2 million tons produced annually worldwide. Its primary source is not from fruit but from the fermentation of crude sugars (such as molasses and corn starch) by the mold *Aspergillus niger*. While it occurs naturally in citrus fruits, the industrial production process is the main contributor to the global supply.

Table 5.1: Organic acids in food items

Name of acid	Food items	Name of acid	Food items
Lactic acid	Curd, milk	Tartaric acid	Unripe mangoes, grapes
Oxalic acid	Spinach, tomatoes	Formic acid	Ant's sting
Citric acid	Oranges, lemons	Acetic acid	Vinegar
Malic acid	Apples	Ascorbic acid	Amla

Mineral acids: *Acids that are derived from an inorganic[1] material or source are called* ***mineral acids.***

Nitric acid, hydrochloric acid and sulphuric acid are examples of mineral acids. Mineral acids may be strong or weak, based on the way they take part in a chemical reaction.

Word Web

[1]**Inorganic**: Made from or containing materials, that do not come from plants or animals

Concentrated and Dilute Acids

Depending upon the volume of water present in acids, they are categorized into concentrated and dilute acids.

Dilute acids: *When water is added to acids, then they are called* ***dilute acids***. For example, 100 mℓ of water added to 10 mℓ of hydrochloric acid produces a dilute acid in the ratio 10 : 1. Dilutions can vary.

Concentrated acids: *When there is no water added or the volume of water added is lesser than that in dilute acids, then it is referred to as* ***concentrated acid***.
Therefore, if a volume less than 100 mℓ of water per 10 mℓ of acid is added, then it is a concentrated acid.

Wonder!

Most of the sour-tasting things contain acids, which make them taste sour. However, some substances may be sour due to the presence of non-acidic substances. For example, unripe fruits such as green grapes or green tomatoes are sour due to the presence of substances called tannins which impart a sour or astringent taste without being acidic.

Properties of Acids

- Acids are sour to taste.
- Acids turn blue litmus red.
- Acids can corrode[1] metals such as aluminium, zinc and iron due to their corrosive nature. That is why acids are stored in glass containers and not in metal containers.
- Most of the mineral acids cause burns, so care should be taken while handling these acids.
- Acids are soluble in water.
- Acids react with metals to form salt and hydrogen gas.

$$Mg + 2HCl \longrightarrow MgCl_2 + H_2$$

Magnesium + Hydrochloric acid ⟶ Magnesium chloride + Hydrogen gas

- Acids react with bases to form salt and water.

$$NaOH + HCl \longrightarrow NaCl + H_2O$$

Sodium hydroxide + Hydrochloric acid ⟶ Sodium chloride + Water

- Acids react with carbonates to form salt and carbon dioxide.

$$CaCO_3 + 2HCl \longrightarrow CaCl_2 + H_2O + CO_2$$

Calcium carbonate + Hydrochloric acid ⟶ Calcium chloride + Water + Carbon dioxide

Science in Context

While diluting acids, acids must always be added slowly to water while constantly stirring and not vice versa. If water is added to a concentrated acid, a large amount of heat is generated. This will cause the liquid to spurt out of the container onto our arms and can cause burns.

Word Web

[1]**Corrode:** To destroy something slowly by chemical action

Uses of Acids

Uses of some acids are given in Table 5.2.

Science in Context

Vinegar is nearly 4–8% of acetic acid by volume.

Table 5.2: Uses of acids

Name of the acid	Uses
Hydrochloric acid (HCl)	• It is used in steel industries to remove rust from iron. • It is used as an active ingredient in the synthesis of many chemicals (example: glue). • It is used to maintain the acidity of a solution and in wastewater treatment. • It is used in the processing of leather and to purify common salt. • It is used in industries to remove deposits formed inside the boilers. This process is called descaling.
Sulphuric acid (H_2SO_4)	• It is used in the manufacture of fertilizers (example: ammonium sulphate). • It is used in the production of nylon. • It is used as an industrial cleaning agent to remove rust from automobiles. • It is used as an electrolyte in the car batteries. • It is used as an ingredient in the manufacture of drugs related to mouth ulcers. • It is used as an ingredient in the acidic dry cleaners to remove grease. • It is used in the refining of oil and processing of wastewater.
Nitric acid (HNO_3)	• It is used in the synthesis of fertilizers (example: ammonium nitrate). • It is used in the production of explosives. • It is used in the purification of gold and silver. • It is used as a main component in liquid-fuelled rockets.
Acetic acid (CH_3COOH)	• It is mainly used in food supplements as a raw material. • It is used as a solvent.

BASES

Some substances such as soaps, shampoos and cleaning agents have a bitter taste and are slippery to touch (Fig. 5.2). This is due to the presence of a substance called 'base' in them. Substances that contain bases are called **basic substances**.

(a) Shampoo (b) Soap (c) Cleaning agent

Fig. 5.2: Some basic substances

Types of Bases

Based on how they take part in a reaction, bases are of two types: strong and weak bases.

Strong bases: Some of the bases are corrosive in nature and may result in skin burns. Such bases are called **strong bases**. Examples of strong bases are sodium hydroxide, calcium hydroxide and potassium hydroxide.

Weak bases: The bases that are not corrosive in nature are called **weak bases**. Examples of weak bases are magnesium hydroxide, ammonium hydroxide and copper hydroxide.

Science in Context

Sweat is an acidic waste excreted *via* skin. It helps to maintain the skin's resistance to bacteria. When we wash the sweat off the skin with alkaline soap, we expose our skin to bacteria.

Properties of Bases

- Bases are bitter to taste.
- Bases turn red litmus blue.
- Bases are slippery to touch.
- Bases soluble in water are called **alkalis** (examples: potassium hydroxide and sodium hydroxide). Bases insoluble in water are not alkalis.
- Bases are corrosive in nature, so they should not be touched with bare hands.

It is essential to note that any chemical/substance should not be tasted without first checking with adults, as these can cause harm.

- Bases react with acids to form salt and water.

NH_4OH	+	HCl	$\longrightarrow$	NH_4Cl	+	H_2O
Ammonium hydroxide		Hydrochloric acid		Ammonium chloride		Water

- Bases react with metals to form salt and hydrogen gas.

$2NaOH$	+	Zn	$\longrightarrow$	Na_2ZnO_2	+	H_2
Sodium hydroxide		Zinc		Sodium zincate		Hydrogen

Uses of Bases

Uses of some bases are given in Table 5.3.

Table 5.3: Uses of bases

Name of the base	Uses
Sodium hydroxide (NaOH) is commonly called 'caustic soda'.	• It is used as a major ingredient in the manufacture of soaps and detergents. • It is used in paper, textile and plastic industries. • It is used in the food processing industries for washing and chemical peeling of fruits and vegetables. • It is used as a cleaning material to unblock clogged drains and to clean waste discharge pipes.
Calcium hydroxide [$Ca(OH)_2$] is commonly called 'slaked lime'.	• It is used as an additive in the cement industry. • It is used in the storage of fruits and vegetables, as it can absorb the extra carbon dioxide and maintain the oxygen to carbon dioxide ratio. • It is used in the processing of water that can be used in soft drinks and alcoholic beverages. • It is used in the treatment of wastewater before it is disposed of. • It is used as the main component in neutralizing the soil, which helps in enhancing the growth of plants.
Ammonium hydroxide (NH_4OH) is commonly called 'aqueous ammonia'.	• It is used as a major ingredient in various cleaning agents. • It is used in the manufacture of fertilizers (example: ammonium nitrate).
Magnesium hydroxide [$Mg(OH)_2$] is commonly called 'milk of magnesia' due to its milk-like appearance.	• It is widely used as an antacid to neutralize acidity in the stomach. • It is used along with hydrochloric acid in fire extinguishers.
Potassium hydroxide (KOH) is commonly called 'potash'.	• It is used in the refining of petroleum. • It is used in the manufacture of fertilizers and soft soaps. • It is used in the preparation of alkaline batteries due to its electrolytic property.

NEUTRAL SUBSTANCES

Substances that are neither acidic nor basic are called ***neutral substances***. These substances do not change the colour of any indicator. For example, common salt or NaCl.

Revise and Recall

Match the following.

1. Citric acid	(a) Potassium hydroxide
2. Nitric acid	(b) A weak base
3. Copper hydroxide	(c) A mineral acid
4. Potash	(d) Found in oranges

ACID-BASE INDICATORS

a

Substances that assist in determining whether a given substance is acidic or basic in nature, with the help of a colour change, are called ***acid-base indicators*** *or simply* ***indicators***.

Indicators help in deciding whether a given substance is acidic, basic or neutral by changing their colour. They will not affect the nature of the solution to be tested and a very little quantity of indicator is sufficient to observe the colour change. There are basically two types of indicators, namely natural indicators and synthetic indicators. Turmeric, China rose and litmus are some examples of natural indicators. On the other hand, phenolphthalein, methyl red and methyl orange are some examples of synthetic indicators. Phenolphthalein, litmus and methyl orange indicators are used commonly in laboratories.

Fig. 5.3: Lichen

Natural Indicators

Litmus: Litmus is the most commonly used natural indicator. It is extracted from lichens (Fig. 5.3). It is available in two forms: in the form of a solution, called 'litmus solution' and as strips of paper called 'litmus paper'.

If acidic substances are added to blue litmus, it turns red, while red litmus turns blue when basic substances are added to it (Fig. 5.4).

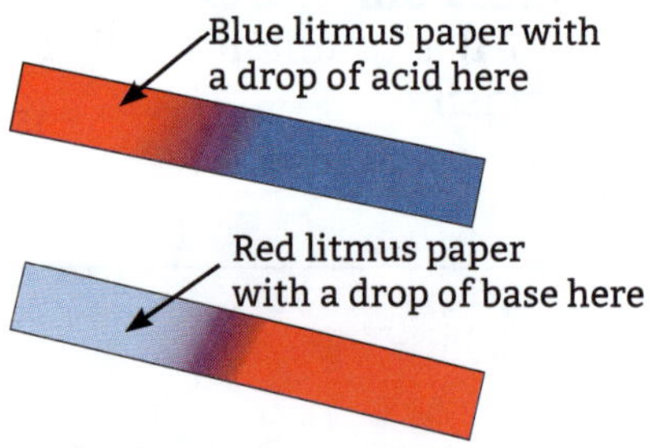

Fig. 5.4: Colour change for litmus paper

Activity 1

Aim: To investigate the nature of a given substance using litmus paper

Materials required: Blue and red litmus papers, beakers, droppers, lemon juice, soap water, tap water, vinegar, tomato juice, baking soda solution, ammonia solution, milk, salt solution and distilled water

Procedure:

1. Take each solution in separate beakers and label them accordingly.
2. Put a clean glass dropper in each of the beakers.
3. With the help of the dropper, add a drop of each solution on to a separate red litmus paper and blue litmus paper.
4. Record your observations in the table given below.

Observation:

Type of solution	Effect on blue litmus	Effect on red litmus	Nature of the solution (acidic/basic/neutral)
Lemon juice			
Soap water			
Tap water			
Vinegar			
Tomato juice			
Distilled water			

Turmeric: Turmeric (*Haldi*) used in the kitchen can also be used as one of the natural indicators for bases (Fig. 5.5).

Turmeric contains a compound called **curcumin**, which is responsible for its vibrant yellow colour and undergoes a change in colour in basic solutions. With acidic and neutral substances, the turmeric solution remains yellow in colour, while with basic substances, it turns brick red in colour (Fig. 5.6).

Fig. 5.5: Turmeric

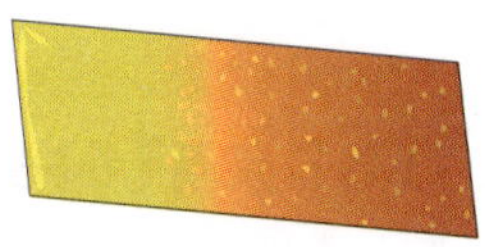

Fig. 5.6: Turmeric strip turns red when tested with a base

China rose: Petals of China rose (*Hibiscus*) contain a pigment, anthocyanin, which changes colour on reacting with a base or an acid. The juice obtained from the petals is used as a natural indicator (Fig. 5.7).
If acidic substances are added, it turns dark pink (magenta) in colour, while adding basic substances makes the juice green (Fig. 5.8).

Fig. 5.7: China rose

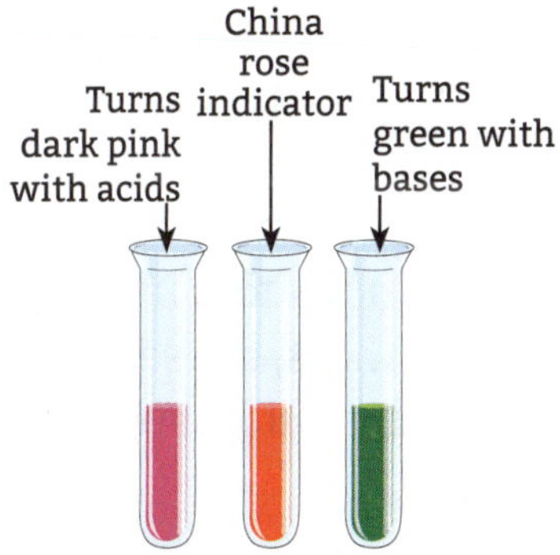

Fig. 5.8: Colour changes for China rose

Know the Scientist

Robert Boyle (1627–1691) was an Irish writer and chemist. He is considered to be the 'Father of Modern Chemistry'. He observed that all acids turn a particular vegetable indicator from blue to red and all alkalis turn the indicator green. He found that some substances did not change the colour of the indicator and concluded that these were neutral. He, thus, provided an operational method of classifying substances.

pH

The pH scale serves as a numerical gauge for assessing the acidic or basic nature of substances, spanning from 1 to 14. Substances with a pH below 7 are classified as 'acids', those above 7 as 'bases' and those at a pH of 7 as 'neutral'. Neutral substances are neither acidic nor basic.

Universal Indicators

Universal indicators are compounds that show a gradual change in colour to indicate the acidity or basicity of a solution. These indicators are available as both strips of paper (called pH paper) and solution. To find the nature of unknown solutions, the change in colour of these substances can be compared with that of the standard colour chart shown here. The colours that indicate the acidity or basicity of a solution after the addition of a universal indicator are given in Fig. 5.9.

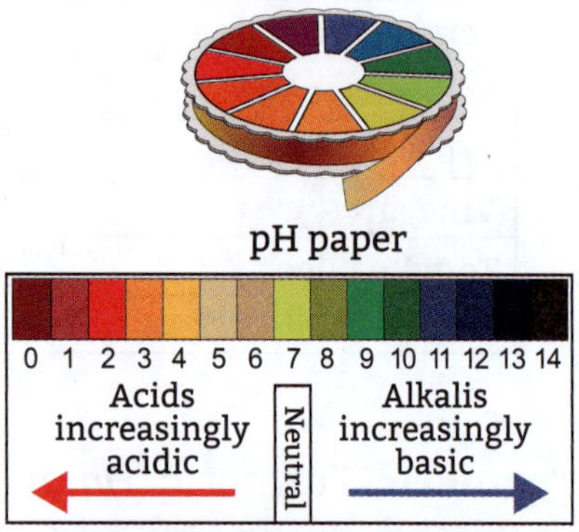

Fig. 5.9: Chart representing the variation of colours for universal indicator

Other Indicators Used in Laboratories

Phenolphthalein indicator: It is one of the commonly used indicators in laboratories. When it is added to basic substances, the solution turns pink (Fig. 5.10), whereas when added to acidic substances, it remains colourless.

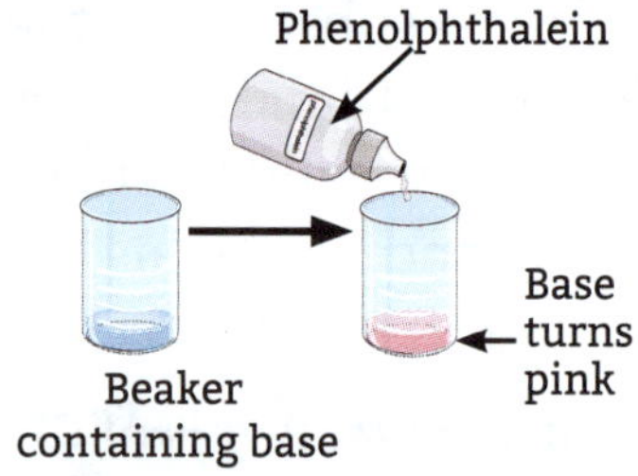

Fig. 5.10: Colour change for phenolphthalein

Methyl orange indicator: It is also one of the commonly used indicators in laboratories. When it is added to basic substances, the solution turns yellow, whereas when added to acidic substances, the solution turns red (Fig. 5.11).

Fig. 5.11: Colour changes for methyl orange

SALTS

When acids react with bases, they can neutralize one another's specific properties (i.e. acidic and basic properties). Substances that are produced as a result of neutralization between acids and bases are called **salts**. *The reactions in which acids react with bases, resulting in the formation of salt and water, are called* ***neutralization reactions***.

Acid + Base ⟶ Salt + Water + Heat

Hydrochloric acid (HCl) + Sodium hydroxide (NaOH) ⟶ Sodium chloride (NaCl) + Water (H_2O) + Heat

Let us perform an activity to observe the process of neutralization.

Activity 2

Aim: To observe the process of neutralization

Materials required: Sodium hydroxide solution, phenolphthalein indicator, lemon juice, 10 mℓ beakers, a test tube, dropper, measuring cylinder and distilled water

Procedure:

1. Prepare sodium hydroxide solution. Take about 20 mℓ of distilled water in a beaker and add 3–4 pellets of sodium hydroxide into it.
2. Prepare 5 mℓ of lemon juice by squeezing one medium sized lemon into a beaker. Add 15 mℓ of water to this juice.
3. Take a test tube.
4. Using a measuring cylinder, add 5 mℓ of sodium hydroxide solution in the test tube.
5. Add a few drops of phenolphthalein indicator into this test tube and stir in. You will observe that the solution turns pink.
6. Now take lemon juice solution in a dropper and add it drop by drop into the test tube.
7. Record your observations. What do you observe? Why?

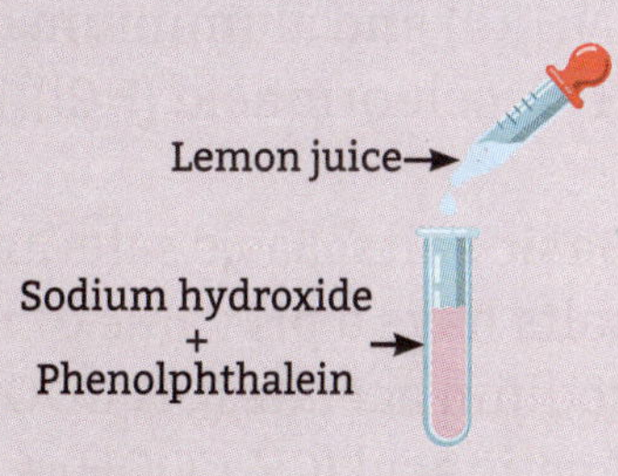

Observation and conclusion: The pink colour disappears in the test tube indicating that base is not present in these solutions. To further confirm whether acid is present or not, use a litmus paper. When an acidic solution and a basic solution are mixed in suitable amounts, both the acidic nature of the acid and the basic nature of the base are destroyed. Therefore, the solution is neither acidic nor basic.

Applications of Neutralization Reactions

Following are some neutralization reactions that we observe in our everyday life.

- **In the treatment of ant sting**: Some people are highly allergic to ant sting as it releases formic acid. It is neutralized by rubbing moist baking soda (sodium bicarbonate) or calamine solution, which contains zinc carbonate, on the affected area.
- **In the treatment of indigestion**: Hydrochloric acid secreted in the stomach helps in the digestion of food. However, its excess secretion could lead to acidity and indigestion. Milk of magnesia (magnesium hydroxide) is used to neutralize the acid.

- **In the treatment of soil**: When the soil is too acidic, it is treated with slaked lime or quicklime, which is a base. If the soil is too basic, it is treated with gypsum or organic matter such as the composts obtained from vegetables or fruits as they are acidic in nature.
- **In the treatment of sewage waste**: The wastes of many factories contain acids. If they are allowed to flow into water bodies, these wastes would affect aquatic organisms. Slaked lime (calcium hydroxide) is often used to neutralize this acidic waste let out from the factories. Calcium hydroxide removes only the acidic contents of the industrial wastes and not any other chemicals that may be present.
- **In the treatment of acid burns**: During acid burns, the affected part of the body should be cleaned with cold water and a dilute solution of baking soda should be applied. It acts as a neutralizing agent to make it harmless. The solution used should be dilute, otherwise it can harm the affected region.

Types of Salts

Salts can be acidic, basic or neutral in nature. Some examples of salts are given in Table 5.4.

- **Acidic salts**: Acidic salts are formed when strong acids react with weak bases. These salts have a pH value of less than 7. Examples are ammonium chloride (NH_4Cl) and aluminium chloride ($AlCl_3$).
  Hydrochloric acid (HCl) + Ammonium hydroxide (NH_4OH) $\rightarrow$ Ammonium chloride (NH_4Cl) + Water (H_2O) + Heat
- **Basic salts**: Basic salts are formed when strong bases react with weak acids. These salts have a pH value of more than 7. Examples are sodium carbonate (Na_2CO_3) and sodium acetate (CH_3COONa).
  Acetic acid (CH_3COOH) + Sodium hydroxide ($NaOH$) $\rightarrow$ Sodium acetate (CH_3COONa) + Water (H_2O) + Heat
- **Neutral salts**: Neutral salts are formed when strong acids react with strong bases. These salts have a pH value of 7. Examples are sodium chloride ($NaCl$), potassium nitrate (KNO_3) and calcium sulphate ($CaSO_4$).
  Hydrochloric acid (HCl) + Sodium hydroxide ($NaOH$) $\rightarrow$ Sodium chloride ($NaCl$) + Water (H_2O) + Heat

Table 5.4: Types of salts

Salts	Obtained from	Example
Sulphates	Sulphuric acid	$CuSO_4$ (Copper sulphate)
Chlorides	Hydrochloric acid	$NaCl$ (Sodium chloride)
Nitrates	Nitric acid	$NaNO_3$ (Sodium nitrate)
Carbonates	Carbonic acid	Na_2CO_3 (Sodium carbonate)

Properties of Salts

- Most of the salts are soluble in water (there are a few exceptions, for example, calcium carbonate).
- Solutions of salts in water act as good conductors of electricity.
- Some salts are white crystals, whereas some are coloured. For example, copper sulphate is blue in colour and ferrous sulphate is green.
- Salts that form crystals contain water molecules inside them; these water molecules are called **water of crystallization**. *The salt crystals that contain water of crystallization are called **hydrated salts*** (example: Blue vitriol [$CuSO_4 \cdot 5H_2O$]).
- Sometimes salts are obtained when more than one base reacts with an acid; or more than one acid reacts with a base. Such salts are called **mixed salts** (example: Alum [$K_2SO_4 \cdot Al_2(SO_4)_3 \cdot 24H_2O$]).

Preparation of Salts

Salts can be prepared by following any of these three methods:

- By making an acid react with a base
- By making an acid react with a metal
- By making vegetable oil react with caustic soda

Uses of Salts

Salts are useful to us in several ways. For example, salts of iodine, calcium, potassium, sodium and magnesium are essential for the growth of our body. Uses of some common salts are given in Table 5.5.

Table 5.5: Uses of some salts

Name of the salt (chemical formula)	Common name	Uses
Sodium chloride ($NaCl$)	Table salt/ common salt	It is used as a major ingredient in cooking and as a food preservative.
Sodium carbonate (Na_2CO_3)	Washing soda	It is widely used as a washing agent.
Sodium bicarbonate ($NaHCO_3$)	Baking soda	It is widely used as a baking agent, in medicines and as a fire extinguisher.
Potassium nitrate (KNO_3)	Nitre	It is used in fireworks and in the manufacture of fertilizers.
Potassium aluminium sulphate ($K_2SO_4 \cdot Al_2(SO_4)_3 \cdot 24H_2O$)	Alum	It is used in the purification of water and in the textile industry.
Copper sulphate (hydrated) ($CuSO_4 \cdot 5H_2O$)	Blue vitriol	It is used as a fungicide and in the textile industry.

Keywords

Acids: Substances that taste sour and change blue litmus paper to red

Organic acids: Acids that are naturally obtained from plant and animal sources

Mineral acids: Acids that are derived from an inorganic source

Bases: Substances that taste bitter and are slippery to touch and change red litmus paper to blue

Alkalis: Bases that are soluble in water

Neutral substances: Substances that are neither acidic nor basic

Indicators: Substances that help to determine whether a given substance is acidic or basic, with the help of a colour change

pH scale: A numerical representation of the acidity and basicity of substances

Salts: Substances that are produced as a result of reaction between acids and bases

Neutralization reactions: The reactions in which acids combine with bases resulting in the formation of salt and water

Water of crystallization: Water molecules found in salt crystals

Hydrated salts: Salts crystals that possess water of crystallization

Summary

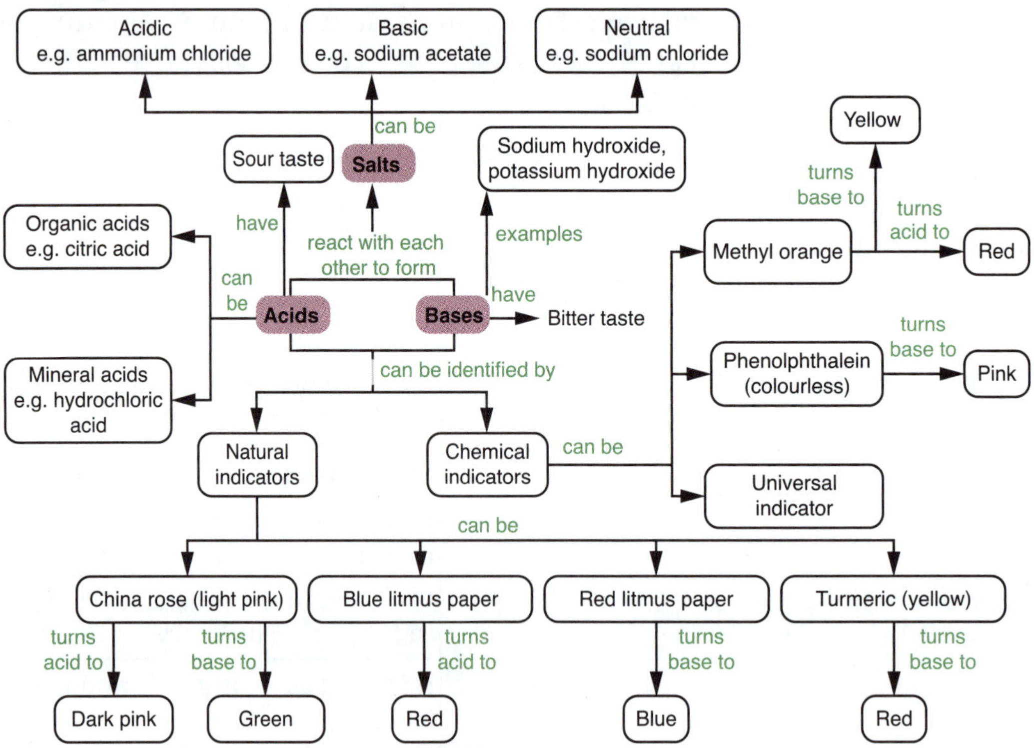

EXERCISE

W

A. Choose the correct option.

1. Which of the following is not an organic acid?
   (a) Malic acid (b) Lactic acid (c) Nitric acid (d) Acetic acid
2. Identify the characteristic of an acid.
   (a) Changes red litmus to blue (b) Reacts with a base to form a salt
   (c) Soapy to touch (d) Bitter to taste
3. Blue litmus paper dipped in an unknown solution remains blue because it is ________________.
   (a) neutral (b) acidic (c) soluble (d) colourless
4. A salt is formed when
   (a) acids react with water. (b) acids react with bases.
   (c) bases react with water. (d) acids or bases react with oxygen.
5. Identify the statement that is *not* correct.
   (a) When the soil is too acidic, it is treated with organic matter.
   (b) Stomach acidity can be treated by ingesting milk of magnesia.
   (c) The effect of ant sting can be neutralized by applying calamine solution.
   (d) Sodium chloride is obtained when hydrochloric acid is added to sodium hydroxide.

B. Fill in the blanks. ia

1. The acid released when an ant stings is ________________. (formic acid/nitric acid)
2. Nitric acid is an example of ________________. (mineral acid/organic acid)
3. Potassium hydroxide is an example of ________________. (alkali/acid)
4. Slaked lime is another name for ________________. (calcium hydroxide/potassium hydroxide)

C. State whether the following statements are true (T) or false (F). ia

1. Salts formed during neutralization are always neutral in nature. ☐
2. Acids are highly corrosive in nature. ☐
3. Ammonium hydroxide is present in most cleaning agents. ☐
4. Phenolphthalein solution has no effect on acids. ☐
5. The pH value of 7 indicates a substance is neutral. ☐

D. Answer the following in one word each.

1. Substances that cause orange, curd and tamarind to have a sour taste
2. Substances that cause soaps to be slippery
3. Substances that are neither acidic or basic

4. The common name of calcium carbonate
5. Substances produced as a result of the neutralization of acids and bases

E. Give reasons for the following.

1. Only few substances can be used as natural indicators.
2. Washing soda is an effective component of detergents not baking soda.
3. Calamine solution is applied on the skin when an ant bites.
4. Neutral solutions do not show any effect on litmus paper.
5. Turmeric stain on white shirt turns to red when it is washed with soap.

F. Answer the following questions briefly.

1. Acids are not stored in metal containers. Why?
2. Why do different substances have different tastes?
3. Distinguish between organic acids and mineral acids.
4. What are universal indicators and what are their uses?
5. Distinguish between strong and weak bases.

G. Answer the following questions in detail.

1. Distinguish between acids and bases.
2. Neutralization reactions play an important role in our daily life. Support the statement with at least two examples.
3. How will you prepare a dilute acid from a concentrated acid?
4. What are indicators? Explain in brief about the various types of natural indicators.

COGNITIVE CORNER

Critical Thinking

1. You are given three test tubes, one of them contains distilled water and the other two contain an acidic solution and a basic solution respectively. If you are given only red litmus paper, how will you identify the contents of each test tube?
2. Milk is basic while the curd obtained from milk is acidic. Why?

Picture Study

Label the pH chart given alongside.

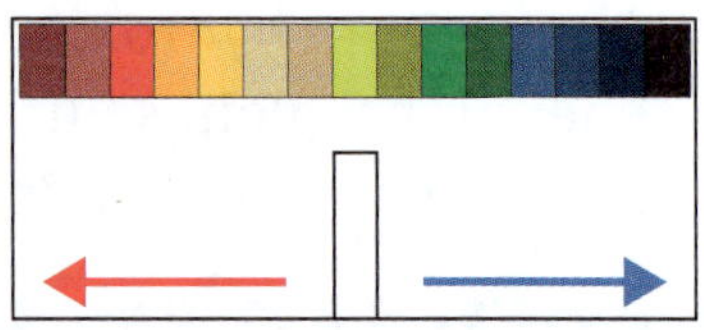

Project

Describe some practical uses of natural indicators in any two industries. Write a note on how the indicators are made/obtained and make a PowerPoint presentation on it. **(C-7.1)**

In the Library

Collect information from your library books about the 'different kinds of acids present in the human body and their functions'. Make a poster to showcase the organs or systems where these acids are found. **(C-7.2)**

In the Laboratory

Aim: To determine the neutralizing ability of an antacid **(C-7.1)**

Materials required: Phenolphthalein indicator, dilute HCl, antacid tablets (500 mg), beaker, spatula, mortar and pestle and dropper

Theory: In order to help in the digestion of food and to protect our stomach against bacterial growth, our stomach secretes gastric juice consisting mainly of hydrochloric acid. Indigestion or an upset stomach is a result of too much of this acid in our stomach. Although our stomach is protected by a mucous lining, it can be damaged if the acidity becomes too high, possibly causing an ulcer.

Treatment of indigestion involves either lowering the production of acid in the stomach or neutralizing it. Antacids neutralize the acid in the stomach by raising the pH level. Thus, they provide quick relief and are less expensive.

Procedure: Add 2–3 drops of phenolphthalein solution with the help of a dropper into a clean glass beaker containing 50 mℓ of dilute HCl. Note the colour. Take six antacid tablets (500 mg) and crush them into a powder using mortar and pestle.

Take 2–3 spatulas (1 g) of the crushed antacid powder and dissolve them into the beaker containing the solution of dilute HCl and phenolphthalein. Since antacid tablet contains other chemical substances, much of the tablet may not dissolve and the solution may be cloudy. Keep adding 2–3 spatulas of antacid powder until the content of the solution in the beaker turns pinkish. Again, add 2–3 drops of HCl with a dropper into the solution and stir it with the help of a glass rod. Observe and note the colour change. Now, add 2–3 more spatulas of powdered antacid into the solution and stir it. Observe and note the colour change.

Record your observations in the table given below.

Solution	Colour change observed
Dilute hydrochloric acid (50 mℓ) and phenolphthalein	
Dilute hydrochloric acid (50 mℓ), phenolphthalein and antacid (in excess when compared to hydrochloric acid)	
Dilute hydrochloric acid (50 mℓ), phenolphthalein and antacid (less when compared to hydrochloric acid)	

Conclusion: Antacids have the ability to neutralize hydrochloric acid.

Life Skills

The addition of some nitrogen-based fertilizers result in the acidification of soil and has a negative impact on fertility and plant productivity. What alternatives do you think can be used instead of nitrogen fertilizers in agriculture to increase crop yield? **(C-7.3)**

Worksheet

The chemical nature of soil has indirect yet far-reaching effects on plants. Every plant has its preferred range of soil acidity. Most plants thrive in slightly acidic soil because it provides them with good access to all nutrients.

Various plant nutrients become available in toxic amounts if the soil turns excessively acidic or basic. This can stunt root growth and interfere with plant's uptake of nutrients.

Ancient Indians found out that alkaline soils were suitable for growing crops such as barley and grapes, while acidic soils were better for paddy cultivation. Ancient Indian farmers used various methods to assess soil fertility and quality. One of the common practices to determine the soil's acidity or alkalinity was to grow certain types of plants as indicators. They knew that certain plants could thrive in acidic soils, while others could thrive in alkaline or neutral soil conditions.

Cauliflower plants need slightly alkaline soil.

Tomato plants need slightly acidic soil.

A. Read about the methods ancient Indian farmers employed to correct the soil pH and soil fertility. Write a short note on it.

____

____

____

B. Do you think combining ancient Indian agricultural practices with modern scientific advancement and soil testing techniques can help us achieve the sustainable development goals on 'Zero Hunger' and 'Responsible Consumption and Production'? Explain.

____

____

6 Heat and Temperature

Curricular Goals

- Explore the world of matter and its constituents, properties and behaviour **(CG-1)**
- Explore the nature and processes of science through engaging with the evolution of scientific knowledge and conducting scientific inquiry **(CG-6)**

Competencies

- Describe changes in matter and use particulate nature to represent the properties of matter **(C-1.2)**
- Observe and explain the phenomena caused due to difference in temperature and density **(C-1.4)**
- Formulate questions using scientific terminology and collect data as evidence **(C-6.2)**

Let's Get Started

Look at the pictures given below and write H against the objects that are hot and C against those that are cold.

☐

☐

☐

☐

We have learnt in the previous classes that the ability to do work is called **energy**. Also, we were introduced to various types of energy such as, heat, light, sound and wind. In this chapter we will learn more specifically about heat energy.

HEAT

Have your ever observed that if you leave a steel spoon in a glass of hot milk for some time, the spoon becomes warm? Have you ever wondered why this happens?

When a hot object and a cold object come in contact with each other, a type of energy flows from the hotter object to the colder one. This energy is called ***heat energy***. The SI unit of heat is joule (J).

An object becomes warm when heat energy flows into it and becomes cold when heat energy flows out of it. Sun is the natural source of heat energy on the Earth.

TEMPERATURE

The sun and a cup of tea are not equally hot. Similarly, snow and a glass of chilled lemonade are not equally cold. There is a difference in the degrees of hotness or coldness of things mentioned above that we can sense.

Science in Context

Heat is a form of energy, but temperature is not the measure of that energy. However, it is possible to find out how much heat energy an object has if we know its temperature.

The degree of hotness or coldness of an object is called its ***temperature***. The SI unit of temperature is kelvin (K). A hot object has more heat energy than a cold object of same mass.

We often touch objects to decide how hot or cold they are. But is our sense of touch reliable? Let us perform a simple activity to understand this.

Activity 1

Aim: To understand whether our sense of touch is reliable to determine how hot or cold objects are

Materials required: Three beakers labelled as A, B and C, warm water, cold water and normal water

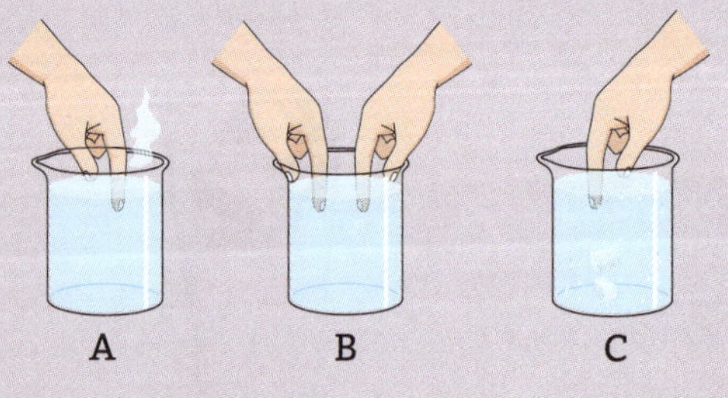

Procedure:

1. Take three beakers (A, B and C). Pour warm water in beaker A and cold water in beaker C. In beaker B, pour water at room temperature.
2. Dip the index fingers of your left and right hands in beakers A and C, respectively, for about a minute. Then dip both the fingers in beaker B.

Observation: You will notice that the water in beaker B feels cold to the left index finger and warm to the right index finger.

Conclusion: This shows that the terms 'hot' and 'cold' are relative. There should be a reference temperature with respect to which we can say whether a given object is hot or cold. Our sense of touch is therefore not reliable in determining how hot or cold objects are.

As shown in activity 1, our sense of touch is not very reliable in deciding how hot or cold objects are. There are more reliable ways to measure the temperature of an object. Let us learn more about them.

Science in Context

In 1593, Galileo Galilei invented a water thermoscope, which, for the first time, measured the variations in temperature.

Measurement of Temperature

The instrument used to measure temperature is called a **thermometer**.

A thermometer consists of the following parts (Fig. 6.1).

Bulb: This is the part which actually touches the object whose temperature is to be measured. The bulb contains either mercury or alcohol.

Let us discuss why mercury is used in thermometers.

Mercury is preferred in most thermometers because it is present in liquid state over a wide range of temperatures. It is silvery grey in colour, therefore it is relatively easy to observe. It does not stick to the glass in which it is enclosed.

However, one drawback of using mercury is that it is very toxic. Any exposure to mercury is very harmful for the body.

Now, let us discuss why alcohol is used in thermometers.

A thermometer that uses alcohol can measure temperature as low as –70 °C. Alcohol is cheaper than mercury.

On the other hand, the drawback of using alcohol in thermometer is that the temperature above 78 °C cannot be measured.

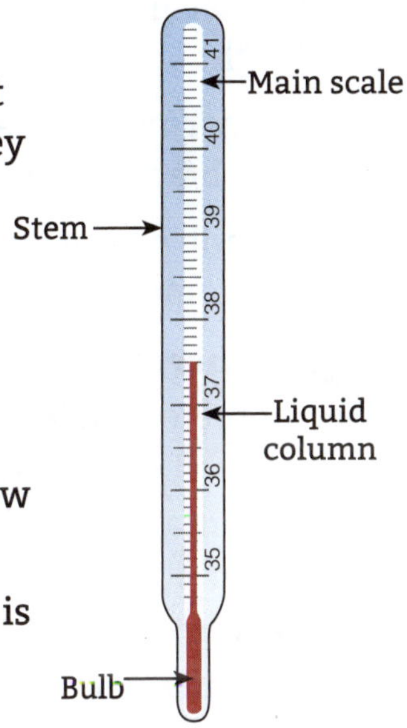

Fig. 6.1: Parts of a thermometer

Stem: It is a glass capillary tube through which the mercury or alcohol rises or falls as the object around the bulb warms or cools.

Scale: The scale marked on the stem indicates the temperature of the substance.

Types of Thermometers

The three commonly used thermometers are as follows:

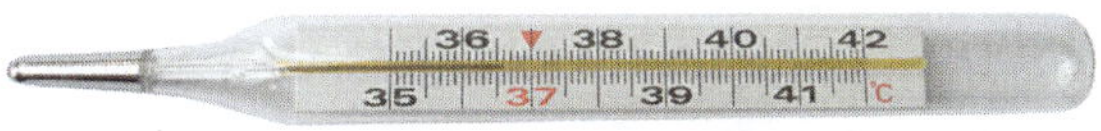

Fig. 6.2: Clinical thermometer

Clinical thermometer: A clinical thermometer is used to measure the temperature of a human body. The normal approximate temperature of a human body is 37 °C or 98.6 °F. However, the human body temperature varies depending on age, activity, time of the day and environmental conditions. It rises or falls under a state of illness. Any rise beyond 40 °C or 104 °F is a medical emergency and requires immediate treatment.

The capillary tube of a clinical thermometer has a kink or bend that does not allow the mercury to flow back into the bulb before the temperature has been read. The mercury column breaks at the kink when it contracts due to a decrease in temperature. It prevents the mercury column from falling beyond this point.

This is the reason why we have to shake the thermometer before taking a new reading. The jerk sends the mercury back into the bulb.

While using a clinical thermometer, the following precautions should be taken:

- The thermometer should be washed before and after use, preferably with an antiseptic solution.
- It should be ensured that before use, the mercury level is below 35 °C or 95 °F.
- The thermometer should be read keeping the level of mercury along the line of sight.
- The thermometer should be handled with care. If it hits against some hard object, it can break.
- The bulb of a thermometer should not be touched while taking a reading. Hold the thermometer by its glass body.

Digital thermometer: Nowadays, electronic thermometers called digital thermometers are widely used for measuring temperature. These do not contain mercury. Hence, there is no risk of mercury being released on breakage. The temperature is easier to read in this type than in conventional thermometers as it is shown as a number on the display (Fig. 6.3).

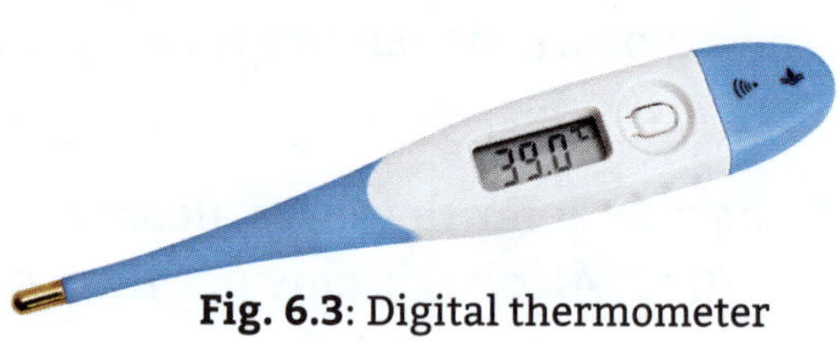

Fig. 6.3: Digital thermometer

Laboratory thermometer: As the name suggests, laboratory thermometers are used in the laboratories during experiments (Fig. 6.4). The range of temperature that a laboratory thermometer can measure is between –10 °C and 110 °C.

The following are some precautions to be taken while using a laboratory thermometer:

- Handle the thermometer with care. If it hits against some hard object, it can break.
- Do not hold the thermometer by the bulb while taking a reading.

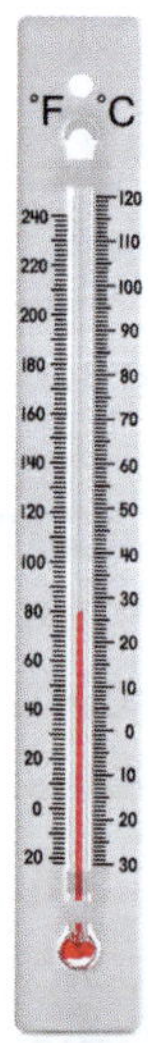

Fig. 6.4: Laboratory thermometer

- The thermometer should be kept upright, not tilted.
- The bulb should be surrounded on all sides by the substance whose temperature is to be measured.
- The bulb should not touch the surface of the container.
- Removing the thermometer from a boiling water bath and immediately immersing it in an ice bath may cause the thermometer to break.

Science in Context

Nowadays, a digital thermometer is recommended for routine use over the traditional glass mercury thermometer. This is because mercury is a toxic substance and is very difficult to dispose of if a thermometer breaks.

Temperature Scales

Temperature is measured using different temperature scales. In a temperature scale, two reference temperatures are chosen (most commonly, the freezing and boiling points of water). The difference between the two reference points is broken down into a certain number of divisions. Each division is taken as one unit of the scale.

The commonly used scales are the Celsius scale, the Fahrenheit scale and the Kelvin scale.

Celsius scale: This scale was developed by Anders Celsius. The unit of this scale is °C (read as degree Celsius). On this scale, the divisions fall between the freezing point of water taken as 0 °C and the boiling point of water taken as 100 °C. 0 °C is also called the lower fixed point, whereas 100 °C is called the upper fixed point. There are 100 divisions between these two points (Fig. 6.5).

Fahrenheit scale: This scale was developed by Daniel Gabriel Fahrenheit. The unit of this scale is °F (read as degree Fahrenheit). The Fahrenheit scale sets the freezing point and boiling point of water at 32 °F and 212 °F, respectively. The lower fixed point is 32 °F and the upper fixed point is 212 °F. There are 180 divisions between these two points (Fig. 6.5).

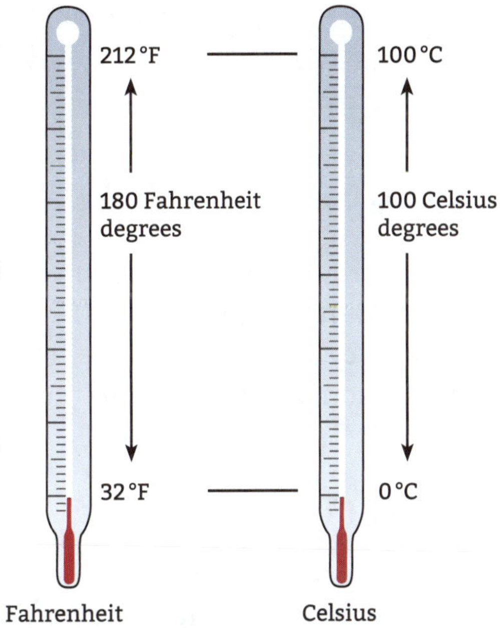

Fig. 6.5: Fahrenheit and Celsius scales

Kelvin scale: This scale was invented by Lord Kelvin. The unit of this scale is K and is the SI unit for measuring temperature. On this scale, the freezing point of water is 273.16 K (approx.) and the boiling point of water is 373.16 K. For convenience it is approximated and written as 273 K and 373 K. It is called the absolute scale of temperature since its 0 K is the absolute zero, that is, the lowest attainable temperature in the universe.

Conversion of scales

The three temperature scales (Celsius, Fahrenheit and Kelvin) can be converted from one to the other, using the following formulae:

$°F = [°C \times \frac{9}{5}] + 32$ is used to convert Celsius to Fahrenheit scale

$°C = [°F - 32] \times \frac{5}{9}$ is used to convert Fahrenheit to Celsius scale

$K = °C + 273$ is used to convert Celsius to Kelvin scale

Revise and Recall

State whether the following statements are true (T) or false (F).

1. The degree of hotness or coldness of objects is called temperature. ☐
2. Our sense of touch is reliable enough to determine the hotness and coldness of temperature. ☐
3. A thermometer need not be handled with care as it is made up of a hard substance. ☐
4. The unit of the Celsius scale is °F. ☐
5. The freezing point of water on the Fahrenheit scale is 45 °F. ☐

TRANSFER OF HEAT

Heat energy always flows from a region of higher temperature to a region of lower temperature, till both attain the same temperature. This phenomenon is called ***transfer of heat***. Heat can be transferred from one object to another by three modes: conduction, convection and radiation.

Conduction

a

Conduction *is the transfer of heat from a hotter part to a colder part of an object due to the collision of its particles without their actual movement from their positions.* Heat transfer through conduction occurs within solids and between solid substances that are in direct contact with each other.

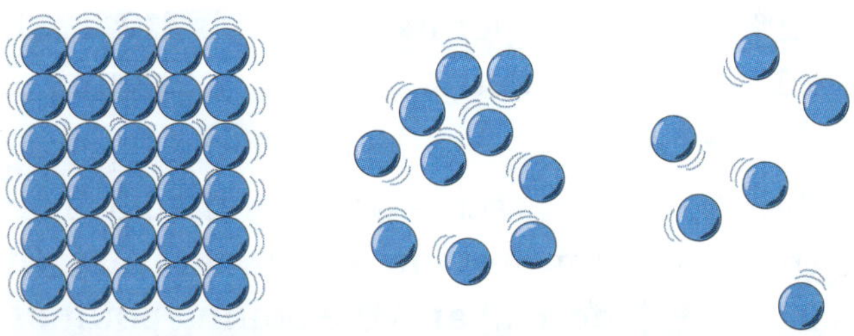

Fig. 6.6: Particle arrangement in solid, liquid and gas

How well a material conducts heat depends on how close the particles are arranged. Therefore, solids are the best conductors of heat, followed by liquids. However, gases are bad conductors of heat.

How does conduction occur?

We know that particles are closely packed in solids, that is, they cannot move freely and can only vibrate at their fixed positions (Fig. 6.6).

(a) When a solid is heated, the particles that are in direct contact with the source of heat start vibrating faster than those that are not in direct contact.

(b) These fast vibrating particles collide with the neighbouring slow vibrating particles and transfer energy to them, thereby making them vibrate faster. They, in turn, collide and transfer the energy to their neighbouring particles, and so on.

(c) In this way, heat is conducted, that is, transferred from one particle to the next, through collision of vibrating particles within substances.

Activity 2

Aim: To understand that heat travels through conduction in good conductors

Note: *This activity must be performed under the supervision of the teacher.*

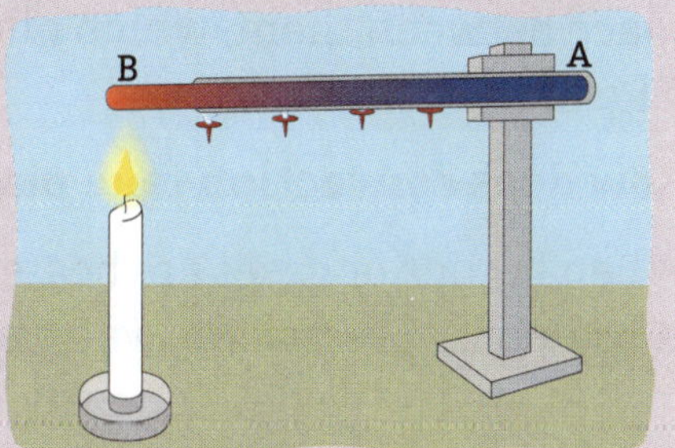

Materials required: Metal rod (good conductor of heat), four board pins, wax, candle, matchbox and clamp

Procedure:

1. Take a metal rod and fix a set of pins to it at regular intervals, using wax.
2. Get one end of the metal rod (marked A) fixed to a clamp.
3. Light a candle so that the other end of the metal rod (marked B) begins to get heated by the flame of the candle.

Observation: You will see that as the rod gets heated, the wax holding the pin nearest to the heated end melts and the pin falls down. Slowly, the rest of the pins too fall, one-by-one.

Conclusion: Heat was transferred from one end of the rod to the other. As the rod got heated, the wax started melting, detaching the pins and making them fall.

The rate of conduction of heat is different in different solids.

In the objects shown in Fig. 6.7, certain parts of these devices (body of the cooker and face of the frying pan) heat up easily, while certain other parts (the handles of all these devices) do not.

Fig. 6.7: Conductors and insulators

Materials that conduct heat easily are called **conductors**. Metals are usually conductors of heat.

Materials that do not allow the conduction of heat are called **insulators** *or* **bad conductors of heat.** For example, wood, cotton, rubber, clay and cork. Air is also an example of insulator as it is a bad conductor of heat. Materials such as wool, feathers and fur act as insulators because the air trapped between their fibres do not conduct heat.

Practical applications of conduction

Following are some practical applications of conduction:

- Pans used for cooking are usually made of metals such as steel, copper or aluminium (good conductors), while their handles are made of plastic (poor conductors).
- Clothes made of fur trap air inside them and this trapped air then acts as an insulator. It prevents heat from escaping, keeping the body warm.

Convection

Convection *is the transfer of heat by the movement of particles.* Convection is the primary mode of heat transfer in fluids (liquids and gases). This is because the constituent particles are loosely arranged with space between them, which allows their movement (Fig. 6.8).

Fig. 6.8: Convection current in a liquid

How does convection take place?

When liquids or gases are heated, the heated molecules rise up. For example, when water is heated in a vessel, the water at the bottom gets heated first. As hot water is lighter, it rises up. The colder and heavier water from the top of the vessel moves downwards. This process continues, setting up circulating streams of hot and cold water in the vessel (convection currents). Thus, the entire volume of water within the vessel becomes hot.

Activity 3

Aim: To understand that heat transfers through convection in liquids

Materials required: Beaker, water, burner and potassium permanganate crystals

Procedure:

1. Take a beaker and fill three-fourth of it with water.
2. Drop a small, single crystal of potassium permanganate in it and heat gently on a low flame.

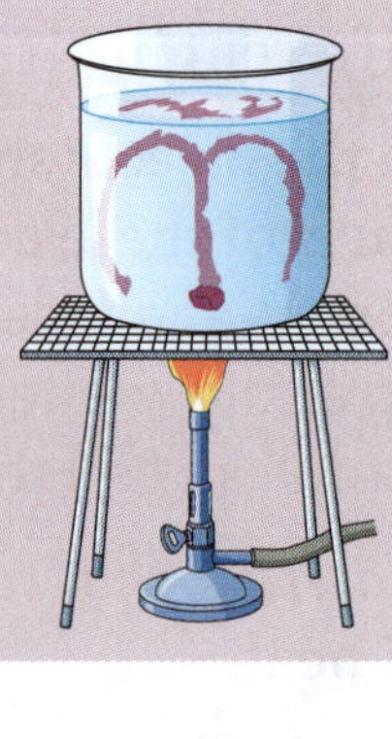

Observation: The colour streaks of potassium permanganate rise up to the surface of the beaker and then sink down after some time.

Conclusion: The rise and fall of the colour streaks of potassium permanganate indicate molecular movement in water when it is heated. This helps in understanding that heat transfers through convection in liquids.

As mentioned earlier, convection also occurs in gases. An example of this is the formation of sea breeze and land breeze in coastal areas (Fig. 6.9). The sun heats up the land during the day much faster than the water in the sea. Therefore, during daytime, the air above the land gets warm and rises up, and the air from over the sea flows in to take its place. This results in sea breeze.

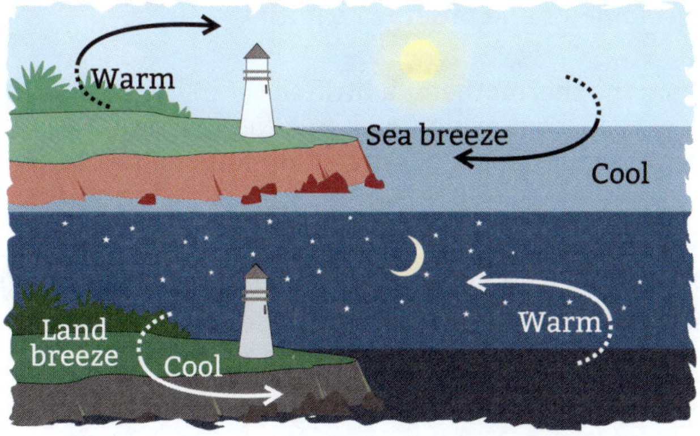

Fig. 6.9: Sea breeze and land breeze

At night, the land cools down faster than the water in the sea. Hence, the air above the sea is hotter than the air above the land. The air above the sea, therefore, rises. The cool air above the land rushes in to take its place resulting in land breeze.

Practical applications of convection

Following are some practical applications of convection:

- Exhaust fans in kitchens are always fitted high, close to the ceiling so that they can remove the hot air that rises up.
- Room heaters are placed on the floor of a room. When the cool air is heated, it rises up and the cold air flows down to the floor. This results in effective heating of the entire room.
- The ventilators of a room are at the top of a window or the door. This is because when the air in the room gets heated, it rises and passes out through the ventilators at the top.

Radiation

Heat energy can travel in the form of waves even if a medium (particles of any material) is absent, that is, it can travel even in a vacuum. *The transfer of heat in the form of rays or waves is called* ***radiation****.*

If you stand outside in the sun for some time, you start feeling warm. How does the heat energy of the sun travel to the Earth and reach us? It does so through radiation.

Although radiation does not require any medium, it is also not obstructed by the presence of any medium. Thus, heat can radiate through air as well as water.

Activity 4

Aim: To understand heat transfer through radiation

Materials required: Candle and laboratory thermometer

Procedure:

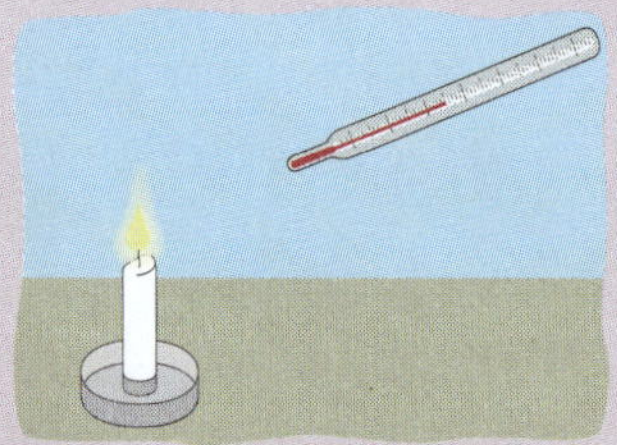

1. Take a laboratory thermometer and observe its initial temperature reading.
2. Light a candle and bring the thermometer a little closer to the flame (never directly expose the thermometer bulb to the flame). Hold the thermometer near the candle but make sure that it does not touch the flame.
3. Note the change in temperature.

Observation: The laboratory thermometer shows a change in temperature.

Conclusion: As there is no other source of heat or any heating by contact, this clearly proves the transfer of heat through radiation.

All hot objects radiate heat. When radiation falls on an object, a part of it is absorbed and the remaining is reflected. The amount of heat absorbed or reflected by an object depends on several factors such as the nature of the surface and its colour. Darker colours are good absorbers while lighter colours are poor absorbers.

Practical applications of radiation

A practical application of solar radiation is solar heater. Solar heaters are designed to use the heat energy from the sun for cooking food and heating water.

Science in Context

In cold places, such as hilly areas, roofs of houses are painted black to maximize the absorption of heat from the sun. Whereas in hotter areas, painting the roof of the house white reflects the heat keeping the house relatively cooler.

SEASONS AND CLOTHES WE WEAR

We experience different seasons on Earth throughout the year. Summers are hotter and winters are colder. This is because we receive a lot of heat energy from the sun during the summer and less heat energy during the winter. Seasons on Earth are caused because the Earth's axis of rotation is tilted at an angle of 23.5 degrees. When the northern hemisphere of the Earth faces the sun, we experience summer in the northern hemisphere and winter in the southern hemisphere. When the northern hemisphere of the Earth faces away from the sun, we experience winter in the northern hemisphere and summer in the southern hemisphere (Fig. 6.10).

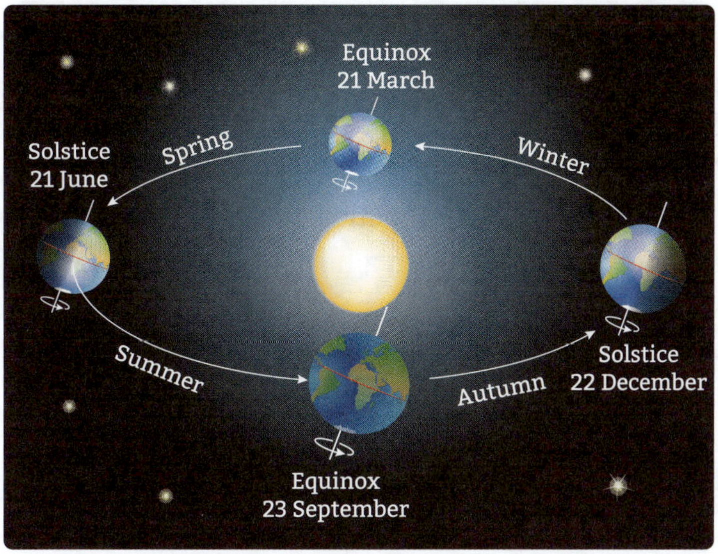

Fig. 6.10: Occurrence of seasons on Earth

During different seasons, we wear different clothes. Why do we prefer wearing light-coloured clothes in the summer? We know that light colours are poor absorbers of heat and reflect most of the heat that falls on them. Therefore, light-coloured clothes absorb very little sunlight which keeps us cool and comfortable during the summer months.

In winter, however, we prefer wearing dark-coloured clothes because they are good absorbers of heat and thus keep us warm. We also use woollen clothes during winter. Wool contains a lot of trapped air between its fibres and hence acts as a poor conductor of heat. This prevents any loss of heat from our body and provides insulation from the cold surroundings.

Working of a Thermos Flask

A thermos flask maintains the temperature of the substance kept in it, that is, it keeps a hot substance hot and a cold substance cold for a long time (Fig. 6.11). Let us understand how it works.

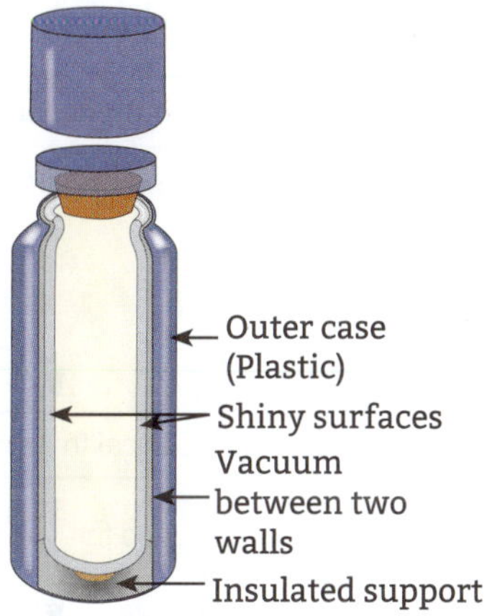

Fig. 6.11: Thermos flask

The outer casing of a thermos flask is made up of plastic (or stainless steel). Plastic, being a poor conductor of heat, acts as an insulator preventing heat loss through conduction. Inside it is a double-walled container made of glass or stainless steel. Both the walls are polished so they are shiny. The space between the two walls is a vacuum; this prevents heat loss through convection since there are no air particles to carry out the transfer of heat. The shiny surface of the walls also prevents heat loss through radiation.

Keywords

Heat: A form of energy that flows from a hot object to cold object

Temperature: The degree of hotness or coldness of an object

Thermometer: The instrument used to measure temperature

Conduction: The transfer of heat from a hotter part to a colder part of an object through the collision of its particles

Conductors: Materials that conduct heat easily

Insulators: Materials that do not conduct heat

Convection: The transfer of heat with the help of actual movement of particles in a liquid medium

Radiation: The mode of heat transfer in which there is no medium required

Summary

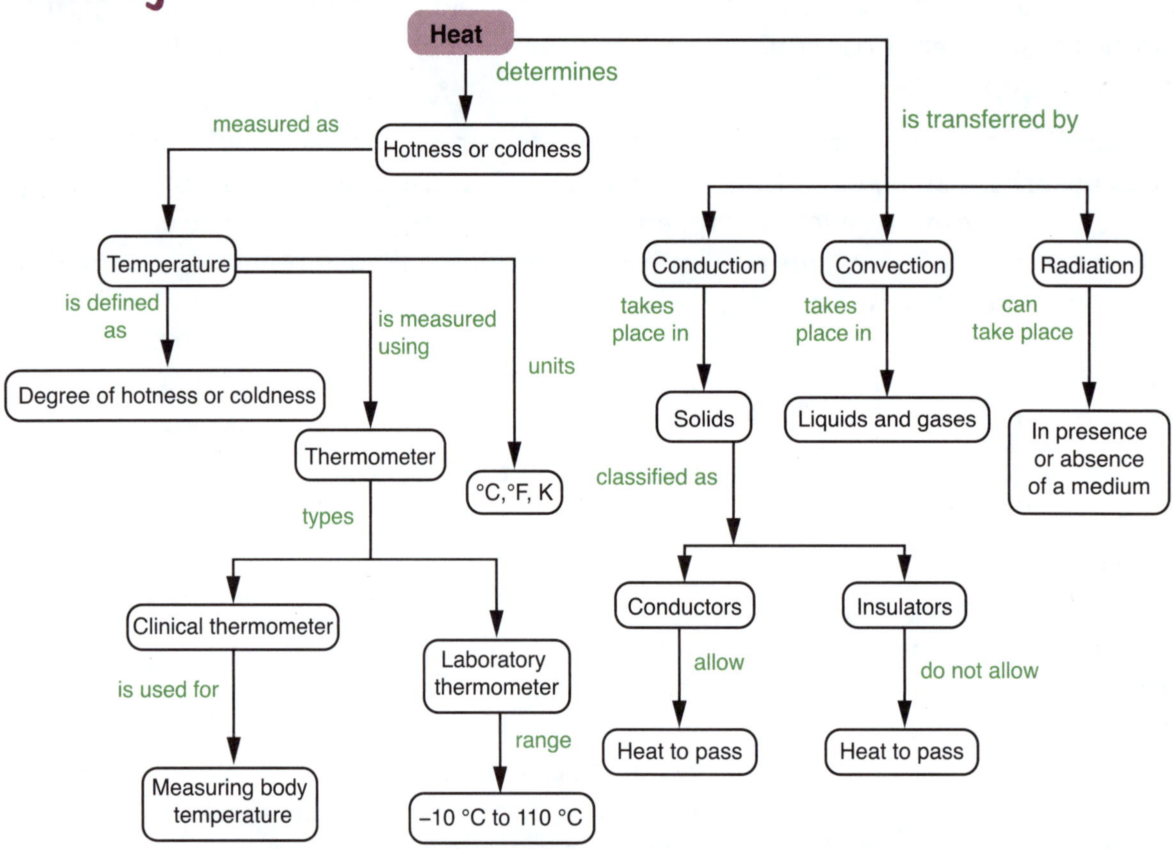

EXERCISE

W

ia

A. Choose the correct option.

1. The form of energy that flows from a hot object to a cold object is called ________.
   (a) temperature (b) thermometer (c) heat (d) light
2. The degree of hotness or coldness in a substance is called ________.
   (a) temperature (b) thermometer (c) heat (d) light
3. In solids, the transfer of heat can take place through ________.
   (a) conduction (b) convection (c) both (a) and (b) (d) none of these
4. The transfer of energy between objects that are in physical contact occurs by ________.
   (a) conduction (b) convection (c) radiation (d) none of these
5. Which of these is a conductor of heat?
   (a) Wood (b) Paper (c) Copper (d) Plastic

B. Fill in the blanks.

ia

1. The ________ in a clinical thermometer prevents the backflow of the mercury into the bulb. (stem/kink)
2. The boiling point of water in the Celsius scale is ________. (32 °C/100 °C)
3. The handles of cooking utensils are made of materials that are ________. (insulators/conductors)
4. The vacuum in a thermos flask reduces the heat loss due to ________. (convection/radiation)
5. Dark colours are good ________ of heat. (reflectors/absorbers)

C. State whether the following statements are true (T) or false (F).

1. Air is a good conductor of heat. ☐
2. Movement of particles takes place during convection. ☐
3. Heat transfer by convection occurs in solids, liquids and gases. ☐
4. The air moving from land to sea is called a sea breeze. ☐
5. Radiation occurs only when two objects are in contact. ☐

D. Answer the following in one word each.

1. The SI unit of heat
2. The SI unit of temperature
3. The instrument used to measure temperature
4. The transfer of heat from a hotter part to a colder part of an object due to vibration of its particles
5. The materials that do not conduct heat

E. Give reasons for the following.

1. It is preferred to use two thin blankets rather than one thick blanket to keep our body warm.
2. It is advised that the outer walls of houses should be painted white in places that have a hot climate.
3. In a mercury thermometer, the level of mercury rises when its bulb comes in contact with a hot object.
4. Retailers selling ice blocks usually cover them with jute sacks.
5. We have to shake a clinical thermometer before taking a new reading.
6. Woollen clothes are preferred during winter.

F. Answer the following questions briefly.

1. Write briefly about any two commonly used temperature scales.
2. What is the relation between the Celsius scale and the Fahrenheit scale?
3. Explain the three modes of heat transfer. Which mode of heat transfer takes place in fluids?
4. Dark colours are good absorbers of heat. Explain.

G. Answer the following questions in detail.

1. Explain the construction and working of a clinical thermometer with the help of a labelled diagram.
2. Explain the formation of sea breeze and land breeze.
3. Explain the construction and working of a thermos flask with the help of a labelled diagram.
4. (a) Convert the given temperatures to °C. (i) 150 °F (ii) 48 °F
   (b) Convert the given temperatures to °F. (i) 150 °C (ii) 32 °C

COGNITIVE CORNER

Critical Thinking

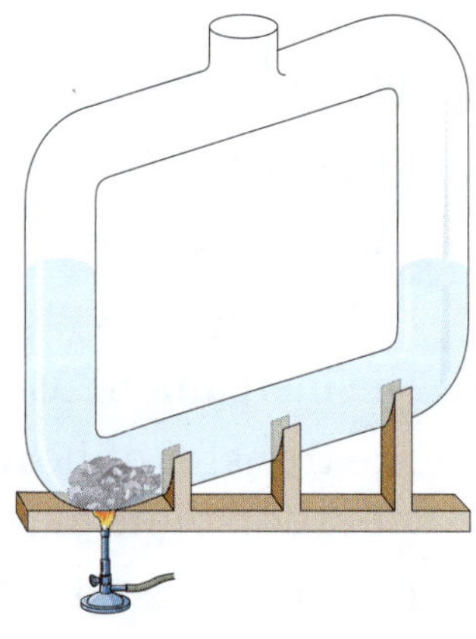

1. The apparatus shown alongside is filled with water and kept slightly elevated on one side. A small crystal of potassium permanganate is placed on the opposite side. Illustrate the flow of convection current when the apparatus is heated from below as shown.
2. If particles are displaced during the transference of heat, what would you call it—convection or conduction of heat?

3. Will the atmospheric heating be at the same rate over the Arctic ocean, the Indian ocean and the Thar desert? Explain.
4. Why should we not use clinical thermometer for measuring the temperature of hot milk?
5. Why do we need three different scales of measurement for the temperature and not just one?

Picture Study

Identify and write whether the objects shown below are conductors or insulators.

Body of pressure cooker

Cotton

Wood

______________________ ______________________ ______________________

Project

Although plastic is considered to be a poor conductor of heat, the handle in many of today's cooking pans can be observed to become warm (or even hot). Why is that? Conduct a research and make a report based on your findings. **(C-6.2)**

In the Library

Ice cubes put inside a thermocol box do not melt fast. Find out the reasons. Can you think of some design modification to the thermocol box to ensure that the ice cubes stay cold even longer? **(C-7.1)**

Life Skills

Before the invention of refrigerators, many households stored their food items in a clay pot fridge that was usually made of porous clay (lined with wet sand) and contained an inner pot within which the food was placed. You can also make your own clay pot fridge by using clay pots, sand and water. Explain how a clay pot fridge prevents ice from melting. **(C-7.1 and C-7.2)**

Worksheet

Global warming from fossil fuel emissions, due to release of carbon dioxide, poses severe and lasting effects on our planet. Addressing rising temperatures and energy needs is crucial. Transitioning to sustainable options, such as solar energy, which is abundant, clean and can be harnessed for thermal or electrical use, is the need of the hour.

Rising sea levels pose a risk to low-lying coastal regions.

Melting of glaciers leads to rise in sea levels.

Solar panels converting solar energy to electricity

A. Imagine you are an energy planner tasked with promoting the use of solar energy in your community. Design a persuasive campaign highlighting the benefits of solar energy over fossil fuels. Consider its environmental impact, sustainability and potential to achieve Sustainable Development Goal 7 (Affordable and Clean Energy). What strategies would you use to encourage people to adopt solar energy solutions?

____

____

____

____

B. Suggest three more alternative sources of energy.

____

____

____

____

7 Weather, Climate and Adaptations of Animals to Climate

Curricular Goals

- Explore the world of matter and its constituents, properties and behaviour **(CG-1)**
- Explore the living world in scientific terms **(CG-3)**
- Explore the nature and processes of science through engaging with the evolution of scientific knowledge and conducting scientific inquiry **(CG-6)**

Competencies

- Observe and explain the phenomena caused due to difference in pressure and temperature **(C-1.4)**
- Analyse patterns of relationships between living organisms and their environments in terms of dependence on and response to each other **(C-3.3)**
- Formulate questions using scientific terminology and collect data as evidence **(C-6.2)**

Let's Get Started

Observe the pictures given below. Select the clothes and accessories from the given box that you would wear in the places shown below.

Leather boots, muffler, woollen gloves, umbrella, polo neck sweater, sandals, hat, cotton pants, jerkin, denims

____

____

____

Weather plays an important role in our lives. While planning our day-to-day activities, we keep the prevailing weather conditions in mind. Even the clothes that we wear reflect the weather. In cold weather we keep ourselves warm by wearing woollen clothes, while in hot weather we wear cotton clothes that keep us cool.

In this chapter, you will learn about the factors that affect the weather and climate, and how animals adapt to the climate of the place they live in.

WEATHER AND CLIMATE

***Weather** is the day-to-day atmospheric condition at any given place with respect to conditions such as temperature, humidity, rainfall and wind speed.*

Climate is the average weather pattern of a long period of time occurring at any given place.

The **weather** may vary from day to day or even from hour to hour. For example, if on one day the weather is cloudy and cool, there are chances that the next day it may be sunny and warm. Sometimes during the day, mornings may be sunny and warm but by evening it may become cloudy and rain heavily.

The **climate** does not vary for short periods but remains constant for several years. For example, the Himalayan region is said to have a cold climate because its weather has been extremely cold for centuries. Similarly, the Western Ghats have had a humid and tropical climate for years.

A **meteorologist** is a person who prepares weather reports by collecting information on conditions such as temperature, wind, humidity and rainfall and predicts the weather conditions of a particular place. In a weather report, the maximum and minimum temperatures are also recorded every day.

Weather reports collected over a long period, say for 25 years, help to predict the climate of the place. If we find the temperature of a particular place is high most of the time, then we can say that the climate of that place is hot. If the temperature of a place is high along with heavy rainfall on most days in a year, then the climate of that place is said to be hot and wet. Likewise, when certain regions receive very less rainfall, the climate is said to be hot and dry.

Table 7.1: Differences between weather and climate

Weather	Climate
Weather is a daily condition including temperature and rainfall.	Climate is the average weather over a long period of time.
Weather can change from minute to minute, day to day, and from year to year.	The overall changes and variations in climate are stable and may take decades or years to change.
Weather may involve just one condition of the atmosphere.	Climate includes all the conditions of the atmosphere such as temperature, precipitation, wind, humidity, cloudiness and pressure.
The scientific study of weather is called meteorology.	The scientific study of climate is called climatology.

FACTORS AFFECTING THE WEATHER OF A PLACE

a

The factors affecting the weather of a particular place are given below:

- **Temperature**: Temperature is the measure of the heat content of the atmosphere. When you wake up in the morning, you may have noticed the pleasant coolness around you even during the summer season. But as the day advances, you begin to feel the air turning warmer. This happens when the sun's rays warm up the Earth along with rocks, soil and water present on the Earth's surface. The maximum temperature is reached during the afternoon. As the sun goes down, the Earth starts getting cooler. It is the coolest during dawn, when the minimum temperature is reached. Hence, the Earth grows warmer by day and cools down at night. Temperature as you have already learned can be measured using a **thermometer.** The common units for measuring temperature are degree Celsius (°C) and degree Fahrenheit (°F). Maximum and minimum temperatures in a day are measured using a special thermometer called **maximum-minimum thermometer** (Fig. 7.1). The maximum temperature of the day occurs generally in the afternoon while the minimum temperature occurs generally in the early morning.

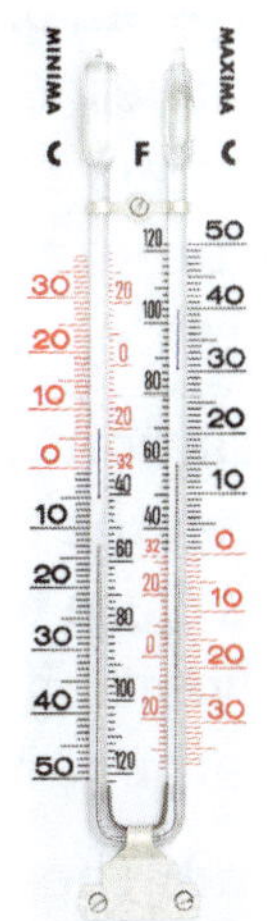

Fig. 7.1: Maximum-minimum thermometer

- **Humidity**: It represents the amount of water vapour in the air. The air can hold only a certain amount of water vapour at a particular temperature. When the air has the maximum possible amount of water vapour present, it is called **saturated** air. As the temperature increases, the capacity to hold water vapour in the air also increases. A **hygrometer** is used to measure humidity in percentage (%) (Fig. 7.2).

Fig. 7.2: Hygrometer

- **Rainfall:** It is the liquid form of water that reaches the surface of the Earth from the atmosphere. When the temperature of the air falls, the water vapour present in it condenses to form tiny droplets of water. Clouds form when condensation takes place at higher altitudes. When the droplets join together and become heavy, they fall down as rain. A **rain gauge** is used to measure rainfall in millimetre (mm) (Fig. 7.3).

Fig. 7.3: Rain gauge

When the temperature in the air is very low, the droplets from the clouds freeze into crystals of ice and come down in the form of **hail** or **snow**. If the droplets pass through very cold layers of air, they freeze and come down as **hailstones**. During winter, the temperature falls after sunset. Water vapour condenses near the ground, and looks hazy to the human eye; this is known as **fog**.

- **Atmospheric pressure:** Atmospheric pressure is the weight of the atmosphere overhead. The pressure created by the weight of the air in the Earth's atmosphere is known as air pressure. Air has weight because it is a mixture of gases such as nitrogen, oxygen, argon, carbon dioxide and a few other gases in the form of small particles. Because of the Earth's gravitational force, the weight of the particles in the air creates pressure. In addition, since there is more air close to the ground, the air pressure is highest on the planet's surface and decreases as the altitude increases.

  Variations in air pressure control the weather events that occur in a given area. When the air pressure is high, the skies are usually clear and blue. When the air gets close to the ground, the high pressure causes it to flow down and fan out, preventing clouds from forming. When the air pressure is low, the air flows together and upward, converges, rises, cools, and forms clouds, causing rainfall.

- **Wind:** The moving air is called wind. Wind is the main reason for the occurrence of cold and warm fronts, clouds, thunderstorms and hurricanes. Wind is formed because of the differences in temperature and atmospheric pressure between nearby regions. Winds tend to blow from areas of high pressure, where it is colder, to areas of low pressure, where it is warmer. The distance between low- and high-pressure regions and the difference in air pressure determine the wind speed and strength.

- **Clouds:** Clouds are one of the quickest ways to determine the current and future weather conditions. Clouds can affect the amount of sunlight reaching the Earth's surface. Cloudy days are cooler than clear ones because clouds prevent more of the sun's radiation from reaching the Earth's surface. The clouds act as a blanket, keeping the Earth warm.

Weather Report

A weather report is a summary of weather conditions often including the predicted conditions for an area. The given data shows a sample of the weather report (Fig. 7.4).

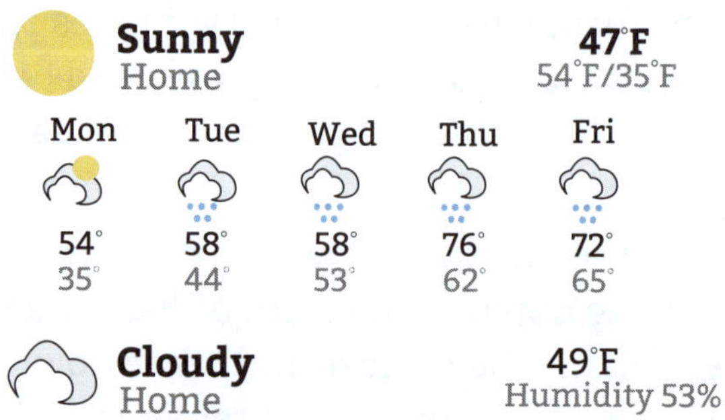

Fig. 7.4: Weather report

Activity 1

Collect the weather reports of the last week from any newspaper. You can also collect weather reports from a library. Now, record the information from the weather reports you collected in the table given below.

Date	Maximum temperature in degree Celsius	Minimum temperature in degree Celsius	Humidity	Rainfall in mm

From the above activity, it is clear that all the parameters are not the same on any two days. Over the course of a week, there may be considerable variation.

Look at the graphs below. Can you read these graphs and describe what they mean?

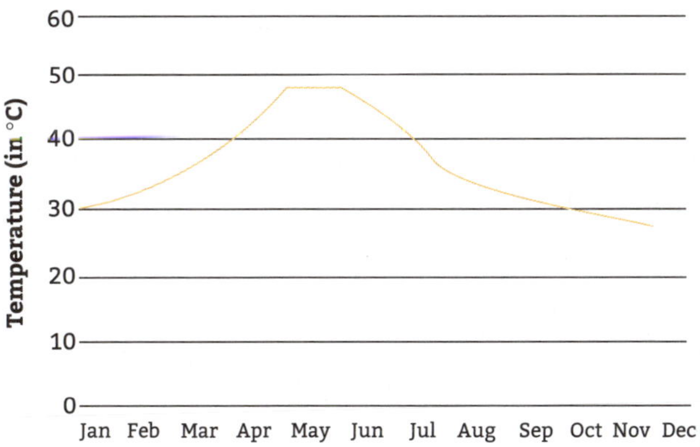

Graph 1

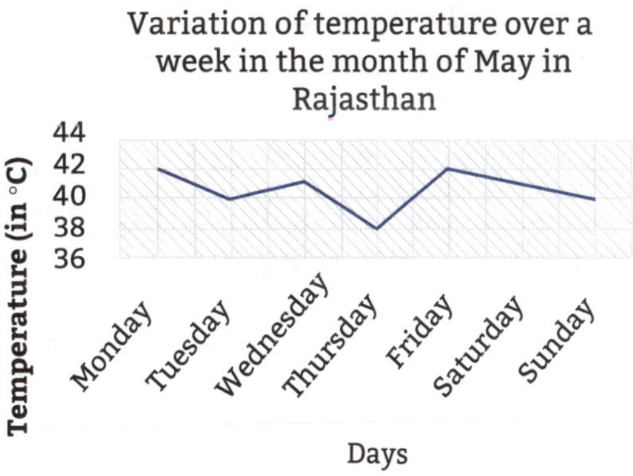

Graph 2

Fig. 7.5: Graphs showing the maximum and minimum temperatures

Graph 1 shows the maximum and minimum temperature recorded in Rajasthan over a year.

Graph 2 shows Rajasthan's average temperature over a week in the month of May.

FACTORS THAT AFFECT THE CLIMATE OF THE EARTH

The Earth has three basic types of climate: tropical, temperate and polar. Let us look at some of the factors that determine the climate of a place.

- **Distance from the sun**: The farther the Earth is from the sun, the lesser the heat obtained from the sun. As the Earth revolves around the sun, only one hemisphere is closer to the sun at a time (Fig. 7.6). So, when the North Pole is towards the sun, it is warmer than the South Pole, and vice versa.

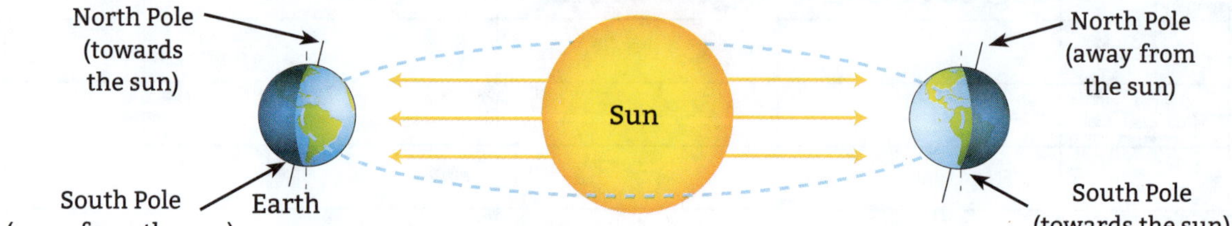

Fig. 7.6: Distance from the sun affects the climate

- **Tilt**: The Earth's axis is not perpendicular to the plane of its orbit. It is inclined at an angle of 23.5°. This causes the northern hemisphere to receive the maximum direct sunlight. Thus, it gets more hours of daylight in June than in December when it receives lesser direct sunlight and lesser hours of daylight (Fig. 7.7). This causes different seasons in a year. In contrast, in the southern hemisphere the seasons are reversed. Thus, it is summer in the northern hemisphere in June; days become longer and the angle of the sun goes higher.

  When the seasons are reversed in the southern hemisphere, the North Pole is tilted away from the sun; the South Pole is tilted towards it. As a result, it is summer in the southern hemisphere. If the Earth did not have a tilt, there would be no seasons and day and night would be of the same length throughout the year. The amount of solar energy reaching any given location on Earth would also be constant throughout the year.

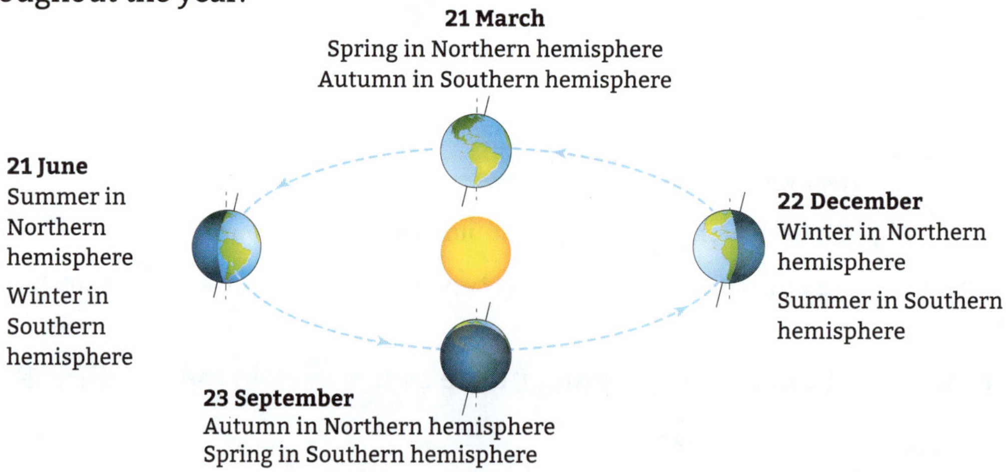

Fig. 7.7: Tilt of the Earth and its movement around the sun cause seasonal changes

- **Sunrise and sunset**: As the Earth revolves on its axis (an imaginary line passing through both the north and south poles) once a day, it gives the appearance of sunrise or sunset (Fig. 7.8).

  As learnt earlier, the axis of the Earth is tilted by about 23.5° to its orbit. This is not only a major cause of the changing seasons, but also has a great impact on the time of sunrise and sunset. If the Earth was not tilted, it would receive the same amount of sunlight each day of the year without causing a difference in the time of sunrise and sunset.

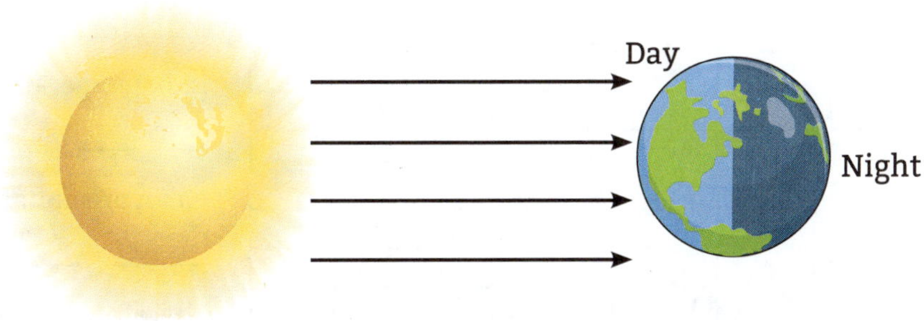

Fig. 7.8: Occurrence of day and night

Factors That Affect the Climate of a Place

The reasons for the differences in temperature and rainfall in these places are because of the factors that affect the climate of a place. Let us look into what these factors are:

- **Distance from the equator**: Different parts of the Earth receive different amounts of heat from the sun. The amount of heat received depends upon the distance of the latitude[1] from the equator. Places located at higher latitudes (far from the equator) receive less sunlight than those at lower latitudes (close to the equator). Due to the curved surface of the Earth, the sun's rays spread over a greater surface area at higher latitudes than at the equator. The rays also have to travel through a greater thickness of atmosphere to reach higher latitudes. Thus, high latitudes receive less sunlight, resulting in cold climates. The tilt of the Earth and its yearly orbit around the sun also contribute to temperature changes. The maximum sunlight is received at the equator, making areas near the equator very warm.

Word Web

[1]**Latitude:** The distance of a place from the equator

- **Height above the sea level**: The climate of a place is influenced by the height of the place above the sea level, which is known as **altitude**. We see differences in the climate, mainly in the mountains and plains. Mountains are cooler as the air is thin and is not able to absorb and retain much heat. Plains are warmer than mountains as the air is thicker and absorbs and retains heat.

Activity 2

Jaipur is a semi-desert region and is situated in the eastern part of Rajasthan (Latitude 26.92° in the north to longitude 75.82° in the east). It has an average elevation of 431 m (1417 ft). Refer to the table and fill in the summary of the climate of Jaipur.

Month	Mean temperatures (°C)		Precipitation (mm)
	Max. Temp.	Min. Temp.	
Jan	23	8	8
Feb	26	11	12
Mar	32	16	6
Apr	37	21	4
May	40	25	16
Jun	40	27	66
Jul	34	26	216
Aug	32	24	231
Sep	33	23	80
Oct	33	19	23
Nov	29	13	3
Dec	24	9	3
Mean			

The climate of Jaipur:

Altitude ____________

Max. temperature:

____________ (°C)

Min. temperature:

____________ (°C)

Mean precipitation:

____________ mm

Therefore, Jaipur has a

____________ climate.

Study the table given below. Is the average temperature and rainfall recorded in all the places given in the table same? What could be the reasons for such differences in these places?

Stations	Temperature	Avg. annual rainfall	Altitude
Chennai (Tamil Nadu)	Max. temp. in summer: 41 °C Min. temp. in winter: 20 °C	1400 mm	6.7 m above sea level
Jodhpur (Rajasthan)	Max. temp. in summer: 51 °C Min. temp. in winter: 10 °C	353 mm	231 m above sea level
Darjeeling (West Bengal)	Max. temp. in summer: 20 °C Min. temp. in winter: 1.9 °C	3200 mm	2042 m above sea level

Revise and Recall

Name the following.

1. The day-to-day atmospheric condition at a place ____________
2. The instrument used to measure the maximum and minimum temperatures in a day ____________
3. The instrument used to measure the amount of rainfall ____________
4. The instrument used to measure humidity in percentage ____________
5. The factor that causes change in seasons ____________

ADAPTATIONS OF ANIMALS TO DIFFERENT CLIMATES

a

*The features and habits developed in plants and animals that enable them to survive in their surroundings are called **adaptation**.*

Let us look at the adaptations some animals have undergone to adjust to different climates.

- **Temperate climate:** Temperate climates are quite pleasantly warm to cold. It becomes pleasantly warm during summers but become quite low during winter months.
  Animals living in these climates are adapted to cope with the heat and cold.
  - Elks undergo a seasonal molting process. In summer, they have a reddish-brown coat that is well-suited for camouflage in temperate forests and grasslands. In winter, their coat becomes darker and thicker, providing better insulation and protection against the cold.

Fig. 7.9: Elk

  - In winter, bisons grow a thick, dense coat of fur, including a warm undercoat. This insulating fur helps them retain body heat in cold weather. During the warmer months, they engage in dust bathing, rolling in dry dirt or dust. This behaviour helps them remove excess moisture and insects from their fur while also providing some cooling relief.
  - Tigers usually live closer to the water bodies to stay cooler and swim during the day.
- **Tropical climate:** Tropical climates are very hot and humid. In this climate, there is abundant rainfall and a considerable amount of sunshine.
  Animals living in these climates are adapted to cope with the excessive humidity and heat.
  - Jaguars have adapted to the wet environment. They are very good swimmers and they seek out water for bathing and swimming. Their fur keeps them camouflaged in the tropical rainforests (Fig. 7.10).

Fig. 7.10: Jaguar

  - Sloths have thick, dense coats. This keeps them dry during heavy downpours. They move very slowly and this helps them avoid being seen by predators.
  - Most monkeys such as the lion-tailed macaque and some apes are smaller in size than other animals, which helps them lose heat more easily.

Animals found in tropical climate	Animals found in temperate climate
Deer	Elk
Jaguar	Bison
Lemurs	Raccoon
Gorilla	Tiger
Sloth	Giant panda
Rhinoceros	Cougar

Science in Context

Human beings are the biggest threat to climate change and global warming, leading to the disappearance of many animal species.

- **Extremely cold climates**: The polar regions are at the farthest distance from the equator and receive the least amount of sunlight. The temperatures are freezing all throughout the year. The soil is covered with snow and thick layers of ice in most of the areas. Animals found in extremely cold climates include the polar bear, Arctic fox, penguin, arctic tern, killer whale, snow goose, beluga whale and seal.
    - **Migration**: Animals such as the caribou, which are unable to cope with the cold, migrate to warmer places such as the Alaskan forests during the winter months. Snow geese fly away to Japan and the arctic terns fly to Antarctica to breed (Fig. 7.11).

Fig. 7.11: Migratory birds

    - **Hibernation**: It is the process of remaining in an inactive state (which resembles deep sleep) in certain animals living in cold climates during winter. Hibernation protects the animal from the cold and reduces the need for food when food is scarce. The animals that hibernate during winters are the polar bear, skunk and chipmunk.
    - Polar bears have wide and large paws, which help them to swim and walk on the snow with ease (Fig. 7.12). They can close their nostrils while under water and stay there for a long time. They have a strong sense of smell and can identify their prey from huge distances. The thick layer of fur in polar bears insulates them from the cold. They also have a thick layer of fat, called **blubber**, under their skin, which keeps them warm.

Fig. 7.12: Polar bear

    - Seal and penguin also have a layer of **blubber** under their skin, which insulates their body from cold (Fig. 7.13). The fat also provides energy to the animal when there is a scarcity of food. Whiskers are used by them to feel and locate fish in murky or deep water. They have two layers of fur; one layer is close to the body and the other layer is longer and waterproof, which not only keeps them warm, but also gives their streamlined body an advantage while swimming. The claws help in grooming the outer fur. The flippers help in blood circulation and regulating the body temperature from time to time.

Fig. 7.13: Seal

    - The long white fur of the Arctic fox, commonly called the snow fox, camouflages it from predators and protects it from cold (Fig. 7.14). During warmer months, the coat colour changes to brown, blending with the environment. The small and round ears, nose and paws of the fox help in preventing heat loss from the body.

Fig. 7.14: Arctic fox

Wonder!

The white fur on polar bears makes them less visible in the snow and makes it easy for them to hunt.

- **Scrubland and deserts:** Scrubland and deserts have very high temperature during most part of the year. Winter lasts only for a few months during which the temperature is quite low. These regions receive very little rainfall and have a typical desert climate.
  - Camels are especially adapted to these climates as they can survive the harsh conditions of the deserts (Fig. 7.15). They are adapted to excrete very less urine to reduce the loss of water. They can also drink large quantities of water and eat plenty of food which can be stored in their hump for later use. Hence, they can survive without food and water for days while travelling in the desert. Their bodies are also adapted to tolerate temperature changes such as heat in the daytime and cold in the night time. Camels have the ability to close their eyes and nostrils to keep out the blowing sand and dust in the desert. They have three eyelids that prevent the sand from entering their eyes.

Fig. 7.15: Camel

  - Many reptiles and other animals, such as fennec fox protect themselves from the extreme temperature by spending their time in burrows during the day and become active during night (being nocturnal). Fennec foxes have distinctive, batlike ears that radiate body heat and help keep them cool (Fig. 7.16).

Fig. 7.16: Fennec fox

  - Some animals such as rat, salamander and tortoise cannot cope with the heat and so undergo aestivation (summer sleep) to escape the heat.
  - Kangaroo rat spends its days in burrows where the air is moist and humid (Fig. 7.17).

Fig. 7.17: Kangaroo rat

Go Green

Using recycled products not only saves trees but also saves the Earth from getting warmer, reducing the climate changes on the Earth and saving endangered species from becoming extinct.

Keywords

Weather: The day-to-day atmospheric condition at a place

Climate: The average weather pattern that prevails over a long period of time in a place

Aestivation: The long sleeping period of animals during summer to escape the heat

Hibernate: A deep sleep that some animals go into, to survive the long and cold winters and a scarcity of food

Blubber: Thick layer of fat stored under the skin of animals living in polar regions that protects their bodies from extreme cold climate and serves as a food reserve

Summary

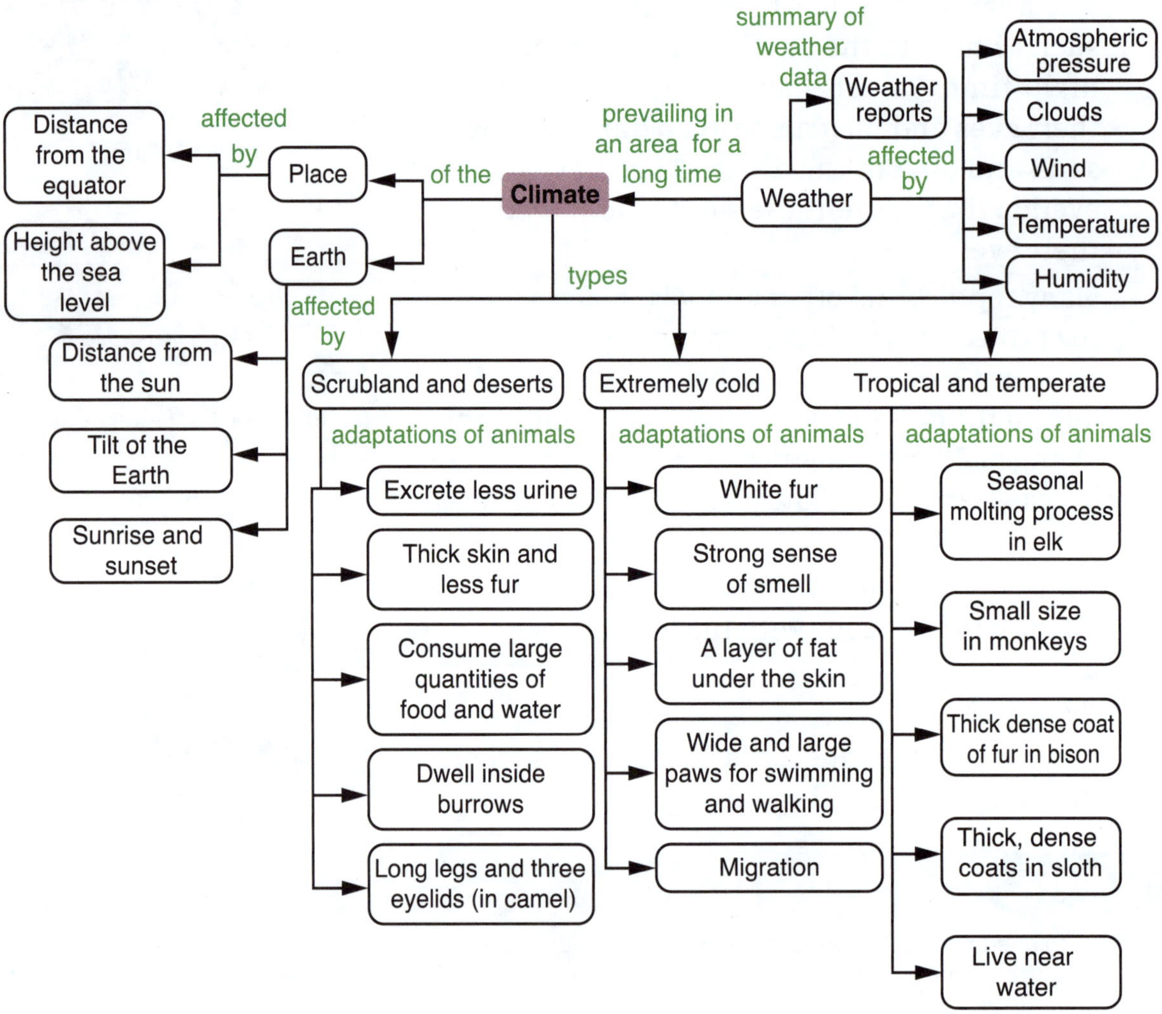

EXERCISE

W

A. Choose the correct option.

ia

1. The climate of a place is predicted with the help of weather reports collected in the past ________.
   (a) 24 hours (b) couple of months (c) one year (d) 25 years at least
2. Polar bears can identify their prey from huge distances because of their ________.
   (a) strong eyesight (b) strong hearing capacity
   (c) strong sense of smell (d) None of these
3. Which of the following best describes a tropical region?
   (a) Hot and humid
   (b) Moderate temperature, heavy rainfall
   (c) High temperature, low rainfall
   (d) Hot and dry
4. Some animals go into deep summer sleep to escape the heat. This summer sleep is called ________.
   (a) hibernation (b) aestivation (c) migration (d) orientation
5. Which of the following terms is associated with adaptations in the polar region?
   (a) Hibernation (b) Blubber (c) Migration (d) All of these

B. Fill in the blanks.

1. The instrument used to measure rainfall is called ________ . (rain sensor/rain gauge)
2. Animals living in the polar regions can withstand ________ climate. (very cold/both hot and cold)
3. The wide and large paws of polar bears help them to ________ . (swim/glide)
4. ________ is the amount of water vapour in the air. (Humidity/Temperature)
5. The ________ the altitude, the cooler is the region. (lower/higher)

C. State whether the following statements are true (T) or false (F).

ia

1. A place that receives very little rainfall and has a high temperature throughout the year will have a hot and humid climate. ☐
2. The height of a place above the sea level is called its latitude. ☐
3. The tilt of the Earth causes the change of seasons in a year. ☐
4. The long white fur of the Arctic fox camouflages it from predators. ☐
5. Kangaroo rat spends its days in burrows to escape the heat. ☐

D. Name the following.

1. An animal that migrates from the polar region
2. An instrument used to measure humidity in percentage
3. An adaptive feature in monkeys that help them to live in temperate climates
4. The angle at which the Earth tilts
5. Two factors that determine the weather of a place

E. Give reasons for the following.

1. One hemisphere of the Earth is warmer than the other.
2. There are different seasons in a year.
3. Plains are warmer than mountains.
4. Camels have three eyelids.
5. Tigers usually live closer to the water bodies.

F. Answer the following questions briefly.

1. What does a meteorologist do?
2. How does the Arctic fox prevent heat loss from its body?
3. What are the common adaptations in animals living in deserts?
4. What do the statements given below refer to—weather or climate?
   (a) 'June will be cold and wet'.
   (b) 'I think we should move to the southern part of the country where it is warmer'.
   (c) 'I don't think my clothes will dry today'.
   (d) 'The mountain cliff was covered with mist in the morning'.
5. List two factors each that affect the climate of a place and the climate of the Earth.

G. Answer the following questions in detail.

1. Explain the differences between weather and climate with examples.
2. What happens due to the tilt of the Earth and how would the Earth be affected if it were not tilted?
3. Do you think having a thick skin, large ears and tusks helps an elephant to survive in a tropical climate? Give reasons to justify your answer.

COGNITIVE CORNER

Critical Thinking

1. A polar bear closes its nostrils while swimming under water. Why?
2. If a camel is kept in very cold climate, would it be able to cope up well? Explain.

Picture Study

Choose the odd one out. Also give reasons for your choice.

Project

Refer to a newspaper and collect one week's weather details such as the temperature, humidity, rainfall and wind speed of the place your area. Prepare a summary using the table format given below. *(Rainfall may be optional depending on the weather.)* **(C-6.2)**

Date	Max. temp. (°C)	Min. temp. (°C)	Humidity (%)	Rainfall (mm)	Wind speed (kmph)

In the Library

Charles Darwin, a British naturalist, proposed the theory of evolution by natural selection: Survival of the Fittest. He pointed out that in the struggle for existence, only the fittest organisms survive in a habitat and others die out. Find out how his theory proved to be accepted from the books in your school library or the Internet. **(C-7.1)**

Life Skills

Global warming is the increase in the Earth's average surface temperature due to the effect of greenhouse gases such as carbon dioxide, which trap heat that would otherwise escape from the Earth.

Global warming has drastically harmed at least two-thirds of all plants and animals on Earth. As an individual, what measures can you take to help prevent the climate changes? **(C-7.1)**

Worksheet

Climate change in the Arctic may be accelerated by global activities that produce greenhouse gases. Melting glaciers, warmer/drier summers and increased precipitation impact the Earth, causing temperature rise, sea-level increase and shifts in weather patterns. Urgent action is needed, such as reducing carbon footprints, to mitigate these effects and prevent further harm.

Melting glaciers

A carbon footprint is the total amount of greenhouse gases, primarily carbon dioxide, and other related emissions produced directly and indirectly by an individual, organization, event or product throughout its life cycle. It measures the impact of human activities on the environment in terms of their contribution to climate change and global warming. Reducing one's carbon footprint involves minimizing the emissions associated with activities such as energy consumption, transportation, food choices and waste generation.

What can you do to reduce your carbon footprints? Make a poster on How to Reduce Our Carbon Footprints?

8 Soil

Curricular Goals

- Explore the living world in scientific terms **(CG-3)**
- Explore the nature and processes of science through engaging with the evolution of scientific knowledge and conducting scientific inquiry **(CG-6)**

Competencies

- Analyse patterns of relationships between living organisms and their environments in terms of dependence on and response to each other **(C-3.3)**
- Illustrate how scientific knowledge and ideas have changed over time and identify the scientific values that are inherent and common across the evolution of scientific knowledge **(C-6.1)**

Let's Get Started

Recall the uses of soil that you have learnt in the previous classes and fill in the blanks for each of the images given below.

For the growth of

____

Home to

____

Source of

____

For making

____

Let us learn more about how soil is formed and what it contains.

SOIL FORMATION

Soil is the uppermost layer of the Earth's surface. It is formed by the breakdown of rocks over thousands of years through a process called weathering.

***Weathering** is the process of breaking down of rocks into smaller particles by the action of wind, water and chemicals; changes in temperature and action of plants.*

Weathering is a continuous and natural process that occurs due to heat, cold, wind, rain and frost, and also due to biological factors such as roots of plants and soil organisms. Snow, sea water and river water are some of the major factors that help in the formation of soil in coastal areas and mountainous regions.

Fig. 8.1: Physical weathering

Weathering is of three types: physical, chemical and biological.

Physical weathering: The breaking down of big rocks into smaller-sized rock particles by agents such as wind, water or change in temperature is called physical weathering. It is also called mechanical weathering.

Chemical weathering: Chemical weathering occurs when rocks are broken down by a chemical change. Rainwater can become slightly acidic by absorbing carbon dioxide in the atmosphere. This reacts with the mineral grains in the rock giving rise to new minerals and salts. The degree of chemical weathering depends on the type of rock. For example, limestone is more readily chemically weathered than granite. Temperature and acid rain also contribute to chemical weathering.

Fig. 8.2: Chemical weathering

Biological weathering: The roots of trees and burrowing of animals inside the soil bring about this type of weathering. Roots of trees and plants grow through the rocks, contributing to weathering. As the roots grow bigger, they penetrate deeper into the ground, forming cracks in rocks and helping in soil formation. Chemicals produced by lichens that grow on rocks also help in breaking down rocks to form soil.

Fig. 8.3: Biological weathering

Soil formation takes place in three main stages:

First stage - Mechanical breakdown: **Parent rocks** or **bedrocks** get broken down into smaller-sized rocks by the action of wind, water or change in temperature (Fig. 8.4).

(a) Effect of sun

(b) Effect of rain

Fig. 8.4: Effect of change in temperature on bedrocks

The rocks are also broken down with the help of the decaying remains of plants and animals present in the parent rock during this stage.

Second stage - Chemical and biological action: Further weathering continues to form smaller rock particles. Thus, soil formation begins. Then as the dead plants and animals present in the soil get decayed by the action of bacteria and other microorganisms, soil begins to get fertile (Fig. 8.5).

Third stage: In this stage, chemical and biological weathering continue. The mineral salts with water percolate and reach deep, thus enriching the nutrients in the soil. This stage completes the process of soil formation (Fig. 8.6).

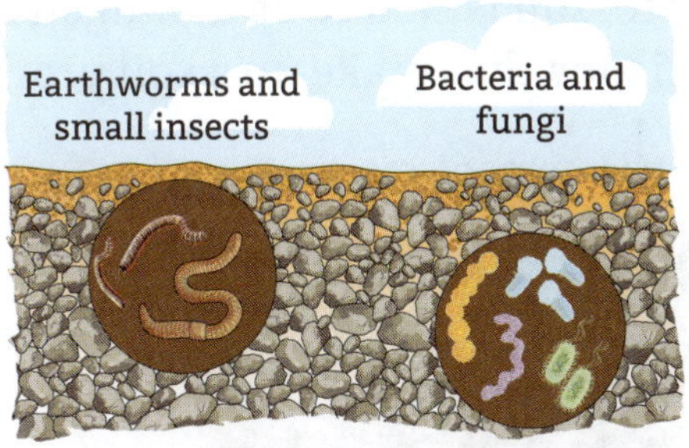

Fig. 8.5: Action of bacteria and microorganisms on soil

Fig. 8.6: Addition of minerals and smaller rocks to soil

Activity 1

Visit different places around your locality and collect different soil samples in small boxes. (Try collecting samples from the surface as well as from different depths.) Take out the samples and observe the differences in each. Analyse their differences and fill the table given below.

	Depth	Colour	Texture	Size	Living/non-living matter
Sample 1					
Sample 2					
Sample 3					

Abiotic Factors Affecting Soil Formation

There are many abiotic[1] factors that affect soil formation:

Climate: Climatic conditions such as harsh wind, rainfall and fluctuating temperature lead to the formation of cracks in the rocks. These cracks deepen with time and eventually cause the rocks to break down into smaller rocks.

Word Web

[1]**Abiotic:** Things in environment that are not living

Landscape: The layer of soil in hilly areas is thinner because the running water washes away the topsoil very often, whereas the layer of soil found in the plains is thicker because water does not wash away the soil very often here. The landscape in the hills facilitates the running down of water, thereby eroding the rocks with more intensity and causing them to break or crack.

Nature of the parent rock: Soil formed will have similar composition as that of the parent rock (the rock from which it is formed). For instance, if the parent rock has a high calcium content, the soil formed will also be rich in calcium.

SOIL PROFILE

If you closely observe a construction site or an area where a well is being dug, you will notice that as workers dig deeper, there are differences in the type of soil in terms of colour and texture. Scientists have also found that the chemical composition of soil also changes as you dig deeper into the ground. Hence, soil is said to be arranged in layers which are called **horizons**. There are four horizons that make up a soil profile.

*A **soil profile** is a vertical section of the soil showing its different layers or horizons.* Figure 8.7 shows the horizons that make up the soil profile.

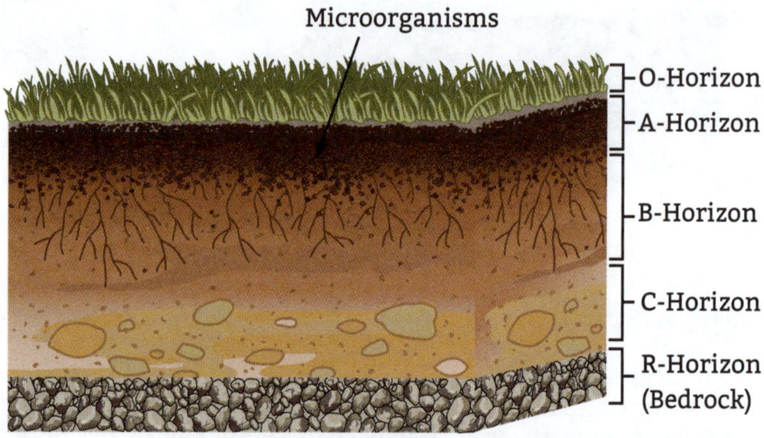

Fig. 8.7: The soil profile

O-Horizon: This is the first layer of a soil profile. This layer is rich in plant residues and other organic matter in their non-decomposed form.

A-Horizon: This is the second layer and is known as the **topsoil**. This dark, soft and porous layer is rich in humus and contains fine particles of soil. Humus is ideal for making the soil fertile and plant roots growing in this layer flourish well. A-horizon not only provides nutrients for the healthy growth of plants but is also home to many animals and insects.

B-Horizon: This layer is found just below the A-horizon and is known as the **subsoil**. This hard and compost layer is rich in minerals but poor in humus. It is lighter in colour than the topsoil. The minerals present in this horizon provide nutrients mainly for plants that have deep roots.

C-Horizon: Below the subsoil is the infertile zone (lacking humus) that contains partially weathered rocks with a lot of cracks and crevices. This layer is the first stage in the formation of soil and eventually forms the upper two layers as weathering takes place.

R-Horizon: This layer is the lowermost layer in the soil profile and is known as the **bedrock** as it contains hard rocks that provide a base to the other three layers. The soil-forming materials are derived from the weathering of this layer.

COMPOSITION OF SOIL

Soil has four main components: parent material, water, air and organic matter (humus). Along with these components, soil also contains soil organisms and minerals.

Parent material: This consists of rock particles of different sizes made of clay, sand or gravel.

Water: Water present around the soil particles is absorbed by plants for photosynthesis.

Air: Air is found around the spaces between the soil particles. Oxygen present in the soil is important for the roots of plants during respiration.

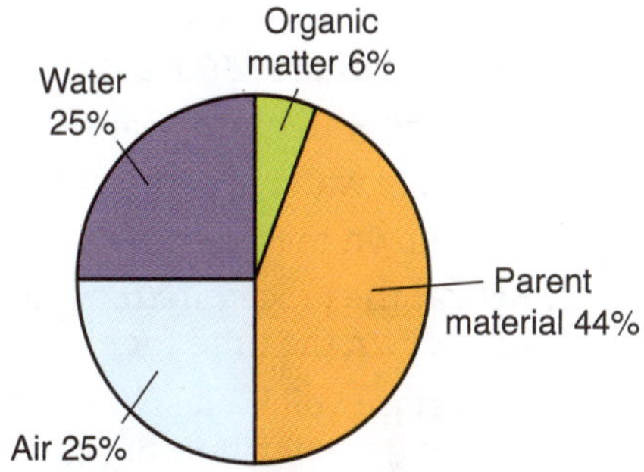

Fig. 8.8: Components of soil

Organic matter (humus): Humus is made up of dead and decaying plant and animal remains. It adds to the fertility of the soil by providing nutrients to it. Humus also increases the texture of the soil and its water-holding capacity.

Soil organisms: Different kinds of microorganisms such as bacteria and fungi are present in the soil. Other organisms such as earthworms, millipedes, ants and termites are also found in soil. These organisms play an important role as they help in aerating and loosening the soil.

> **Wonder!**
>
> Scientists have estimated that every gram of soil contains about a billion of bacteria.

Minerals: Clay and sand contain minerals such as silica, iron, magnesium, potassium and calcium, which are necessary for the growth of plants and are absorbed by the hair present at the root surfaces.

TYPES OF SOIL

Soils are of different types because of their water-holding capacity. This is because of the difference in the size of the particles in each type of soil. Sand, silt and clay are three primary types of soil particles.

Sand: Largest particles, ranging from 0.05 to 2.0 millimeters in diameter

Silt: Medium-sized particles, with diameters from 0.002 to 0.05 millimeters

Clay: Smallest particles, less than 0.002 millimeters in diameter

Activity 2

Aim: To identify different types of soil

Materials required: Three beakers, soil samples from different places, water, a stopwatch, a measuring cylinder

Procedure:

1. Label the three beakers as A, B and C.
2. Fill exactly half of each beaker with different soil samples.
3. Measure exactly 50 mℓ of water in a measuring cylinder.
4. Pour the water into beaker A and simultaneously start the stopwatch.
5. Once the water is completely absorbed by the soil, stop the stopwatch.
6. Note down the time in your notebook.
7. Repeat the procedure for samples B and C and note down the time for each in the given table.

Sample	Time taken to absorb water
Sample A	
Sample B	
Sample C	

Conclusion: Soil is classified into three main types based on its water-holding capacity: sandy soil, clayey soil and loamy soil.

Sandy soil contains large coarse particles, which we call sand. It is gritty, with very little humus and lot of air spaces between the particles. Hence, this type of soil is well aerated and cannot hold water for long. This soil is mainly found in places with warm climates such as deserts and marshy areas.

Fig. 8.9: Sandy soil

Loamy soil contains large and fine particles of sand, silt and clay. This is the most fertile type of soil and is considered to be ideal for plant growth. This soil is well aerated and contains a lot of humus. Silt is a type of soil formed due to its depositions in river beds.

Fig. 8.10: Loamy soil

Clayey soil contains fine particles made of clay. The soil particles have little air spaces between them. Water will not drain quickly compared with sandy soil. Hence, the water in this soil will get logged, making the soil sticky. Waterlogging reduces the availability of air between the soil particles, making the soil infertile.

Though sandy soil and clayey soil are not considered good for the growth of crops, they can be used for growing crops by adding clay or sand, respectively, to them along with humus. This will alter their water-holding capacity as well as increase their fertility due to the addition of humus. This is done as some plants such as groundnut and potato are found to grow well in them.

Fig. 8.11: Clayey soil

PROPERTIES OF SOIL

- **Moisture**: Take 2 g of soil (try samples from the surface as well as from different depths) in a dry test tube and heat it. What do you observe? Tiny droplets of water will be seen near the mouth of the test tube. Moisture is the amount of water present in the soil. Since different soils have different water-holding capacities, the amount of moisture present in each type of soil will be different. Water can easily pass through sandy soil, which is also well aerated. So, it allows water to drain out quickly and does not retain moisture for long. Clayey soil takes up water slowly but can hold a lot of water. Since they cause water to stagnate and collect above its surface, especially after a heavy rain, they cause waterlogging, choking the plant roots and finally leading to the death of plants. Loamy soil holds the right amount of moisture for plant growth. Humus and silt present in these soils help in holding adequate amount of water required for plant growth.
- **Absorption**: *The ability of a particular type of soil to absorb and retain water is called its **water-holding capacity**.*

  Let us do the following activity to know the water-holding capacities of different soil types.

Activity 3

a

Aim: To calculate the amount of water absorbed by different soils

Materials required: Two 250 mℓ conical flasks, soils of two types (sand and clay), two funnels, two filter papers, water and a measuring cylinder

Procedure:

1. Take two 250 mℓ conical flasks.
2. Place a funnel on each of the conical flasks.
3. Fold both the filter papers and fix one in each funnel.
4. Place 10 g of sand in one funnel and 10 g of clay in the other.
5. Pour 25 mℓ of water in each funnel and observe the amount of water collected in each conical flask after 5 minutes.
6. Measure the amount of water collected in each conical flask using a measuring cylinder.
7. Calculate the amount of water absorbed by using the formula given.
   Amount of water absorbed = Initial amount of water – Water collected in the conical flask

Observations: Note down your observations in the given table.

Soil sample	Amount of water collected
Clay	
Sand	

The more water collected in the conical flask, the lesser the water-absorption capacity of the given soil sample.

Conclusion: The water-absorption capacity of clay is more than that of sand.

- **Percolation rate**: *Percolation is the process of movement of water through the soil.* ***Percolation rate*** *is the rate (speed) at which water flows through the pores in the soil.* The soil with a high water-holding capacity has a low percolation rate and vice versa. Let us find out the percolation rates in different types of soils by performing the following activity.

Activity 4

Aim: To find the percolation rate of water in different soils

Materials required: Three plastic syringes, three conical flasks, sandy, clayey and loamy soil samples, water, a measuring cylinder, a stopwatch

Procedure:

1. Take three transparent disposable plastic syringes and label them as A, B and C.
2. Take 10 g of sandy, clayey and loamy soil samples and fill each of them into the three syringes and place each over a conical flask.
3. Measure 25 mℓ of water using a measuring cylinder.
4. Pour the water into syringe A.
5. Start the stopwatch as you start pouring the water into the syringe containing the soil sample.
6. Note down the time. Stop the watch when no more water is seen to percolate into the conical flask.
7. Pour water into syringes B and C containing the respective samples.
8. Record the time as done for syringe A.
9. Using the measuring jar, find the volume of water that has percolated into each conical flask and note it down.
10. Calculate the percolation rate of water for all three samples using the formula.

Percolation rate = Amount of water in (mℓ)/Time in minutes

Observations: Note down the percolation rate for each sample in the given table. Find out if your observation and record justify the qualities of soil described earlier.

Sample	Percolation rate
Sample A	
Sample B	
Sample C	

Conclusion: The percolation rate varies from soil to soil.

Science in Context

Soil with a poor percolation rate will retain excessive water for extended periods, which can be detrimental to plants because their roots require adequate aeration for proper growth.

Revise and Recall

Match the following.

1. Rate of movement of water into the soil	(a) O-Horizon
2. First layer of the soil	(b) Chemical weathering
3. Change in the chemical nature of soil	(c) Percolation rate
4. Lowermost layer of the soil	(d) Humus
5. Organic matter made of dead organisms	(e) Bedrock

SOIL DISTRIBUTION AND CROPS IN INDIA

Have you ever observed the type of soil present in the areas around your home or the types of crops grown in your kitchen garden? Have you wondered why some crops grow well in some types of soil, while others do not?

Soil is an important natural resource for crop production. Successful crop production depends on the suitability of soil types for the crops that need to be grown. Most crops need well-drained, moderately fine-to-medium textured soil with optimum physical and chemical properties.

The kind of minerals present in the soil, the acidity and alkalinity of the soil and humus are the factors that play an important role in the growth of crops.

In the Indian subcontinent, many types of soil are available (Fig. 8.12), each with different characteristics. Each one is ideal for a specific set of crops. Let us learn about different types of soil and their suitability for different crops.

Alluvial soil: The alluvial soil is made of particles such as clay, sand and slit. Alluvial soil is highly fertile because it has an adequate amount of potash, lime and phosphoric acid. Alluvial soil is found in the deltas of different rivers such as the Mahanadi, Kaveri, Godavari and Krishna in peninsular India. Alluvial soil has a light green colour, and crops cultivated in alluvial soil are wheat, maize, sugarcane, rice, pulses and oilseeds. Alluvial soil is found in the northern plains, beginning from Punjab to West Bengal and Assam.

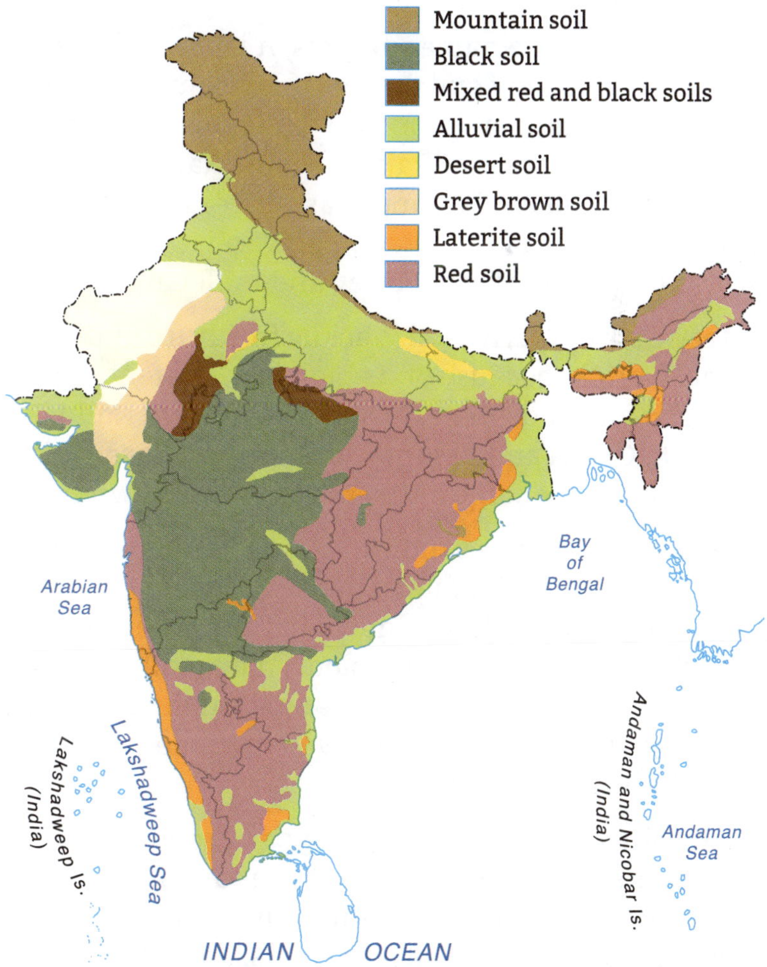

Fig. 8.12: Soil distribution in India

Black soil: The major crop grown in black soil is cotton. This soil is rich in potash, lime, magnesium carbonate and calcium carbonate, which are adequate for growing cotton crops. Black soil is mostly found in Gujarat, Maharashtra and Madhya Pradesh. It is also found in the southern part of India, in the states of Andhra Pradesh, Karnataka and Tamil Nadu.

Black soil holds a lot of moisture and has a higher water-holding capacity. Crops such as cotton, wheat, millet and tobacco can be grown in black soil.

Red soil: It is formed by the weathering of metamorphic and igneous rocks. The soil is known as red soil because it has a high iron content, which gives it its red colour. Red soil is rich in potash but lacks nitrogen phosphate and humus content. The texture of red soil is sometimes sandy and clayey. This type of soil is found in some parts of Karnataka, Orissa, Jharkhand, Madhya Pradesh, Tamil Nadu and Maharashtra.

Groundnut, potato, maize or corn, rice, ragi, wheat, millets, pulses, sugarcane, oilseeds, fruits such as oranges and mangoes, and vegetables are some of the best crops grown in this soil.

Desert soil: As the name suggests, it is found in desert areas with low rainfall. This type of soil is sandy and dry, with some quantities of nitrogen. Generally, only drought-resistant crops such as millet and barley can grow in this soil. This type of soil is found in areas of Rajasthan, the Rann of Kutch in Gujarat, adjoining regions of Haryana and Punjab, and coastal areas of Kerala, Tamil Nadu and Orissa. This soil covers about 4% of the total Indian land. Only drought-tolerant crops are suitable to grow in this type of soil. Barley and millet are two such examples.

Laterite soil: Laterite soil is acidic in nature and rich in iron. This kind of soil is used to make bricks because of its high iron content. It is low in organic matter, calcium, nitrogen and phosphate. It is found in Tamil Nadu, Karnataka, Kerala, Madhya Pradesh, Orissa and Assam. Cotton, wheat, rice, pulses, rubber, tea, coffee, coconut and cashews are some of the major crops grown in laterite soil.

Arid soil: Arid soil is sandy and has a low clay content. Arid soil is low in organic matter and humidity due to the heavy evaporation in arid regions. Due to high salt content, this soil is saline in nature and nitrogen content is low. However, it is abundant in plant oils. The colour of dry soil varies from red to brown. It is found in Aravalli West. Saline-resistant and drought-tolerant crops are suitable to be grown in this type of soil. Barley, maize, wheat, millets, cotton and pulses are some of the crops that can be grown in this soil.

Mountain and forest soil: This type of soil is rich in organic matter but poor in nutrients such as potash, phosphorus and lime. Crops grown in this soil require the right fertilizers. Along with this, it is acidic in nature. It is available in the Himalayan area, the Western and Eastern Ghats, and a few areas of the Peninsular Plateau. Wheat, barley, maize, tea, coffee, spices, and tropical and temperate fruits are some of the forest soil crops.

SOIL EROSION

***Soil erosion** is the gradual removal or wearing away of the Earth's soil surface by natural agents such as running water, wind, waves and snow.* It takes away the fertile topsoil, making the soil infertile and unsuitable for plant growth. Soil erosion is more severe in areas where there are destructive human activities and less (or loss of) vegetation cover. The soil covering the surface of the Earth has taken millions of years to form.

For every 100 to 400 years, soil is formed at a rate of only 1 cm and it takes 3,000 to 12,000 years to build enough soil to produce a suitable land for cultivation. This means that soil once lost would take at least a hundred years to restore!

Fig. 8.13: Soil erosion

Causes of Soil Erosion

- The loss of protective vegetation through deforestation, overgrazing, ploughing and forest fire makes the soil susceptible to being swept away by strong wind and running water.
- Inappropriate farming techniques such as deep ploughing the land two or three times a year to produce annual crops can lead to soil erosion.
- Overcultivation of crops and overgrazing by animals can cause the soil to lose its structure and binding capacity, which makes it easier to erode. Once the nutrient-rich topsoil is washed away, only a few plants can survive and grow in the soil and the land becomes desert-like. This process of loss of vegetation and soil is called **desertification**. It is very difficult and often impossible to restore desertified land.

Prevention of Soil Erosion

When rain falls on soil with no vegetation cover, it easily washes the topsoil away. The main role of plants in preventing soil erosion is that their roots bind the soil particles and slow down the water flowing over the land (called run-off), thus allowing the rain to percolate into the ground.

Humus helps the soil from getting eroded by acting as a glue that binds the soil particles together. Thus, the organic matter that forms the humus plays an important part in preventing soil erosion.

Preventing overgrazing and undertaking crop rotation are some other methods to prevent soil erosion in cultivable lands. Afforestation, step farming and constructing river embankments also prevent soil erosion.

SOIL POLLUTION

Soil pollution is the presence of unwanted substances in the soil that can be harmful for all living beings. It has become a threat to the living organisms inhabiting the soil.

Causes of Soil Pollution

Fig. 8.14: Soil pollution

Solid wastes, excess use of chemicals such as fertilizers, pesticides and insecticides, and acid rain are the main contributors to soil pollution (Fig. 8.14). Solid wastes such as human excreta, biomedical wastes, plastics and metal objects, which come from homes, cattle sheds, agricultural fields, industries and many other places get accumulated in the form of heaps. Harmful chemicals and microorganisms from these heaps percolate into soil polluting it. Acid rain is caused when the polluted air mixes with rainwater. This is mainly seen near industrial areas as highly harmful gases coming out from the chimneys of factories remain mixed with the air. Excessive use of chemical fertilizers, insecticides and pesticides affect the soil as they get absorbed by the plants, affecting the entire food chain. Materials such as untreated sewage sludge and human excreta used as manure are also contributors to soil pollution. Plastic, electronic, metal and biomedical wastes such as packaging materials, mobiles, earphones, electronic chargers, tins, metal casings, masks and gloves act as breeding grounds to germs and take long time to decay.

Prevention of Soil Pollution

- Farmers should be encouraged to use **bio-fertilizers**, **bio-pesticides** and **fungicides**. The microorganisms used in these fertilizers help in increasing the fertility of the soil. Industrial toxic waste should be treated to reduce its toxicity before it is disposed of into water bodies or lands.
- The best way to prevent soil pollution is to prevent the use of harmful chemicals. Recycling and reusing wastes not only help in reducing the felling of trees but also help in decreasing soil pollution.
- Deforestation is a major concern to be dealt with as the loss of trees is resulting in the removal of the topsoil by different agents of nature such as wind and water.
- Measures also need to be taken to prevent overgrazing and overcropping as they lead to soil erosion.
- Biomedical wastes should be disposed of in a closed biodegradable garbage bag. The metallic objects such as syringe needles, plastic gloves, hair caps and plastic should be segregated from the wet biomedical waste such as bandages, plaster of paris castings, cotton and masks.

Keywords

Weathering: The process of breaking down of rocks into smaller particles

Humus: A dark brown or black mass of partially decomposed organic matter

Erosion: The wearing away of topsoil by agents such as wind, running water and human activities on the surface of the Earth

Desertification: A process by which fertile land turns into a desert

Summary

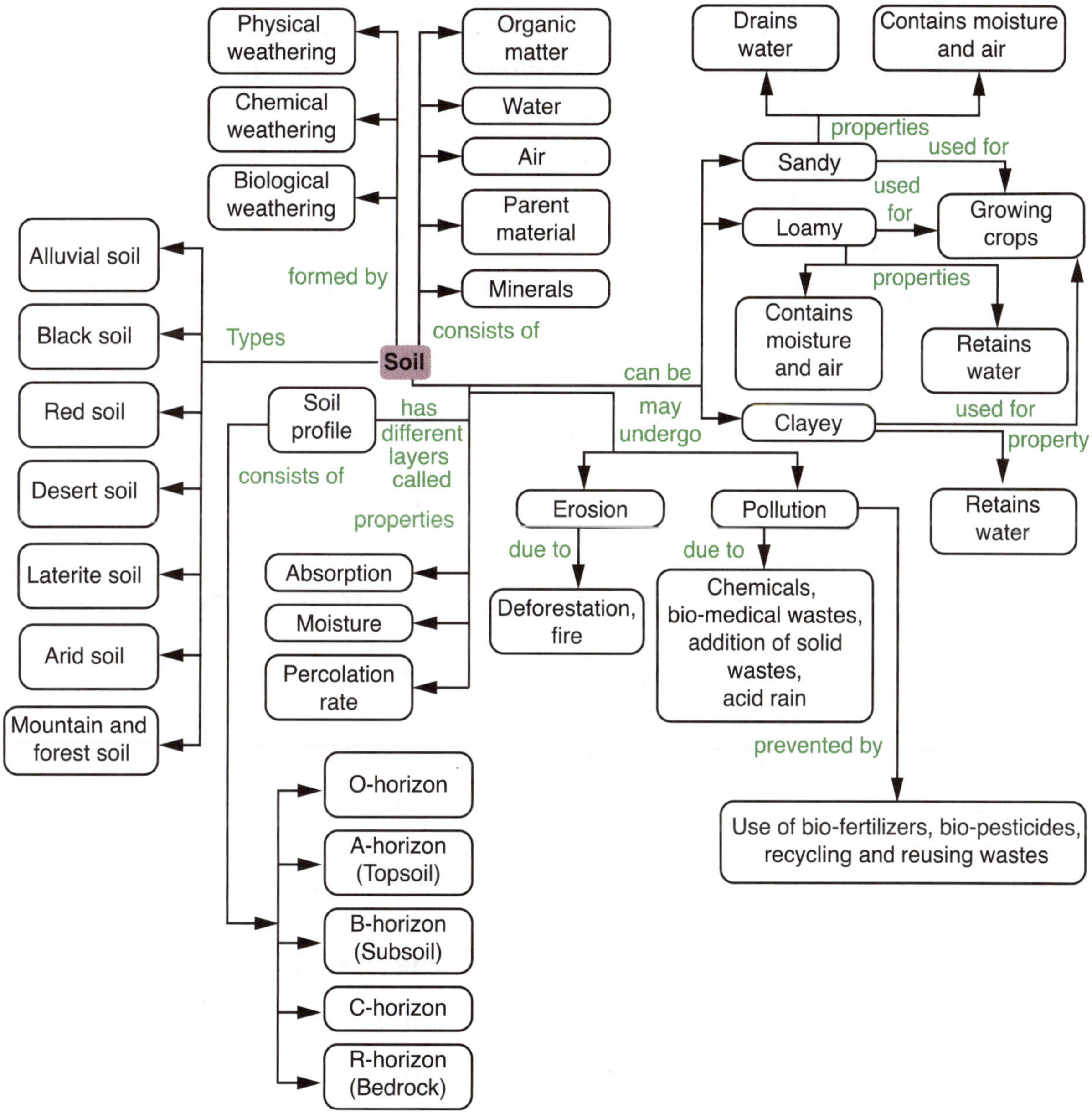

EXERCISE

W

A. Choose the correct option.

1. The upper layer of the soil is generally dark in colour because ______________.
   (a) crops grow in it (b) organisms live in it
   (c) it is rich in humus and minerals (d) it is a mixture of clay and loam
2. What is percolation rate of the soil?
   (a) The rate at which water evaporates from the soil
   (b) The rate at which the soil loses water
   (c) The rate at which water is absorbed by the soil
   (d) The rate at which water enters and moves through the soil
3. Which of the following determines the type of crops that might grow in any soil?
   (a) Water retention and water percolation property
   (b) The climate of that place
   (c) Moisture in the soil and components of soil
   (d) All of these
4. It took 25 minutes for 400 mℓ of water to percolate through a soil sample. What is the percolation rate?
   (a) 16 mℓ/s (b) 16 mℓ/min (c) 16 s/mℓ (d) 16 ℓ/min
5. Which of the following factors does not affect soil erosion?
   (a) Wind (b) Temperature
   (c) Rainfall (d) Grazing of cattle

B. Fill in the blanks. ia

1. ______________ makes soil fertile and provides nutrients to the plants. (Bedrock/Humus)
2. Soil that has the greatest proportion of large coarse particles is called ______________ soil. (sandy/clayey)
3. ______________ soil is the best soil for plant growth. (Clayey/Loamy)
4. ______________ is one of the ways to prevent soil pollution. (Pesticides/Bio-pesticides)
5. Breaking down of rocks by the action of wind, water and climate is called ______________. (weathering/erosion)

C. State whether the following statements are true (T) or false (F). ia

1. The C-horizon layer is generally soft and porous, and can retain more water. ☐
2. Loamy soil is well aerated and also contains a lot of humus. ☐

3. The large spaces between particles of sand get filled with water. ☐
4. Percolation rate is the highest in sandy soil. ☐
5. The main causative agents for soil erosion are wind and water. ☐

D. Answer the following in one word each.

1. The horizontal layers of soil one below the other in a vertical cross-section
2. The lowermost layer in the soil profile
3. Soil with the highest percolation rate
4. A type of soil formed due to deposition in riverbeds
5. Soil considered the best for agriculture in India
6. The soil also called cotton soil

E. Give reasons for the following.

1. Humus plays an important part in preventing soil erosion.
2. Manure is suggested for use over chemical fertilizer.
3. Clayey soil is used to make pots.
4. Plants help in development of soil fertility.
5. Clay along with humus is added to sandy soil.

F. Answer the following questions briefly.

1. How is humus formed?
2. What is weathering? List the different types of weathering.
3. How is soil classified based on its absorption capacity? Give one property for each type.
4. Give two differences between sandy soil and loamy soil.
5. Mention two ways by which a farmer's field could get eroded.

G. Answer the following questions in detail.

1. With the help of diagrams, explain the stages of soil formation.
2. Explain the different layers in a soil profile.
3. Explain the different properties of soil.
4. List the types of soil suitable for the growth of crops. Give two examples of crops that can be grown in each type.
5. What is soil pollution? Name three causes and preventive measures of soil pollution.
6. With the help of a political map of India, explain different crops grown in different parts of our country.

COGNITIVE CORNER

Critical Thinking

1. How might a farmer choose the most suitable soil type for cultivating a specific crop? What factors and strategies should be considered to maximize crop yield in different soil types?
2. How might the choice of soil type impact the stability of a building's foundation, and what precautions should be taken in areas with clay-rich soils?

Picture Study

Number the following figures of soil formation in the correct sequence.

Project

1. Collect samples of different types of soil and fill them into different flower pots each. Make sure you have at least three different soil samples. Plant a few groundnut seeds into each of the soil samples. Keep the pots in sunlight and water them every day. Find out which of these soil samples is the best for plant growth. **(C-7.2)**
2. Are all medical wastes hazardous? Take any three examples and suggest suitable methods for their safe disposal. Make a poster highlighting the reasons for your choice of methods. **(C-7.1)**

In the Library

Different soils contain different quantities of the minerals. These minerals determine the agricultural potential of the soil. Collect information about the minerals found in different soils in different states of India from the books in your school library. Write an article based on your findings. **(C-7.1)**

Life Skills

Visit some nearby farm in your area and check what kind of fertilizers the farmers are using for their farm. Advise farmers on using bio-fertilizers and bio-pesticides to improve the fertility of the land and explain the long-term side effects of excessive use of chemical fertilizers and pesticides. Find out and list a few bio-fertilizers and bio-pesticides in your notebook. Read about these so that you can advise their use to the farmers during your visit. **(C-6.1)**

Worksheet

Chemical fertilizers have been used since the middle of the 20th century to increase the production of healthy crops. Fertilizers provide nutrients for healthy plant growth and development. They are generally classified according to their NPK content, representing the concentrations of nitrogen, phosphorous and potassium. However, the use of chemical fertilizers is emerging as one of the greatest issues throughout the world.

Farmer spraying fertilizer

A. Chemical fertilizers seep into the groundwater and other water sources. What will be its impact on the aquatic species?

____

____

____

B. Chemical fertilizers supply plants with elements that may be missing or in short supply. This makes the plants grow faster. However, such plants miss out on important minerals such as calcium, zinc and iron. What effect will this have on human health when these plants are eaten by them?

____

____

____

C. Often chemical fertilizers seep through the soil. From there, these toxic chemicals are absorbed by the plants and eventually enter human bodies. What can be the long-term effect of this?

____

____

____

9 Respiration in Organisms

Curricular Goals

- Explore the living world in scientific terms **(CG-3)**
- Understand the interface of science, technology and society **(CG-5)**

Competencies

- Analyse patterns of relationships between living organisms and their environments in terms of dependence on and response to each other **(C-3.3)**
- Distinguish the characteristics of living organisms from non-living things **(C-3.2)**
- Explain the conditions suitable for sustaining life on Earth **(C-3.4)**
- Illustrate how science and technology can help to improve the quality of human life **(C-5.1)**

Let's Get Started

We eat food to build and maintain our body and to get energy for carrying out all life activities. Observe the images given below and number them in the increasing order based on the level of energy required to carry out each activity.

Running

Reading

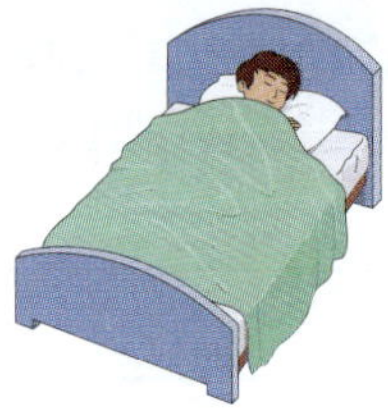

Sleeping

Swimming

Lifting weights

You might have noticed that when we exercise or run fast, we start breathing faster. Why does running or exercising make a person breathe faster? To answer this question, we must first know why we breathe. Breathing is a part of a process called respiration. In this chapter, we will learn about respiration and the organs involved in carrying out respiration in living organisms.

BREATHING AND RESPIRATION

Living beings take in air rich in oxygen and give out air that has more carbon dioxide than oxygen. The taking in of oxygen-rich air into our body is called **inhalation** and the giving out of carbon dioxide-rich air is called **exhalation**.

Inhalation and exhalation are collectively called **breathing**. The oxygen inhaled is used by all the cells in the body to break down food and release energy.

***Respiration** is the process of using oxygen to break down food to release energy, carbon doixide and water.*

Respiration is also called the **universal chemical process** as every living cell respires to survive. Thus, respiration and breathing are vital for the survival of living things.

Table 9.1: Difference between respiration and breathing

Respiration	Breathing
There is release of energy at the end.	There is no release of energy.
It is an intracellular process. (It takes place inside the cells.)	It is an extracellular process. (It takes place between the organism and its environment.)
It is a biochemical process involving the breakdown of digested food.	It is a physical process involving inhalation and exhalation.

ORGANS FOR BREATHING IN ANIMALS

Different animals have different organs and mechanisms for the exchange of gases. Some of these are discussed below.

Through the skin: In animals that live in the soil, such as earthworms and leeches, the exchange of gases takes place through the slimy surface of the skin (Fig. 9.1).

The walls of the skin in earthworms allow gaseous exchange. The skin is rich in blood vessels. The blood transports the gases throughout the body.

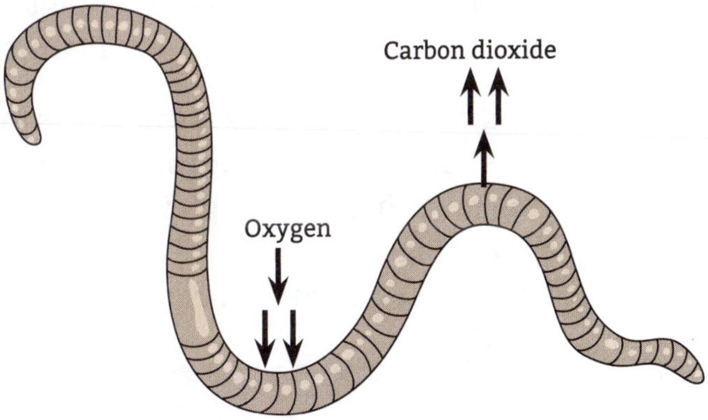

Fig. 9.1: Respiration in an earthworm

Through air holes: In insects such as grasshoppers and cockroaches, exchange of gases occurs through small openings or pores called **spiracles** present on the sides of their body. These pores are the openings of a network of air tubes called **trachea**, which carry the oxygen to different parts of the body (Fig. 9.2). Carbon dioxide diffuses out through the trachea and exits through the spiracles.

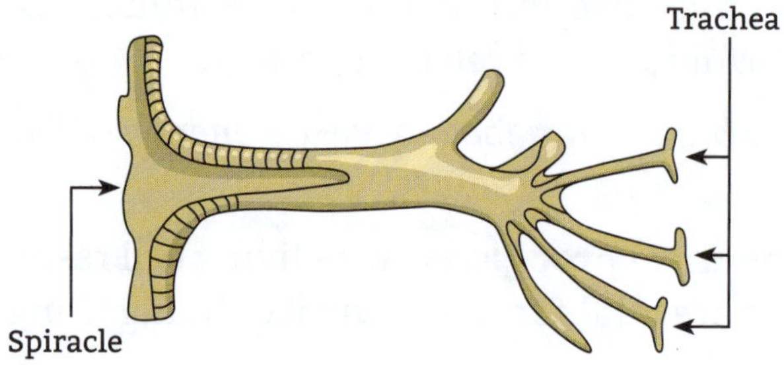

(a) Structure of a spiracle

(b) Spiracles on the body of an insect

Fig. 9.2: Respiration in insects

Through gills: Aquatic animals such as fish live in water and get oxygen dissolved in water. Fish have a special structure called **gills** on either side of their mouth. The water along with dissolved oxygen enters the mouth, and the absorption of oxygen takes place through the gills (Fig. 9.3). Carbon dioxide diffuses into the water which is released through the openings in the gills.

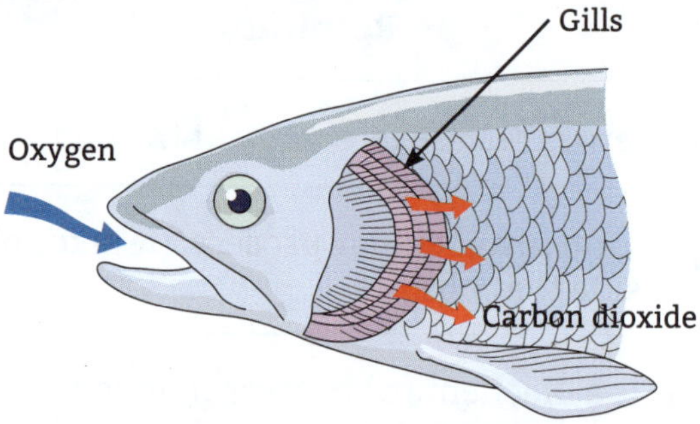

Fig. 9.3: Respiration in fish

Fig. 9.4: Cutaneous respiration in frogs

Through lungs: Amphibians such as frogs, newts and salamander are both aquatic and terrestrial. Frogs have **lungs**, but they use their skin for the exchange of gases when in water. They use their lungs when on land (Fig. 9.4). Reptiles, birds and mammals also breathe through lungs.

Respiration through the lungs is known as **pulmonary respiration** and respiration through the skin is known as **cutaneous respiration**. When at rest or floating on water, a frog takes in air through its nostrils into the buccal cavity. The gaseous exchange takes place through the lining of the buccal cavity. This method of respiration is known as **buccal respiration**.

Wonder!

In humans, the right lung is a little larger than the left lung, which shares space in the chest with the heart.

Revise and Recall

State whether the following statements are true (T) or false (F).

1. Respiration is the process of taking in oxygen to get energy without the breakdown of food. ☐
2. The trachea in cockroaches carries the oxygen to different parts of the body. ☐
3. The buccal cavity in frogs is used for breathing when they float on water. ☐
4. Earthworms respire through gills. ☐
5. Respiration through the lungs is known as cutaneous respiration. ☐

RESPIRATORY SYSTEM IN HUMAN BEINGS

The organs for breathing in human beings are shown in Fig. 9.5.

When air is inhaled, it passes through our nostrils and enters the **nasal cavity**. From the nasal cavity, the air enters the windpipe (**trachea**). The windpipe branches into two smaller tubes called **bronchi** (singular: bronchus). Each bronchus enters into a lung. In the lungs, each bronchus branches out into smaller tubes called **bronchioles** (Fig. 9.6). At the end of these tubes, there are tiny air sacs called **alveoli** (singular: alveolus). The walls of the alveoli are lined with a network of blood vessels and capillaries to facilitate the exchange of gases.

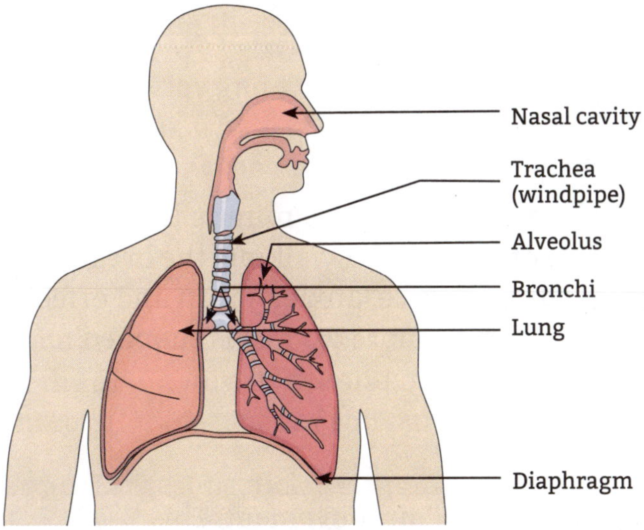

Fig. 9.5: The organs for breathing in humans

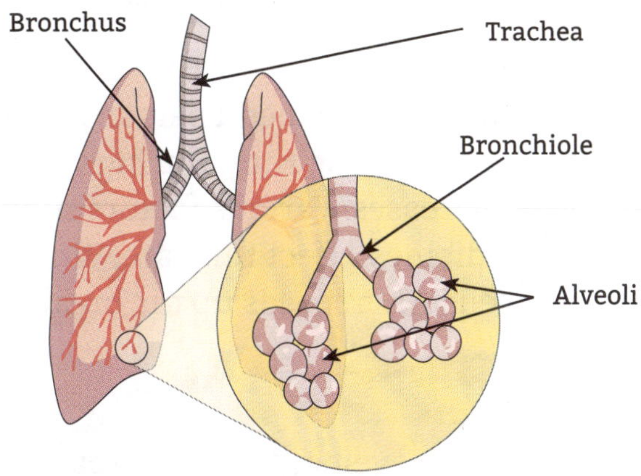

Fig. 9.6: The organs involved in exchange of gases

Lungs are present in the chest cavity, which is surrounded by ribs on the sides. The ribs form a cage-like structure called the **ribcage**.

A large tissue sheet with muscles at its ends is called **diaphragm** that forms the base of the ribcage. The dome-shaped diaphragm separates the stomach and other organs of the digestive system from the chest cavity.

Wonder!

Each lung in the human body contains about 300 million alveoli.

Mechanism of Breathing

During inhalation, the diaphragm contracts and moves down. The ribcage moves upwards and outwards (expanding the chest cavity). This causes the volume inside the chest cavity to increase and reduces the pressure inside it. When the pressure inside the lungs gets reduced, the air from outside rushes into the lungs. During exhalation, the diaphragm relaxes as it moves up and returns to its normal dome shape. The ribcage also returns to its normal position. This reduces the volume within the chest cavity. The reduction in volume inside the lungs increases the pressure inside it, expelling (pushing) the air out (Fig. 9.7).

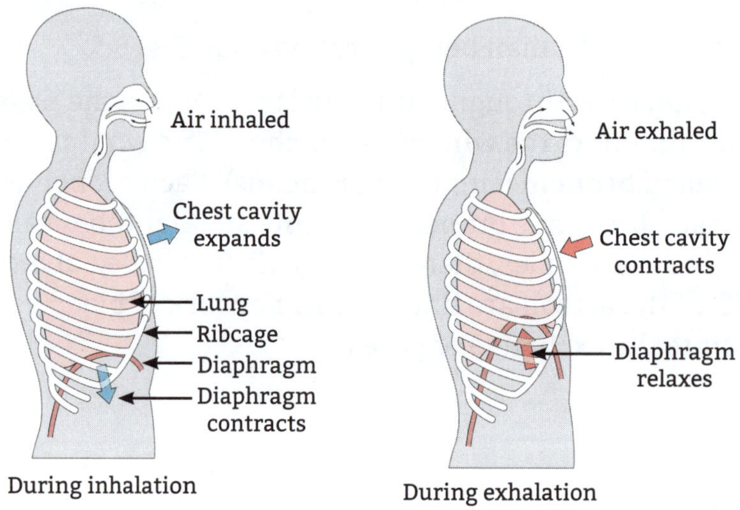

Fig. 9.7: The process of breathing

The number of times a person breathes (inhales and exhales) in a minute is termed as the **breathing rate**. During vigorous exercise or while brisk walking, the breathing rate increases. Various factors such as age, gender, exercise, anxiety, pain and effect of medicines affect this rate. When one breathes faster, more oxygen is supplied to our cells. This speeds up the breakdown of food, releasing more energy.

Wonder!

Chest movement during breathing is not the result of air movement. This is because of the movement of the ribs which is connected to the diaphragm—a thin sheet of dome-shaped structure that separates chest and abdomen. Muscles attached to the ribs contract and straighten to move them up and down.

Activity 1

Aim: To understand the working of human lungs and diaphragm

Materials required: A soda or a plastic bottle, a cutter, a Y-shaped tube, a rubber sheet, a string, balloons

Procedure:

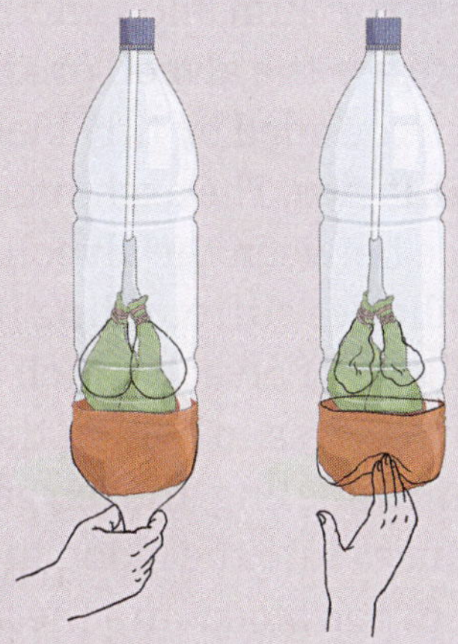

1. Drill a hole in the lid/cap of a soda plastic bottle.
2. Make sure that the hole is just as big as the diameter of the Y-shaped tube.
3. Cut the base of the bottle using the cutter and close the lid of the bottle.
4. Fit the Y-shaped tube through the bottom hole into the lid of the bottle.
5. Fix the balloons to each of the arms of the Y-shaped tube through the open base of the bottle.
6. Tie them with rubber bands or strings, so that they are held tightly.
7. Fix a rubber sheet to the bottom of the bottle and tie it with a string or a rubber band to make sure that it is held tightly.
8. Pull and push the rubber sheet to observe the inflation and deflation of the balloons.
9. The balloons can be compared with the lungs, the rubber tube to the diaphragm, the Y-shaped tube to trachea and the bronchi.

Let us look into the role of each respiratory organ, starting from the organ the air enters in.

Structures	Functions
Nasal cavity	It helps in filtering air and prevents the entry of harmful substances.
Trachea	It is also called the windpipe and helps in the movement of air.
Bronchi	These are branches of trachea and carry air to the lungs.
Lungs	These are present in the chest cavity. Inside lungs, the bronchi branch into bronchioles, which have alveoli at their ends.
Alveoli	These are thin, tiny air sacs in the lungs where the exchange of gases takes place.

Other structures which support breathing are given below:

Structures	Functions
Ribs	These help in the protection of the chest cavity and the process of inhalation and exhalation.
Intercostal muscles	Attached to the ribs, these muscles help in the process of inhalation and exhalation.
Diaphragm	It forms the floor of the chest cavity and help in the process of inhalation and exhalation.

Science in Context

Lungs are the only organ in the human body to have buoyancy. When all the alveoli are filled with air, the lungs become the only organ in the human body that can float.

Exchange of Gases

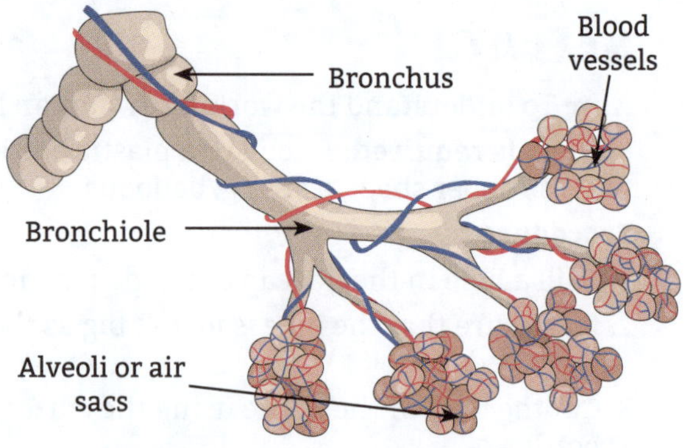

Fig. 9.8: Internal respiration

The structural and functional unit of the lungs are the alveoli or air sacs. Each alveolus is surrounded by tiny blood vessels called **capillaries**. The exchange of gases takes place between the alveoli of the lungs and the capillaries surrounding it. Each lung contains millions of alveoli which produce a very large surface area to help in the exchange of gases. While inhaling, the oxygen from the alveoli diffuses into the blood in the capillaries. The carbon dioxide present in the blood passes out of the blood into the alveolus, which is then exhaled (Fig. 9.8).

Cellular Respiration

The oxygen that enters the capillaries from the alveoli enters the red blood cells (RBCs) of blood. The RBCs contain a protein called **haemoglobin** which binds with the oxygen and forms a compound called **oxyhaemoglobin**. Oxyhaemoglobin is carried through the blood to all the cells of the body. In the cells, oxygen is released from oxyhaemoglobin. Cells use this oxygen to break down glucose (sugar) to form carbon dioxide and water. During this process, energy is released, which is used for the movement of muscles, for the growth and repair of cells, for bringing about chemical reactions and so on.

$$\underset{\text{Glucose}}{C_6H_{12}O_6} + \underset{\text{Oxygen}}{6O_2} \longrightarrow \underset{\text{Water}}{6H_2O} + \underset{\text{Carbon dioxide}}{6CO_2} + \text{Energy}$$

The carbon dioxide generated diffuses into the blood. The blood carries it back to the lungs from where it is expelled during exhalation.

Wonder!

Carbon monoxide has a higher affinity for haemoglobin than oxygen, leading to the formation of a compound called carboxyhaemoglobin that prevents red blood cells from carrying oxygen to our body cells. This lack of oxygen can cause sickness or even death. To prevent this, it is important to avoid places with high levels of carbon monoxide and ensure proper ventilation.

AEROBIC AND ANAEROBIC RESPIRATION

Have you wondered what would happen if oxygen did not reach the cells in the body? Can energy be obtained without oxygen? Yes, in some cases, energy can be obtained without oxygen reaching the cells. Let us learn how it takes place.

When food (glucose) is broken down in the presence of oxygen, it is called **aerobic respiration.**

Glucose + Oxygen ⟶ Carbon dioxide + Water + Energy

Carbon dioxide is liberated and water is used up for other cellular functions. Aerobic respiration is the most common type of respiration exhibited by most organisms. It is also the most efficient form of respiration.

Food can also be broken down in the absence of oxygen, which is called **anaerobic respiration**. Anaerobic respiration is exhibited in some organisms such as yeast and certain bacteria. Muscles in animals and humans also respire anaerobically when oxygen supply falls, such as during vigorous exercise or sprinting.

Glucose ⟶ Alcohol + Carbon dioxide + Energy

Anaerobic respiration in muscles takes place only for short durations. Aerobic respiration produces more energy than anaerobic respiration.

Science in Context

Alcohol produced by anaerobic respiration gets further degenerated by **enzymes** in organisms such as yeast and bacteria. We exploit this ability of yeasts and bacteria to produce alcoholic beverages such as beer and wine.

Activity 2

Aim: To demonstrate aerobic respiration

Materials required: Germinating seeds, dry seeds, lime water, two test tubes, two conical flasks, stoppers, bent glass tubes

Procedure: Distribute lime water equally into the test tubes (make sure that it does not come in contact with the carbon dioxide in the air).

Experimental set-up 1:

1. Place 30 g of germinating seeds in one of the conical flasks.
2. Cover the conical flask with the two-holed stopper.
3. Insert a bent glass tube into one hole and the long tube into the other hole.
4. Connect the bent tube to a test tube with lime water through the one-holed stopper.

Experimental set-up 1

Experimental set-up 2:

1. Place 30 g of dry seeds in one of the conical flasks.
2. Cover the conical flask with the two-holed stopper.
3. Insert a bent glass tube into one hole and a long tube into the other hole.
4. Connect the bent tube to a test tube with lime water through the one-holed stopper. Make sure that the bent tube is immersed inside the lime water.

Experimental set-up 2

Observation: Lime water gradually turns milky in experimental set-up 1.

Conclusion: In experimental set-up 1, the lime water turning milky is an indication of the liberation of carbon dioxide. In the experimental set-up 2, the lime water will not turn milky. This is because the germinating seeds respire actively and at a faster rate whereas dry seeds do not respire. That is why carbon dioxide was not liberated in experimental set-up 2.

Activity 3

Aim: To prove that anaerobic respiration takes place in the absence of oxygen

Materials required: Oil, warm water, yeast, glucose, lime water, one test tube, one conical flask, two-holed rubber cork for conical flask and one-holed rubber cork for test tube, bent glass tubes

Procedure:

1. Pour the warm water into a conical flask and add glucose and yeast. Mix well.
2. Pour oil over the surface of the solution (to prevent the entry of air). Do not shake the set-up once the oil is poured.
3. Close it with the one-holed stopper by fitting it with a bent glass tube.
4. Connect the bent tube to a test tube with lime water through a one-holed stopper.

5. Leave the set-up undisturbed for 15–20 minutes. Make sure that the bent tube is immersed inside the lime water.

Note: Yeast also ferments sugar in the presence of oxygen.

Observation: Lime water gradually turns milky.

Conclusion: The yeast cells are kept in an anaerobic condition but still the lime water turns milky. This is because yeast cells are capable of respiring even under anaerobic conditions.

Note: Use a freshly prepared lime water. Lime water will not turn milky if it is not freshly made or is more than 2 days old.

The muscle cells in our body normally carry out aerobic respiration. But when we run fast or exercise vigorously, the muscle cells work faster and require more energy. To meet this energy demand, the muscle cells switch over to anaerobic respiration. But in this case, instead of alcohol, lactic acid is produced. The partial breakdown of glucose produces lactic acid.

Glucose ⟶ Lactic acid + Energy

The accumulation of lactic acid causes muscle cramps, which can be relieved by a hot water bath or a massage as it improves the blood circulation. The supply of oxygen to the muscle cells increases, resulting in complete breakdown of lactic acid into carbon dioxide and water.

Science in Context

Epiglottis is a flap of cartilage that prevents the food and water from entering the windpipe (trachea). This is situated at the tongue base obliquely on the voice box. This prevents us from choking, especially while swallowing without chewing.

RESPIRATION IN PLANTS

Plants also respire by taking in oxygen and giving out carbon dioxide. The leaves of most plants have tiny pores called **stomata** (singular: stoma) on the underside. Stomata bring about the exchange of oxygen and carbon dioxide in plant cells.

Guard cells on either side of the stomata regulate their opening and closing (Fig. 9.9).

Science in Context

The stem bark also has tiny openings called **lenticels** which help in gaseous exchange during night-time (as the stomata close during the night).

Wonder!

It is not advisable to stay under trees during night-time because you will be breathing more carbon dioxide than oxygen.

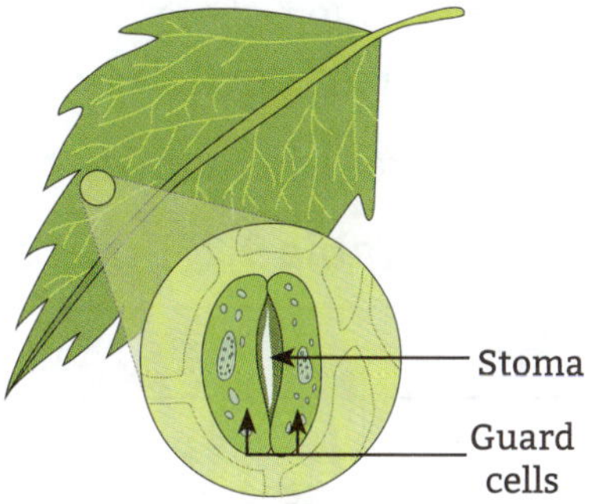

Fig. 9.9: Structure of stomata

Aerobic respiration in plants

$C_6H_{12}O_6$	+	$6O_2$	⟶	$6CO_2$	+	$6H_2O$	+	Energy
Glucose		Oxygen		Carbon dioxide		Water		(Energy out)

The rate of exchange of gases in plants is much slower than in animals. The energy released during respiration is used by the organism. The rest is lost as heat. Let us prove this by conducting the following activity.

Activity 4

Aim: To show that heat is liberated during the process of respiration

Materials required: Two thermos flasks, germinating seeds, cotton, thermometers, a beaker

Procedure: Take equal quantities of germinating seeds.

1. Place one portion of the germinating seeds in one thermos flask (Flask A). Make sure that the seeds are moist.
2. Boil another portion of the seeds in a beaker so that the seeds stop germinating.
3. After the boiled seeds are cooled, place them in another thermos flask (Flask B).
4. Insert a thermometer into each of the flasks (making sure that the thermometer bulb reaches the seeds and is surrounded by them).
5. Plug both the openings of thermos flasks with moist cotton plugs.

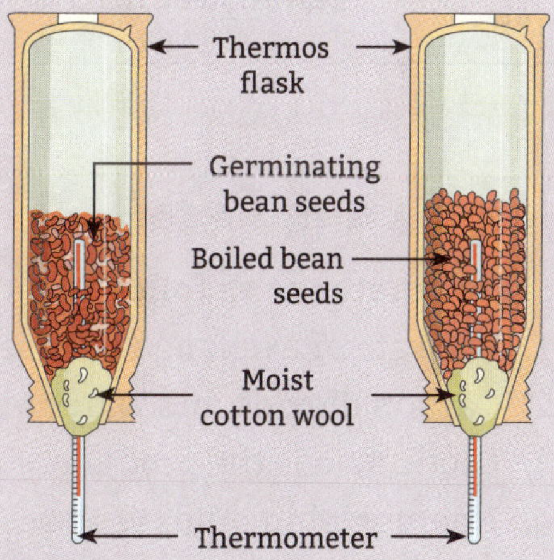

Note down the initial temperature in both the cases.

Check the temperature at regular intervals for 3–4 days and record your observations.

Observations: The temperature of Flask A, which contains germinated seeds, rises while that of Flask B, which contains boiled seeds, remains the same.

Conclusion: The boiled seeds do not have living cells to respire. Hence, the temperature of Flask B remains the same. On the other hand, germinating seeds taken in Flask B have living cells that respire. The rise in temperature in Flask B indicates the release of heat. Hence, heat is liberated during respiration.

Like all other living cells of plants, the root cells also need to breathe to produce energy. The spaces between the soil particles trap the air and this air is utilized by the plant roots. Due to this reason, farmers and gardeners frequently turn around the soil so that fresh air particles can get trapped in the soil.

Table 9.2 gives the main differences between respiration in plants and photosynthesis.

Table 9.2: Differences between respiration and photosynthesis

Parameters	Photosynthesis	Respiration
Definition	It is the process by which plants prepare their own food in the presence of sunlight, chlorophyll, carbon dioxide and water.	It is the process of obtaining energy from food in the presence (or some time even absence) of oxygen.
Products formed	Glucose (a carbohydrate) is formed. Oxygen and water are given out.	Glucose is broken down. Energy along with carbon dioxide and water are released.
Equation	Carbon dioxide + Water $\xrightarrow{\text{Sunlight} \mid \text{Chlorophyll}}$ Carbohydrate + Oxygen + Water	Glucose + Oxygen $\rightarrow$ Carbon dioxide + Water + Energy
Takes place during	Daytime	All the time and is a continuous process
Structures involved	Leaves, stem, roots	All cells in the plant

Revise and Recall

State whether the following statements are true (T) or false (F).

1. The rate of exchange of gases in plants is much faster than in animals. ☐
2. Carbon dioxide and water are the only products of aerobic respiration. ☐
3. Lactic acid is the product of anaerobic respiration in muscle cells. ☐
4. Haemoglobin binds with respiratory gases and circulates in the body. ☐
5. Lungs are protected by ribs and diaphragm. ☐

Keywords

Spiracles: Small openings on the sides of the bodies of insects through which the exchange of gases takes place

Trachea (in insects): Air tubes that are connected to a network of spiracles, and that carry the oxygen to different parts of the body of an insect

Trachea (windpipe): A tube that connects the pharynx (throat cavity) and larynx (voice box) to the lungs

Bronchi: Tubes that branch out from the trachea and enter each lung

Alveoli: Tiny air sacs present at the end of the bronchioles in human lungs

Diaphragm: A structure that separates the chest cavity from the abdominal cavity where stomach and other organs such as kidneys are present

Aerobic respiration: Respiration that takes place in the presence of oxygen

Anaerobic respiration: Respiration that takes place in the absence of oxygen

Stomata: Small pores in the cells of leaves of plants through which the exchange of gases takes place

Summary

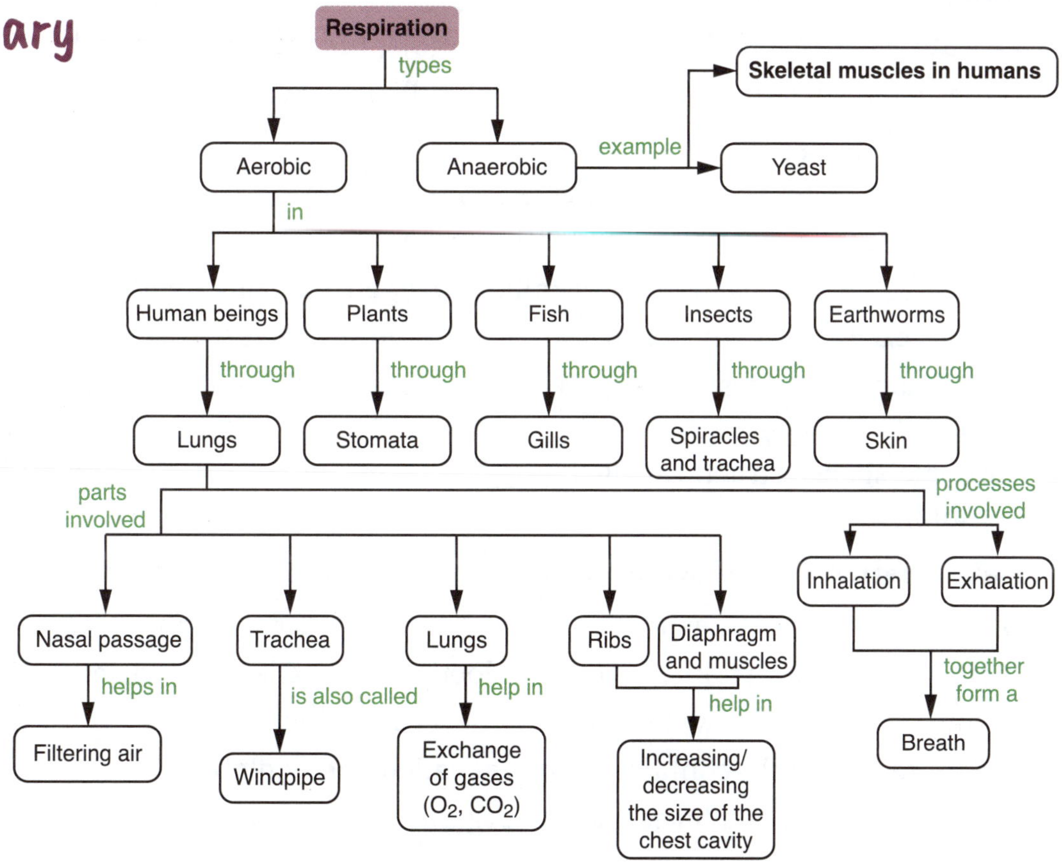

EXERCISE

A. Choose the correct option.

1. In earthworms, the exchange of gases takes place through ______________.
   (a) the skin (b) both skin and lungs
   (c) buccal cavity (d) spiracles
2. Anaerobic respiration produces ______________.
   (a) alcohol and water (b) only water
   (c) carbon dioxide and water (d) alcohol and carbon dioxide
3. Anaerobic respiration in human beings takes place during ______________.
   (a) eating (b) sleeping (c) rigorous exercise (d) cooking
4. Muscle cramps occur due to
   (a) accumulation of glucose in the muscles.
   (b) accumulation of oxygen in the muscles.
   (c) accumulation of lactic acid in the muscles.
   (d) accumulation of carbon dioxide and water in the muscles.
5. Respiration through the skin is called ______________.
   (a) cutaneous respiration (b) pulmonary respiration
   (c) buccal respiration (d) dermal respiration

B. Fill in the blanks.

1. The breakdown of food in cells using oxygen with the release of energy is called ______________ respiration. (anaerobic/aerobic)
2. ______________ turns lime water milky. (Oxygen/Carbon dioxide)
3. Gaseous exchange in insects takes place through __________. (trachea/spiracles)
4. The exchange of gases in the leaves of plants takes place through ______________. (stomata/lenticels)
5. The dome-shaped structure called ________ forms the base of the chest cavity. (diaphragm/alveolus)

C. State whether the following statements are true (T) or false (F).

1. When at rest or floating on water, frogs undergo buccal respiration. ☐
2. Every alveolus is surrounded by tiny blood vessels called capillaries. ☐
3. During inhalation, the volume of the chest cavity increases. ☐
4. The white blood cells contain a pigment called haemoglobin. ☐
5. Anaerobic respiration takes place in organisms such as yeast. ☐

D. Differentiate between the following.

1. Respiration and breathing
2. Pulmonary respiration and cutaneous respiration
3. Inhalation and exhalation
4. Aerobic respiration and anaerobic respiration
5. Photosynthesis and respiration

E. Give reasons for the following.

1. During heavy exercise we get cramps in legs.
2. Amphibians can respire through skin.
3. A person breathes faster while brisk walking.
4. The size of the chest cavity increases during inhalation.
5. We get relief from muscle cramps after a hot water bath or a massage.

F. Answer the following questions briefly.

1. What is the role of stomata in plant cells?
2. Explain the role of haemoglobin in cellular respiration.
3. Explain how respiration takes place in a cockroach.
4. How does respiration take place in muscles? Give the equation for the same.

G. Answer the following questions in detail.

1. With the help of labelled diagram, explain the mechanism of breathing in humans.
2. Name the structures of the human respiratory system and write their functions starting from the organ through which the air enters.
3. How does the exchange of gases take place inside the cells of living organisms?

COGNITIVE CORNER

Critical Thinking

1. Why do we choke and cough sometimes when we swallow food?
2. What would happen if a potted plant having underground roots is overwatered?
3. Why do fish die when taken out of water?
4. Why do we sneeze when we inhale a lot of dust-laden air?

Picture Study

Label the given diagram.

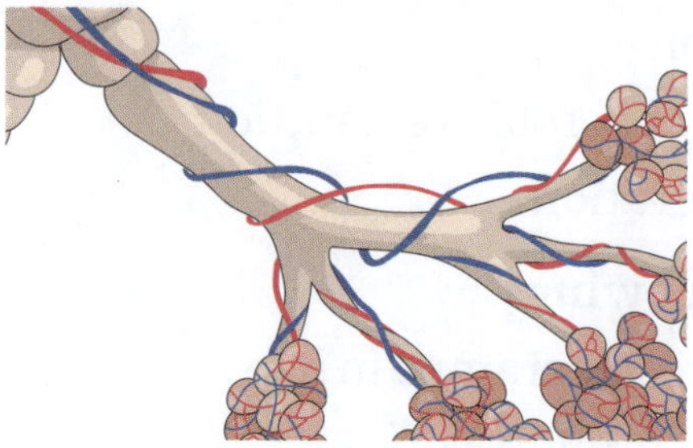

Project

Visit a general physician and collect necessary information on the harmful effects of smoking. You can also collect materials on this topic from sources on the Internet. Seek help from your teacher or parents and find out the percentage of people in your area who smoke. Confront smokers in your family, relatives or family friends and make them aware of the harmful effects of smoking as a part of an anti-smoking club. **(C-7.1)**

In the Library

Are there any organisms which die in the presence of oxygen? What are they called? Find out the names of these organisms. **(C-7.1)**

In the Laboratory

Take a Rhoeo leaf and peel the lower side of the leaf (pink in colour) using a forceps. Place the peel on a glass slide with a drop of water. Place a coverslip over the peel to keep the cell moist. Observe the stomatal cells under a microscope. **(C-7.1)**

Rhoeo plant

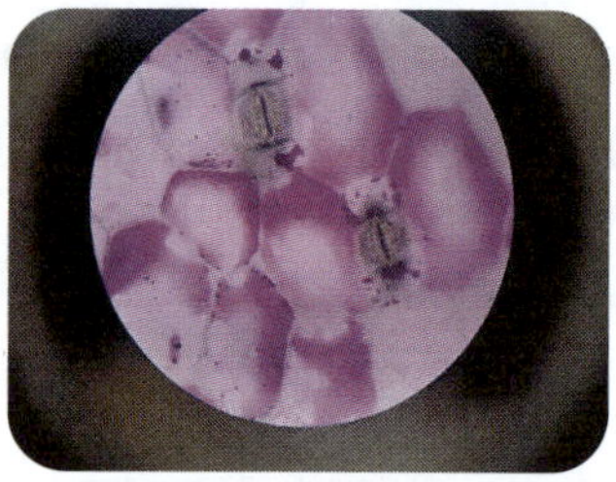

Stomatal cells of Rhoeo leaf

Life Skills

Our lungs, respiratory tract, nose and alimentary canal produce mucus or phlegm, a sticky substance that aids in removing dust and germs from inhaled air. Throat and nose are cleared by coughing and sneezing phlegm.

List the diseases that could spread from the phlegm of an infected person to others. **(C-7.3)**

Worksheet

Oil spills from damaged tankers, pipelines or rigs have immediate and lasting impacts on the environment. Floating oil coats aquatic birds' feathers, preventing flight and disrupting waterproofing, while ingestion harms internal organs. Marine life is affected as oil blocks sunlight and oxygen, leading to death of marine organisms and ecological damage.

Oil spill

Shipwreck

A penguin covered in oil

A. How can technology and innovative strategies be adopted to prevent and effectively respond to oil spills? Consider the role of robotics, remote sensing and international collaborations in addressing these challenges while aligning with Sustainable Development Goal 14 (Life Below Water).

____

____

____

____

____

B. Create taglines highlighting the plight of marine animals that come in contact with oil spills.

10 Transportation of Substances in Plants and Animals

Curricular Goals

- Explore the living world in scientific terms **(CG-3)**
- Explore the nature and processes of science through engaging with the evolution of scientific knowledge and conducting scientific inquiry **(CG-6)**
- Communicate questions, observations and conclusions related to science **(CG-7)**

Competencies

- Distinguish the characteristics of living organisms from non-living things **(C-3.2)**
- Explain the conditions suitable for sustaining life on Earth **(C-3.4)**
- Formulate questions using scientific terminology and collect data as evidence **(C-6.2)**
- Design and build simple models to demonstrate scientific concepts **(C-7.2)**

Let's Get Started

All living organisms need water and nutrients in order to survive. The picture alongside shows a plant. Draw arrows to show how water is taken up by the various parts of a plant for it to remain healthy.

The transport system of plants works like the circulatory system in our body. However, plants do not have a pumping organ like the heart. Therefore, they use other ways to transfer substances from one part of the plant to another.

The food and water that we take in do not just enter and leave the body. The nutrients in them are digested and then absorbed into the body for carrying out various life processes.

How are these nutrients and water carried and transported within the body of plants and animals? Let us learn about transportation of substances in plants and animals in this chapter.

Transportation is important in living organisms to carry oxygen, food, water and other substances to all parts of the body, and also to eliminate waste products from the body. Depending on the size and the body structure, living organisms have different kinds of transportation systems.

In animals, the transportation system is called the **circulatory system** and in plants, the transportation takes place through tissues that form pipe-like connections called **vascular bundles.**

TRANSPORTATION OF SUBSTANCES IN ANIMALS

Unicellular organisms such as *Amoeba, Paramecium* and bacteria do not need a circulatory system. The substances move in and out of the cell through the cell membrane that covers the cell. Depending on the concentration of the substances inside the cell body, the membrane selects whether to take in or to let out the particles. The substances move from a region of higher concentration to a region of lower concentration. For example, if the volume of oxygen present inside the *Amoeba's* cell is lower than its surroundings then oxygen will move into the cell. If the volume inside the cell is more than its surroundings then the membrane will prevent any more oxygen from coming in. This type of transportation of substances occurring in unicellular organisms is called **diffusion**. Diffusion also allows substances to move within the cell and in and out of the nucleus. Figure 10.1 shows the transportation of gases and nutrients within a single cell.

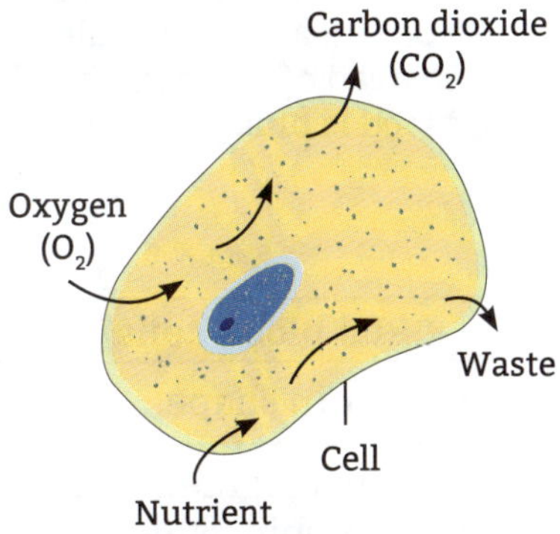

Fig. 10.1: Transportation within a single cell

In aquatic organisms, including some multicellular organisms such as sponges, jellyfish and *Hydra*, the oxygen and nutrients are transported into the body and waste products are removed by water by the process of diffusion.

TRANSPORTATION OF SUBSTANCES IN HUMANS

In higher multicellular organisms such as humans, diffusion is too slow to transport substances to all the cells. Hence, a fluid medium called **blood** always circulates throughout the body within narrow tubes or channels called **blood vessels**.

The transportation system in humans is known as the **circulatory system** as the transporting fluid—blood circulates throughout the body, transporting the substances at the same time.

The heart, blood and blood vessels together make up the circulatory system in humans.

Blood

Blood is a red-coloured fluid that transports respiratory gases, nutrients, secretions as well as waste materials from one part of our body to another.

Blood consists of a pale yellow liquid called **plasma** in which many cells float. Cells that are found in the plasma are the **red blood cells** (RBCs), **white blood cells** (WBCs) and **blood platelets** (Fig. 10.2).

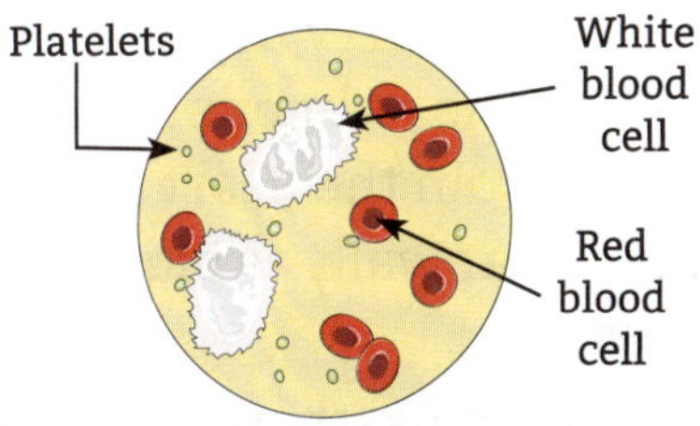

Fig. 10.2: Composition of blood

Science in Context

Some molluscs and crustaceans (crabs) contain a pigment called **haemocyanin** instead of haemoglobin; hence their blood is **blue** in colour.

Science in Context

The cells in the blood rush to injured sites of the body and stop the bleeding by clumping together, resulting in the formation of clots.

Table 10.1: Features of blood cells

Red blood cells	White blood cells	Blood platelets
1. Circular in shape	1. Irregular in shape	1. Small, irregularly shaped
2. Contain a pigment called haemoglobin, which gives blood a red colour	2. Colourless as they do not contain any pigment	2. Colourless
3. Transport oxygen and carbon dioxide to different parts of the body	3. Fight and destroy the germs that enter our body	3. Clot blood and stop the bleeding in wounded areas
4. Also called **erythrocytes**	4. Also called **leucocytes**	4. Also called **thrombocytes**

Blood performs several functions:

- It **transports** digested food, hormones, enzymes and other products to different parts of the body.
- It **carries oxygen** from the lungs to the cells and carbon dioxide from the cells to the lungs. It also carries waste products from the cells to the kidneys for their removal from the body.
- It **protects** the body against infection by destroying disease-causing germs.
- It **clots** blood when there is an injury or cut, preventing the excess loss of blood.

Blood Vessels

The blood in our body moves through tube-like structures called ***blood vessels***. Blood vessels are of three types: arteries, veins and capillaries (Fig. 10.3).

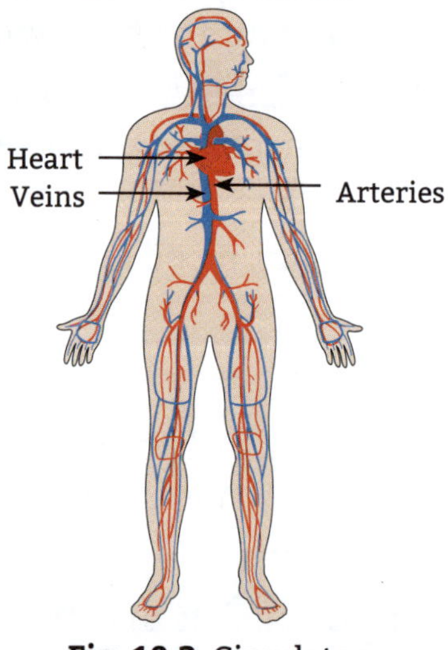

Fig. 10.3: Circulatory system in a human being

Arteries: Arteries (shown in red in Fig. 10.3) transport blood from the heart to the different organs and tissues. They generally carry **oxygenated** blood (blood rich in oxygen) except the pulmonary artery, which carries deoxygenated blood from the heart to the lungs. They have thick elastic muscular walls as blood flows through them under high pressure.

Veins: Veins (shown in blue in Fig. 10.3) bring blood to the heart from all parts of the body.

Veins generally carry deoxygenated blood, except the pulmonary vein, which brings oxygenated blood from the lungs to the heart. Veins have thinner walls compared to arteries. Veins have **valves**, structures that prevent the blood from flowing back to the organs (Fig. 10.4). Veins lie closer to the skin surface and can be seen as greenish-blue lines in our hands and legs.

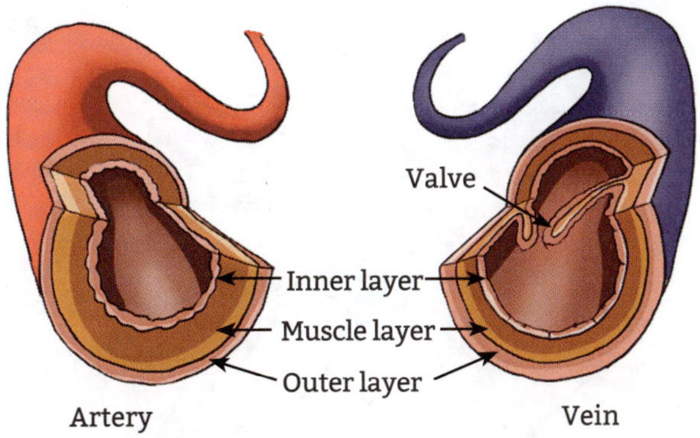

Fig. 10.4 Structure of artery and vein

Capillaries: When an artery reaches an organ, it branches into smaller vessels called **arterioles** which further branch into form a network of extremely thin blood vessels called capillaries (Fig. 10.5). The capillaries join together to form larger vessels called venules, which in turn join to form veins.

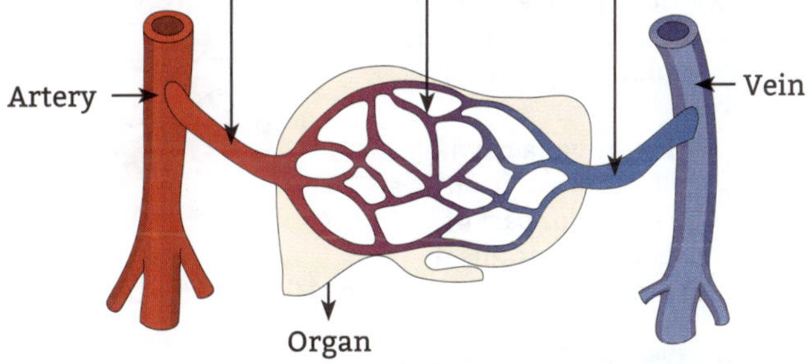

Fig. 10.5: A network of capillaries

Exchange of materials such as nutrients, chemical substances and gases between the blood and the cells occurs in capillaries. The blood pressure in capillaries is lower than that in arteries.

Science in Context

The blood capillaries are so small that it takes 10 capillaries to equal the thickness of one human hair.

The Heart

The heart is a fist-sized muscular organ having an average weight of around 250–350 grams. It is located in the chest cavity tilted towards the left lung. It pumps blood to all parts of the body. It beats 60–80 times a minute throughout our life.

The heart is made up of four chambers (Fig. 10.6). The upper left and right chambers are the **atria** (singular—**atrium,** also called **auricle**), and the lower left and right chambers are the **ventricles**. The atria and ventricles are separated from each other by walls or partitions which have **valves** in them. Valves allow the blood to flow in only one direction. The right auricle opens into the right ventricle and the left auricle into the left ventricle.

Due to this, the right side of the heart remains completely separated from the blood on the left side of the heart. The blood rich in carbon dioxide flows through the right side of the heart, while the blood rich in oxygen flows through the left side of the heart. A partition called **septum** separates the left side of the heart from the right, preventing the mixing of oxygenated blood with the deoxygenated blood.

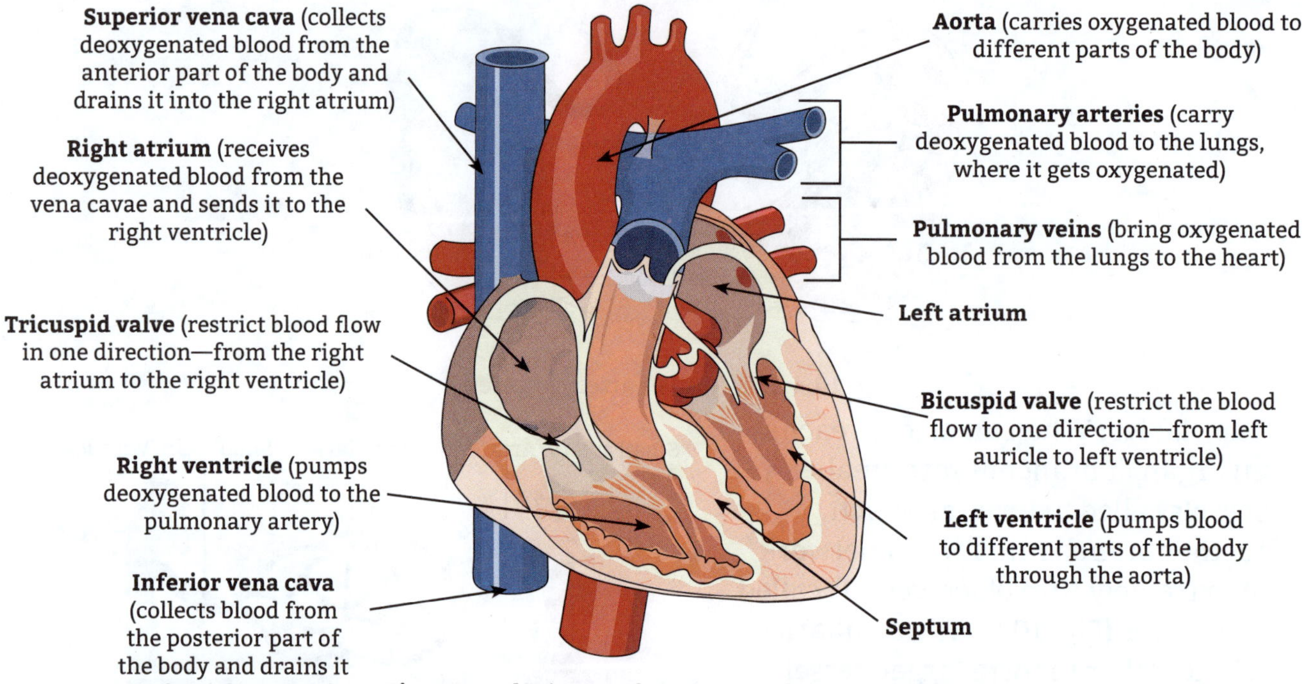

Fig. 10.6: The internal structure of the human heart

Science in Context

Squeeze a tennis ball as hard as you can with your fist. This is approximately the same amount of force your heart applies every time it pumps blood. Even when you are at rest, it works twice as hard as the leg muscles.

The arteries and veins in the heart connect to other parts of the body. The blood vessels that enter or leave the heart are:

Vena cava: It is a large vein that collects blood rich in carbon dioxide from all parts of the body through other smaller veins and empties the blood into the right atrium.

Pulmonary artery: It carries blood rich in carbon dioxide from the right ventricle of the heart to the lungs.

Pulmonary vein: It brings oxygenated blood from the lungs to the left atrium of the heart.

Aorta: It is the largest artery which receives blood rich in oxygen from the left ventricle. The oxygenated blood is then circulated to different parts of the body.

Science in Context

In human beings, blood is carried by blood vessels from the heart to all the cells and back again. It never leaves the blood vessels. Hence, it is also called a closed blood system.

Heartbeat and Pulse

The heart works by contracting and relaxing its muscles. The contraction and relaxation follows a rhythm called **heartbeat**. Therefore, a heartbeat is one complete cycle of contraction and relaxation.

Our heart normally beats 70–80 times per minute. When you place your hand on your chest, you can count the number of times your heart beats in a minute. Another way to count the number of times your heart beats in a minute is by measuring your pulse. **Pulse** is the throbbing sensation of an artery at each beat of the heart. It can be felt where an artery is close to the surface of the skin such as the wrist and the neck. A doctor uses an instrument called the **stethoscope** to listen to your heartbeat. He can also count your pulse rate by feeling the pressure of the movement of blood through the artery.

Activity 1

Aim: To examine the effect of exercise on the heartbeat and the pulse rate

Procedure:

1. Pulse rate

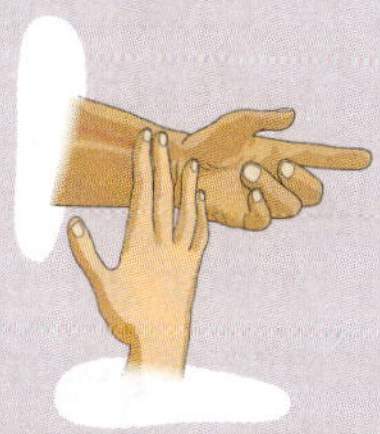

(a) Partner with a friend and take turns at being the subject and the tester.

(b) Place the middle and index finger over the inner side of the subject's left wrist just below the base of the thumb (to find the pulse).

(c) Count the beats for 60 seconds to obtain the number of beats per minute.

(d) Next, the subject must jog on the spot for about five minutes and repeat the above procedure.

2. Heartbeat

(a) Each student in the group can take turns at being the subject and the tester.

(b) Insert the ends of a stethoscope into your ears and place the mouth of the funnel on the subject's chest slightly to the left side.

(c) Carefully listen to the heartbeat.

(d) Count the beats for 60 seconds to obtain the rate of heartbeat.

(e) Now make the subject jog on the spot for about five minutes and repeat the above procedure.

Sl. no.	Name of the student	During rest	After exercise (jogging for 5 minutes)
		Pulse rate (beats per minute)	Pulse rate (beats per minute)

How many pulse beats were you able to count? *The number of beats per minute is called the* ***pulse rate***. After performing Activity 1, you find that the rate of heartbeat and pulse rate is more during exercise as compared to the rate before exercise. Heartbeat and pulse rate increase due to the increase in the muscular activities.

BLOOD PRESSURE

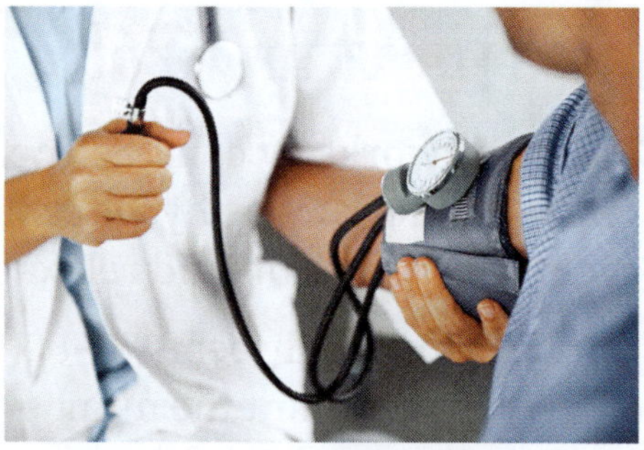

Fig. 10.7: Measuring blood pressure using sphygmomanometer

Blood pressure is the force or pressure exerted by the blood against the walls of the blood vessels. It is similar to the pressure in a water pipe when water flows through it. Blood pressure is measured using a device called a **sphygmomanometer** (Fig. 10.7). Blood pressure can vary from person to person and change throughout the day.

Maintaining a healthy blood pressure is important because low blood pressure can cause dizziness and fainting, while high blood pressure can strain the heart and blood vessels and make them work harder. It can also damage the blood vessels by exerting too much pressure on their walls. Over time, this can lead to the accumulation of fatty deposits inside the blood vessels, narrowing them and hindering blood flow, which can result in a stroke affecting movement, speech, and cognitive abilities. In severe cases, high blood pressure can even lead to death.

To keep blood pressure in a healthy range, it is important to eat a balanced diet, exercise regularly, manage stress and avoid smoking. Regular check-ups with a doctor can help monitor and manage blood pressure to ensure good overall health.

Science in Context

The actual amount of blood the heart pumps in a day, also called **cardiac output**, varies from person to person but typically falls between 4,000 and 6,000 litres for a healthy adult. Can you come up with any variables that could affect the amount of blood it pumps in a 24-hour period?

Revise and Recall

Fill in the blanks.

1. Blood contains a pale yellow liquid called __________. (lymph/plasma)
2. Our heart beats __________ times per minute. (40–50/70–80)
3. The vein that collects blood rich in carbon dioxide from all the parts of the body is the __________. (vena cava/aorta)

TRANSPORTATION OF SUBSTANCES IN PLANTS

In plants, transportation of substances occurs through diffusion, vascular tissues, and conduction. These processes enable the movement of water, nutrients and other substances throughout the plant.

Diffusion: The movement of substances from a region of higher concentration to a region of lower concentration is called **diffusion**. Diffusion is the major method by which transport of materials occurs in single-celled organisms such as ***Chlamydomonas*** and simple multicellular plants such as ***Spirogyra***. It plays a crucial role in the transportation of gases, such as carbon dioxide and oxygen, across plant cells. Through small pores called **stomata** on the leaves and stems, gases diffuse in and out of the plant.

Vascular tissues: Like animals, plants also need to transport water, minerals, salts and nutrients to all of their parts through specialized vascular tissues. **Xylem** and **phloem** are the two main types of vascular tissues responsible for this transport.

Once the water and minerals are absorbed from the soil by the roots, they move up the stem and leaves through tube-like tissues called the **xylem**. Absorption and transportation of water are continuous processes that occur with the help of transpiration. ***Transpiration** is the process in which plants lose water in the form of water vapour through the stomata.* This results in water loss in the cells of the leaves and creates a pressure. The pressure helps to pull the water from the roots through the xylem of the stem to reach all the way to the leaves.

*The food manufactured in the leaves during photosynthesis reaches all parts of the plant through a process called **translocation***. This occurs through another set of tube-like tissues called the **phloem**.

Xylem and phloem are called conducting tissues or **vascular bundles** (Fig. 10.8).

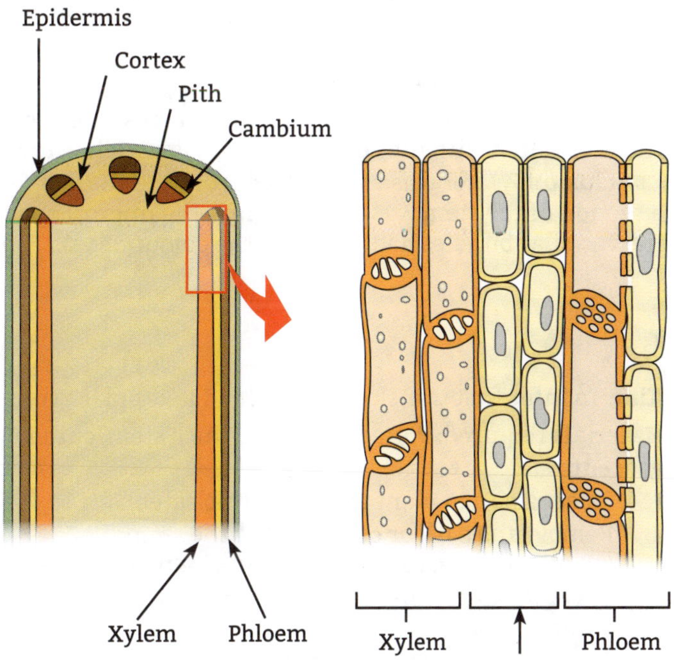

Fig. 10.8: The conducting tissues in dicot plants

Conduction: In plants, substances can be transported from one cell to another through a process called conduction. This helps in the distribution of water, minerals and nutrients. Conduction occurs in different parts of the plant, including the **cortex** (outer layer) located in the stem (Fig. 10.8) and root. It carries water and minerals from the roots to other parts of the plant. The **pith** (centre) also assists in the movement of substances. Furthermore, gaps called **pits** in the cell walls aid in the transfer of substances between adjacent cells. These plant structures have pathways that aid in the movement of substances. Through conduction, plants efficiently transport water, minerals and nutrients, ensuring their proper growth, development and survival.

Activity 2

Aim: To infer that transportation of water and minerals takes place through the xylem

Materials required: Two glass beakers, water, two plants, stain/ink, cover slip, blade, slide, microscope

Procedure:

1. Take two clean glass beakers and fill them up to three-fourths with water.
2. Place one plant in each of the beakers containing water and label them as Set-up A and Set-up B.
3. Add a few drops of stain or ink into the beaker labelled as Set-up B. Observe and record your observations.
4. Cut a thin section of the plant stems from both the set-ups with the help of a blade.
5. Transfer the sections to a clean glass slide.
6. Place a cover slip and focus the slide under the microscope with the help of your teacher. Observe the sections under the microscope.

Observation: The stem in Set-up A looks transparent because the water was colourless. In Set-up B, tubes coloured with the colour of the ink are visible towards the centre of the section.

Conclusion: Water was transported from the stem to the leaves through xylem vessels and when a section of the stem was viewed under the microscope, it showed that a few parts of the tissues in the vascular bundles had absorbed the colour or ink. These are the xylem tissues.

Activity 3

Aim: To infer that translocation of food takes place through the phloem

Materials required: Potted plant with thick stem, cutter or steel ruler

Procedure:

1. Select a potted plant that has a thick stem.
2. Remove the bark or outer part of the stem (about 5 inches) carefully with the help of a cutter.
3. Leave the experimental set-up for about 10 days and water the plant regularly.
4. Observe the stem part after 10 days and record your observations.

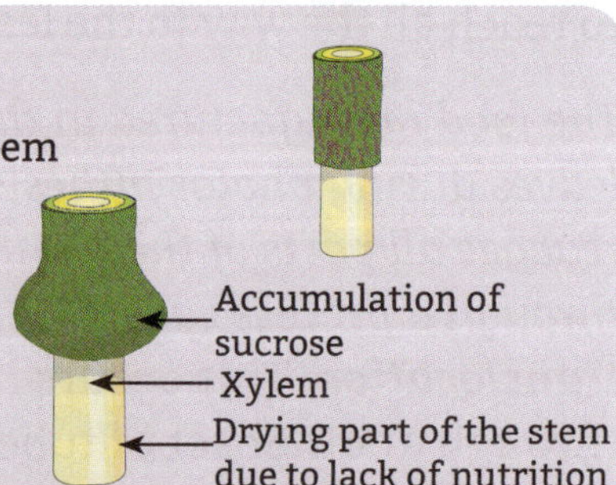

Accumulation of food materials observed in the portion above the point where the bark has been cut off

Observation: The portion of the stem above the point where the bark was cut off shows swelling and the leaves will look fresh and green due to the accumulation of food. The portion of the stem below the point where the bark is cut off starts dying and the leaves wither away due to the blockage of the movement of food downwards.

Conclusion: This activity proves that phloem is responsible for the translocation of food in plants.

EXCRETORY SYSTEM

All living organisms produce chemical waste materials which are the by-products of various life processes that take place in the body. These waste products are often toxic and hence need to be removed from the body. *The process by which metabolic waste products are removed from the body is called* ***excretion***. The organs involved in excretion form the **excretory system**.

Science in Context

Each segment in the body of an earthworm has a pair of excretory organs called nephridia that form the excretory system.

Excretion in Animals

In unicellular organisms such as *Amoeba*, *Paramecium* and lower animals such as *Hydra* and sponges, some of the waste products are excreted by the process of diffusion through their body surface. *Hydra* excrete excess fluids and waste through its mouth. Sponges have special cells to push excess wastes out. Larger animals have special organs for excretion.

Excretion in Humans

The organs involved in removing wastes in human beings are the skin, lungs and kidneys. Lungs are responsible for excretion of gaseous wastes from the body. The main waste gas excreted by lungs is carbon dioxide, which is a waste product of respiration in cells throughout the body. Skin helps in excreting excess water and salts, in form of sweat. Excretion of nitrogen-containing wastes (for example, urea and uric acid) in humans is carried out mainly by the urinary system, which includes the kidneys, the ureters, the urinary bladder and the urethra (Fig. 10.9). Human beings have one pair of bean-shaped kidneys which filter waste products from the blood and form urine.

Each kidney consists of a large number of coiled tubes called **nephrons**. The nephrons filter out waste products from the blood. Hence, nephrons are considered the functional units of the kidney.

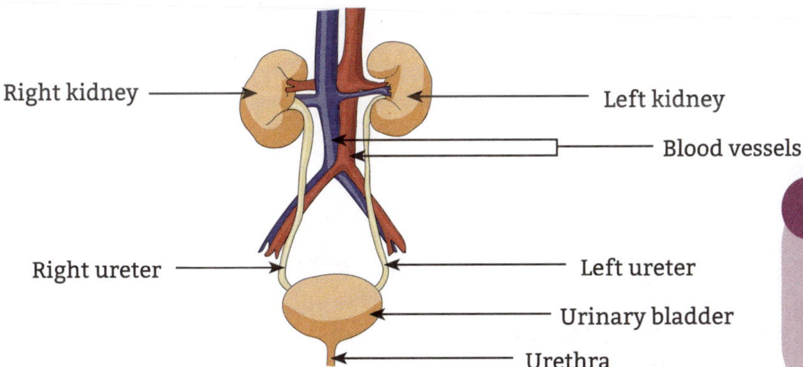

Fig. 10.9: The urinary system in human beings

Wonder!

A person needs at least one healthy kidney in order to lead a healthy life.

A narrow tube called **ureter** runs from the inner side of each kidney. The two ureters from the two kidneys are connected to a large sac called the **bladder**. The urine passes out from the kidneys through the two ureters into the urinary bladder where it is stored. From the bladder, the urine passes through another muscular tube called the **urethra** and is finally passed out through a urinary opening at the end of the urethra. The sphincter muscle in the urethra helps in the passing of urine.

Dialysis

Sometimes, due to infection, genetic conditions or injury, the kidneys may stop functioning properly, resulting in the accumulation of waste substances within the body. This condition, known as kidney failure or end-stage renal disease, can be fatal[1]. In such cases, a treatment called **dialysis** becomes necessary to remove waste products and excess fluid from the body.

Word Web

[1]**Fatal:** Capable of causing death

Dialysis is a process that mimics the function of the kidneys by filtering the blood and removing waste substances. It is often referred to as an artificial kidney machine or renal replacement therapy. During dialysis, blood is carefully and safely circulated through a machine called a dialyzer. The dialyzer contains a special filter called a **dialyzer membrane** or **artificial kidney**. This membrane allows waste products, excess fluid and toxins to pass through while retaining essential substances such as red blood cells and proteins. The dialyzer is designed to mimic the natural filtration process that occurs in the kidneys.

The dialysis machine consists of components such as a blood pump, dialyzer (an artificial kidney), dialysis solution, dialyser pipes and filters (Fig. 10.10).

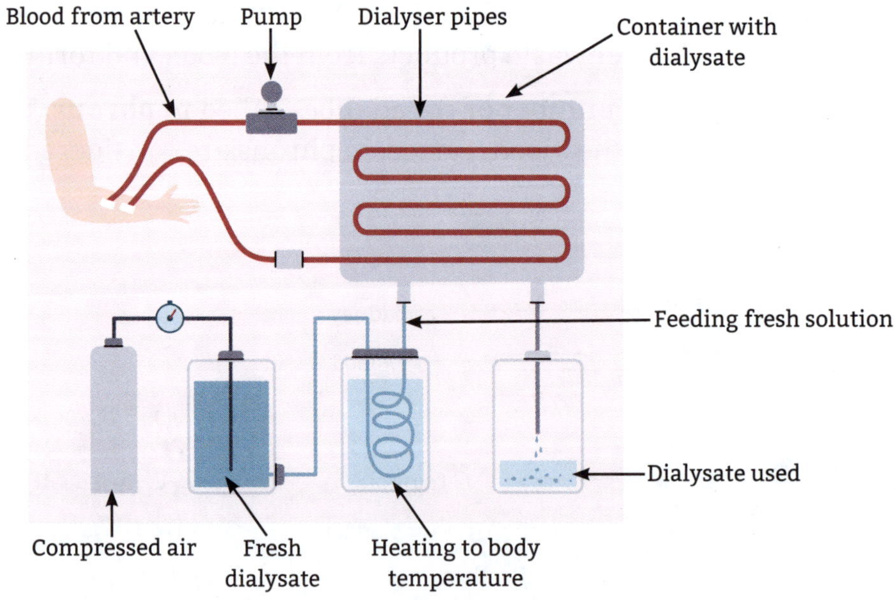

Fig. 10.10: A dialysis machine at work

The machine circulates the patient's blood through the dialyzer, where waste substances are filtered out and the clean blood is returned to the body. This helps maintain the balance of essential substances in the body and supports the overall health of individuals with kidney failure.

Dialysis treatments are usually performed on a regular basis, with the frequency and duration determined by the individual's specific needs. The goal of dialysis is to help individuals with kidney failure maintain a stable and relatively normal life by managing the levels of waste substances and fluid in their bodies.

While dialysis is a life-sustaining treatment, it is important to note that it is not a cure for kidney failure. It serves as a temporary solution to support individuals until a kidney for transplant becomes available (a kidney transplant is a surgical process in which the failed or diseased kidney is replaced with a healthy kidney from a donor) or until their own kidneys regain their function.

Excretion in Plants

Plants too excrete waste products from their body. The main wastes excreted by plants are given below:

- **Gases**: Oxygen and carbon dioxide are given out during the process of photosynthesis and respiration, respectively.
- **Excess water**: The excess water taken in through the roots is lost by the plant through the stomata, through the process of transpiration.
- **Excess salts**: The excess salts obtained either from the soil or water in the ground are excreted and they get deposited on plant surfaces such as the leaves or the stem in the form of small crystals.
- **Gums, resins and latex** are excretory products from plants. We use these substances as adhesives, paints, varnishes and rubber.

Wonder!

Anti-transpirants (substances that reduce water loss from the plants) when sprayed on the stem and leaves protect the evergreen plants from dry winter winds.

Keywords

Diffusion: The movement of molecules from a region of high concentration to a region of low concentration

Blood: A red fluid in vertebrates containing RBCs, WBCs, platelets and plasma

Plasma: The pale yellow liquid part of blood in which the red blood cells, white blood cells and platelets are suspended

Haemoglobin: The red-coloured pigment present in the red blood cells

Ventricles: The lower two chambers of the heart with thick muscular walls

Valves: Muscular flaps that allow the blood to flow in only one direction

Atria or **Auricles**: The two upper chambers of the heart with comparatively thinner walls

Xylem: Tube-like tissues through which water and minerals are transported in plants

Translocation: The process of transportation of food from the leaves to the other parts of the plant

Phloem: Tube-like tissues through which food is transported in plants

Nephrons: The functional units of the kidney which filter waste products from the blood

Summary

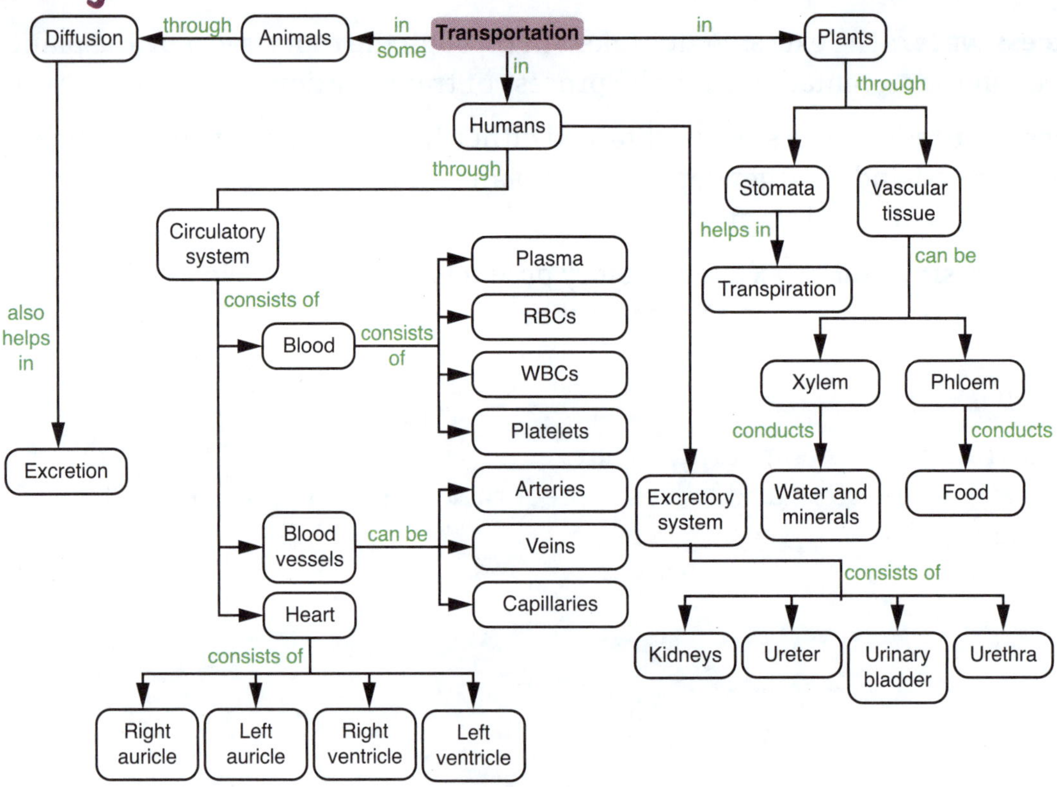

EXERCISE

W

ia

A. Choose the correct option.

1. Which of these structures help in preventing the blood from flowing back?
   (a) Capillaries (b) Valves (c) Arteries (d) Veins
2. Which of the following structures transports water and minerals in plants?
   (a) Xylem (b) Phloem
   (c) Blood vessel (d) None of these
3. The pulmonary artery carries ____________ blood.
   (a) oxygenated (b) deoxygenated
   (c) carbonated (d) partially oxygenated
4. Which of the following blood cells destroy the germs that enter our body?
   (a) Platelets (b) Red blood cells
   (c) White blood cells (d) Antibodies
5. Which of the following is not a waste material excreted by plants?
   (a) Gum (b) Resin (c) Urine (d) Latex

ia

B. Fill in the blanks.

1. The ____________ receives oxygenated blood from the left ventricle. (vena cava/aorta)
2. The tissue that transports food in plants is the ____________. (phloem/xylem)
3. The contraction and relaxation of the heart is called the ____________. (heartbeat/pulse rate)
4. The lower chambers of the heart are called the ____________. (auricles/ventricles)
5. The loss of water from the stomata is called ____________. (transpiration/translocation)

C. State whether the following statements are true (T) or false (F).

1. All the living organisms have the same kind of transportation system. ☐
2. Transportation of substances in plants occurs through blood. ☐
3. The force created by transpiration in plants pulls the groundwater up to greater heights. ☐
4. The veins have thicker walls than the arteries. ☐
5. Nephrons are the functional units of the heart. ☐

D. Name the following.

1. The red-coloured fluid medium that transports substances in our body
2. The process by which food is transported in plants by phloem tissues
3. The organ that filters waste from blood to form urine
4. The process in which blood is passed through an artificial kidney machine to remove waste products
5. The upper left and right chambers of the heart

E. Give reasons for the following.

1. Human blood is red in colour.
2. Veins have valves.
3. Capillaries are thin walled.
4. Translocation is a vital process in plants.
5. Gums, resins and carbon dioxide are given out by plants during metabolic processes.

F. Answer the following questions briefly.

1. Why is the transportation of materials necessary in organisms?
2. What are the different types of cells found in blood?
3. List the functions of blood.
4. What are xylem and phloem? What are their roles?
5. What are the products excreted by plants during transpiration?
6. What is the difference between transpiration and translocation?

G. Answer the following questions in detail.

1. Draw a neat and labelled diagram of the human urinary system and explain the function of kidneys.
2. Explain how the transportation of food, water and minerals happens in plants.
3. Differentiate between arteries, veins and capillaries on the basis of wall type, valves, function and blood flow.
4. What is dialysis and how does it help individuals with kidney failure?

COGNITIVE CORNER

Critical Thinking

1. How are new blood cells produced and how are the damaged red blood cells removed from the body?

2. Blood transfusion is the process of replacing blood lost during an injury or a surgery. From which of the blood vessels is blood drawn during blood transfusion? Why?
3. Why does the weight of the human heart vary among individuals?

Picture Study

Identify and label the different blood cells in the diagram given alongside.

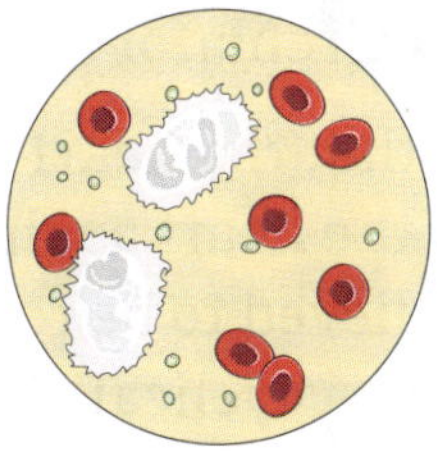

Project

Make your own stethoscope.

Materials required: Two polythene tubes, cellophane tape, funnel, balloon, string and rubber tube

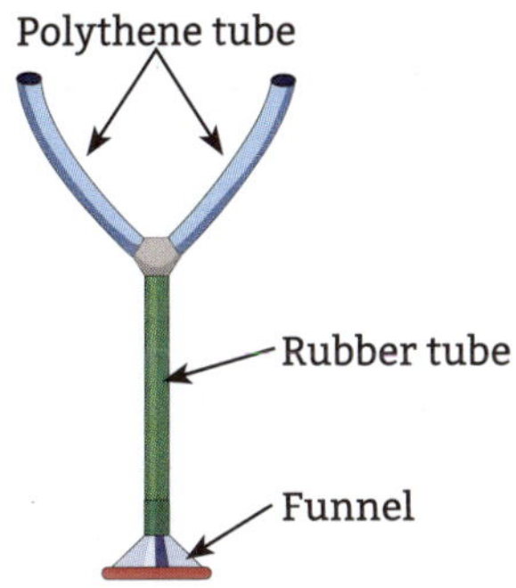

Procedure: Join the tubes together with the help of a cello tape. Attach them to the rubber tube as shown in the picture. Fix the funnel at the open end of the rubber tube. Cut a piece of rubber from the balloon and stretch it over the mouth of the funnel. Secure the piece of balloon by tying it with a string. Place the two ends of the polythene tubes in your ears and hold the funnel against your chest and hear your heartbeat. **(C-7.2)**

In the Library

1. From which part of the plant are latex, resins and gums obtained? How are they useful to us? Find this out from the books in your library or the Internet. **(C-7.1)**
2. Water is absorbed by the roots of the plants from the soil by a process called osmosis. Find out about osmosis from your books and the Internet. Use this knowledge to design and build simple models that can effectively demonstrate the process of osmosis. **(C-7.2)**

Life Skills

People who exercise regularly, eat a healthy diet that consists of low-fat foods and consume more vegetables and fruits can reduce the risk of heart diseases. Find out and list atleast three measures to reduce the risk of heart disease. **(C-7.3)**

Worksheet

According to Ayurveda, the human body consists of channels *srotas* through which various substances, including blood, flow. These channels are responsible for carrying vital energy, oxygen and nutrients throughout the body. The main channel associated with blood circulation is known as circulatory system. The ancient Indians not only knew about the organs of the circulatory system such as the heart, arteries and veins, but also the diseases associated with circulatory system such as clogged arteries.

Ancient Indian scholars recognized that the heart played a crucial role in the circulation of blood. They described the heart as the seat of consciousness and the centre of life force. The heart was believed to be responsible for pumping blood and distributing it throughout the body in a cyclical manner.

A. Read more about ancient knowledge about the functions and purpose of heart and blood circulation. Write in the space given below.

____

____

____

____

____

____

____

B. Do you think combining ancient knowledge with modern advancements in technology can be used to improve people's health conditions? How?

____

____

____

____

____

____

____

____

11 Reproduction in Plants

Curricular Goals

- Explore the living world in scientific terms **(CG-3)**
- Understand the interface of science, technology and society **(CG-5)**
- Explore the nature and processes of science through engaging with the evolution of scientific knowledge and conducting scientific inquiry **(CG-6)**
- Communicate questions, observations and conclusions related to science **(CG-7)**

Competencies

- Describe the diversity of living things observed in the natural surroundings, including at a smaller scale **(C-3.1)**
- Explain the conditions suitable for sustaining life on Earth **(C-3.4)**
- Illustrate how science and technology can help to improve the quality of human life **(C-5.1)**
- Formulate questions using scientific terminology and collect data as evidence **(C-6.2)**
- Use scientific vocabulary to communicate science accurately in oral and written form, and through visual representation **(C-7.1)**

Let's Get Started

Observe the parts of the plant in the image given below and match their functions given in the help box by writing the numbers against each part in the boxes provided.

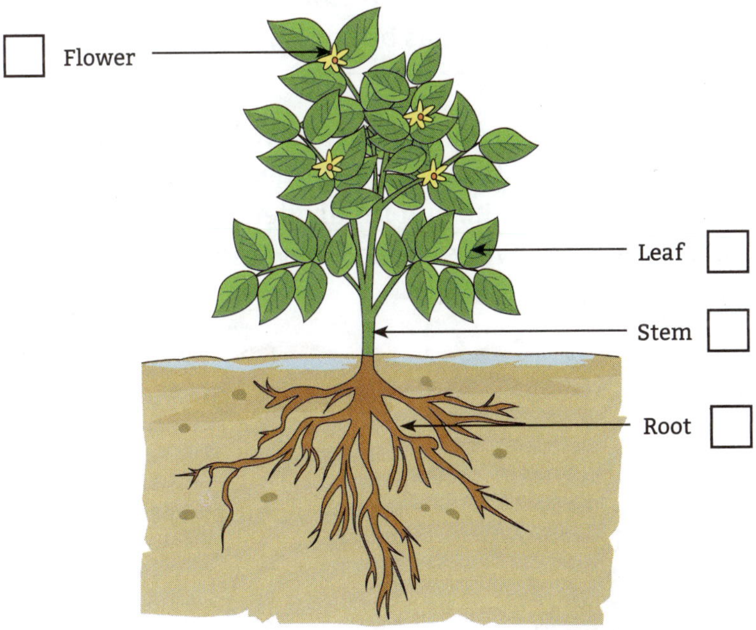

Help Box

1. Contains the reproductive organs
2. Makes food using sunlight, water and carbon dioxide by photosynthesis
3. Provides support and transports food
4. Anchors the plant to the ground and absorbs water and minerals

In earlier classes, you have studied that one of the characteristics of living things is that they *reproduce*. For example, a dog can give birth to puppies that slowly grow into adult dogs. Similarly, plants have the ability to produce seeds that germinate into young plants. As these young plants continue to grow, they develop into fully mature plants.

Reproduction *is a fundamental characteristic of living organisms, which refers to their ability to produce young ones of their own kind.*

IMPORTANCE OF REPRODUCTION

Living organisms have a specific lifespan. For example, an annual plant such as a sunflower completes its entire life cycle in approximately one year. On the other hand, a perennial plant such as a neem tree has a lifespan that extends over many years. It is essential for organisms to reproduce during their lifespan to ensure the continuation of their own kind. Without reproduction, once organisms die, there would be no way for producing new organisms, ultimately resulting in the extinction of their own kind.

In this chapter, we will learn the different ways of reproduction in plants. Plants undergo both asexual and sexual reproduction methods. Let us learn about these in detail.

ASEXUAL REPRODUCTION AND ITS METHODS

Asexual reproduction *is a kind of reproduction in which only a single parent is involved.* There are different forms of asexual reproduction such as budding, fragmentation and spore formation. These are commonly seen in algae and fungi.

Budding: Budding is seen in organisms such as yeast. A bulb-like projection protrudes from the body of the parent cell and is called a 'bud'. This bud continues to grow. Some of the contents from the parent cell flows into the bud. The bud finally detaches itself from the parent cell. The detached cell then continues to live as a whole new individual cell. The new cell formed is identical to the parent cell (Fig. 11.1).

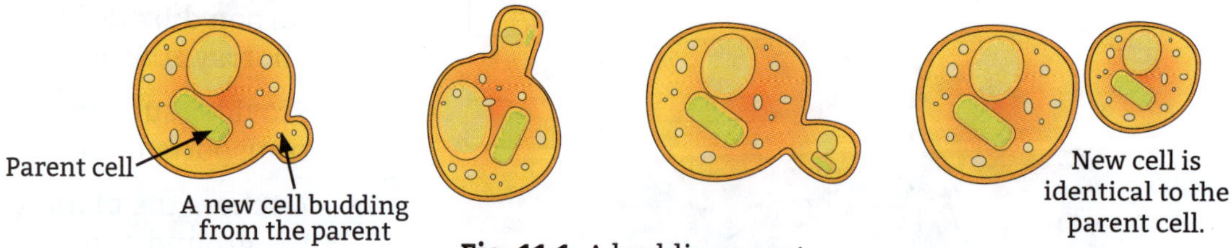

Fig. 11.1: A budding yeast

Fragmentation: Fragmentation is seen in algae such as *Oscillatoria* and *Spirogyra* (Fig. 11.2 and 11.3). The body of the parent organism breaks into 'fragments' and each fragment can grow to function as a new individual. (*Note*: Yeast is a type of fungus. Fungi and algae were earlier classified as plants, but they have now been put into separate groups.)

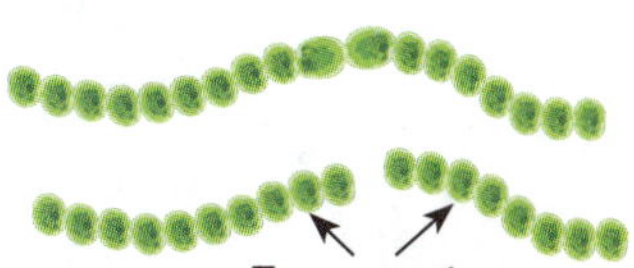

Fig. 11.2: Fragmentation in *Oscillatoria*

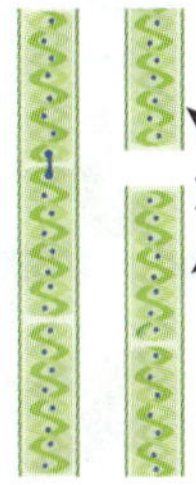

Fig. 11.3: Fragmentation in *Spirogyra*

Spore formation: Spores are tiny, spherical, single-celled bodies produced for the purpose of reproduction. They are produced and released from specialized structures of the plant body. These spores can remain dormant[1] during harsh weather conditions. They grow into a new plant under favourable conditions. Mosses, ferns, fungi, etc. reproduce by this method (Fig. 11.4).

Word Web

[1]**Dormant**: Alive but not active

Fig. 11.4: Spores under the leaflets of fern

VEGETATIVE PROPAGATION

Have you noticed small projections or green shoots coming out from potatoes or onions? They can grow into new plants. New plants are found to grow from the vegetative parts of the parent plant such as root, stem or leaf. This type of reproduction is called **vegetative propagation**. Vegetative propagation can take place naturally and can also be carried out by artificial means. Let us look at different examples of vegetative propagation.

Vegetative Propagation by Natural Means

In nature, most plants reproduce vegetatively with the help of stems, roots or leaves.

From stems

New plants can grow either from horizontal stems or from underground stems. Some types of vegetative propagation through horizontal stems are discussed below.

(a) **Runners**: A runner is a slender branch that creeps some distance away from the mother plant on the ground, roots itself at the nodes and grows into a new plant (Fig. 11.5). Examples: wood-sorrel and grass

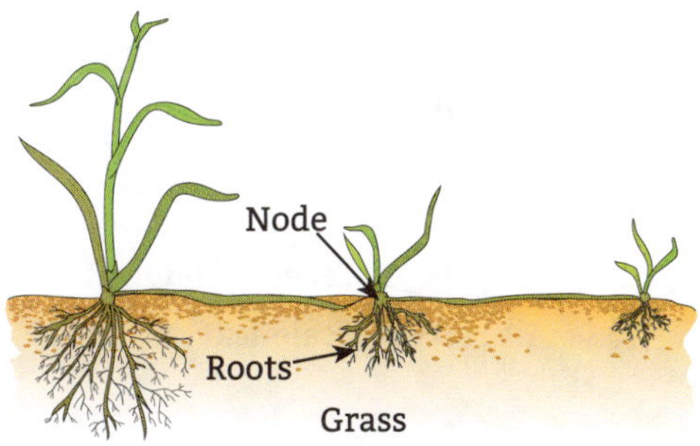

Fig. 11.5: Reproduction in a runner

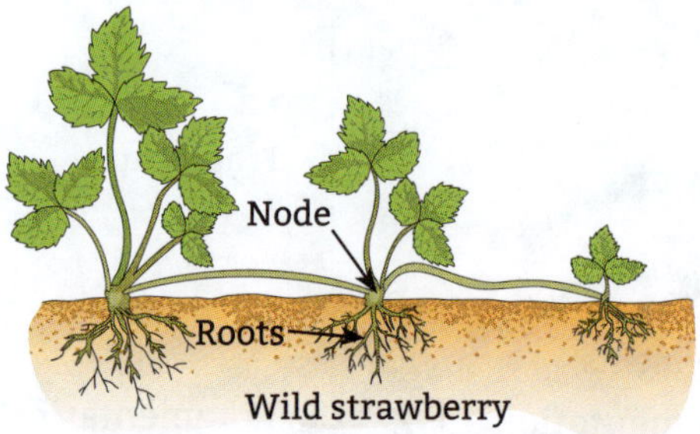

Fig. 11.6: Growth of a stolon

(b) **Stolons**: Stolons are lateral slender branches that arise from the base of the stem. Stolons initially grow upwards and slowly drop to the ground. These stems root at the nodes, producing buds that soon grow into daughter plants (Fig. 11.6). Examples: wild strawberry and peppermint

(c) **Offset**: An offset is a short horizontal branch that arises from the axil of a leaf (leaf axil is where the leaf stalk attaches to the stem). The branch elongates to a certain length and then produces leaves at the node and a cluster of roots that fix to the ground. The offset then breaks away from the mother plant, leaving the daughter plant which then grows into an independent plant body (Fig. 11.7). Example: water lettuce

Fig. 11.7: Reproduction in an offset plant

Fig. 11.8: *Chrysanthemum*

(d) **Suckers**: Suckers grow from the underground part of the main stem, develop roots underground and then grow obliquely upwards giving rise to new plants (Fig. 11.8). Example: *Chrysanthemum*

Some plants have underground stems that are swollen to store food and have buds which can grow into new plants. Some examples of reproduction through underground stems are discussed below:

(a) **Tubers**: If you observe a potato which is a few days old from the time it is harvested, you will notice small projections on the skin surface. These are called 'eyes'. If a piece of the potato containing the eye is cut and planted in the soil, it will develop roots and shoots and grow into a new plant (Fig. 11.9).

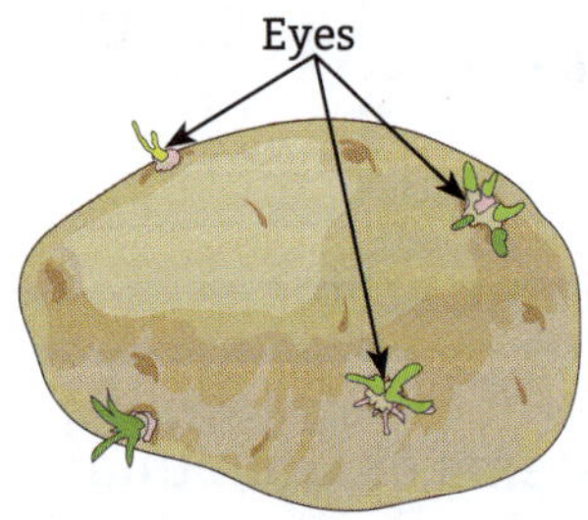

Fig. 11.9: A potato tuber

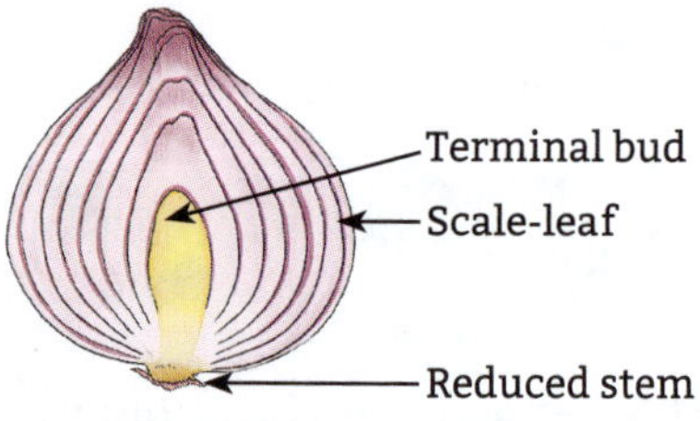

Fig. 11.10: An onion bulb

(b) **Bulbs**: In an onion bulb, there is a terminal bud at the centre (Fig. 11.10). Fleshy scale leaves that store food surround the bud. In the growing season, new shoots arise from the bud. Examples: onion, garlic, lily, tulip, amaryllis and iris

(c) **Rhizome**: Rhizomes are underground stems that have scaly leaves at their nodes. The axil of the scaly leaf has buds that grow into new shoots upwards (Fig. 11.11). Examples: ginger, asparagus and water lily

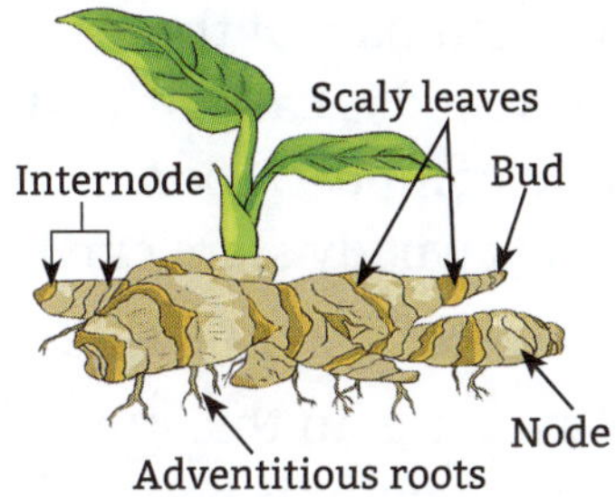

Fig. 11.11: A ginger rhizome

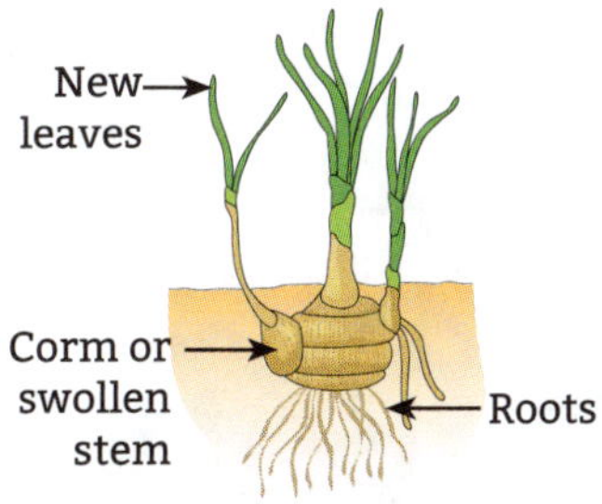

Fig. 11.12: Reproduction in a crocus

(d) **Corm**: Corms are swollen stems. They bear buds on the axil of their scaly leaves which grow into new plants (Fig. 11.12). Examples: yam, colocasia, crocus and gladiolus

From roots

Some plants such as sweet potato and dahlia have swollen roots without any shape. These roots are called tuberous roots (Fig. 11.13). These roots have small buds which give rise to a new plant when they are planted into the soil.

Fig. 11.13: Tuberous roots in sweet potato

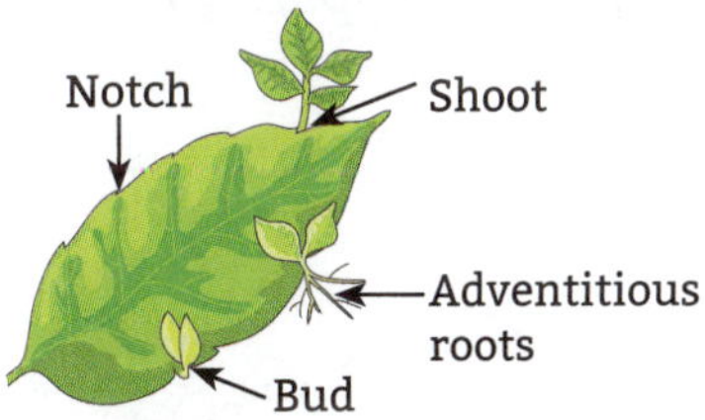

Fig. 11.14: Vegetative propagation through a leaf

From leaves

Plants such as *Bryophyllum* produce buds from the margin of the leaves (Fig. 11.14). These buds drop off from the leaves and fix themselves to the ground and later grow into new plants.

Vegetative Propagation by Artificial Means

Vegetative propagation can also happen under artificial conditions to form new plants. Some methods are discussed below:

Cutting: This method is carried out in plants such as *Hibiscus*. The stem of the plant is cut and planted in a new pot or soil. The cut stem eventually develops roots and shoots and grows into a new plant.

Grafting: Grafting involves two plants of the same species. A bud or a stem cutting from one plant is inserted into a groove of the second plant which is rooted to the ground (Fig. 11.15).

Fig. 11.15: The steps involved in grafting stem

The cut part of the stem is called the **scion**. The second plant to which the scion is attached is called the **stock**. The grafted areas are then covered with a layer of soil and compost. Soon, the stock and scion join together to form one plant. Plants with a thick woody stem can be easily used for grafting. Varieties of fruit-bearing trees are developed by grafting.

Layering: In this method, a part of the branch on the plant is bent down and covered with soil. The remaining part of the branch remains above the ground. A heavy brick is placed over the layered soil which is watered regularly. Once the roots start developing, new shoots will start to grow from the ground. The branch can then be cut from the parent plant. Layering is often done in plants such as jasmine which have long and slender branches. Plants that have a flexible stem can be propagated through this method (Fig. 11.16).

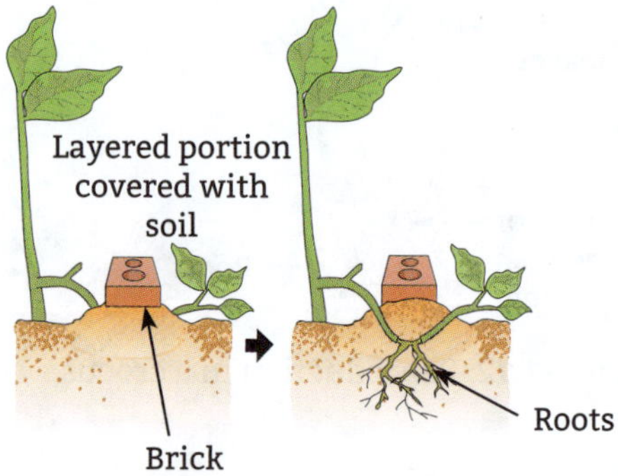

Fig. 11.16: The steps involved in layering

Tissue culture: In this method, the growing tips of plants are cut and planted in an artificial medium kept inside a conical flask or a test tube. The medium provides all the necessary nutrients for plant growth. Once the roots develop, they are planted in suitable soil. From here, they grow into whole new plants.

Advantages of vegetative propagation

- Vegetative propagation is very useful for plant growers as they can get large quantities of new plants in a short time.
- The newly reproduced plants have the exact characteristics as that of their parent plants.
- It is easy to produce new varieties of plants with the required characteristics.
- Vegetative plants grow faster than the plants grown from seeds and need less attention during the early stages of growth.
- Fruits without seeds, disease and drought-resistant plants can be produced using these methods.

Wonder!

- The largest flower is the stinking corpse lily (*Rafflesia*) which can grow up to 90 cm in diameter.
- The tallest flowering plant is the *Eucalyptus* which can reach up to 132 m in height.
- The smallest flowering plant is the duckweed called *Wolffia*. It is 0.5 mm long.

SEXUAL REPRODUCTION

Sexual reproduction is a type of reproduction where a new plant develops from the fusion of male and female gametes. Before we learn about sexual reproduction in plants, let us recall the parts of a flower (Fig. 11.17), as sexual reproduction in plants takes place in the flowers.

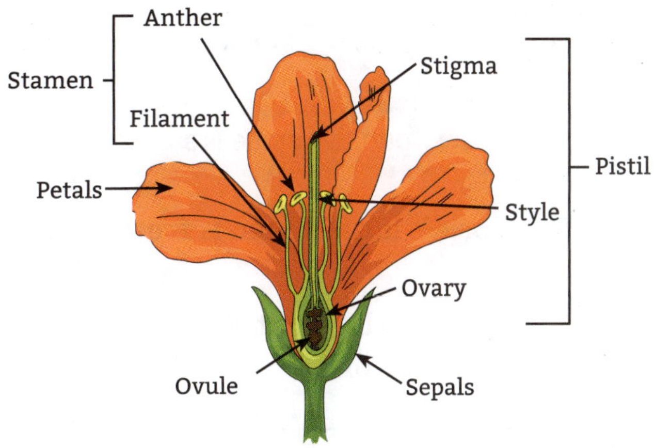

Fig. 11.17: Structure of a flower

Structure of a Flower

Stamen is the male part of the flower. It has a long filament with a elongated sac-like structure at its tip called the anther. The anther holds the pollen sacs inside which pollen grains are found.

Pistil is the female part of the flower. It has a tube-like structure called the style. The style is oval-shaped at the base. This is the ovary. The tip of the style is sticky. It is called the stigma. It helps to attach the pollen grains during pollination.

Flowers with both stamens and pistils are called **bisexual flowers**. They are also called **complete flowers**. Some examples of bisexual flowers are *Hibiscus*, wild rose, *Vinca rosea*, etc. Flowers with only the male or the female reproductive part are called **unisexual flowers**. They are also called **incomplete flowers**. Some examples of unisexual flowers are watermelon and cucumber.

Pollination

a

During sexual reproduction in plants, there is a fusion of the male and female gametes. Pollination must take place so that the male and female gametes can meet to fuse. *The process of transfer of pollens from the anthers of a stamen to the stigma of the pistil is called **pollination***. Pollination can be either self- or cross-pollination (Fig. 11.18).

Self-pollination: It occurs when the pollen is transferred to the stigma of the same flower or the stigma of a different flower in the same plant.

Cross-pollination: It occurs when the pollen is transferred to the stigma of another flower of another plant of the same kind.

Fig. 11.18: Methods of pollination

Wonder!

- The strawberry is a false fruit, but it is covered by tiny dry fruits, each with a seed.
- The most expensive spice is saffron, which is the dried stigma of the flower itself.
- The world's largest seed is from Coco de Mer. It weighs about 17.6 kg.

Pollination may be brought about by insects, wind and water which are called the **agents of pollination**.

Means/Agents of pollination	How does it occur?
Insects	Pollination occurs by means of insects. Insects move from one flower to the other with pollen sticking to their body and their legs. This pollen gets dropped on to the other flowers.
Wind	Pollination occurs by wind. Wind carries the pollen which reaches the stigma of another flower.
Water	Pollination occurs by water. Water currents carry the pollen to reach the stigma of the other flowers.

Some flowers are brightly coloured, while some are dull; some have long protruding structures, while some do not.

Wind-pollinated flowers are generally small and not always brightly coloured (Fig 11.19). They lack nectar and odour. The pollens are very light, smooth and produced in large quantities. The anthers are usually exposed out of the flowers. The stigma also hangs out of the flower and is usually feathery in order to catch the pollen.

Fig. 11.19: Wind-pollinated flower

Fig. 11.20: Insect-pollinated flower

Insect-pollinated flowers are usually bright because the petals are large and brightly coloured (Fig. 11.20). These flowers are showy, with a sweet odour and contain nectar. The pollens are sticky or have spikes. The anthers are firm and are inside the flower to brush against the body of the insect. The stigma is firm and inside the flower, with a sticky surface.

Water-pollinated flowers get pollinated through water. Some aquatic plants release their pollen grains (often hydrophobic and float on the water's surface) in the water which are carried by the flowing water. The stigma is typically feathery or branched to help in capturing pollen grains carried by water currents.

Fertilization: Soon after fertilization, the pollen grain on the stigma develops a tube. This thin tube called the **pollen tube**, contains the male gamete. It grows through the style right down to reach the ovary. Once inside the ovary, it enters the ovule. The male gamete travels through this tube and fuses with the female gamete. *The process of fusion of the male and female gamete is known as **fertilization***. The fertilized cell is known as the **zygote**. The ovule develops into a seed and the ovary into the fruit. The zygote is the first cell formed after fertilization. The zygote divides and develops to form an embryo. Cells inside the embryo then become differentiated and develop into shoots and roots (Fig. 11.21).

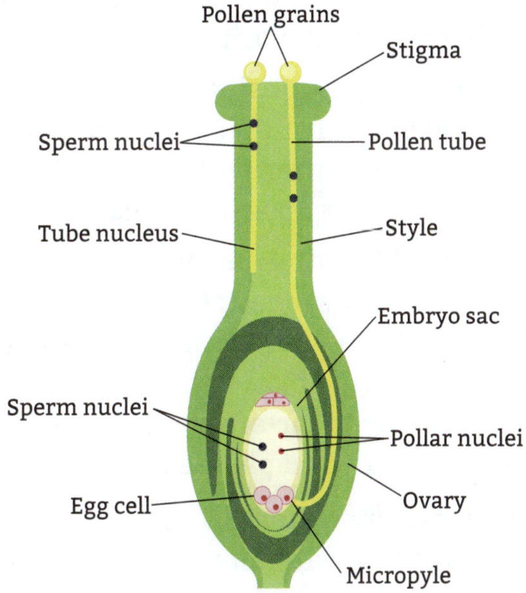

Fig. 11.21: Fertilization in a flower

Fruit and seed formation: The function of the flower is to help in fertilization. After fertilization, the flower becomes redundant. So, the sepals wither, the corolla (petals) wither, followed by the stamens, stigma and style. The ovary then develops into a fruit and the ovules develop into seeds (Fig. 11.22).

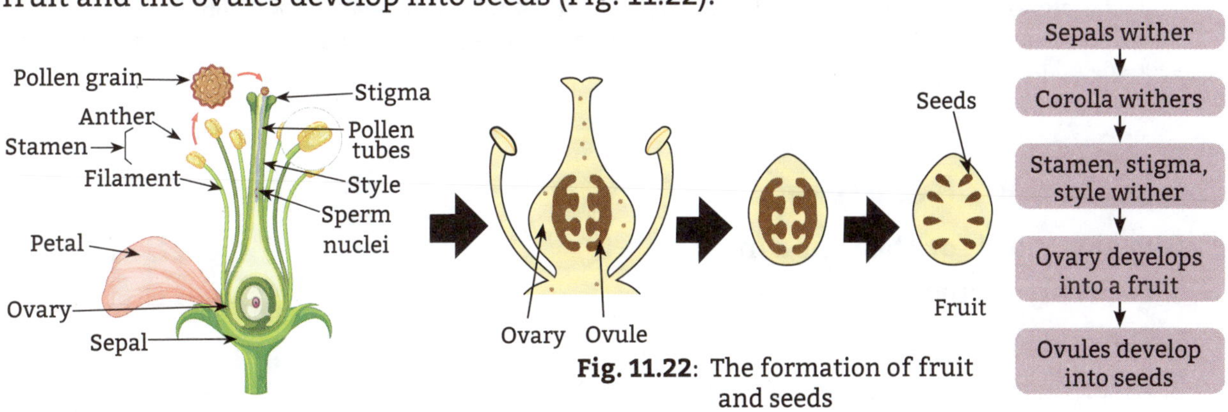

Fig. 11.22: The formation of fruit and seeds

SEED DISPERSAL

Once the seeds dry, they get dispersed. ***Seed dispersal** is the scattering of seeds over a large area by various means.* The different means of seed dispersal are wind, water, animals and the explosion of fruits.

Different means of seed dispersal help the plants as it helps the seeds to reach a suitable medium for germination, far away from the parent plant (Fig. 11.23).

Dispersal by explosion: In this method, the pod or the fruit bursts open with great force, scattering the seeds inside it. Examples: balsam and pea plants

Dispersal by wind: Seeds that are dispersed by wind have winged structures or tuft of hair that aid in being carried away by wind. When the wind blows, these seeds are easily blown away to far-off places. Examples: dandelion and maple seeds

Dandelion (dispersal by wind)

Coconut (dispersal by water)

Cocklebur (dispersal by animals)

Peas (dispersal by explosion)

Fig. 11.23: Different means of seed dispersal

Dispersal by water: Seeds that are dispersed by water have a spongy coat or a layer of fibre that makes them light. This property helps them to float on water. The flowing water then carries them to far-off places. Examples: coconut, foxglove and willow

Dispersal by animals: Some animals eat fruits and discard the seeds. Animals such as squirrel bury the seeds in the soil to hide them and then forget about it. Some birds eat the fruits along with the seeds and pass them out through their excreta. These seeds then germinate into new plants under favourable conditions.

Activity

Collect different kinds of seeds/seed pods/fruits such as Tridax, *Bidens pilosa* (cobbler's pegs), *Xanthium* (cocklebur), drumstick, balsam and Singapore cherry fruit. Draw the structure of the seeds/seed pods/fruits and write their means of dispersal.

Revise and Recall

Give one word for the following.

1. The reproductive part of a plant ____________
2. The male part of a flower ____________
3. After fertilization, the ovary develops into this ____________
4. The part of a flower that develops into seeds ____________
5. The structure that is carried from flower to flower during pollination ____________

Keywords

Reproduction: The process of producing new offspring of one's own kind

Asexual reproduction: Reproduction in which a single parent is involved

Vegetative propagation: New plants produced from vegetative parts such as root, stem and leaf of the parent plant

Unisexual flowers: Flowers that contain either stamen or pistil

Bisexual flowers: Flowers that contain both stamen and pistil

Pollination: The transfer of pollen grains from the anther to the stigma of the same flower or different flowers

Pollen tube: A hollow tube that develops from a pollen grain after pollination and grows down the style to the ovule, carrying the male gametes to bring about fertilization

Gametes: The male (pollen) and female (ovule) sex cells in a flower

Fertilization: The process of fusion of the pollen and egg cells to form the zygote

Seed dispersal: Scattering of seeds to far-off places by various means

Summary

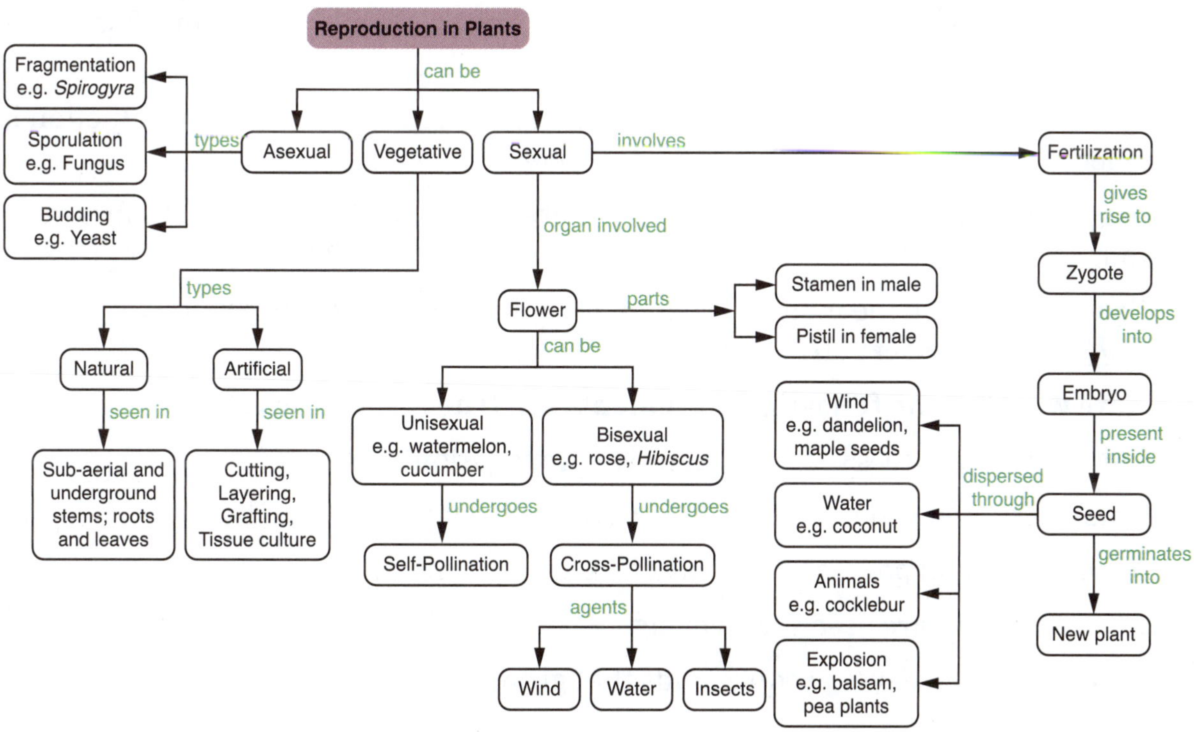

EXERCISE

W

ia

A. Choose the correct option.

1. Maria placed a leaf of *Bryophyllum* plant on moist sand. Several weeks later, she observed small leaflets growing from the edges of the leaf. This type of reproduction is called ______________.
   (a) fragmentation (b) vegetative propagation
   (c) budding (d) sporulation
2. The process of fusion of the male and the female gametes is called ______________.
   (a) fertilization (b) pollination (c) zygote (d) seed
3. Which of the following is not a characteristic of insect-pollinated flowers?
   (a) Spiky pollens (b) Bright, colourful petals
   (c) Dull coloured flowers (d) Sticky stigma
4. Seeds of maple and dandelion are dispersed by ______________.
   (a) wind (b) water (c) explosion (d) animals
5. Mature ovary forms the ______________.
   (a) seed (b) stamen (c) pistil (d) fruit

B. Fill in the blanks.

1. Asexual reproduction does not take place by ______________. (seeds/budding)
2. Flowers having both stamens and pistils are called ___________ flowers. (bisexual/unisexual)
3. If a new plant has to grow from an underground stem, the type of reproduction is called ________________ reproduction. (vegetative/asexual)
4. The process of vegetative propagation where the stem of a herb or a shrub is cut and planted in the ground is called ________________. (layering/cutting)
5. Flowers with only the male or the female reproductive part are called ______________. (bisexual/unisexual)

C. State whether the following statements are true (T) or false (F). ia

1. The 'eyes' in potatoes help in vegetative propagation. ☐
2. Stolons are lateral slender branches that arise from the base of the stem. ☐
3. Fertilization and pollination always take place at the same time. ☐
4. Stock and scion are used for layering. ☐
5. In *Bryophyllum*, leaves produce buds that grow into new plants. ☐

D. Name any two plants that undergo the following.

1. Asexual reproduction ______________ ______________
2. Vegetative propagation from stems ______________ ______________
3. Grafting ______________ ______________
4. Sexual reproduction ______________ ______________
5. Disperal of seeds by wind ______________ ______________

E. Give reasons for the following.

1. Coconut is a huge fruit but it floats on water.
2. Birds help in seed dispersal.
3. Sexual reproduction in plants involve the fertilization of gametes.
4. Pollination is essential for the formation of fruits.
5. Fungal spores remain dormant until favourable conditions are met.

F. Answer the following questions briefly.

1. List three examples of reproduction in plants through underground roots.
2. With the help of a diagram, explain how pollination leads to fertilization.
3. Explain sexual reproduction in a *Hibiscus* flower.

G. Answer the following questions in detail.

1. Compare and contrast the different types of asexual reproduction on the basis of the process, structures formed and the organisms in which it is found.
2. Explain how layering is different from grafting in the artificial method of reproduction in plants.

COGNITIVE CORNER

Critical Thinking

1. What will happen if the pollens of *Hibiscus* flower reach the stigma of a rose flower?
2. Do you think insect-pollinated flowers can also be pollinated by wind? Give reasons.

Picture Study

Correlate the structures of the flowers with the type of pollination most likely to occur.

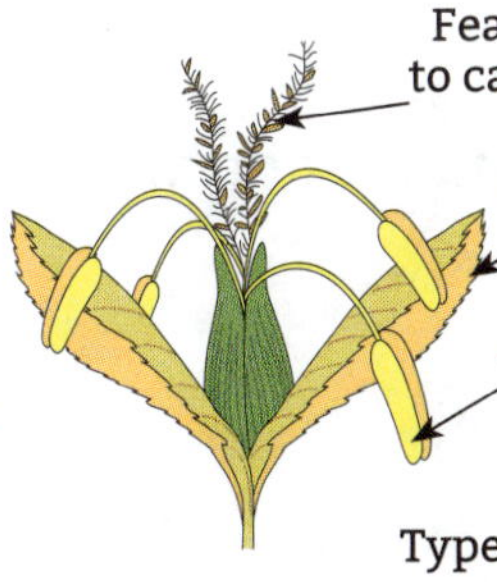

Type of pollination: ______________

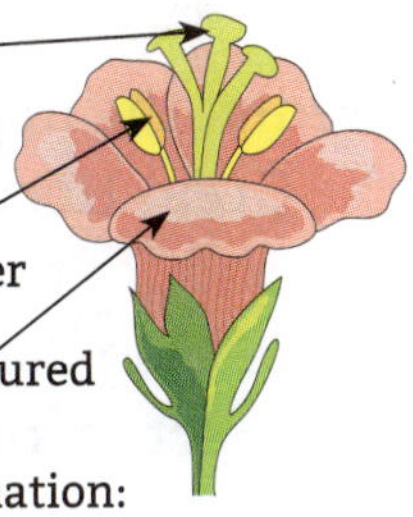

Type of pollination: ______________

Project

As a part of Eco Club activity, explore the process of reproduction in the commonly found money plant or any other plant available in your garden. Take about 20 cm of money plant and cut the stem into pieces of 5 cm length each. Place the cuttings in different pots or plant them near your classroom and water them regularly for some days until you notice the growth. Record the growth rate and the conditions you provided for growth. Can you vegetatively grow any other plant found near your school? **(C-7.2)**

In the Library

Find out the steps involved in artificial pollination and its advantages in horticulture. Share your inferences precisely with your classmates. **(C-7.1)**

In the Laboratory

Aim: To understand different modes of seed dispersal **(C-7.2)**
Materials required: 4–5 plastic beads (1 cm diameter), brown paper or wrapping sheet, two small-sized (5 cm diameter) plastic balls, water, one small (6”–10”) plastic tub, velcro sheets, 10 small (0.2 mm diameter) plastic beads, a pair of scissors, fevicol, double-sided tape
Procedure:

1. Wind dispersal: Cut a piece of brown paper in the shape of a maple seed wing and paste it on to the plastic beads.
2. Water dispersal: Place the plastic ball over the surface of water to show that it floats on water just like the water-dispersed seeds.
3. Animal dispersal: Paste the velcro sheet over the surface of the small plastic ball using glue or double-sided tape. This mimics the seeds with spikes.
4. Explosion of fruit: Put the smaller beads inside the balloon and blow it until it bursts, releasing the beads.

Life Skills

Predict the impact of destruction of forest habitat on any particular species such as the Great Hornbill. Reflect on the following:

A. Food for the birds and other species
B. Nesting places
C. Effect on the web of life

Conduct research on the same. Write a brief report based on your findings. **(C-7.3)**

Worksheet

Rose cultivation is practised as a hobby by many enthusiasts who try to create roses of new colours by combining rose plants of existing colours. The most popular method used is by grafting.

Rose cultivation is becoming more and more popular because of its increase in demand as cut flower and higher commercial gains. Hybrid Teas are one of the most recognized and popular cut flowers. Some of the other popular cut flowers are Ottavia Missoni, Pretty Lady, etc.

A rainbow rose

Stem Grafting

A. What are the other advantages of this method?

____

____

____

____

____

____

____

____

____

____

____

B. Which characteristic should belong to the two parts involved in stem grafting?

1. The plant should be hardy and resistant to diseases ____________________
2. The flowers should be delicate and pretty ____________________

12 Time and Motion

Curricular Goals

- Explore the physical world in scientific and mathematical terms **(CG-2)**
- Explore the nature and processes of science through engaging with the evolution of scientific knowledge and conducting scientific inquiry **(CG-6)**
- Communicate questions, observations and conclusions related to science **(CG-7)**

Competencies

- Describe one-dimensional motion using physical measurements through mathematical and diagrammatic representations **(C-2.1)**
- Formulate questions using scientific terminology and collect data as evidence **(C-6.2)**
- Use scientific vocabulary to communicate science accurately in oral and written form, and through visual representation **(C-7.1)**
- Represent real world events and relationships through diagrams and simple mathematical representations **(C-7.3)**

Let's Get Started

Look at the pictures given below and answer the questions that follow.

(a) At what time do you wake up in the morning? ____________________

(b) At what time do you get ready for school? ____________________

(c) How long does it take to reach your school? ____________________

(d) How long is each period in your school? ____________________

(e) At what time do you come back home? ____________________

(f) At what time do you go to bed? ____________________

Is time measurement necessary in our life? What will happen to most of the activities that we do on a routine basis in the absence of time measurement?

MEASUREMENT OF TIME

In the absence of accurate time measurement, it will be difficult for us to do things on time such as waking up, getting dressed and going to school on time. In ancient times, when there were no time-measuring devices such as clocks, people relied on natural phenomena to keep track of time.

Our ancestors depended on natural, repetitive events such as sunrise and sunset, phases of the moon and revolution of the Earth to measure time.

The time interval between one sunrise to the next was considered as a **day**. The time interval between one sunset to the next immediate sunrise was considered as **night**. The time interval between one new moon and the next was considered as a **month**. The time taken by the Earth to complete one revolution around the sun was considered as a **year**.

Evolution of the Clock

As time progressed, the need to measure time intervals much shorter than a day was felt; this paved the way for the evolution of clocks. Many devices have been invented to measure time. The study of these devices as well as the study and measurement of time is called **horology**. Some instruments used for the measurement of short intervals of time are discussed below:

Sundial: A sundial has a circular plate with a triangular metallic plate called **gnomon** (pronounced as nō-man) fixed at its centre, pointed at an angle (Fig. 12.1). The device is placed in open sunlight in such a way that the gnomon points in the north-south direction. The shadow of gnomon on the circular plate indicates the time.

Fig. 12.1: Sundial

The major drawback of using a sundial is that the device cannot be used during night time and cloudy days when there are no sunrays falling on the device.

Wonder!

The Jantar Mantar in Jaipur has the largest sundial in the world. The Jantar Mantar was built by Maharaja Sawai Jai Singh II of Jaipur. He was a visionary ruler known for his significant contributions to various fields, particularly astronomy, mathematics and architecture.

Water clock: The Greeks invented water clocks to measure time at night. It was based on the rising and falling of a liquid column. Time was measured by the regulated flow of liquid into or out of a vessel. The drawback with water clocks was that they required regular monitoring as the rate of flow of water would vary with temperature (Fig. 12.2).

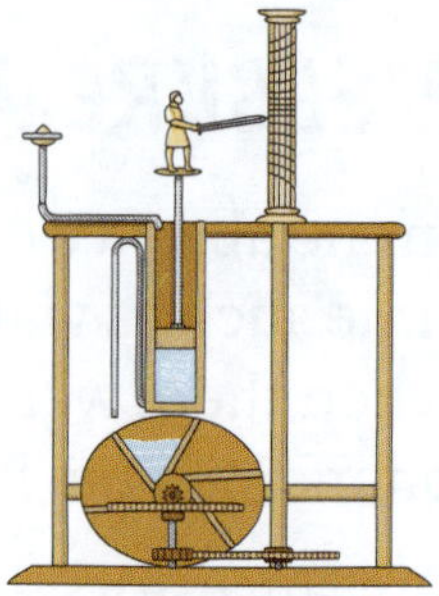

Fig. 12.2: Water clock

Sand clock: A sand clock is also known as an **hourglass**. It was invented by a French monk called Liutprand in the 8th century AD. It measures the passage of a few minutes or an hour of time.

A sand clock has two vertical glass bulbs allowing a regulated trickle of sand from top to bottom. Once the top bulb is emptied, it can be inverted to begin timing again. These days hourglasses are ornamental or used as egg timers for cooking and for board games (Fig. 12.3).

Fig. 12.3: Sand clock

Pendulum clock: As the name suggests, a pendulum clock is based on a pendulum. Let us first understand what a pendulum is and then learn how it is used in pendulum clocks.

A **simple pendulum** has a metallic bob suspended from a rigid stand by a thread. The rest position of the bob is called the mean position or equilibrium position. When displaced, the bob of the pendulum undergoes a 'to-and-fro motion'.

The pendulum is said to have completed one oscillation when the bob moves from one extreme position (A) to the other (B) and back (Fig. 12.4).

*The time taken by the pendulum to complete one oscillation is called the **time period.***

The time period of a simple pendulum varies with the length of the thread, but does not vary with the mass of the bob or with the distance of the bob from the mean position (for small distances).

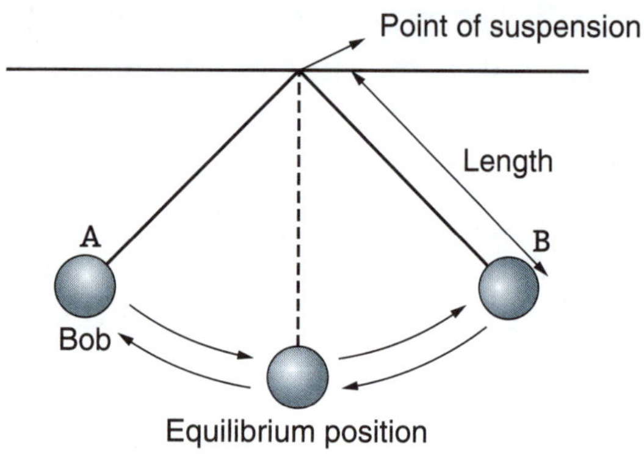

Fig. 12.4: Pendulum

The oscillations of a simple pendulum are periodic, that is, they repeat themselves at fixed intervals. Such a motion is called **periodic motion**. In pendulum clocks, the periodic motion of a pendulum is used to move the hand, which indicates the time.

The pendulum in a pendulum clock swings continuously under the influence of wound up springs (or batteries) and controls the action of its hands.

Science in Context

It is said that famous Italian astronomer Galileo Galilei was sitting in a church when he happened to notice that a lamp suspended from the ceiling with a chain was moving slowly from one side to the other. He was surprised to find that his pulse beat the same number of times during the interval in which the lamp completed one oscillation. Galileo experimented with various pendulums to verify his observation. He found that a pendulum of a given length always takes the same time to complete one oscillation. This observation led to the development of pendulum clocks. Although Galileo made these observations, he did not go on to complete it. The pendulum clock was invented in 1656 by Dutch scientist and inventor Christiaan Huygens.

Activity

Aim: To verify constancy of time period of a pendulum

Materials required: Retort stand, string measuring 1 metre, split rubber cork, pendulum weights of different masses and stopwatch

Procedure:

1. Set up a simple pendulum using the retort stand, metallic bob and the string. Use the split rubber cork at the suspension point of the retort stand so that the string is suspended firmly. Make sure that it moves freely.
2. Keep the stopwatch ready. Pull the bob a little away to your left from the mean position and hold. Release the bob gently and start the stopwatch simultaneously.
3. Measure the time taken for five oscillations.
4. Perform two more trials.
5. Record your observation and tabulate your readings.

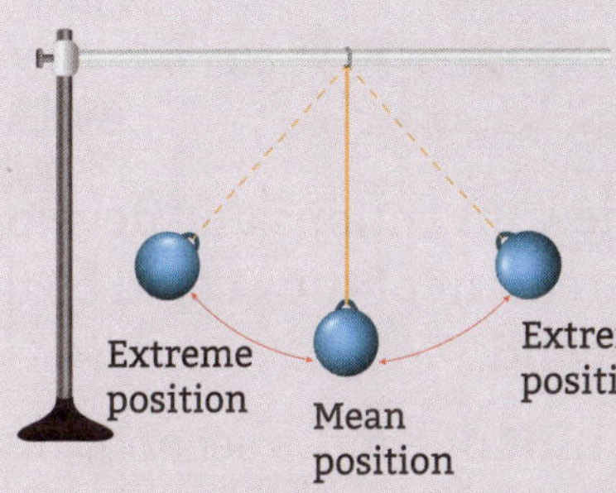

S. no.	Time taken for 5 oscillations	Time period
1.		
2.		
3.		

Conclusion: Time taken by the pendulum remains constant.

Quartz clock: With the invention of quartz crystal in 1921 and the quartz clock in 1927, timekeeping accuracy was highly improved, replacing pendulum clocks (Fig. 12.5).

Fig. 12.5: Quartz clock

Wonder!

Quartz crystals are piezoelectric, which means that they generate an electrical charge when mechanical pressure is applied to them. They also vibrate when placed in an electric field. These vibrations are converted by suitable means to measure time.

Science in Context

A quartz timepiece can keep time accurately to about one second every 10 years.

Atomic clock: An **atomic** clock is a device that uses an electronic transition frequency in the ultraviolet region of the electromagnetic spectrum of atoms as the standard. Atomic clocks are the most accurate timekeeping devices (Fig. 12.6).

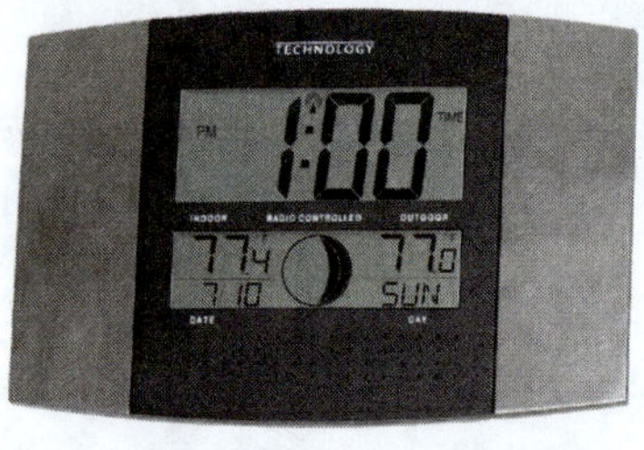

Fig. 12.6: Atomic clock

Quartz clocks and atomic clocks are considered as accurate time-measuring devices, atomic clocks being more accurate than quartz clocks.

Science in Context

Atomic clocks are also called **caesium clocks**. Their working is based on the radiation released by each of the atoms present in the material. The Indian Space Research Organisation (ISRO) has developed an atomic clock that will be used in navigation satellites to measure precise location data.

Units of Time

With new inventions and developments in the time-measuring devices, the measurement of time could be taken beyond a day to the level of an **hour**, **minute** and **second**.

The **SI unit** of time is second.

The relationship between various time-measuring units is given below:

1 day = 24 hours, 1 hour = 60 minutes and 1 minute = 60 seconds

Different units of time are used based on the requirement. For example, it is appropriate to mention the age of a person in years, the time for short travelling distances in hours and the running time of an athlete in minutes or seconds.

7 days = 1 week

4 weeks = 1 month

12 months = 1 year

10 years = 1 decade

10 decades = 1 millennium

Science in Context

Nowadays, there are special clocks which can measure time less than a second. These clocks are used in scientific research.

1 second = 10^6 microsecond

1 second = 10^9 nanosecond

SLOW AND FAST MOTION

Figure 12.7 shows some vehicles moving on a road in the same direction. Among these vehicles, which is the fastest and the slowest?

The distance moved by an object in a given interval of time or the time taken for covering a fixed distance will help us decide whether a vehicle is moving faster or slower.

Therefore, vehicle D moves the fastest as it covers the distance of 500 m in 19 seconds and vehicle B moves the slowest as it covers the same distance in 25 seconds.

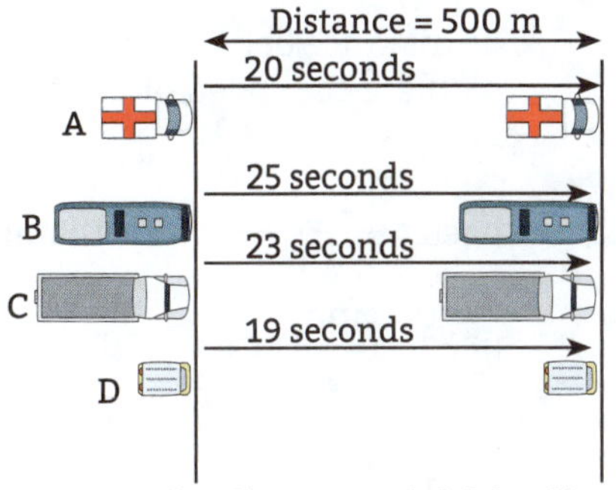

Fig. 12.7: Initial and final positions of vehicles

Speed

The distance covered by a body in unit time is called **speed**.

$$\text{Speed} = \frac{\text{Distance travelled}}{\text{Time taken}}$$

If we say that an object is moving at the speed of 50 km/h, it means that the object covers a distance of 50 km in one hour.

Units of speed

Usually, speed is denoted by kilometre per hour (km/h), but the SI unit of speed is metre per second (m/s). The unit of speed can be converted from km/h to m/s and vice versa.

$$1\ \text{km/h} = \frac{1000}{3600}\ \text{m/s}$$

$\frac{1000}{3600}$ can be simplified as $\frac{5}{18}$.

To convert km/h to m/s, the value needs to be multiplied by $\frac{5}{18}$.

$$\text{And } 1\ \text{m/s} = \frac{\frac{1}{1000}\ \text{km}}{\frac{1}{3600}\ \text{h}}$$

$\frac{3600}{1000}$ can be simplified as $\frac{18}{5}$.

To convert m/s to km/h, the value needs to be multiplied by $\frac{18}{5}$.

Wonder!

A fighter jet aircraft can travel at a speed of about 2400 km/h (666.6 m/s), which is almost 2.35 times the speed of sound.

Solved Example

The distance between two stations is 120 km. A train takes about 3 hours to cover the distance. Calculate the speed of the train.

Solution:

Speed = $\frac{\text{Distance}}{\text{Time}}$ Distance covered = 120 km Time = 3 h

Speed = $(\frac{120}{3})$ km/h = 40 km/h

Every vehicle has a speedometer console, which consists of a speedometer and an odometer. The speedometer indicates the instantaneous speed of the vehicle while the odometer displays the distance travelled (Fig. 12.8).

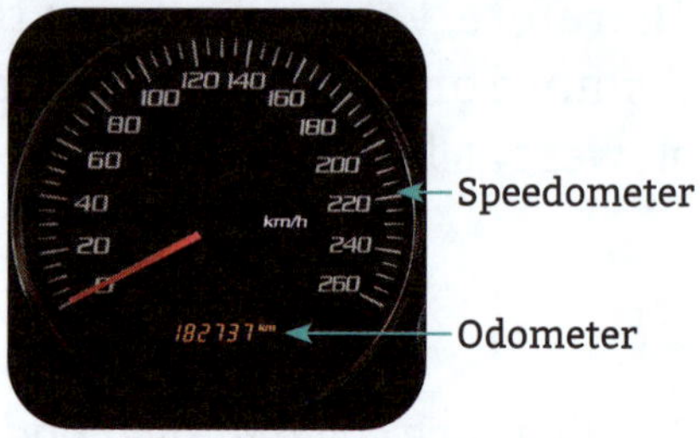

Fig. 12.8: Speedometer console

Uniform and Non-Uniform Speed

Observe some vehicles moving on the road. Do they cover equal distances in equal intervals of time? You will find that vehicles keep changing their speed throughout their motion. Vehicles generally do not move with a constant speed.

If an object covers equal distances in equal intervals of time (however small it is), it is said to be moving with **uniform speed** *or* **constant speed**. *Such an object is said to be in* ***uniform motion***.

If an object covers unequal distances in equal intervals of time or equal distances in unequal intervals of time, it is said to be moving with **non-uniform speed** *or* **varying speed.** *Such an object is said to be in* ***non-uniform motion.***

In daily life, it is rare to find any object moving with a constant speed, and so we calculate the average speed of the objects in motion.

$$\text{Average speed} = \frac{\text{Total distance travelled}}{\text{Total time taken}}$$

DISTANCE–TIME GRAPH

a

The distance travelled and time taken can be presented in many forms. The simplest of all is a table as shown alongside:

Distance (metres)	Time (seconds)
0	0
5	1
10	2
15	3

The data given in the table can also be presented as a line graph shown alongside. A line graph is drawn by plotting the data into *X*- and *Y*-axes and joining the points. In the line graph shown here, the distance covered has been taken on the *Y*-axis and the time taken to cover that distance on the *X*-axis.

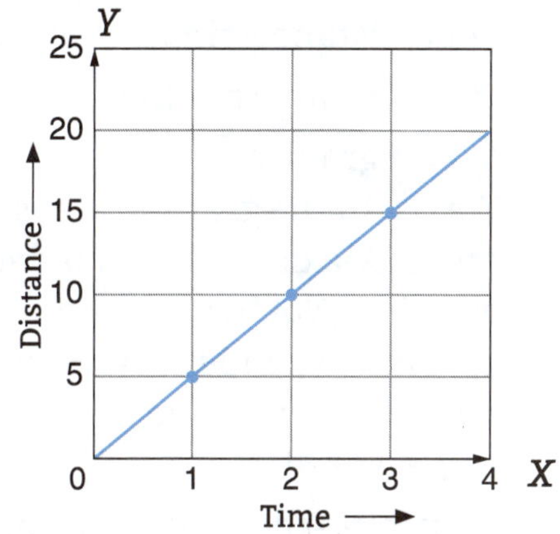

If an object is stationary (that is, at rest) with respect to time, then we get a horizontal line (parallel to the time axis) on the distance–time graph. Time increases to the right, but distance does not change (Fig. 12.9 (a)).

If an object is moving at a steady speed, it covers equal distances over equal intervals of time. Time increases to the right and distance increases steadily with time. This is the condition of uniform speed. The distance–time graph for uniform motion gives a straight line (Fig. 12.9 (b)).

If an object is moving with varying speed, it covers unequal distances for equal intervals of time. Time increases to the right and distance increases unsteadily with time. This is the condition of non-uniform speed. The distance–time graph for a non-uniform motion is a curve (Fig. 12.9 (c)).

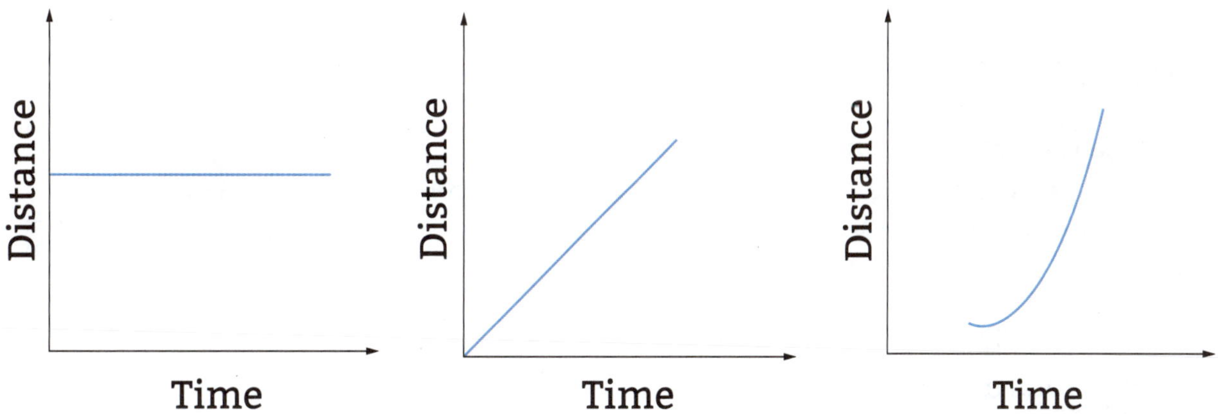

(a) Stationary object (b) Object moving with uniform speed (c) Object moving with non-uniform speed

Fig. 12.9: Distance–time graph

Plotting a distance–time graph

To plot a distance–time graph, follow the steps given below:

1. Tabulate your readings.
2. Take a graph sheet, draw *X*-axis and *Y*-axis. In the graph, always plot time on the *X*-axis as it is an independent variable. Plot distance on the *Y*-axis as it is a dependent variable. Time is measured in seconds (s) and distance is measured in metres (m).
3. Distribute the values appropriately for distance and time on the graph.
4. Look into the tabular column and identify the points on the graph where the body reaches a certain a distance at a particular time. Do the same for all the values of distance and time.

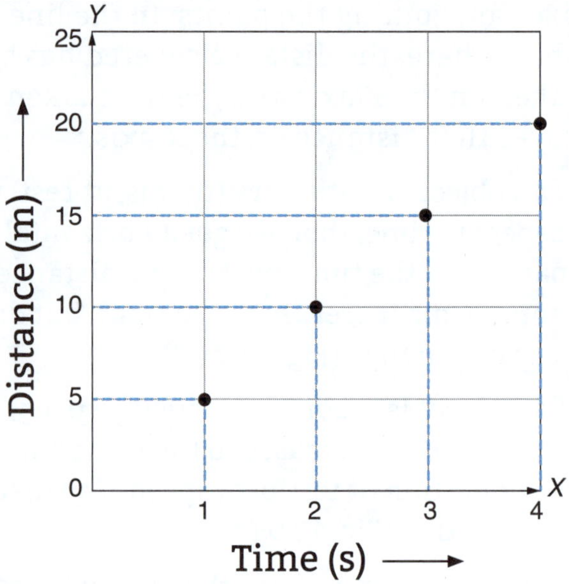

Distance (m)	0	5	10	15	20
Time (s)	0	1	2	3	4

Revise and Recall

Choose the correct option.

1. A car travels with a uniform speed of 60 km/h. What would be the time taken by the car to travel a distance of 180 km?
   (a) 1 h (b) 2 h (c) 3 h (d) 4 h
2. Average speed is calculated by
   (a) $\frac{\text{Total distance}}{\text{Total time}}$ (b) $\frac{\text{Total time}}{\text{Total distance}}$
   (c) $\frac{\text{Speed 1} + \text{Speed 2}}{2}$ (d) None of these
3. A boy has to cover 20 km in 2 h. What should be his speed?
   (a) 10 km/h (b) 20 km/h (c) 1/10 km/h (d) 40 km/h

Keywords

Time period: The time taken by a pendulum to complete one oscillation

Oscillation: One complete to-and-fro motion of a pendulum bob from its mean position

Speed: The distance covered by a body in unit time

Speedometer: A device that measures the speed of a vehicle

Odometer: A device that measures the distance travelled by a vehicle

Uniform speed: The speed of a body that covers equal distances in equal intervals of time

Non-uniform speed: The speed of a body that covers unequal distances in equal intervals of time or equal distances in unequal intervals of time

Summary

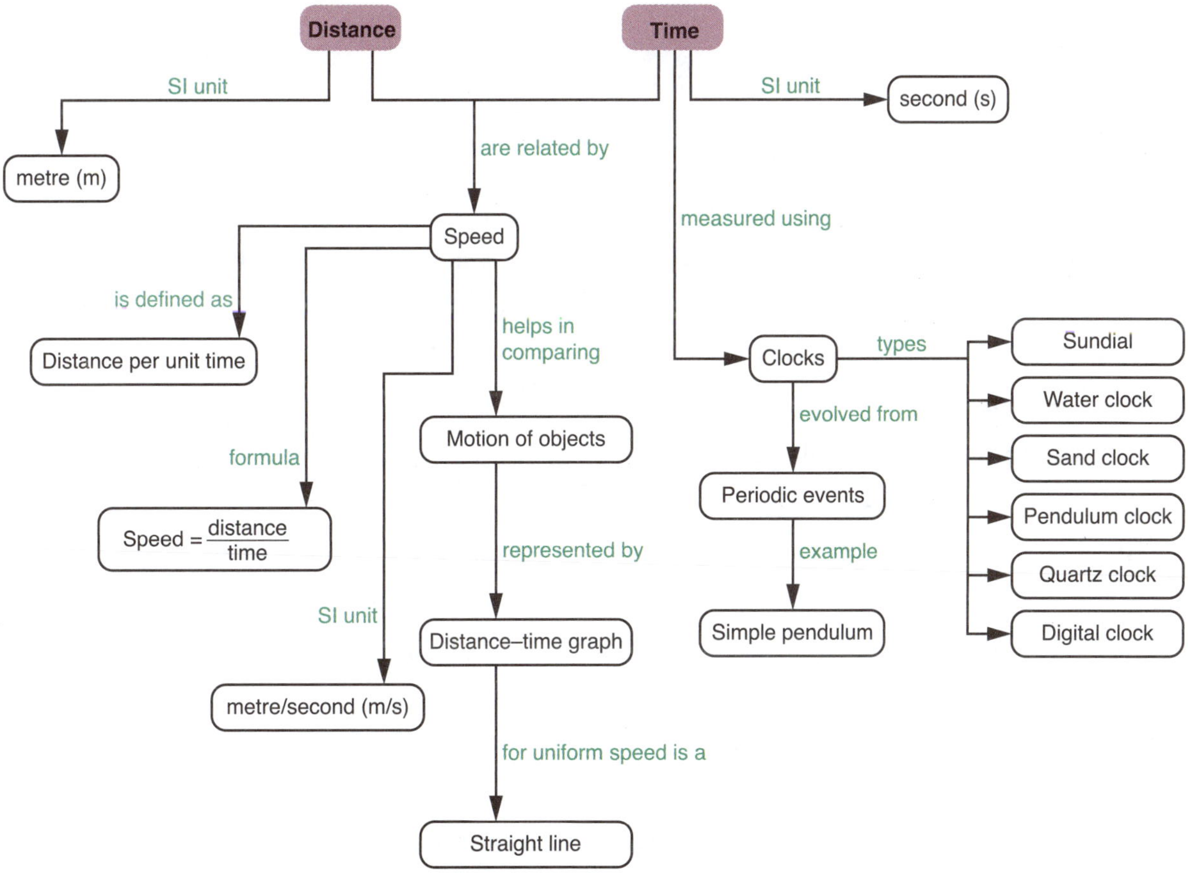

EXERCISE

A. Choose the correct option.

1. The SI unit of speed is ______________.

   (a) m/s (b) km/h (c) km/min (d) m/min

2. Which of the following formulae is used to calculate distance?

   (a) $\frac{\text{Speed}}{\text{Time}}$ (b) Speed × Time

   (c) $\frac{\text{Time}}{\text{Speed}}$ (d) 1/(Time × Speed)

3. Which of the following devices was invented by the Greeks to measure the time at night?

   (a) Sundial (b) Hourglass (c) Water clock (d) Atomic clock

4. The distance–time graph for an object at rest is:

   (a)
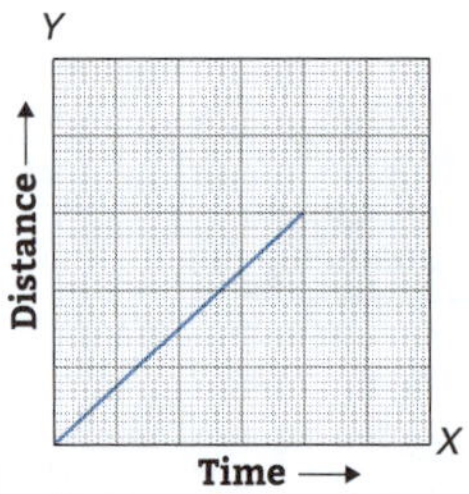

   (b)
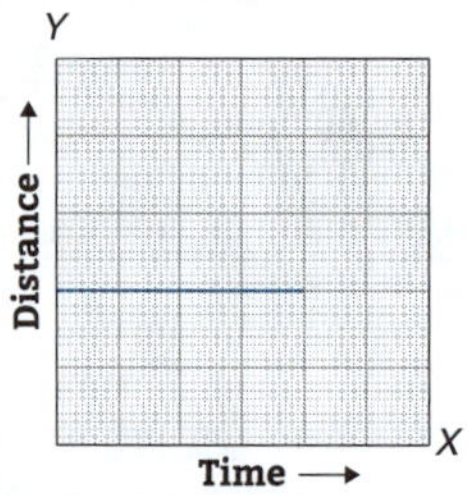

   (c)
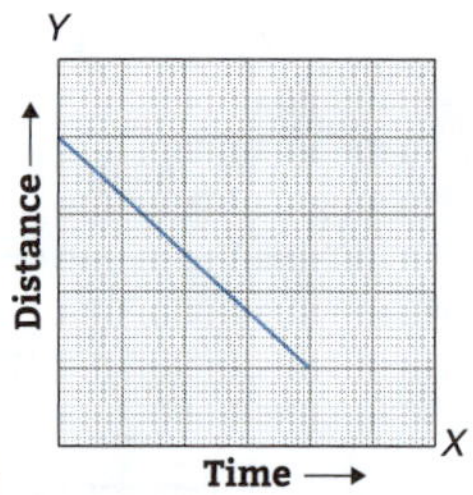

   (d)
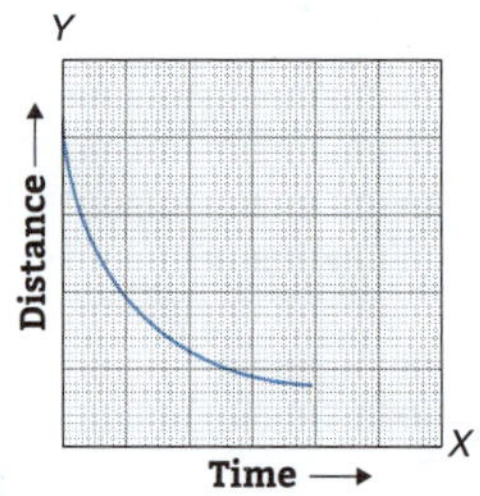

5. John takes 10 minutes to reach his school from his house. The distance of his school from his house is 1.2 km. What is his speed during this journey?

   (a) 2 m/s (b) 2 km/min (c) 20 m/min (d) 20 km/h

B. Fill in the blanks.

1. The time taken by a simple pendulum to complete one oscillation is called ______________. (speed/time period)
2. The object suspended at the free end of the string of a simple pendulum is called ______________. (bob/gnomon)
3. The distance moved by an object in unit time is called ______________. (time period/speed)
4. A simple pendulum completes 15 oscillations in 30 seconds. The time period of the pendulum is ______________ seconds. (2/30)
5. If the speed of an object in motion is constant, such a motion is called ______________. (uniform/non-uniform)

C. State whether the following statements are true (T) or false (F).

1. Speed is the distance covered by a body in unit time. ☐
2. The distance–time graph for uniform motion is always a curve. ☐
3. Sundials could not be used at night for timekeeping. ☐
4. Periodic motion of a pendulum has been used to make clocks and watches. ☐

D. Define the following terms.

1. Day
2. Gnomon
3. Time period
4. Speed
5. Horology
6. Uniform motion

E. Give reasons for the following.

1. The time period of a given simple pendulum is constant.
2. Sundial cannot be used on a cloudy day or at night.
3. In our day-to-day life, it is rare to find an object moving with constant speed.
4. The distance-time graph for uniform motion gives a straight line.
5. A car is moving with a speed of 25 m/s and and a bus is moving with a speed of 90 km/h. Both the vehicles are moving with the same speed.

F. Answer the following questions briefly.

1. Graphically represent the nature of the distance–time graph of motion of the given objects.
   (a) An athlete running with constant speed
   (b) A train waiting at a station for another train to pass by
2. A water clock is better for measuring time than a sundial. Why?
3. Differentiate between periodic and non-periodic motion with examples.
4. Define speed. Mention the SI unit of speed.

G. Answer the following questions in detail.

1. (a) The length of a simple pendulum is increased. What happens to its time period?
   (b) The mass of the pendulum bob is doubled. What will happen to its time period?
2. What is distance–time graph? What is the nature of the distance–time graph of a body in the following cases? Represent graphically.
   (a) The body is at rest
   (b) The body is moving with constant speed
   (c) The body is moving with varying speed

COGNITIVE CORNER

Critical Thinking

1. Identify biological process in our body that is nearly periodic and that can be used to measure time.
2. A pendulum takes 1 second to move from one extreme end to other extreme end. This pendulum is used in a clock to move the seconds hand. How many oscillations are required to make the seconds hand to complete 1 minute?
3. Car X covered 125 m in 5 s. Car Y covered 150 m in 15 s.
   (a) Which car will cover a greater distance in 30 s?
   (b) Which car has a higher speed?

Picture Study

The picture given here is the speedometer console of a sports car. What is the speed of the car?

Project

Find out the average speed with which you travel from your home to school daily (consider a situation where you don't take breaks during your journey).

Each type of vehicle has a speed limit on the road, that is, they can travel at a certain speed and should not cross the speed limit. Look up the speed limit of the vehicle you have chosen from the Internet and make a note of it and show it to your teacher. **(C-7.3)**

In the Library

Speedometer gives us the information on the speed with which the vehicle is moving. Find out how the speedometer measures the speed of the vehicle when it is moving. Make a report on the same. **(C-7.1)**

Life Skills

Look at a two-wheeler or four-wheeler at your home or at your neighbours' and try to find out the total distance travelled by the vehicle from the date of purchase. Also, try to find the name of the device fixed to the vehicle which gives you the information on distance travelled. **(C-7.1)**

Worksheet

A pedometer is an instrument for estimating the distance travelled on foot by recording the number of steps taken.

A portable and usually an electronic device, pedometer measures our steps because our body swings from side to side as we walk. Each swing counts as one step.

Research has shown that pedometers are effective tools in encouraging a healthy and active lifestyle. Walking is often an overlooked exercise, as it looks ordinary, but it can be the tool you need to achieve healthy lifestyle.

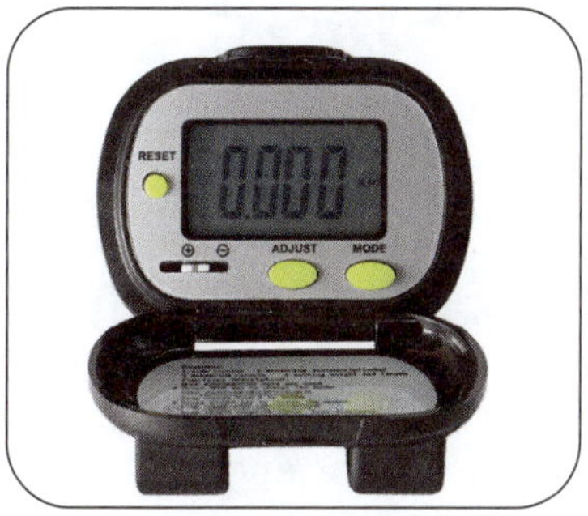

Pedometer

A woman jogging with a pedometer

Be your own pedometer!

Take a few steps and measure the distance between the steps in centimetres. ________________

Convert the value to kilometres. ________________

Now write down how much distance you wish to cover each day in kilometres. ________________

How will you calculate the total steps that you need to take?

Just divide the distance by the measurement of your stride. ________________

You can now set a goal of the distance you wish to walk each day and count off the steps as you walk!

This is what the pedometer does electronically. It displays the number of steps you have taken and displays the distance you have walked by multiplying the number of steps with the length of your stride.

13 Electric Current and its Effects

Curricular Goals

- Explore the physical world in scientific and mathematical terms **(CG-2)**
- Understand the interface of science, technology and society **(CG-5)**
- Explore the nature and processes of science through engaging with the evolution of scientific knowledge and conducting scientific inquiry **(CG-6)**

Competencies

- Describe how electricity works through manipulating different elements in simple circuits and demonstrate the heating and magnetic effects of electricity **(C-2.2)**
- Illustrate how science and technology can help to improve the quality of human life (judicious consumption of resources) **(C-5.1)**
- Formulate questions using scientific terminology and collect data as evidence **(C-6.2)**

Let's Get Started

Electricity has an important role in our day-to-day life. It is used for running computers and most appliances, home heating and even for transportation. It is the most useful form of energy and can be converted to other forms of energy such as heat, light, chemical or mechanical energy.

The pictures given below show various sources of energy used to produce electricity. Identify these sources.

__________ __________ __________

__________ __________ __________

ELECTRIC CURRENT

You already know that a cell or a battery is a source of electrical energy. Electrical energy is converted into light energy when a bulb is connected across a cell circuit. This is possible because of the constant flow of charges from one terminal to the other terminal of a cell through the external circuit.

The flow of charges through a circuit is called ***electric current***. The SI unit of electric current is **ampere** and is denoted by **A**. The direction of the electric current is conventionally from the positive terminal to the negative terminal of a cell.

Electric Circuit

An electric circuit is a complete path for the flow of electric current. It consists of a source of electrical energy (cell or battery), devices which use the electrical energy, a switch and connecting wires. These are called the **components** of the circuit or **circuit elements**.

If any part of a circuit is broken or disconnected, electric current does not flow through it. This type of circuit is called an **open circuit** (Fig. 13.1).

If there are no breaks in a circuit, then it provides a continuous or closed path for the flow of electric current. This type of circuit is called a **closed circuit** (Fig. 13.1). Electric current can flow only through closed circuits.

Open circuit Closed circuit

Fig. 13.1: Open and closed circuits

Components of an Electric Circuit

Cell or battery: A cell is a source of electric current. It has a positive and a negative terminal. When two or more cells are connected such that the positive terminal of one cell touches the negative terminal of the other, it forms a battery.

Switch: A switch is used to close or open a circuit. When the switch is in the OFF position, the circuit is open and no current flows through it. When the switch is in the ON position, the circuit is closed allowing the current to flow.

Electrical appliance: An electrical appliance is a device that uses the electric current flowing through it to function. Electric bulb, electric iron, fan and electric motor are some commonly used electrical appliances in our daily life.

Wires: Wires connect the elements of the electric circuit. They are made up of materials that are good conductors of electricity.

Circuit Diagram

A schematic diagram that represents an electric circuit using the standard symbols of the components used in the circuit is called a ***circuit diagram****.*

Table 13.1: Standard symbols for some components of electric circuits

Component	Standard symbol
Electric cell	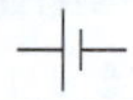
Battery	
Electric switch (open)	
Electric switch (closed)	
Electric bulb	
Electric fuse	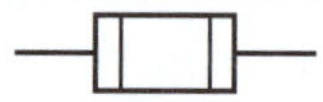
Connecting wire	———

HEATING EFFECT OF ELECTRIC CURRENT

When electric current is passed through an electric circuit, does it produce any heat? Let us examine this with the help of a simple activity.

Activity 1

Aim: To understand the heating effect of electric current

Precaution: Do this activity only in the presence of an adult.

Materials required: A dry cell, torch bulb, wires and switch

Procedure:

1. With the help of an adult, make a circuit using the torch bulb, battery cell and a switch as shown in the figure.
2. Touch the bulb before you turn the switch on and feel the temperature.
3. Now, turn on the switch and let the bulb glow for some time, say 10 seconds.
4. Turn off the switch and touch the bulb again.
5. Wrap a cloth around your hand or wear cotton gloves before touching the hot bulb.

Observation: The bulb becomes hot when electric current is passed through it.

Conclusion: Electric current produces heat as it passes through an electric bulb.

Note: An electric bulb produces light due to the heating effect of current as the current flows through the filament of the bulb. This kind of bulb is called an incandescent bulb. This activity also proves that other forms of energy can be obtained from electrical energy.

In Activity 1, we saw that the bulb got heated up when current was passed through it. When electric current is passed through a conductor, it produces heat in the conductor and this effect is called the **heating effect of electric current**.

Word Web

[1]**Resistance**: The property of an electrical component to resist the flow of electric current

Electric irons, immersion heaters, hot plates, geysers and electric kettles are some of the electrical appliances used, which work on the heating effect of the electric current. All these devices consist of a tightly wound coil (called the heating element) that produces heat when current is passed through them. The heating element is made up of a metal alloy called **nichrome** (alloy of 80% nickel and 20% chromium). Nichrome wires have high resistance[1] to electric current and can withstand high temperatures. Due to these properties, it is a good material for making heating elements.

Electric Fuse

What would happen to a small torch bulb if you connect it across many cells? The filament of the bulb would get damaged due to the excess amount of current flowing through it. Such a damaged bulb is usually called a fused bulb. The filament of a fused bulb is broken or burned due to the flow of excess current (Fig. 13.2).

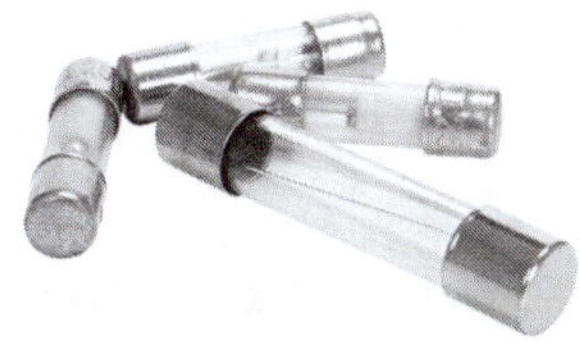

Fig. 13.2: Electric fuse

A large current can cause damage to electrical appliances and electric circuits in our homes. *A **fuse** or an **electric fuse** is a safety device made of a material with low melting point.* It is used to protect the electric circuit as well as devices in the circuit from the excess current passing through them.

Electric fuse works on the principle of the heating effects of electric current. The quantity of heat produced in a conductor by a current depends on the amount of current flowing through the conductor. There is a maximum limit on the current which can safely flow through a circuit. If by accident the current exceeds this safe limit, the wires may become overheated and may cause fire. The fuse wire is made from an alloy of tin and lead and melts easily when heated due to the passage of excess current. So, a proper fuse will blow off and break the circuit in such cases. Therefore, it prevents damages to electrical circuits and possible fires. The main characteristics of a fuse wire are that it must have a low melting point and relatively high resistance. Sometimes, fuse wires are covered by a glass case for added protection to ensure that they do not burn and cause damage.

Science in Context

A miniature circuit breaker (MCB) is a device that has one or more switches. It is an automatically operated switch, that moves to the OFF position when excess current flows through the circuit. It can be reset easily by pushing it back to the ON position unlike a fuse.

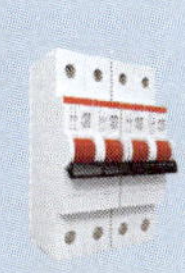

Revise and Recall

Fill in the blanks.

1. The flow of charges through a circuit is called ______________. (electrical energy/electric current)
2. Electric current can flow only through _______ circuits. (open/closed)
3. _______ is used to make the heating element. (Bauxite/Nichrome)
4. The SI unit of current is _________. (ampere/volt)

MAGNETIC EFFECT OF ELECTRIC CURRENT

a

In class 6, you have studied about magnets and their properties such as attraction and repulsion, and also the directional property. These properties are not restricted only to magnets. Electric current passing through a conductor can also show magnetic properties. Let us perform an activity to understand this.

Activity 2

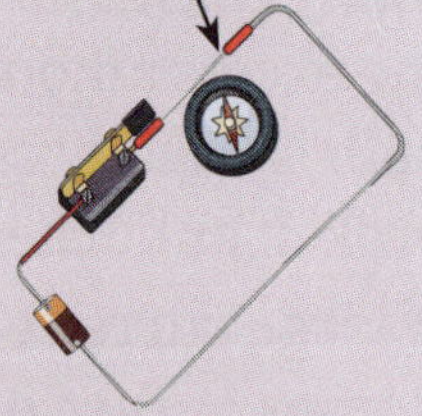

Aim: To show that an electric current passing through a conductor produces a magnetic effect

Precaution: Do this activity only in the presence of an adult.

Materials required: Dry cell, insulated copper wire, a switch and small magnetic compass

Procedure:

1. Keep the magnetic compass on the table and place the insulated copper wire next to it.
2. Connect the ends of the wire across a cell through a switch.
3. Note the position of the needle in the compass.
4. Turn on the switch and observe what happens to the needle.
5. Toggle the switch off and on, and observe the movement of the needle in the magnetic compass.

Observation: When a magnetic needle is placed near a current-carrying conductor, the needle shows deflection.

Conclusion: A current flowing through a conductor produces a magnetic effect.

Activity 2 shows that a current-carrying conductor produces the same effect as produced by the magnetic field of a magnet. This effect of current is called the **magnetic effect of electric current**.

Science in Context

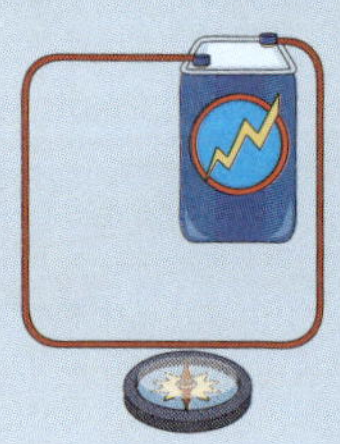

In 1820, Hans Christian Oersted, a Danish physicist and chemist experimentally proved that a current passing through a conductor produces magnetic effect. He performed an experiment using a magnetic needle kept close to a conductor carrying current. He noticed that the magnetic needle deflected whenever a current was passed through the conductor. He reversed the current and noticed that the magnetic needle deflected in the opposite direction when the direction of the current was reversed. This famous experiment is known as Oersted's experiment.

Solenoid

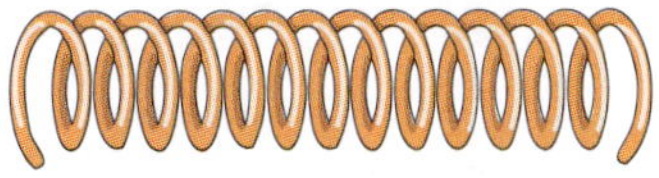

Fig. 13.3: Solenoid

A cylindrical-shaped coil that exhibits magnetic properties, similar to that of a bar magnet, when current is passed through it is called a **solenoid** (Fig. 13.3).

The strength of the magnetic field shown by a solenoid depends on the amount of current flowing through it and the number of turns of the coil.

Activity 3

Aim: To show that the strength of magnetic field of a solenoid depends on the current flowing through it and the number of turns of the coil

Materials required: Dry cells, insulated copper wire, switch, small magnetic compass and two small pipes of length about 5 cm and diameter about 2 cm

Procedure: Wind the insulated copper wire on one of the small pipes and make a solenoid of 10 turns. Wind the insulated copper wire on the other small pipe and make a solenoid of 20 turns.

Case 1:

1. Place the magnetic compass near any one end of one of the solenoids.
2. Connect the solenoid to a single cell.
3. Switch on the circuit and notice the deflection of the needle in the compass.
4. Now, connect two cells to the solenoid and observe the deflection of the needle in the compass. What change in the deflection do you observe?

Case 2:

1. Place the magnetic compass near the solenoid of 10 turns.
2. Connect the solenoid to a single cell and notice the deflection in the magnetic needle of the compass.
3. Repeat the same using the other solenoid of 20 turns and connecting across the same cell.
   What change in the deflection do you observe?

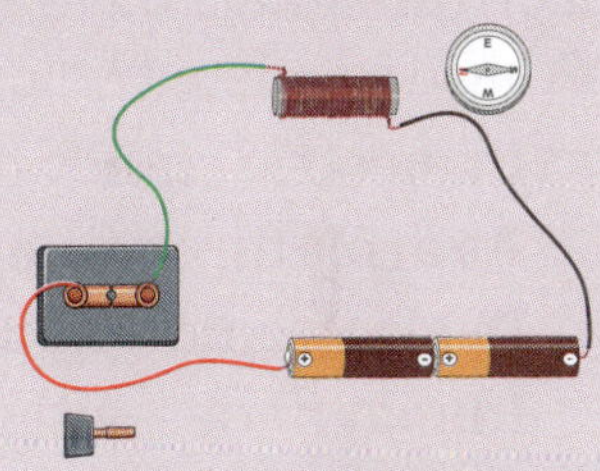

When switch is open

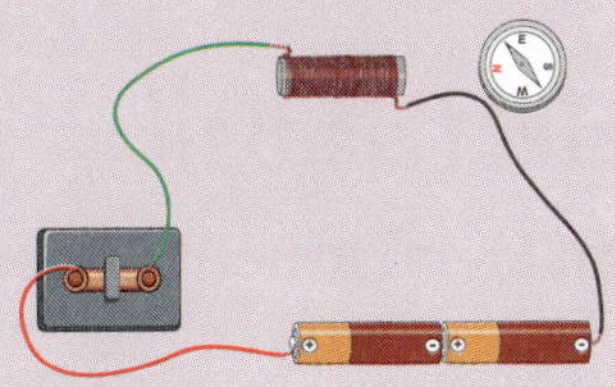

When switch is closed

Observation:

Case 1: Deflection in the needle of the compass is more when more cells are connected.

Case 2: Deflection in the needle of the compass is more when solenoid of more turns is used.

Conclusion: The strength of the magnetic field of a solenoid depends on the amount of current flowing through it and the number of turns.

Electromagnet

An ***electromagnet*** *is a device that acts as a magnet when a current flows through its coil.* It consists of a magnetic material such as a soft iron piece and a coil of insulated copper wire tightly wound around it. The material on which the insulated wire is wound is called its **core**. It is a temporary magnet that loses its magnetic properties when the current through the circuit is withdrawn.

Activity 4

Aim: To construct a simple electromagnet and to show that it is a temporary magnet
Materials required: Iron nail, insulated copper wire, switch, ball pins and dry cell
Procedure:

1. Wind the insulated copper wire on the iron nail from one end to the other.
2. Remove the insulation at the free ends of the copper wire.
3. Connect the ends of the wire across the terminals of a cell through a switch.
4. Bring one end of the iron nail near the ball pins kept on a table. What do you observe?
5. Now turn off the switch (disconnect the cell) and see what happens to the ball pins again.

Observation: Ball pins stick to the iron nail when the cell is connected to the coil. The pins fall down as soon as the cell is disconnected from the coil.

Conclusion: An electromagnet acts as a magnet as long as the current flows through it. It loses its magnetic property when the current through the circuit is withdrawn.

Note: Switch should not be kept in the ON position for a long time, in order to protect the cell. Large current flowing through the circuit discharges the cell soon.

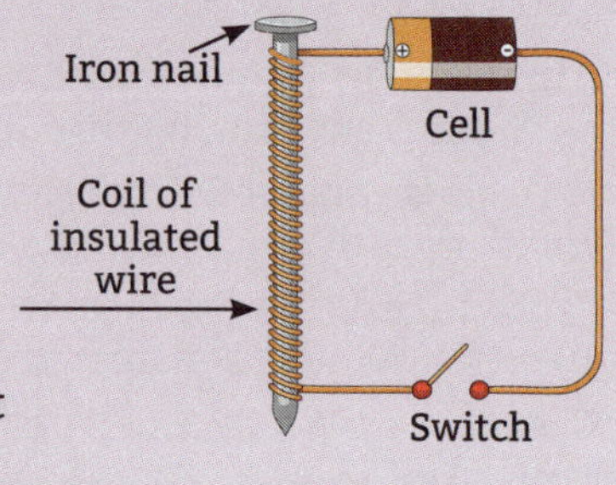

Applications of Electromagnets

Electromagnets have a variety of applications in industries and in our daily life. Some of these are listed below:

- In electric cranes to lift scrap iron
- As armature of electric motors
- In electronic devices such as television, radio and tape recorder
- In magnetic levitation trains, mechanical relay circuits and electric bells
- In CT/MRI scanning for medical diagnosis

Electric Bell

An **electric bell** is a device that works by the means of an electromagnet. A schematic diagram of an electric bell is shown in Fig. 13.4. It consists of an electromagnet, an armature made of thick iron bar fixed on a spring, a make-and-break arrangement with a screw S and an iron strip P.

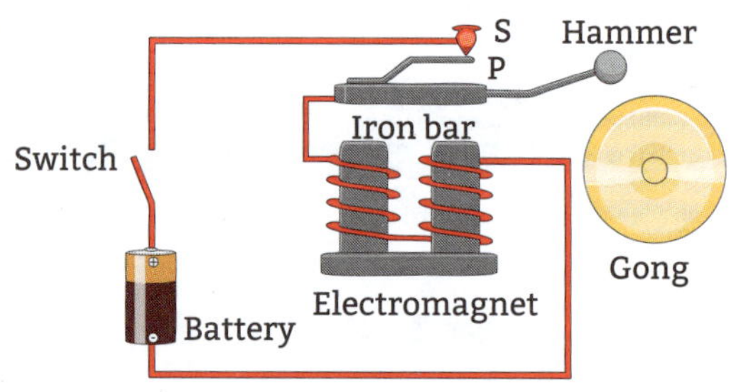

Fig. 13.4: Electric bell

When the switch is pressed, the current flows through the coil of the electromagnet. At this moment, it acts as a magnet and pulls the iron bar towards it. The hammer attached to the iron bar strikes the gong due to the motion of the iron bar towards the electromagnet. As the iron bar moves towards the electromagnet, the iron strip P loses its contact from the screw S. Hence, the circuit becomes a broken circuit and the current flowing through the coil is stopped.

Due to this, the electromagnet loses its magnetic power and the iron bar attached to the spring moves back to its initial position. In this position, it comes in contact with the screw again, closing the circuit. When the circuit is closed, the hammer will again hit the gong. This making and breaking of circuit continues till the switch is kept pressed and the hammer will repeatedly hit the gong to produce the ringing sound.

Keywords

Electric current: The flow of charges through circuit

Electric circuit: A closed path for the flow of electric current

Electric fuse: Safety device used to protect the devices and circuit from overloading and short circuits

Circuit diagram: A schematic diagram that represents an electrical circuit using the standard symbols of the components used in the circuit

Solenoid: A cylindrical-shaped coil which behaves like a magnet when electric current is passed through it

Electromagnet: A device that acts as a magnet when an electric current flows through its coil

Summary

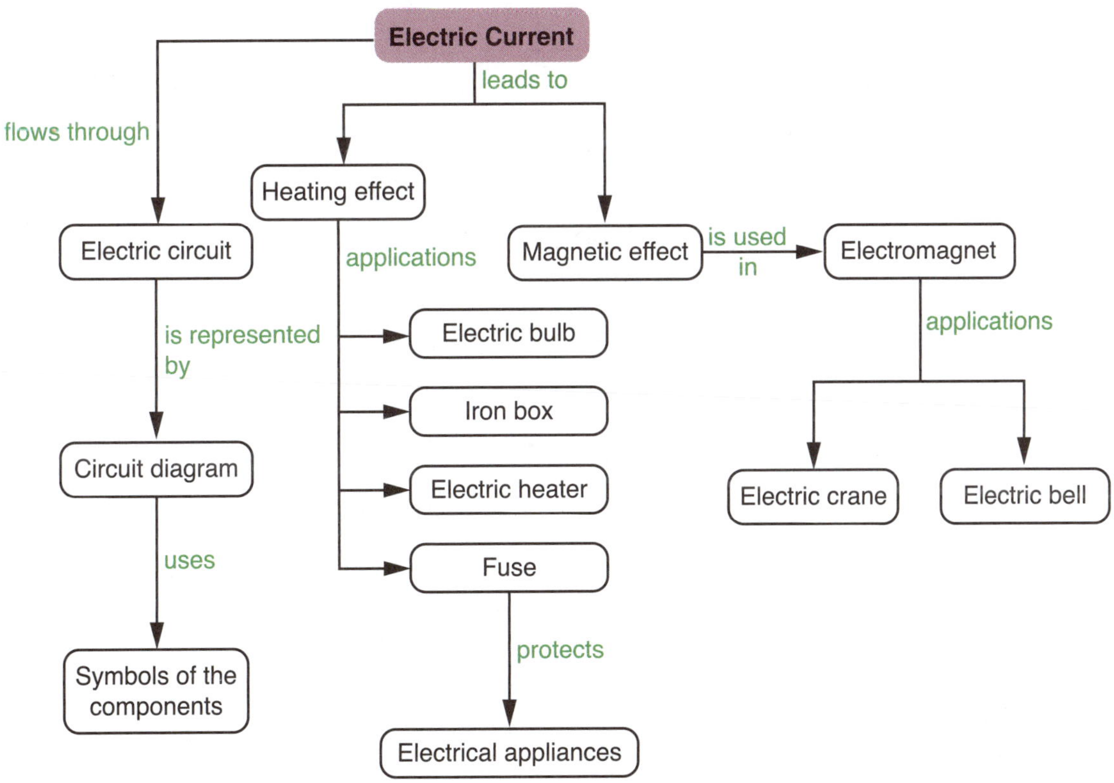

EXERCISE

W

ia

A. Choose the correct option.

1. An electric bulb produces light by the ______________ effect of current.
   (a) magnetic (b) heating
   (c) chemical (d) mechanical
2. Which of the following is a safety device?
   (a) Electric iron (b) Electric bulb (c) Electric oven (d) Electric fuse
3. Which of the following devices works on the magnetic effect of electric current?
   (a) Electric iron (b) Electric bulb
   (c) Electric bell (d) Electric kettle
4. A piece of soft iron is inserted into a solenoid carrying current. Now, the magnetic field strength of the solenoid ______________.
   (a) increases (b) decreases
   (c) remains the same (d) first increases and then decreases
5. The coil of an electric iron is made up of ______________.
   (a) steel (b) brass (c) bronze (d) nichrome

B. Fill in the blanks.

1. A closed path for the flow of electric current is called __________. (electric circuit/ electric bulb)
2. A fuse wire is an alloy of lead and __________. (tin/iron)
3. When an iron nail is inserted into a solenoid carrying a current, the magnetic strength of the solenoid __________. (increases/decreases)
4. An electromagnet is a __________ magnet. (permanent/temporary)
5. Electromagnets are not used in a __________. (kettle/motor)

C. State whether the following statements are true (T) or false (F).

ia

1. A current flowing through a conductor produces heat in it. ☐
2. A thick copper wire can be used as a fuse wire in an electric fuse. ☐
3. Electric fuse works on the principle of the magnetic effect of current. ☐
4. Electric bulb produces light by the heating effect of current. ☐
5. An electromagnet can retain its magnetic power even after the current passing through it is switched off. ☐

D. Give one word for each of the following.

1. A closed path for the flow of electric current
2. The SI unit of electric current
3. A cylindrical-shaped coil that exhibits magnetic properties when current is passed through it
4. A device that acts as a magnet when current flows through its coil
5. A device that works by the means of an electromagnet

E. Give reasons for the following.

1. We should never use a copper wire instead of the fuse wire in an electric fuse.
2. An electric bulb gets heated up when current is passed through it.
3. An electric motor works when you connect it to a battery and stops immediately when you disconnect the battery.
4. The strength of an electromagnet is increased when more number of cells are connected to to it.
5. A fused bulb does not glow.

F. Answer the following questions briefly.

1. What are open and closed circuits?
2. How does an electric bulb produce light?
3. What do you mean by the heating effect of electric current?
4. What do you mean by the magnetic effect of electric current?
5. What is a solenoid?

G. Answer the following questions in detail.

1. What is an electric fuse? Explain how a fuse helps to protect a circuit.
2. What is an electromagnet? Suggest any two methods to increase the strength of an electromagnet.
3. Explain one experiment to show the magnetic effect of electric current.
4. Describe the construction and working of an electric bell.

COGNITIVE CORNER

Critical Thinking

1. Does the heating effect of electric current cause wastage of electricity? Explain.
2. When the fuse blew off, the electrician quickly fixed it with a copper wire because he did not have a proper fuse wire. Do you think he did the right thing? Explain.

Picture Study

Identify the following symbols used in a circuit diagram.

 ____________

 ____________

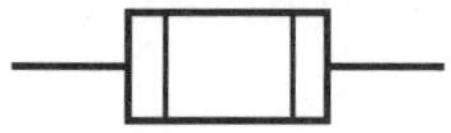 ____________

 ____________

Project

You may have seen the electricity bills at your home. What are the information recorded in it? Analyse three consecutive bills and find out the difference in the amount in them. Plan and implement activities to reduce the consumption of electricity. As a part of the Science Club activity, prepare a chart on the activities you have done to reduce the consumption of electricity. **(C-5.1)**

In the Library

Collect detailed information about the different sources of electrical energy. Among these sources, find out which are renewable sources. What are their advantages over non-renewable sources of electricity? **(C-7.1)**

Life Skills

It is important to take safety precautions when working with electricity. The following are some of the safety measures that will help you while working with electricity.

(a) Always wear rubber sandals while handling electrical appliances. In case of any short circuit, the sandals will act as an insulator and protect us from any electric shock.

(b) Do not touch electrical appliances, electric plugs and sockets with wet hands. Water is a conductor of electricity and increases the chances of electric shock.

Write at least five safety measures to prevent electric shocks. Find out how the safety standards have evolved with the improvement in technology. **(C-5.1)**

Worksheet

Most of us are familiar with heating devices that work on electricity. Which of the following devices produce heat?

Toaster

Electric oven

Mixer-grinder

The devices use electricity to heat water in the geyser, heating coils in the heater or cook food in the oven. But you must have noticed that, after a time, the device switches off on its own and again switches on? It does this to maintain the heat at the temperature the user has specified. This happens with the help of a component called thermostat.

A thermostat usually has two pieces of different metals bolted together to form a strip (known as bimetallic strip).

When electricity passes through this, both the metals get heated. When a metal gets heated, it expands. But different metals expand to different degrees. Here, one metal expands slightly more than the other. As a result, the strip bends breaking the electric circuit.

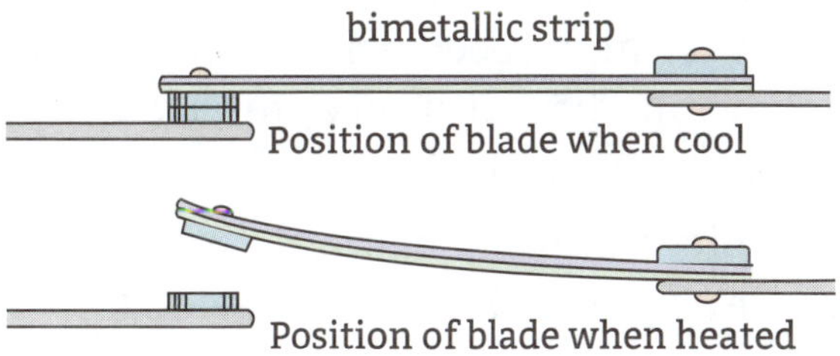

A. What do you think will happen to the device?

____

____

B. As the strip cools down, the metal comes back to the original place and connects to the circuit. What will happen now?

____

____

14 Winds, Storms and Cyclones

Curricular Goals

- Explore the world of matter and its constituents, properties and behaviour **(CG-1)**
- Explore the nature and processes of science through engaging with the evolution of scientific knowledge and conducting scientific inquiry **(CG-6)**
- Communicate questions, observations and conclusions related to science **(CG-7)**

Competencies

- Observe and explain the phenomena caused due to difference in pressure, temperature and density (formation of winds) **(C-1.4)**
- Formulate questions using scientific terminology and collect data as evidence **(C-6.2)**
- Use scientific vocabulary to communicate science accurately in oral and written form, and through visual representation **(C-7.1)**

Let's Get Started

A natural disaster or calamity can severely impact us as it could lead to loss of lives, disrupt normal activities and damage the economy of a country. Wind blowing at a very high speed can wreak havoc on the people caught in them and on the environment. In this chapter, we will study about wind, types of wind and the various hazards caused by it.

The pictures of the natural disasters associated with wind are given below. Write their names in the space provided.

____

____

____

It was the winds and an unyielding will that helped the mariner named Vasco da Gama to sail thousands of kilometres from Europe to find a sea route to India. The role of winds in that voyage which changed the course of our land's history is worth reading. How do winds influence us? Let's learn about the different types of wind, their formation, and effects.

AIR PRESSURE

You may have noticed people filling air in the tyres of vehicles, cycles, etc. How does the air inside the tyres help? Why does a balloon get inflated when you blow air into it?

Tyres and balloons are made up of elastic materials that can expand when air or gas is pumped into them. When air is pumped into tyres, the pressure exerted by the air inside the tyres keeps them inflated and enables them to carry the vehicle (Fig. 14.1). Similarly, the pressure exerted by the air inside the balloons keeps the balloons inflated. *The pressure exerted by air is called* ***air pressure***. Air exerts pressure in all directions and on all objects. The pressure exerted by air depends on temperature and altitude.

Fig. 14.1: Role of air pressure in everyday life

Atmosphere of the Earth

The Earth is surrounded by an envelope of air called the **atmosphere**. The atmosphere exerts pressure on the Earth due to the weight of the air. This is known as the **atmospheric pressure**. We live in the lowest layer of the atmosphere where atmospheric pressure is the maximum. Atmospheric pressure decreases with increase in altitude. The magnitude of the atmospheric pressure on top of a mountain is less than the pressure at sea level. Atmospheric pressure is measured using an instrument called **barometer**.

Activity 1

Aim: To show that air exerts pressure

Materials required: Transparent cup/glass and a cardboard/ plastic sheet big enough to cover the mouth of the glass/cup

Procedure:

1. Fill a glass with water up to the brim, with no trapped air bubble inside.
2. Cover it with a cardboard lid.
3. Place your one hand gently on the lid and turn it upside down.
4. Now, slowly remove your hand.

Cardboard sheet stays in place due to air pressure

Observation: The cardboard sheet does not fall down and the water in the glass does not spill.

Conclusion: This happens because the air pressure pushing up on the cardboard prevents the cardboard from falling off. This shows that air exerts pressure.

Activity 2

Aim: To show the presence of atmospheric pressure

Materials required: A metal tin/can with a tight cap, water, burner/stove and a pair of tongs

Procedure:

1. Fill about one-third of the can with water.
2. Keep the can without its cap on the stove or burner and boil the water for sometime till a lot of steam escapes.
3. Using a pair of tongs, remove the can from the stove and immediately close the can's mouth with the cap tightly.
4. Now, pour cold water on the can and observe what happens.

Metal can Crushed can

Observation: The can gets crushed when cold water is poured on it.

Conclusion: This happens because the steam produced during boiling of water pushes out most of the air inside the can. When cold water is poured, the steam left in the can condenses to form water. So, the pressure of air inside the can becomes much less than the pressure of air outside it. This greater atmospheric pressure crushes the can from all sides, thus indicating the presence of atmospheric pressure.

Science in Context

In 1656, a German scientist and mayor of Magdeburg, Otto von Guericke, designed an experiment to demonstrate the concept of atmospheric pressure. He took two metallic hemispheres of about 50 cm in diameter. He placed these two hemispheres together such that they made a complete sphere and removed the air present in between them. Sixteen horses were required to pull the two hemispheres apart.

When the air inside was removed with a vacuum pump, the air pressure inside the sphere became much less compared to the pressure outside the sphere, that is, the atmospheric pressure. Hence, there was a net large inward force acting on the sphere, which kept the two hemispheres together, making it almost impossible to pull them apart.

Air Expands on Heating

The volume of a given amount of air depends on its temperature. As the temperature of air increases, its volume also increases because its particles start vibrating more and move apart, that is, air expands on heating. Air becomes lighter as it expands due to a decrease in its density and thus rises up in the atmosphere. Activity 3 demonstrates that air expands on heating.

Activity 3

Aim: To show that air expands on heating

Materials required: A balloon, 2-litre water bottle and a bowl/pan of hot water

Procedure:

1. Fix a slightly inflated balloon on the mouth of the 2-litre bottle.
2. Place the bottle with the balloon into the bowl/pan of hot water. Observe the change.

Observation: The balloon gets inflated when the bottle is kept in hot water.

Conclusion: The hot water heats the air in the bottle. The air expands and inflates the balloon. This shows that air expands on heating.

Bottle with balloon kept in hot water

WIND AND FORMATION OF WIND

The flow of air in the atmosphere of the Earth is called **wind**. When air on the surface of the Earth is heated by the sun, it expands and rises up creating a low-pressure region below. Air from the nearby high-pressure regions flows into these low-pressure regions and causes wind. The hot air that rises up cools and sinks down. This continues and a cycle of airflow is formed, which is called the **wind current** (Fig. 14.2).

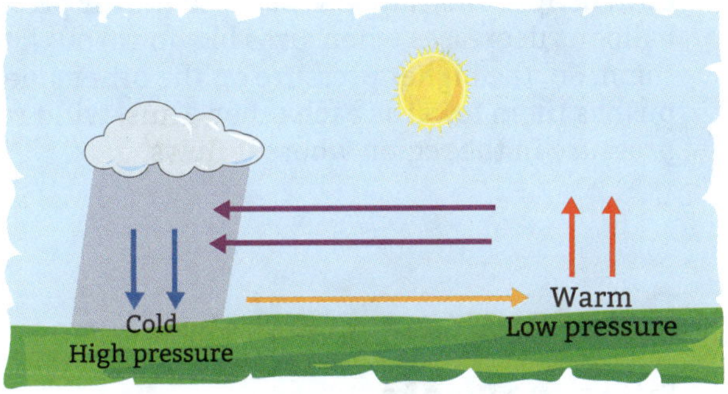

Fig. 14.2: Wind current

High Speed Wind Reduces the Pressure

Wind flowing over a region reduces the air pressure in that particular region. The more the speed of the wind, the lower will be the pressure. This interesting fact was observed by Swiss mathematician and physicist, Daniel Bernoulli.

This can be easily demonstrated by using a piece of paper. Hold a piece of paper near your mouth and blow air over it. You can see that the paper lifts up when you blow air. It happens so because the air pressure decreases above the paper due to the flow of air with some speed (created by blowing). The air pressure below the paper, being higher, pushes the paper up. Therefore, we say that moving air can provide a lift (Fig. 14.3).

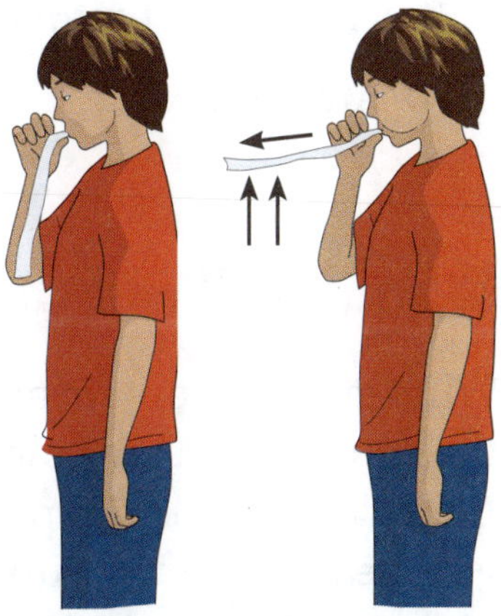

Fig. 14.3: High speed wind reduces air pressure

Why do roofs of houses get blown away during strong winds? The principle behind this is the lift provided by the wind flowing over the roof. When the wind blows, the air pressure above the roof decreases. The pressure exerted by the air below the roof is so high that it lifts the roof, which then gets blown away.

Activity 4

Aim: To demonstrate that wind reduces the air pressure in the region where it flows

Materials required: Two balloons, thread and stand

Procedure:

1. Inflate two balloons and hang them using threads from the stand.
2. Keep some distance between them while hanging.
3. Blow air through the gap between the two balloons.
4. Observe what happens to the balloons.

Observation: The balloons move towards each other.

Conclusion: This happens because the air pressure between the balloons decreases when air is blown through the gap between them. So, the higher pressure on the other side of the balloons pushes them towards each other. Thus, wind reduces the air pressure in the region where it flows.

Balloons move towards each other when air is blown between them.

Revise and Recall

Fill in the blanks.

1. The envelope of air around the Earth is called ______________. (atmosphere/ air pressure)
2. The flow of air in the atmosphere of the Earth is called ______________. (cyclone/wind)
3. Moving air provides a ______________. (lift/drag)
4. Air pressure ______________ as altitude increases. (increases/decreases)

Why are Wind Currents Formed?

a

Wind currents are formed due to the uneven heating of the Earth's surface between the equator and the poles. The equatorial regions receive more sunlight compared to the polar regions. Therefore, the air near the Earth's surface in the equatorial regions gets heated and rises up. This process creates low-pressure regions. Cold air from the high-pressure regions on either side of the equator, up to the latitude of 30°, flows into the low-pressure regions near the equator.

The warm air, which rises up, cools and sinks down in the regions of latitude nearly 30° north and south of the equator. As the cool air sinks, this area becomes a high-pressure region. Once again, wind flows from these high-pressure regions to the equatorial and polar regions. As the wind flows towards the poles, at regions of latitude around 60° from the equator, it meets the cold air from the poles and rises up creating low-pressure regions in these areas. The cold air from the polar regions flows again towards these low-pressure regions.

Due to the effect of rotation of the Earth, the wind flowing in the northern hemisphere of the Earth bends towards its right and the wind in the southern hemisphere bends towards its left (with respect to an observer on the ground). This is due to the origin of a force called the **Coriolis force** caused by the rotation of the Earth about its own axis. The direction of the Coriolis force in the northern hemisphere is towards right and in the southern hemisphere, it is towards left.

Wind Speed and Direction

The **wind speed** is the rate[1] of flow of wind in the atmosphere of the Earth. It is commonly measured using a device called **anemometer** and expressed in kilometre per hour (km/h).

Word Web

[1]**Rate:** How fast or how often something happens

The commonly used anemometer is a cup anemometer. It has four cups hoisted on a vertical pole at right angles to each other. When the wind blows, the wind presses on the inner side of the cup, rotating it. The speed with which it rotates depends on the speed of the wind.

The direction of wind is determined by the direction from which the wind originates. Wind direction is found by using devices such as the wind vane and a windsock (Fig. 14.4). The wind vane consists of an arrow hoisted on a vertical rod or a pole that can rotate. The rear part of the arrow is broad providing more surface area for the wind. Thus, the wind hits the rear part with more force. This causes the wind vane to align in such a way that the pointed part of the arrow always faces the direction of the wind.

Fig. 14.4: (a) Cup anemometer, (b) wind vane and (c) windsock

The wind is named according to the direction from which it flows. The wind flowing from the North is termed Northerly wind and the wind flowing from the South is termed Southerly wind. The following table (Table 14.1) shows the effects of wind blowing at different speeds.

Table 14.1: Different wind speeds and their effects on land

Wind speed (km/h)	Condition of wind	Effect on land
1–6	Light air	Wind motion visible in smoke
7–11	Light breeze	Leaves move
12–19	Gentle breeze	Leaves in constant motion
13–18	Moderate breeze	Dust is raised
19–24	Breezy	Small trees sway
25–31	Strong breeze	Large branches move
32–38	Near gale	Whole trees in motion
39–46	Gale	Twigs break
47–54	Strong gale	Light damages to the structures, such as formation of cracks in the buildings and bridges
64–73	Storm	Trees get uprooted
74–95	Violent storm	Wide range of damage such as uproot of trees, collapse of roofs of buildings, small objects are flown off
55–63	Hurricane	Excessive damage such as flood, landslide, damage to building and roads, threat to life

THUNDERSTORMS AND CYCLONES

A **thunderstorm** is a turbulent[1] weather condition formed by lightning and thunder. Thunderstorms are usually accompanied by strong winds and heavy rains. They are mainly of four types: single-cell, multicell cluster, multicell lines and supercell. The supercell thunderstorms are the strongest among all and are responsible for severe weather conditions.

Word Web

[1]**Turbulent**: Changing direction suddenly and violently

When the air near the surface of the Earth gets heated by the sun, it rises up. The hot rising air carries moisture. As this air reaches the cooler regions of the atmosphere, the water vapour in the air gets condensed to form tiny droplets of water.

These tiny droplets join together to form clouds. When clouds become heavy with water droplets, these water droplets fall as rain. As they fall, they collide with each other and the air rising up. This friction between the droplets and the air particles charges the clouds. The charging of clouds causes electrical discharge between clouds or between a cloud and the ground. This discharge of electricity through the atmosphere of the Earth causes huge sparks known as **lightning**. Due to lightning, the air in the path of discharge of electricity is heated up, causing the air in this region to expand suddenly with a huge sound called **thunder**.

A thunderstorm can cause a lot of damage to living beings and property. Some precautions that need to be taken during thunderstorms are as follows:

- If you are inside your house or any building, stay inside till the thunderstorm stops.
- If you are outside, do not hold an umbrella and walk during thunderstorm.
- Do not take shelter under a tree as it creates an easy path for the discharge of electricity during lightning.
- If you are sitting inside a vehicle, do not come out of the vehicle.

Formation of Cyclones

Cyclones are caused by warm, moisture-bearing air over the oceans. Cyclones are usually formed in low-pressure regions where air gets easily heated by the sun. Warm air rises up carrying water vapour. As this moisture-laden air rises and reaches the cooler regions of the atmosphere, the water vapour gets condensed into small water droplets, which form high thunderclouds. When water vapour condenses into droplets, a lot of heat is released into the air, which heats this air further. Hot air further rises and creates a low-pressure region. When the hot air rises up, the cold air rushes into the low-pressure region created by the rising hot air. The wind thus flows in a spiral manner at a very high speed. The airflow becomes spiral due to the effect of rotation of the Earth about its own axis. This process continues and produces a very low-pressure region, causing winds to move still faster. This rotating wind forms a huge spiral of diameter ranging from a few kilometres to a few hundred kilometres.

A **cyclone** is a low-pressure area surrounded by a high-pressure region of swirling air. The centre of a cyclone is called its **eye** (Fig. 14.5). The eye of the cyclone has the lowest pressure and it is a calm and cloudless area.

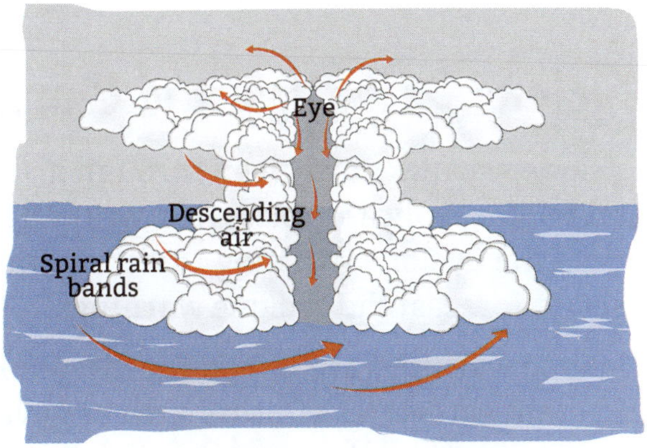

Fig. 14.5: Cyclone flow pattern

The diameter of the eye is around a few kilometres. Heavy winds and rains are formed around this eye of the cyclone. As the cyclones develop in the sea, they start moving towards the land near the ocean with a high speed. This high-speed wind creates large and strong sea waves which may be several metres high. These waves are strong enough to cause destructions to the shore.

Cyclones are called by different names in different countries. In America, it is called a **hurricane** and in Japan and Philippines, it is called a **typhoon**.

In the month of October 2013, a severe tropical cyclone named **Phailin** made landfall in the north-east region of India (Fig. 14.6). It was the second strongest tropical cyclone ever to have landfall in India.

Fig. 14.6: Cyclone Phailin at its peak intensity

Destruction by cyclones

Huge waves, produced by strong winds, accompanied by rains, hit shores and cause heavy floods in the nearby areas. The strong winds can damage buildings, uproot trees and disrupt electrical and communication lines, etc.

As the cyclone reaches the land, it becomes weaker due to the lack of moisture on land and friction with land. The eastern coast of India is more vulnerable to cyclones than the western coast.

Some safety precautions to be taken during cyclones are given below.

- Stay tuned to the local radio for updated news regarding thunderstorms and cyclones.
- Do not use gas or electrical appliances which have been in flood water without checking for safety.
- Do not go outside your house and do not walk through the flood water.
- Always keep drinking water separately as water sources can get contaminated during floods.

Cyclone Detection and Warning

Cyclone warnings are given through a variety of media such as radio, television, fax and telefax, police wireless networks and newspapers. A specially designed system called the Cyclone Warning Dissemination System that works on INSAT satellite is used to forecast the cyclone warnings.

Cyclone warnings are issued for the general public, fishermen, farmers and different categories of users such as government officials responsible for disaster management, road transport and railway department.

Usually, cyclone warnings are given in two stages. The first stage is known as a **cyclone alert** or **cyclone watch**, which is issued 48 hours in advance of any expected cyclone or storm; the second stage is called a **cyclone warning**, issued 24 hours in advance.

TORNADOES

A **tornado** is a violently rotating column of air that extends from the clouds to the ground. It appears as a spinning funnel-shaped cloud that travels very fast. Tornadoes can appear from any direction. They mostly move from south-west to north-east direction or west to east direction.
A tornado can last from a few seconds to an hour. Most tornadoes last for less than 10 minutes.

Tornadoes are very violent in nature. They can completely destroy even the strongest buildings, uproot trees, damage lives and hurl objects through the air. The intensity of a tornado is measured in **Fujita scale** with ratings between F0 that causes minimal damage and F5 that causes maximum damage. The speed of the wind in a strong tornado is almost 500 km/h. Tornadoes that form in the ocean are called **waterspouts**. Figure 14.7 shows a typical tornado.

Fig. 14.7: Tornado

Science in Context

Tornado Alley is the term for the area in the United States where tornadoes are most frequent.

Precautions to be Taken During Tornadoes

A tornado funnel can engulf objects from the surface of the Earth (due to low pressure inside) and throw these back, causing destruction. Some necessary precautions to be taken during tornadoes are given below:

(a) Avoid opening windows and doors of houses. Occupy the ground floor and small rooms in your house.

(b) If you are outside or travelling in a vehicle, get out of it quickly and protect yourself by lying close to the ground and keeping your fingers interlocked, closing the ear and the neck, as shown in figure 14.8.

Fig. 14.8: Protecting oneself from a tornado

Keywords

Wind: The flow of air in the atmosphere of the Earth

Thunderstorm: A climatic condition with lightning and thunder mostly accompanied by rain

Cyclone: A low-pressure area surrounded by a high-pressure region of swirling air

Tornado: A dark funnel-shaped swirling cloud extending from the sky to the ground

Summary

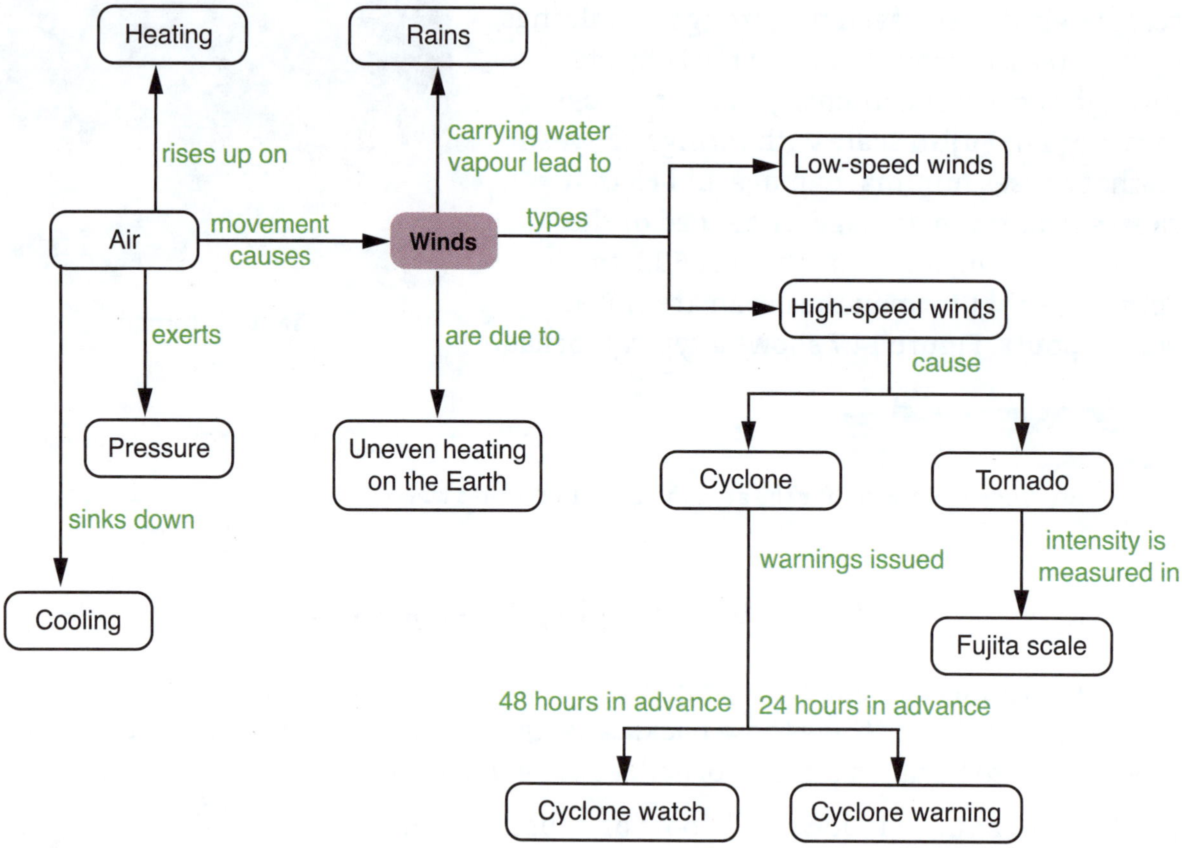

EXERCISE

W

A. Choose the correct option.

1. When air on the Earth is heated by the sun, it ________.
   (a) rises up (b) comes down
   (c) does not move (d) None of these
2. The instrument used to measure the wind speed is called ________.
   (a) manometer (b) anemometer (c) barometer (d) speedometer
3. A dark funnel-shaped cloud that extends from the sky to the ground is called a ________.
   (a) thunderstorm (b) cyclone (c) monsoon wind (d) tornado
4. Select the correct statement about winds.
   (a) High speed winds reduce the air pressure in the region of wind flow.
   (b) High speed winds increase the air pressure in the region of wind flow.
   (c) Wind increases the density of the air in the region of wind flow.
   (d) None of these.
5. The centre of a cyclone is called its ________.
   (a) head (b) eye
   (c) focus (d) None of these

B. Fill in the blanks.

1. Air exerts ________ in all directions. (pressure/speed)
2. The intensity of a tornado is measured by the ________ scale. (Richter/Fujita)
3. A ________ is a low-pressure area surrounded by a high-pressure region of swirling air. (tornado/cyclone)
4. Wind direction is found using a ________. (anemometer/wind vane)
5. Winds are generated due to the ________ on the surface of the Earth. (uniform heating/uneven heating)

C. State whether the following statements are true (T) or false (F). ia

1. Wind is a flow of air from a high-pressure region to a low-pressure region of the atmosphere. ☐
2. Air taken in a container exerts pressure on the walls of the container. ☐
3. During a thunderstorm, it is safe to stay in an open place. ☐
4. The eye of a cyclone is the most turbulent area. ☐
5. Warm air in the atmosphere sinks down. ☐

D. Answer each of the following in one word.

1. The pressure exerted by air on other objects
2. The rate of flow of wind in the atmosphere of the Earth
3. The instrument used to measure the wind speed
4. Climatic condition formed by lightning and thunder mostly accompanied by rain
5. A low-pressure area surrounded by a high-pressure region of swirling air

E. Give reasons for the following.

1. Smoke coming out of a chimney always rises up.
2. Sea breeze occurs during the day and land breeze occurs during the night time.
3. When high speed wind blows, an umbrella held upright at times gets upturned.
4. We should not take shelter under a tall tree during lightning.
5. A cyclone becomes weaker as it approaches the land.

F. Answer the following questions briefly.

1. Hot air rises up and cool air sinks down. Explain why.
2. What do you mean by an eye of a cyclone?
3. As the cyclone hits the land, it becomes weak. Why?
4. How are thunderstorms formed?
5. Write the precautions to be taken during tornadoes.

G. Answer the following questions in detail.

1. Explain the formation of wind and wind currents with the help of a diagram.
2. Explain how a cyclone is formed.
3. Explain the disastrous effects of a cyclone.
4. Write the precautions to be taken during thunderstorms.
5. A strong wind can blow off the roofs of buildings. Explain how.

COGNITIVE CORNER

Critical Thinking

1. The wings of an aeroplane are designed in such a way that the upper part of the wing is curved and the bottom part is almost flat. Why do you think these are designed in such a manner?
2. If you have to choose a place to fix a wind vane, which of these would you choose: a verandah, a rooftop or a pit in the ground. Give reasons for your answer.
3. Tornadoes are relatively rare in India compared to some other parts of the world. Why is it so?

Picture Study

Label the diagram given below.

Project

You may have seen an egg in a bottle in a science exhibition. You can insert a boiled egg into a bottle whose mouth is smaller than the size of the egg. The procedure to demonstrate this is as follows.

Take a glass bottle with a mouth slightly smaller than the boiled egg. Light a piece of paper with a matchstick and drop it inside the bottle. Place the boiled egg on the mouth of the bottle as shown in the figure. Wait for some time and you will observe the egg going inside the bottle. What makes the egg go inside the bottle? Give reasons. **(C-7.2)**

In the Library

You may have seen a cricket ball rising high when hit by a batsman. This is due to the reduced air pressure on the top side of the ball than the bottom side of the ball. The spinning ball drags air near its surface. As the ball moves with speed, the net speed of the air above the ball will be more than the speed of the air below the ball. Therefore, the pressure above the ball becomes less than the pressure below the ball. This high pressure below the ball pushes it up.

The principle that explains this phenomenon is 'Bernoulli's principle' given by Daniel Bernoulli. Collect more details about Bernoulli's principle and its applications. Make a presentation and present it in the class. **(C-7.1)**

Life Skills

Super Cyclonic Storm Amphan was a powerful tropical cyclone that caused widespread damage in Eastern India, specifically West Bengal, in May 2020.

(a) Collect information and prepare a poster on the distress caused by the cyclones Amphan and Nisarga (in June, 2020).

(b) Suggest measures to mitigate the impact of such disasters in future by collecting information from Internet and other sources. **(C-7.1)**

Worksheet

A lightning rod is a metal strip or rod used to protect buildings from a violent lightning strike. Lightning rods are made of a good conducting metal. Copper being a very good conductor, is used for making lightning rods.

A lightning rod is a single component of the lightning protection system. The lightning rod is connected with a cable to the Earth below, where it can channel the charge to a safe place. These rods are placed atop roofs to attract lightning and protect buildings from lightning strikes.

If lightning hits the structure, it will preferentially strike the rod and be conducted to ground through the wire, instead of passing through the structure, where it could start a fire or cause electrocution. The lightning rod requires a connection to Earth to perform its protective function.

A. Can plastic be used instead of copper for making lightning rods?

____

____

____

B. A steel skyscraper does not need lightning rods. Why?

____

____

____

C. What precautions would you take to provide protection against the lightning?

____

____

____

15 Light

Curricular Goals

- Explore the physical world in scientific and mathematical terms **(CG-2)**
- Explore the nature and processes of science through engaging with the evolution of scientific knowledge and conducting scientific inquiry **(CG-6)**
- Communicate questions, observations and conclusions related to science **(CG-7)**

Competencies

- Demonstrate rectilinear propagation of light from different sources, verify the laws of reflection through manipulation of light sources and objects and the use of apparatus and artefacts (plane and curved mirrors) **(C-2.4)**
- Formulate questions using scientific terminology and collect data as evidence **(C-6.2)**
- Use scientific vocabulary to communicate science accurately in oral and written form, and through visual representation **(C-7.1)**
- Design and build simple models to demonstrate scientific concepts **(C-7.2)**

Let's Get Started

We are all familiar with light and its uses. Light is the form of energy that makes things visible to us. In our daily life, we see light from many sources such as the sun, stars, electric bulb, torch, candle, TV, monitor of a computer and mobile phone display. In earlier classes, you have learnt about some properties of light such as formation of shadows, reflection of light from mirrors and formation of images.

Identify the phenomena associated with light in the pictures given below.

______________________ ______________________

In this chapter, we will learn about some more properties of light.

RECTILINEAR PROPAGATION OF LIGHT

Shine a laser torch onto a wall during night and observe its path. What is the nature of the path of light? Is it straight or curved? You can see the straight line path of the light clearly. Does light always travel in a straight line? Let us find out.

Activity 1

Aim: To demonstrate that light travels in a straight line

Materials required: Small cardboard sheets, three stands, candle and candle stand

Procedure:

1. Make small holes at the centre of the three cardboard sheets.
2. Fix the cardboard sheets on the three stands and arrange them in a straight line as shown in the figure.
3. Light the candle and place it in front of the hole made on the first cardboard sheet.
4. See the candle flame through the hole of the third cardboard sheet.

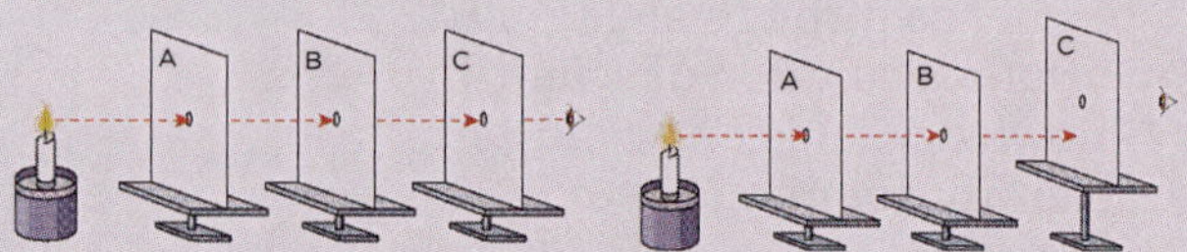

5. Now, move the third stand a little away from the line. Observe the candle flame again.

Observation: Candle flame is visible when the holes of all the cardboard sheets are in a straight line. The flame is not visible when the second cardboard sheet is moved away.

Conclusion: Light travels in a straight line.

Activity 2

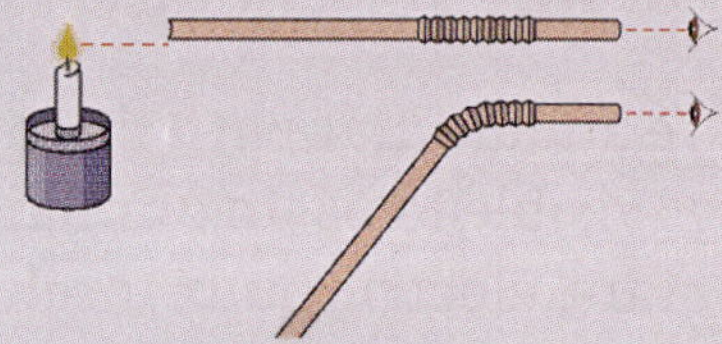

Aim: To show that light always travels in a straight line

Materials required: Straw, candle and candle stand

Procedure:

1. Light the candle and fix it on a candle stand.
2. Keep the straw straight and observe the flame of the candle through the straw.
3. Now, bend the straw and see the flame again. Are you able to see the flame now?

Observation: Candle flame is visible when the straw is straight and aligned with the path of the candle flame. It is not visible when we bend the straw as the alignment gets changed.

Conclusion: This proves that light always travels in a straight line.

From the above two activities, we can conclude that light can travel only in a straight line and not in a curved path. The property of light that it always travels in a straight line is called the **rectilinear propagation of light**.

REFLECTION OF LIGHT

When light falls on a surface, a part of it hits the surface and returns like a ball that bounces back. This phenomenon in which light falling on the surface of an object is sent back by that surface is called the **reflection of light**.

Polished surfaces reflect more light compared to rough surfaces. A mirror can reflect almost the entire amount of light falling on it. Therefore, a mirror shines. Any object or surface that can reflect most of the light falling on it is a shiny object or surface.

IMAGES

An ***image*** *is an optical representation of an object.* An image can be either real or virtual. *The images that can be formed on a screen are called* ***real images****. The images that cannot be formed on a screen are called* ***virtual images***. The light rays falling on a mirror can converge at one point after reflection, or diverge away after reflection. The converging rays of light form a real image and the diverging rays of light form a virtual image.

Science in Context

When we stand in front of a mirror, only one image is formed. What happens if you use two mirrors? Have you ever been to a trial room in a shop? Many trial rooms have more than one mirror such that you are standing between two mirrors.

Since one mirror forms one image, you will say two mirrors will form two. But the number of images formed will be many. This phenomenon is called **multiple reflections**. As you decrease the angle between the mirrors, the number of images formed will increase. A kaleidoscope works on the principle of multiple reflections.

Image Formed by a Plane Mirror

Stand in front of a plane mirror; brush your teeth using your left hand. Which hand of your image is doing the same? Now, lower the left hand and raise the right hand. What change occurs to the image? Doesn't our right side appear left and our left side appear right in the image?

This property of reversal of the sides of an image formed by a plane mirror is called **lateral inversion**. You might have observed that the word **AMBULANCE** on an ambulance vehicle is written in reverse. This is because when the reversed word **AMBULANCE** gets reflected in the rear-view mirror of a vehicle moving ahead of the ambulance, the driver can read the word correctly (AMBULANCE) and give way to it (Fig. 15.1).

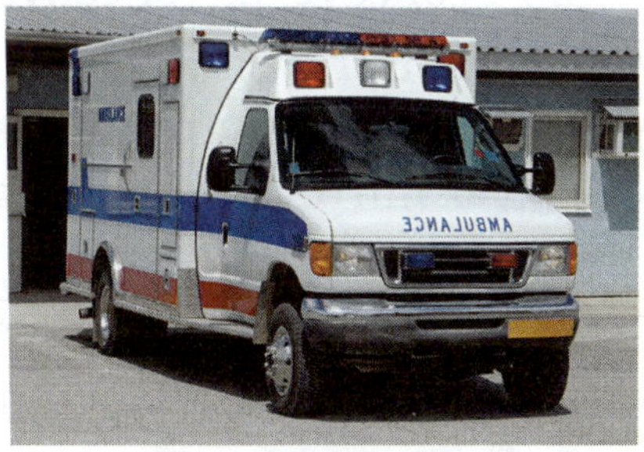

Fig. 15.1: Lateral inversion

Characteristics of the image formed by a plane mirror

- The image formed by a plane mirror is always virtual and erect.
- The image undergoes lateral inversion.
- The size of the image formed by a plane mirror is the same as that of the object.
- The distance of the object from the mirror is equal to the distance of the image from the mirror (that is, image distance = object distance).

Activity 3

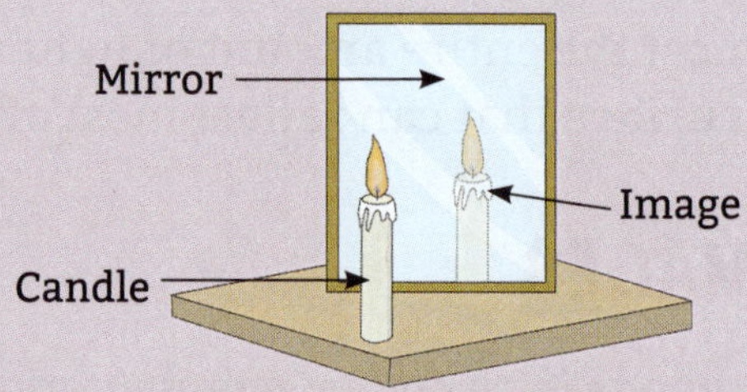

Aim: To understand the characteristics of the image formed by a plane mirror

Materials required: A plane mirror, candle and scale

Procedure:

1. Place a plane mirror perpendicularly on a table.
2. Place the candle in front of the mirror. (This distance between the candle and the mirror should be greater than the height of the candle.)
3. Observe the image. Is the size of the object and the image the same?
4. Keeping a scale in front of the mirror, place the candle at different positions and observe. Does the distance of the image change when the distance of the candle from the mirror is increased?

Observation: The image formed by a plane mirror is always virtual and erect. The size of the image will be the same as that of the object. The distance between the image and the mirror is equal to the distance between the object and the mirror. The image undergoes lateral inversion.

SPHERICAL MIRRORS

Have you ever observed reflecting surfaces which are not plane? Most of the kitchen utensils such as steel vessels and spoons are curved reflecting surfaces. Take a polished steel spoon and look at both the surfaces. You will see an upright image at the back of the spoon and an inverted image in the hollow part of the spoon (Fig 15.2). These curved reflecting surfaces form spherical mirrors.

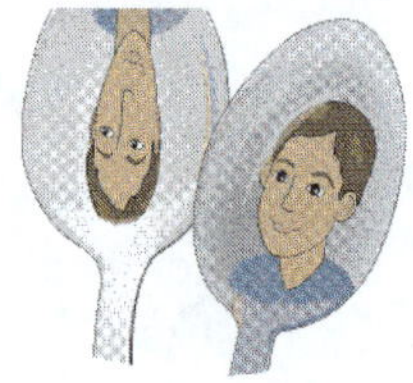

Fig. 15.2: Images formed on two sides of a spoon

Spherical mirrors are of two kinds: concave and convex.

A **concave mirror** is a spherical mirror whose reflecting surface is on the inner side. It is also known as a **converging mirror,** as a parallel beam of light after reflection from a concave mirror converges at a point (Fig. 15.3).

A **convex mirror** is a spherical mirror whose reflecting surface is on the outer side. It is also known as a **diverging mirror,** as a parallel beam of light after reflection from a convex mirror diverges (Fig. 15.4).

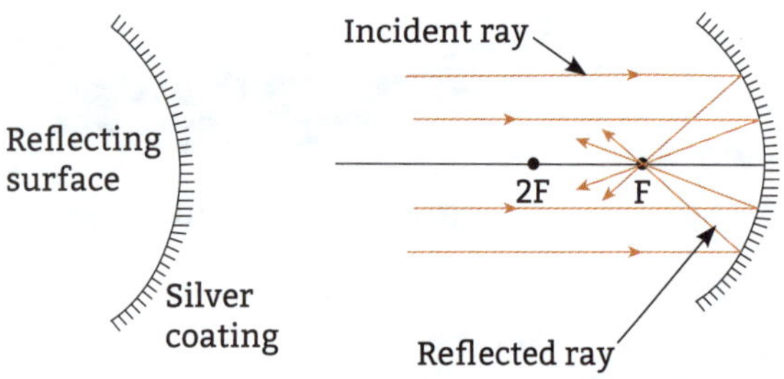

Fig. 15.3: Representations of concave mirror

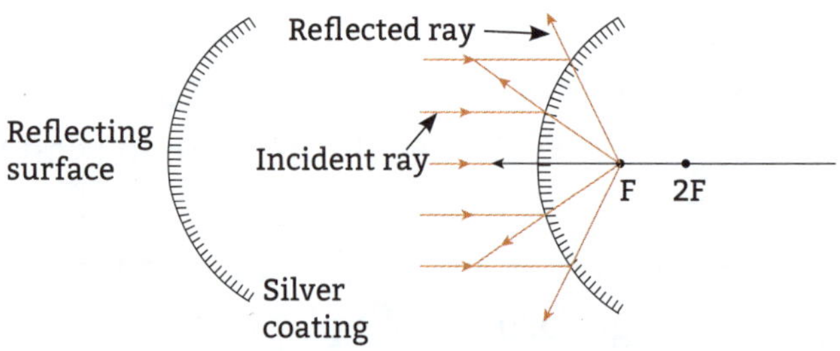

Fig. 15.4: Representations of convex mirror

In the above ray diagrams, 'F' represents **focus** of the mirror. The distance between the focus and the mirror is called the **focal length** of the mirror. '2F' represents the point with distance twice the focal length.

Activity 4

Aim: To show that a parallel beam of light after reflection from a concave mirror converges at a single point in front of the mirror

Materials required: Concave mirror and a sheet of paper

Note: This experiment is best done in a dark room.

Procedure:

1. Hold the concave mirror in your hand so that the reflecting surface of the mirror faces the sun.
2. Hold the paper in the other hand such that it faces the mirror.
3. Adjust its position such that a clear single spot of light is formed on the paper.

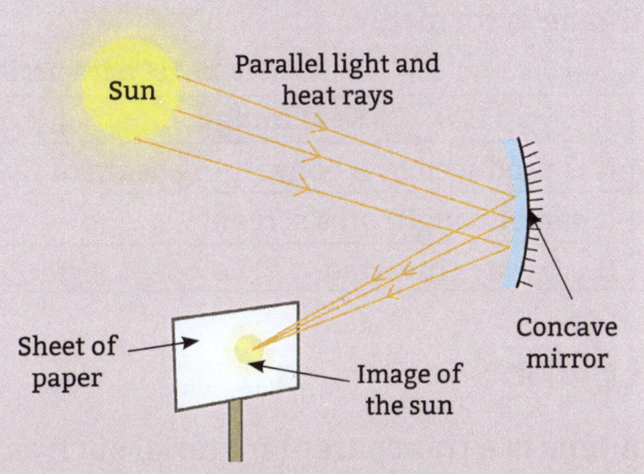

Observation: You will find that the paper starts burning if you keep the mirror in this position for some time.

Conclusion: A parallel beam of light after reflection from a concave mirror converges at a single point.

Uses of spherical mirrors

- Concave mirrors of large focal lengths are used as shaving mirrors.
- Concave mirrors are used as reflectors in headlights of vehicles, search lights, etc.
- Concave and convex mirrors are used in reflection telescopes. Concave mirrors are used in devices such as solar cookers.
- Convex mirrors are used in buses to help the driver see the whole bus.
- Convex mirrors are used as rear view mirrors of vehicles.
- Convex mirrors are used as field view mirrors in supermarkets as they cover a wider range of vision.

Real and Virtual Images

When you see a mirror, you can see your image in the mirror. This image is virtual and cannot be projected on a screen. In a movie theatre, the light from a projector falls on a screen and an image is formed on the screen, which is real.

Hold a concave mirror in front of a distant object and direct the reflected light towards a wall or a white screen. Move the mirror in such a way that the image is clear. You can observe the peculiarities of the image.

Repeat this experiment using a convex mirror. Conduct the same experiment using a plane mirror. Which of these mirrors will produce an image on the screen?

The image which can be obtained on a screen is called real image and the image that cannot be obtained on a screen is called virtual image. A real image can be formed using a concave mirror.

An image formed by a converging beam of light is called a real image. Here, the light rays actually meet at a point to form the image.

An image formed by a diverging beam of light is called a virtual image. Here, the light rays do not meet at a point but they appear to diverge from a point where the virtual image is formed.

Table 15.1: Characteristics of real and virtual images

Real image	Virtual image
It is produced by a converging beam of light.	It is produced by a diverging beam of light.
It can be caught on a screen.	It cannot be caught on a screen.
It is always inverted.	It is always erect.

LENSES

A **lens** is a transparent material such as glass, with two surfaces out of which at least one is a spherical surface.

There are two types of lenses: convex lens and concave lens.

Double convex　Plano convex　Concavo convex

Fig. 15.5: Three types of convex lenses

Convex lenses are also called **converging lenses** since they converge a given parallel beam of light passing through them. They are thicker at the middle and thinner at the edges (Fig. 15.5).

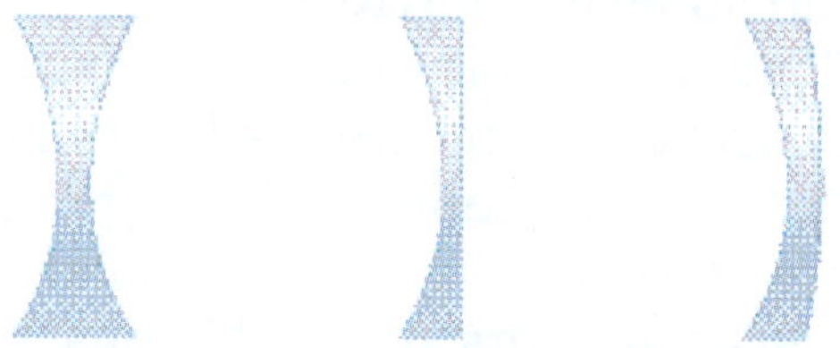

Double concave　Plano concave　Convexo concave

Fig. 15.6: Three types of concave lenses

Concave lenses are also called **diverging lenses** since they diverge a parallel beam of light passing through them. They are thinner at the middle and thicker at the edges (Fig. 15.6).

Activity 5

Aim: To demonstrate that a convex lens brings the light rays passing through it close to each other (converges) while a concave lens separates the light rays passing through it (diverges)

Materials required: Laser torches, a transparent vessel with water, milk or soap

Procedure:

1. Take a transparent vessel containing water. Add some milk or soap to the water to make the path of light rays clearer.
2. Shine the light into the water using two laser torches. You can see the light travelling in a straight line.
3. Now place a convex lens in the path of light outside the vessel but close to it. What change has taken place in the path of light?
4. Now replace the convex lens with a concave lens and observe. Is there any change in the path of light now?

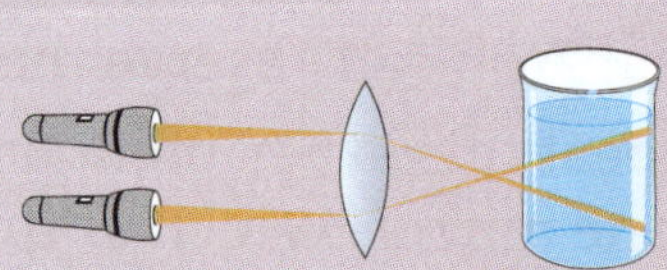

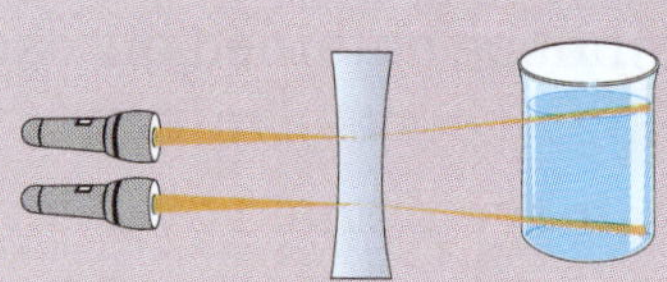

Observation: If we place a convex lens in between the vessel and light source, the light rays passing through the vessel converges.

If we place a concave lens in between the vessel and light source, the light rays passing through the vessel diverges.

Conclusion: A convex lens brings the light rays passing through it close to each other (converges). A concave lens separates the light rays passing through it (diverges).

Images Formed by Lenses

Lenses form images of different types depending on the nature of the lens, the distance of the object from the lens and the distance of the object from the source of light.

Consider the example of a magnifying glass. A magnifying glass is a convex lens. It makes things appear larger and helps in observing tiny objects.

Activity 6

Let us perform an activity to understand more about real and virtual images.

Hold a convex lens against a distant object and try to capture the image on a wall. Increase or decrease the distance between the lens and the wall. Don't you get a clear image? What type of image is obtained? Repeat the experiment using a concave lens. Can the image be captured on the wall?

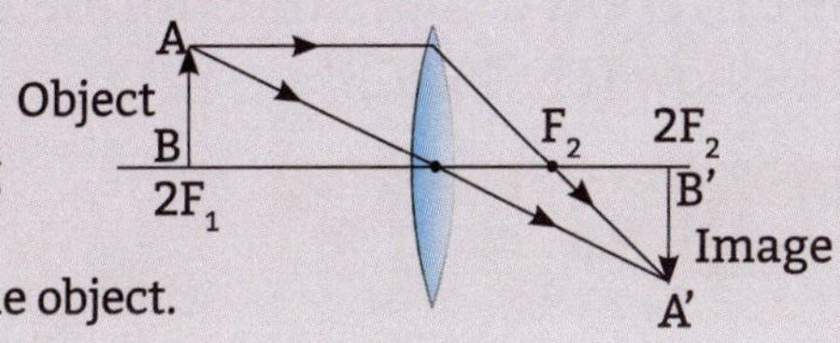

By using a convex lens, we get a real and inverted image of the object.

Uses of convex and concave lenses

- Convex lenses are used as magnifying glasses (simple microscope).
- Convex and concave lenses are used for correcting the defects of the eye.
- Concave lens is used as a peephole.
- Convex and concave lenses are used for cameras and projectors.
- Convex and concave lenses are used in binoculars, telescopes and microscopes.

DISPERSION OF LIGHT

We have all seen a rainbow. A rainbow has different colours. Why are there different colours in a rainbow? How are these colours formed in the rainbow?

Take a compact disc (CD) and expose it to sunlight. You can see different colours.

You can see the colours when you pass sunlight or white light through a prism. Why are these colours formed when white light is passed through the prism? It is because white light consists of seven colours. When a beam of white light is passed through a prism, it splits into its component colours (Fig. 15.14). This phenomenon is called **dispersion of light**.

Fig. 15.14: Spectrum of white light

A prism used commonly in the laboratory is a triangular prism. This is an optical element that has flat, polished and shining surfaces which can refract (change the direction) light. If you project the light that passes through the prism on a white screen, you will see a sequence of seven colours in the following order: violet, indigo, blue, green, yellow, orange and red. The range of colours obtained is called the **spectrum**.

Can we combine these seven colours to produce white light again? Let us try. Place two prisms as shown in figure 15.15.

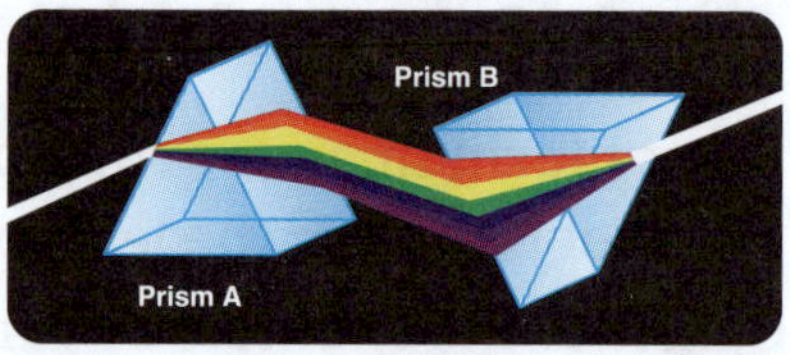

Fig. 15.15: Recombination of the colours of light

When white light is passed through the first prism, it splits into seven colours. As these rays are passed through the second prism, they combine to form white light.

Sunlight appears to be white but it is a combination of seven colours. The different colours in a **rainbow** are formed due to the dispersion of sunlight as it passes through small water droplets in the air after rain. The small droplets of water act as prisms. The different colours thus formed appear in the form of a large curve in the sky called a rainbow (Fig.15.16).

Know the Scientist

It was Sir Isaac Newton who showed that white light can be split into different constituent colours by passing through a prism. He was conducting experiments on images of heavenly objects. He noticed colours at the edges of the images formed. He performed the famous prism experiment at Trinity College, Cambridge. In this experiment he passed a narrow beam of sunlight through a prism. He could observe that the white beam of sunlight was split into seven colours.

Fig. 15.16: A rainbow formed in the sky

A **Newton's disc** can also be used to show how the seven colours can again be combined to form white colour. The area of the disc is divided into seven equal parts and each part is coloured using each of the seven colours (Fig. 15.17). If you rotate the disc fast, it appears white in colour.

Fig. 15.17: Newton's disc

Revise and Recall

State whether the statements are true (T) or false (F).

1. We can obtain an enlarged and erect image by a concave mirror. ☐
2. A convex lens always forms a virtual image. ☐
3. The image formed by a plane mirror is always virtual. ☐
4. A real image can be obtained on a screen. ☐
5. Convex lens is used as a peephole. ☐

Keywords

Rectilinear propagation: The property that light always travels in a straight line

Reflection: Bouncing of light from a surface

Real image: Image that can be projected on a screen

Virtual image: Image that cannot be projected on a screen

Dispersion: Splitting of light into its seven component colours

Spectrum: The sequence of colours obtained when light undergoes dispersion

Summary

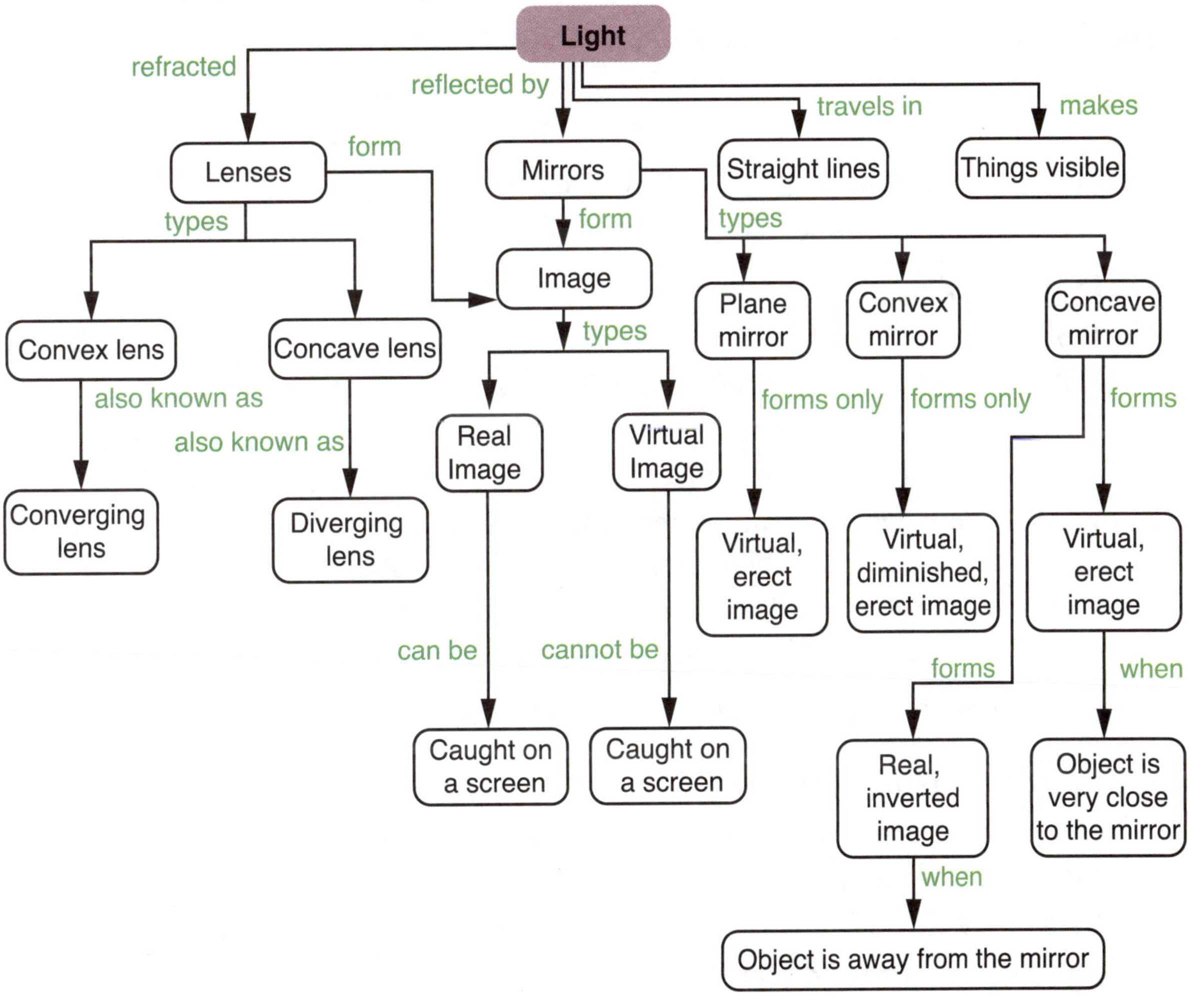

EXERCISE

W

ia

A. Choose the correct option.

1. Which mirror is used as the rear view mirror of vehicles?
   (a) Plane mirror (b) Concave mirror
   (c) Convex mirror (d) Cylindrical mirror
2. The mirror which can form both real and virtual images is a ____________.
   (a) convex mirror (b) concave mirror
   (c) plane mirror (d) All of these
3. The property of reversal of the sides of an image formed by a plane mirror is ____________.
   (a) dispersion (b) lateral inversion
   (c) reflection of light (d) rectilinear propagation of light
4. The device used for making peepholes in the doors of houses is a ____________.
   (a) convex lens (b) concave lens
   (c) convex mirror (d) concave mirror
5. Newton's disc consists of ____________ colours.
   (a) eight (b) seven (c) six (d) five

B. Fill in the blanks.

1. The lens used in simple microscope is ____________. (concave lens/convex lens)
2. The mirrors used in buses to help the driver see inside the whole bus are ____________. (convex mirrors/concave mirrors)
3. An image that can be obtained on a screen is ____________. (real/virtual)
4. A mirror that always forms an image of the same size as that of the object is a ____________. (plane mirror/concave mirror)
5. The splitting of white light into its constituent colours is called ____________ of light. (dispersion/reflection)

C. State whether the following statements are true (T) or false (F). ia

1. An erect image is always virtual. ☐
2. A convex mirror can be used to obtain enlarged erect image of an object. ☐
3. A rainbow is formed due to the dispersion of sunlight by the water droplets in the sky. ☐
4. Sunlight is a mixture of different colours of light. ☐
5. The erect image formed by a concave mirror can be obtained on a screen. ☐

D. Answer the following in one word each.

1. The mirror that forms only diminished image
2. Bouncing of light from a surface
3. A lens that converges a ray of light
4. Image that can be projected on a screen
5. The phenomenon of splitting of light into its component colours

E. Give reasons for the following.

1. Concave and convex mirrors are called spherical mirrors.
2. We cannot form a real image using a convex mirror.
3. Convex mirrors are used as side mirrors in vehicles.
4. An object can be seen only if it either reflects or emits the light.
5. A shopkeeper uses convex mirror to have maximum view of his shop.

F. Answer the following questions briefly.

1. What is a spectrum?
2. What is the difference between a real image and a virtual image?
3. What is principle axis of a concave mirror?
4. How can we differentiate between a convex mirror and a concave mirror?
5. What is lateral inversion?

G. Answer the following questions in detail.

1. Mention the characteristics of an image formed by a plane mirror.
2. With the help of an experiment, show that light cannot bend from its path.
3. Write an activity to show that the light ray converges when it passes through a convex lens.
4. Explain the uses of convex and concave lenses.

COGNITIVE CORNER

Critical Thinking

Can you observe the images of distant objects using different convex lenses? How and why can this be done?

How can this be practically applied in real-world scenarios? What considerations would need to be taken into account for such applications?

Picture Study

Identify the types of lenses used (A, B and C) and justify your answer.

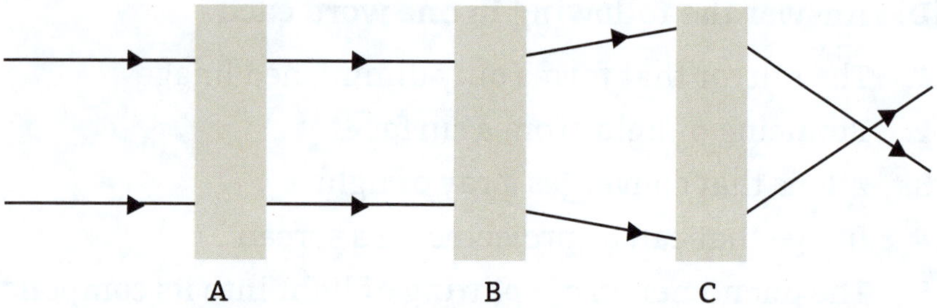

Project

Telescope is an instrument used to view heavenly objects such as moon, planets and stars. As a part of Science Club activity, make your own telescope using two convex lenses. **(C-7.2)**

Materials required: Two convex lenses of focal length about 10 cm and 100 cm, cardboard sheet and glue

Procedure:

1. Roll the cardboard to form a tube whose diameter is equal to that of the lens with a smaller focal length (that is, 10 cm). Fix the lens at the end of this tube using a tape.
2. Make another cardboard tube slightly bigger in diameter than the first tube and fix the other lens at the end of the tube using the tape.
3. Insert the free end of one tube into the free end of the other tube. Now, you can move the tubes and focus the telescope to a distant object.

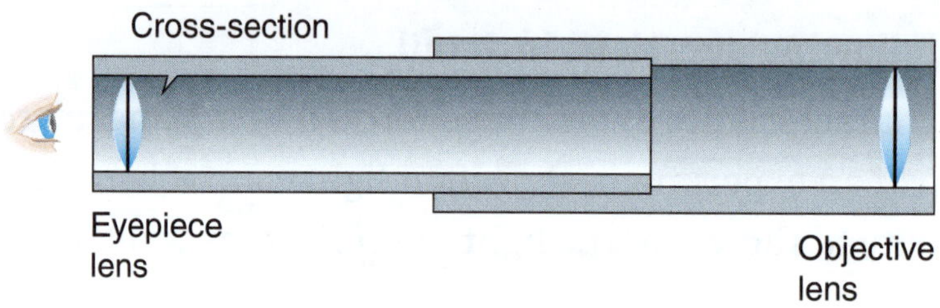

In the Library

Sir Isaac Newton was the first to propose a theory to explain light. His theory is known as the corpuscular theory of light. Later, many theories were developed to explain the behaviour of light. Learn more about the different theories of light. **(C-7.1)**

Life Skills

A rainbow is an optical illusion. This means that a rainbow does not actually exist in a specific spot in the sky. Its appearance depends on where you are standing and where the sun (or other source of light) is shining from. Create a rainbow in your class. Can a rainbow be produced by moonlight? Read about it and discuss in your class. **(C-7.1)**

Worksheet

Telescopes are instruments that allow us to see far off objects such that they appear nearby. Terrestrial telescopes are used in tourist spots to see distant mountain ranges and views from atop a hill spot. They have three convex lenses in a cylindrical body.

Astronomical telescopes may have two convex lenses or a combination of concave and convex mirrors. Trying to see heavenly bodies through astronomical telescopes have various disadvantages. The atmosphere distorts the passage of light from distant stars and weather conditions also affect the visibility. Another type of astronomical telescope is the space telescope. Hubble telescope is the most famous space telescope launched by USA which is still performing.

Terrestrial telescope

Astronomical telescope

Hubble space telescope

All large telescope (and many small ones) use a large concave mirror at the bottom of the telescope and a small plane mirror at the top.

A. Why do you think a large concave mirror is used at the bottom of a telescope?

____

____

____

B. Prisms are used in binoculars. Why are prisms used in binoculars instead of mirrors? Find out.

____

____

____

C. A concave mirror is mounted near the base of a microscope. Find out its purpose.

____

____

____

16 Water

Curricular Goals

- Explore the world of matter and its constituents, properties and behaviour **(CG-1)**
- Explore the living world in scientific terms **(CG-3)**
- Understand the interface of science, technology and society **(CG-5)**
- Communicate questions, observations and conclusions related to science **(CG-7)**

Competencies

- Describe changes in matter and use particulate nature to represent the properties of matter and the changes **(C-1.2)**
- Explain the conditions suitable for sustaining life on Earth and other planets (properties of water) **(C-3.4)**
- Illustrate how science and technology can help to improve the quality of human life (judicious consumption of resources) **(C-5.1)**
- Use scientific vocabulary to communicate science accurately in oral and written form, and through visual representation **(C-7.1)**

Let's Get Started

Look at the pictures given below and identify these sources of water.

________________ ________________ ________________

One of the main reasons for the presence of life on Earth is water. Water is one of the most essential constituents of life. In the previous class, you have studied about the availability and uses of water. In this chapter, we will study about the sources of water, its distribution in various regions and the need and conservation of water.

WATER - A PRECIOUS RESOURCE

Water is one of the essential substances without which life on the Earth cannot exist. All living organisms are dependent on water. Human beings drink around four litres of water a day. Water is also an irreplaceable resource for our agriculture and industries. Water grants us food and livestock security, maintains organic life, and helps in industrial production.

Our Earth consists of 70% water, of which 97.5% of water is found in the oceans and is salty, and only 2.5% is potable freshwater. Thus, even though water is a necessity for all living beings on Earth, having enough healthy drinkable water is a precious commodity across the globe.

Physical Properties of Water

Water is composed of elements hydrogen and oxygen and exists in gaseous, liquid and solid states. It has the chemical formula H_2O. Some of the common observable physical properties of water are as follows:

- Water is a colourless and odourless compound.
- Water is a tasteless liquid in its natural state.
- The boiling point of water is 100 °C.
- The freezing point of water is 0 °C or 32 °F.
- Water is referred as the universal solvent due to its ability to dissolve most substances.

WATER IN DIFFERENT FORMS

Water exists in three different forms: solid, liquid and gas. The three forms of water are interchangeable. Ice is the solid form of water. It melts at 0 °C and changes into liquid water. Water, which is a liquid, boils at 100 °C and changes to steam. *The change in the physical state of water from solid to liquid is called* ***melting****. The change in the physical state of water from liquid to gas is called* ***vaporization****.* Water vapour changes to liquid water when the temperature decreases or it is cooled. *The change in the physical state of water from gas to liquid is called* ***condensation****.*

Liquid water solidifies into ice when it is further cooled. *The change in the physical state of water from liquid water to ice is called* ***freezing*** (Fig. 16.1).

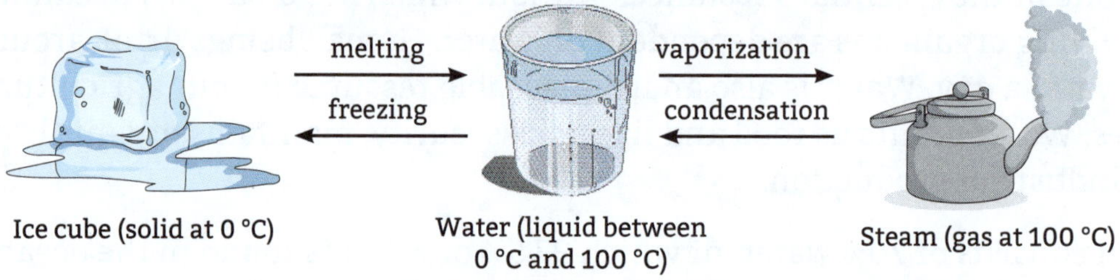

Fig. 16.1: Forms of water

In nature, water takes the forms known by different names as shown in the adjacent box.

Forms of water on Earth

Solid	**Liquid**	**Gas**
Glaciers	Rain	Fog
Icebergs	Dew	Steam
Snow	Mist	Water vapour
Hail		
Frost		

Glacier: It is a large chunk of ice that moves like a river over the surface of land. Glaciers are found moving from high mountains and are a source of freshwater.

Iceberg: It is a large piece of ice that has broken off a glacier and floats in seas and oceans.

Snow: It is a form of precipitation in which crystals of ice fall on the ground.

Hail: These are hard lumps of ice falling from the sky during precipitation.

Frost: It is formed when water vapour solidifies and gets deposited on plants, trees, houses, vehicles, etc.

WATER CYCLE

The continuous circulation of water from the Earth's surface to the atmosphere by evaporation and back to the Earth by condensation is known as the **water cycle**. In this process, water gets converted into all the three states of matter (solid, liquid and gas) but in different stages.

Water from water bodies and moist soil evaporates and rises up in the air in the form of **water vapour**. In the daytime, evaporation is at its highest due to the heat of the sun. Plants also give out water from their leaves in high amount as a result of transpiration. Water vapour is the gaseous state of water. When this vapour rises up, it condenses to form clouds. In the clouds, the vapour cools down to form water droplets. When further condensation takes place, the water droplets become bigger in size. When the clouds get too saturated with water, they pour down as rain. This process where clouds pour down as rain is called **precipitation**. This is the liquid state of water in the water cycle. In colder regions, water drops freeze and fall as hail or snow. Rainwater is the main source of water on the Earth.

The rainwater that falls into seas, rivers, lakes, etc. increases their water level. Some water freezes to form ice on the mountaintops during winter. This ice melts during the summer months to feed the river, which then flows into the sea. The water from these water bodies evaporates back into the atmosphere, completing the water cycle (Fig. 16.2).

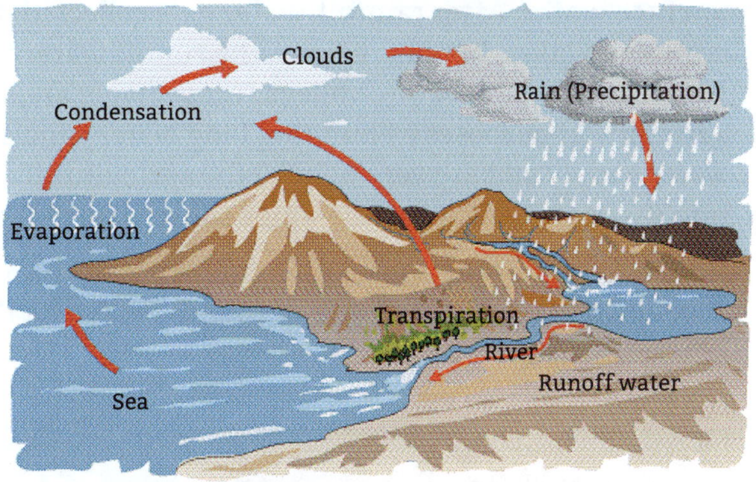

Fig. 16.2: The water cycle

USES OF WATER

Water is required for a variety of purposes. Some of these are discussed below:

Body functions: Plants, animals and human beings need water for their survival. Plants need water to prepare their own food and for the germination of seeds. They absorb water from the soil through their roots. Animals and human beings need water for the digestion and absorption of nutrients.

Domestic use: We need water for drinking, cleaning, cooking, bathing, washing, etc.

Agricultural use: Agriculture in India is mainly dependent on the rains. If there is less rainfall, the crops for the season do not grow properly, creating huge losses for farmers. Crops such as paddy, wheat and sugarcane need a large amount of water to grow.

Industrial use: In many parts of the world, water from rivers is used to produce electricity, which is known as hydroelectric power. Many industries require water for washing, cleaning and as an ingredient in their products. Industries also use water as a coolant.

Use in transport: Huge ships transport goods, containers and people all around the world through rivers, seas and oceans.

As a habitat: Different freshwater and marine water bodies are the habitats for different kinds of plants, animals, fish and microorganisms.

SOURCES OF WATER

Rainwater gets stored in the soil below the ground. Some of the rainwater that falls on the land surface may flow into rivers, streams or oceans. This is called **runoff water**. The runoff water either flows into rivers or gets stored in lakes to form a freshwater source.

Surface water: After rainfall, water gets collected in the low-lying areas to form ponds and lakes. In hilly regions, the runoff water falls from higher areas to form rivers that flow into valleys. These rivers are diverted to distribute water for agricultural purposes by building long water canals. These canals form a network of water supply and are very helpful for agricultural activities. The rivers further flow into seas or oceans. All these water sources form the surface water of the Earth.

Underground water: During the summer season or in case of failure of rainfall, people depend on the water from underground sources for domestic and agricultural purposes.

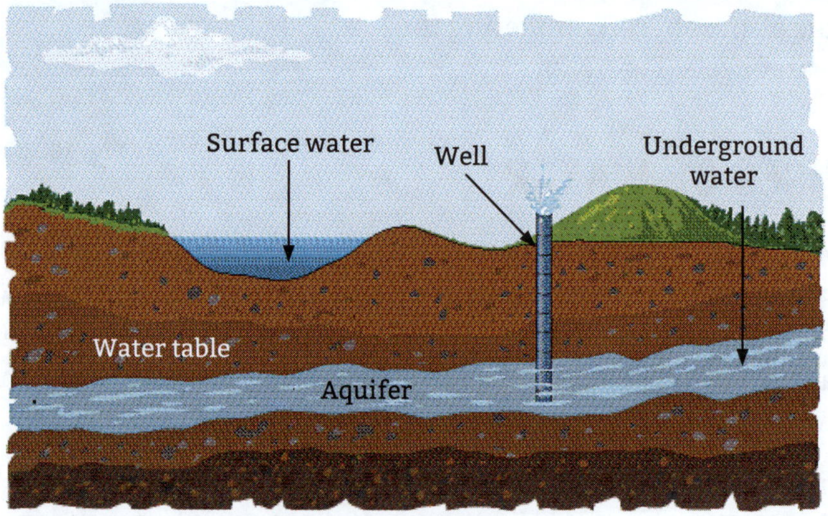

Fig. 16.3: Underground water

Rainwater gets collected in the soil by seeping (leaking) into the gravel and rocks at the bottom. The seepage of rainwater from the surface of the soil is called **infiltration**. The underground level where all the space between the soil particles and rocks is filled with water is called the **water table**. An **aquifer** is the groundwater stored between the hard rock layers below the water table (Fig. 16.3). When this water comes out forcefully under pressure, it forms a spring. Groundwater can also be obtained by digging wells. People depend on groundwater when there is a shortage of surface water. Borewells are constructed by boring or drilling a hole in the Earth until an aquifer is reached.

NATURAL DISTRIBUTION OF WATER IN INDIA

The movement of wind influences rainfall in India. The amount of rainfall is not uniform at all the places. Uneven rainfall leads to floods and droughts.

Some regions such as the north-eastern states of Meghalaya, Sikkim and Manipur get torrential rainfall during the monsoon season. Some coastal states such as Andhra Pradesh, Odisha and West Bengal get rainfall due to the cyclones in the sea and high winds. The heavy rainfall in these regions causes floods, destroying life and property.

However, the western regions of Rajasthan, Gujarat and Madhya Pradesh do not get sufficient rainfall, leading to drought conditions.

Dams are built to maintain and distribute water supply. Artificial walls are built across rivers that control the flow of water in them. It holds a reservoir whose water content is maintained by the opening and closing of the gates. When water is needed in the nearby areas of the dam, the gates are opened to release it from the reservoir. The Bhakra Nangal dam is built on the river Sutlej and provides water to the states of Punjab and Haryana.

The Annual Average Rainfall Map of India

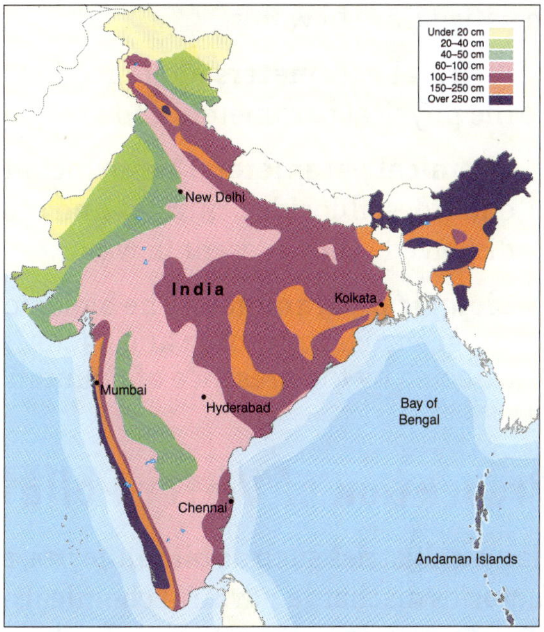

Activity

Collect information about the region where you live and answer the following questions.

1. In which part of India do you live?
2. Does this place receive sufficient rainfall?
3. Does it rain here throughout the year?
4. If not, during what time of the year does it receive rainfall?
5. Is rainfall uniform in all the regions of India? Write your observations after studying the map of India.

Science in Context

A rain gauge is a simple instrument used to measure the amount of rainfall received in a particular area at a given point of time. The amount of rain is measured by using any of these units: millimetre, centimetre or inch.

WATER POLLUTION

Water pollution is the contamination of waterbodies such as rivers, streams, lakes, seas, oceans and underground water by substances which are harmful for living beings. Rapid industrialisation and population explosion are the two important factors for causing water pollution. A large amount of untreated water is discharged back into the water sources after domestic and industrial usage.

Water may be called polluted when the following parameters reach beyond a specified limit in water.

- **Physical parameters:** Colour, odour, turbidity, taste and temperature constitute the physical parameters and are good indicators of contamination of water.
- **Chemical parameters:** These include the amount of carbonates, sulphates, chlorides, fluorides, nitrates and other metal ions. These chemicals form the total dissolved solids present in water.
- **Biological parameters:** The biological parameters include presence of algae, fungi, viruses, protozoa and bacteria. These life forms present in water are affected by the presence of pollutants.

Prevention of Water Pollution

Many industries such as oil refineries, sugar mills, and paper, textile and chemical factories discharge harmful chemicals into rivers and streams, causing the pollution of water. These industries release chemicals such as arsenic, fluoride and lead which make the water toxic.

By adopting some measures, we can prevent water pollution.

- Strict regulations should be made so that sewage is not discharged directly into local waterbodies.
- Every industry should have a water treatment plant so that the industrial discharge is treated before disposing it to a water source.
- We should not dispose household chemicals or cleaning agents down the sink or toilet.
- We should not pour fat or oil from cooking or grease down the sink.
- We should use minimum amount of detergent or bleach when washing clothes or dishes. We should prefer using phosphate free soaps and detergents.
- We should minimise the use of pesticides, herbicides and fertilizers in agriculture.

SCARCITY OF WATER

Water scarcity is a condition of shortage of water when there is not enough water to carry out even the basic necessities of life such as drinking, cooking and washing.

Even though 71% of the Earth is covered with water, the available freshwater is only 2.5%, which exists in the form of rivers, lakes, ice caps and groundwater. Of this, nearly 2% is frozen as ice or snow in the glaciers.

Thus, of the 2.5% freshwater found on the Earth, only 0.7–0.8% of groundwater and 0.01% of surface water are available to all the life forms for their needs. This shows that water is a precious resource.

Freshwater has to be treated to make it potable for human population. An increase in the population creates a greater demand for the construction of houses, shops, offices, industries, roads, etc., leading to overuse of the water resources and thus water scarcity.

Fig. 16.4: (a) Women fetching water from far-off places (b) Water tanker distributing water to areas affected with water shortage

Science in Context

- Wastage of water at homes happens when water taps are left running while brushing teeth, shaving or washing dishes.
- A common toilet uses 8 litres of clean water in a single flush.
- A dripping tap can waste 90 litres of water a week.

People face serious water shortage in both urban and rural areas. In urban areas, people sometimes have to wait for 2–3 days to get their supply of water from the civic authorities (Fig. 16.4). During times of scarcity, civic authorities supply water through tankers to the affected localities and people stand in queues to get their share of water.

In rural areas, lakes, rivers and wells dry up, leading to the shortage of water for household use and for animals. In certain areas, irrigation gets badly affected, leading to crop losses.

Causes of Water Scarcity

There are many causes of water scarcity such as increase in population and demand for more water. The use of water as a coolant in industries and for washing causes scarcity and leads to the pollution of water sources. This causes water to become unfit for use. Deforestation leads to less rainfall. Agriculture in India is mainly dependent on rainfall. However, rainfall is unseasonal and irregular, which causes the scarcity of water and eventually leads to crop loss. Leaking pipes, taps and overflowing tanks are the major contributors to water wastage in the cities. Water gets wasted due to ignorance, wrong attitudes and a general apathy—lack of responsibility. The only effective way to stop the wastage of water is through proper education and by creating awareness about the importance and methods of conserving water.

Excessive usage of borewell technology for accessing groundwater is seen all around the world. Farmers dig many borewells at their farms to use groundwater for agricultural activities (Fig. 16.5).

Fig. 16.5: Borewell used for irrigation in agriculture

When monsoons fail, the farmer is forced to depend on groundwater. Soon, these borewells become dry due to excessive use. The farmers then dig more borewells, which further reduces the water table, but the worst offenders in the misuse of groundwater are the industries and, to some extent, the urban householders.

Due to the failure of rain and the conversion of catchment areas into utility places such as malls, bus stands, hospitals and railway stations, water is in short supply in the cities. House owners and industrialists dig borewells that affect the water table. A rapid increase in population has led to a greater demand for water. This has led to a greater dependence on groundwater, causing its rapid depletion due to an excessive use. In the cities, the amount of underground water is less. This is because the seepage of rainwater into the soil is obstructed due to the construction of concrete pavements and buildings. Deforestation on a large scale leads to poor rainfall, affecting the water table.

Consequences of Water Scarcity

On humans: Unavailability of clean drinking water, which leads to health problems and unhygienic conditions.

On plants: Plants need water to carry out photosynthesis. They wither and die when there is a lack of water.

On land: Soil dries up and the land eventually becomes barren when water is not available.

METHODS OF CONSERVATION OF WATER

The amount of fresh potable water is decreasing day by day at an alarming rate. Due to a rapid increase in population, the demand for potable water is also increasing. So, every drop of water is important for human activities. Economical use and the conservation of water are the two main methods to save water.

Proper storage, management and distribution of water from sources such as rivers and lakes should be undertaken by constructing dams and reservoirs. A huge amount of potable water is lost during the distribution of water because of leakage in the main water pipelines. Fixing these leakages can save a lot of water from going into the drains.

Pollution of water sources is a major problem, which leaves them unusable due to the presence of contaminants in them. Wastewater treatment should be done before letting it flow into the rivers and lakes.

Care should be taken not to pollute the lakes and ponds by using them for washing clothes, bathing animals and other human activities.

A lot of rainwater goes into storm drains during the rainy season. This water can be conserved for use or to replenish the groundwater levels by **rainwater harvesting** (Fig. 16.6). Rainwater harvesting is the practice of storing rainwater that falls on the roofs of houses and buildings. From there, it passes into the gutters, lining the edge of the roofs. It flows through the gutters and pipes into the tanks built on the ground or under the ground. This water is stored in the tanks until required. It is drawn up by pumps. It can be used for domestic purposes as well as for agricultural use.

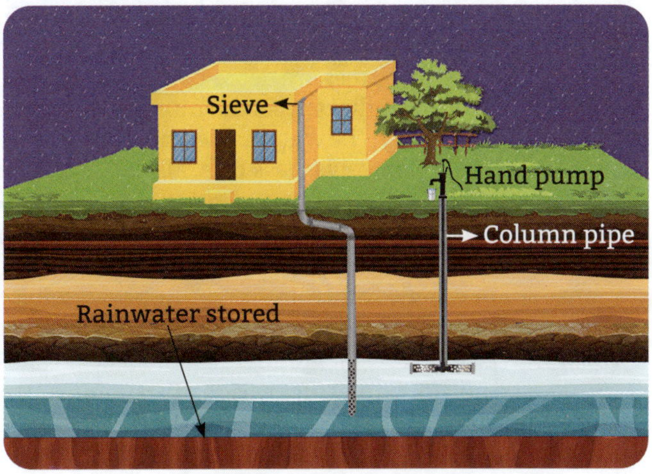

Fig. 16.6: Rainwater harvesting

Government policies should encourage the use of rainwater harvesting by making it a mandatory requirement in houses and buildings in urban areas.

Another simple and effective method to reduce the usage of water is by **recycling the water** from industries and using it for horticultural purposes. A lot of water is wasted in our households. This can be prevented by fixing the leaking taps, pipes and overflowing tanks. The water used for washing vegetables in homes can also be used to water the plants.

Drip irrigation (Fig. 16.7) in agricultural lands can save a lot of water. Crops and plants are given sufficient amount of water without any wastage through this process.

Fig. 16.7: Drip irrigation

A major remedy to lessen the problem of scarcity of water is afforestation. Large areas of forests are being wiped out due to an ever-increasing population. Planting trees and increasing the forest cover would lead to good rainfall and less pollution.

Proper management of water should be done by the methods of drip irrigation, rainwater harvesting and replenishing the groundwater table. We must all practise and promote the economical use of water.

Case Study: Overcoming the Situation of Water Scarcity in Chennai City—A Success Story

Chennai is one of the major metropolitan cities in India. The land area of the city is 76 sq km, consisting of extremely flat coastal plains. Chennai has an average annual rainfall of around 1250 mm. A very high amount of rainfall is received during the months from October to December.

Chennai is home to many multinational companies and attracts job seekers from across the country. This has increased the population of the city, which far exceeds the availability of infrastructural facilities. The demand for residential land, drinking water and electricity has also increased. But water and other resources are decreasing. Unavailability of drinking water has led to an increased dependence on groundwater. As the number of borewells increased and the prices of water supply increased alarmingly, the water table and groundwater aquifers became saline and depleted. In the year 2001, Chennai received less rainfall, causing further water scarcity and a drought-like situation.

In July 2001, the concept of rainwater harvesting was promoted and people realized the need of the hour, as they had severe shortage of drinking water. This system of harvesting rainwater was implemented by institutions and public buildings as well as individual households. During monsoon, the rainwater from the rooftop was collected through drainpipes and diverted to a storage tank through a filter unit. The excess water from this tank was connected either to an existing well or recharge pits constructed for this purpose.

In 2003, rainwater harvesting was made compulsory by law. The government made it mandatory for all buildings to have rainwater harvesting throughout Tamil Nadu. It was implemented not only in the new but also in the existing, old buildings. This initiative by the Tamil Nadu government has helped in improving the groundwater table as well as the quality of groundwater. Moreover, during the rainy season, the dependence of the people of Chennai on the municipal water agency has come down.

Thus, a city known for its acute scarcity of drinking water and the exploitation of groundwater has now moved towards water security achieved by the application of affordable and environmentally sustainable solutions created in situ and with social benefits. Several rainwater harvest structures are constructed by different NGOs across the city with successful initiation of restoration of ground water. Chennai managed to implement the simplest possible solution of installing rainwater harvest structures in a large proportion of homes and buildings.

The director of Rain Centre calculates and says Chennai's average annual rainfall of around 140 cm and if maintained the same, is sufficient to meet domestic water needs. Farmers in coastal area are countering salinity caused by droughts and groundwater depletion through the rain water harvesting and by reviving traditional organic farming practices.

SEAWATER AND ITS DESALINATION

Around 97% of the water present on our planet is salt water. By using innovative techniques, we can remove salt from the saline water and make it suitable for our use. This can also help us tackle the problem of water scarcity.

A technique used for this purpose is called desalination. **Desalination** is the process by which the mineral salts dissolved in water are removed. Many areas affected by freshwater scarcity are close to the sea and this is where the concept of desalination helps. Currently, this process is one of the most used techniques to obtain freshwater for human consumption or agricultural purposes.

Desalination also occurs naturally during the water cycle. The evaporation of seawater forms clouds in the sky and leaves salt behind on the shores.

Keywords

Glaciers: Large chunks of ice that float in oceans

Infiltration: The seepage of rainwater from the surface of the soil

Surface water: The water found in the rivers, streams, lakes, ponds and oceans

Water table: The level underground where all the space between the soil particles and rocks is filled with water

Aquifer: The groundwater stored between the hard rock layers below the water table

Rainwater harvesting: A method used to collect and conserve rainwater for further use and for replenishing groundwater

Drip irrigation: A method of irrigating agricultural land with minimal water wastage

Rain gauge: An instrument used to measure rainfall

Water pollution: The contamination of waterbodies by substances harmful for living beings

Desalination: The process by which the mineral salts dissolved in water are removed

Summary

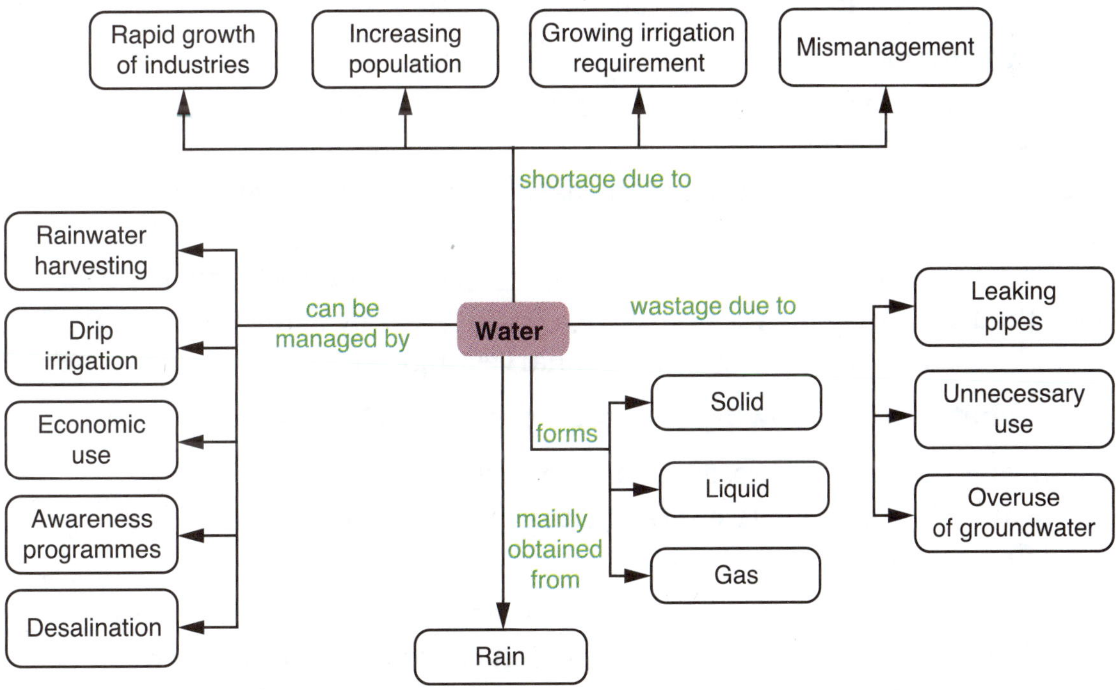

EXERCISE

A. Choose the correct option.

1. A large chunk of ice that moves like a river over the surface of the land is called __________.
   (a) an iceberg (b) a glacier (c) a hail (d) a frost
2. The water on the Earth remains constant due to the continuous circulation of water between
   (a) the three forms of water. (b) the two forms of water.
   (c) water vapour and the oceans. (d) water vapour, glaciers and oceans.
3. Which of the following is not a form of precipitation?
   (a) Frost (b) Glacier (c) Snow (d) Hail
4. The process by which water from water bodies rises up in the form of vapour is called __________.
   (a) transpiration (b) condensation (c) precipitation (d) evaporation
5. Even though facilities such as irrigation ponds and canals are present, they are not sufficient and the farmers depend on groundwater. Why?
   (a) Because of uneven rainfall
   (b) Because of poverty
   (c) Because of too much of water in the agricultural fields
   (d) Because groundwater is best suited for crops

B. Fill in the blanks.

1. A majority of farmers in India depend on __________ for irrigation of their crops. (rainwater/borewells)
2. The groundwater stored between the hard rock layers is known as __________. (aquifer/water table)
3. Transpiration turns water into the __________ state. (solid/gaseous)
4. A method of conserving water used in agriculture is by using the process of __________. (drip irrigation/rainwater harvesting)

C. State whether the following statements are true (T) or false (F).

1. Freshwater is a limitless resource on the Earth. ☐
2. The availability of freshwater is equal to the amount of the water available on Earth. ☐
3. Water can be found in its gaseous state in the form of vapour in the air. ☐
4. The main reason for groundwater depletion is less consumption and too much seepage of the water into the ground. ☐
5. Afforestation increases the forest cover, leading to good rainfall. ☐

D. Define the following forms of water.

1. Glacier 2. Iceberg 3. Snow 4. Hail 5. Frost

E. Give reasons for the following.

1. Judicial use of water is a necessity.
2. Leaking water pipelines or taps must be repaired immediately.
3. Rainwater harvesting is compulsory in Chennai.
4. Rainwater harvesting can increase water table.
5. Bhakra Nangal dam is one of the main sources of water for irrigation in nearby areas.

F. Answer the following questions briefly.

1. What are the reasons for an increase in the demand of water?
2. How does afforestation help in improving groundwater?
3. What is rainwater harvesting?
4. Write a note on the natural distribution of water in India.
5. What are the uses of water?
6. List the physical properties of water.
7. Mention some ways to prevent water pollution.

G. Answer the following questions in detail.

1. What are the causes of water scarcity in India?
2. Suggest a few ways to conserve water.
3. Explain the term 'underground water'.
4. How does an increasing population cause scarcity of water?
5. Explain the water cycle and the forms of water in nature.

COGNITIVE CORNER

Critical Thinking

1. Recently, parts of Odisha were flooded and created a scarcity of drinking water. When floods bring in a lot of water, how can there be scarcity of water?
2. Will the water table in all regions of the Earth hold the same quantity of water? Give reasons for your answer.
3. Should water be treated to make it potable for human use? Why?

Picture Study

Identify the following methods of irrigation. Write or discuss about their advantages and disadvantages.

Project

As a part of Eco Club activity, write slogans to spread a message about water conservation. The slogans should be short and to the point. Draw an image that also conveys the meaning or a part of the meaning of the statement along with the slogans. An example for a slogan: 'Today's wastage is tomorrow's shortage'. Also, create awareness among people about various water conservation methods. **(C-7.1)**

Life Skills

Turn off the taps when they are not in use or while you are brushing your teeth. You can save a lot of water by avoiding the regular use of bathtub as it consumes a high volume of water. **(C-5.1)**

Answer the following:

1. In the school canteen, your friend washes his hands and leaves the tap running. What do you do and why?
2. What time of the day is best for watering the plants and why?
3. What can be done to the water left in the water bottle that you carry to school?
4. How can we reuse the water that has been used for washing vegetables?

Worksheet

Life thrives on Earth due to favourable temperature, oxygen and water. The unique properties of water, such as its heat retention and ice's buoyancy, influence climate and aquatic survival. Water's insulating ice layers shield aquatic life in cold regions, maintaining warmer temperatures beneath frozen surfaces.

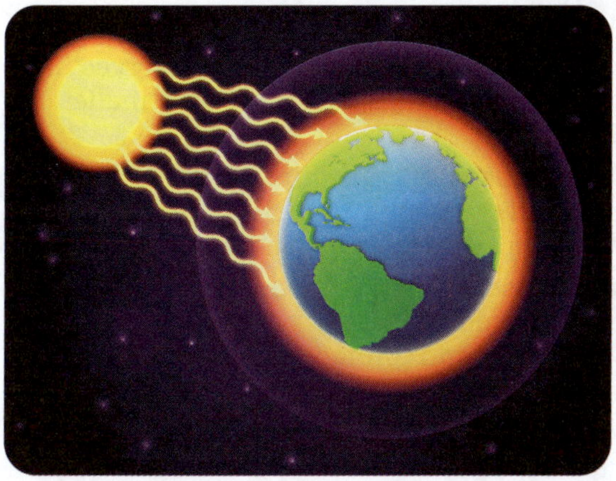

Uneven solar heating of Earth's surface

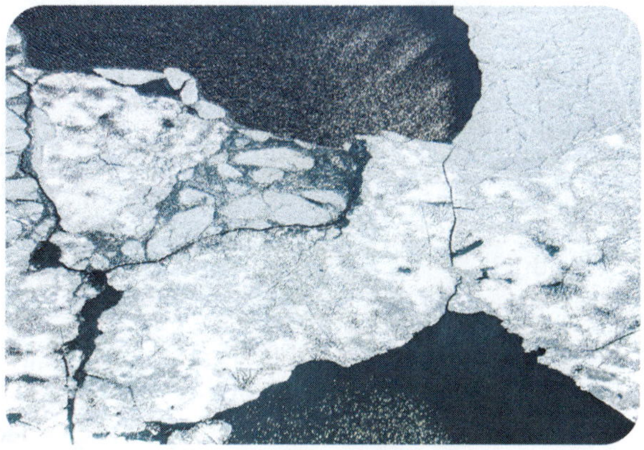

Ice floating on a lake

A. In the context of Sustainable Development Goal 14, how might the understanding of water's unique properties influence conservation efforts and policies aimed at protecting marine ecosystems? Discuss the potential implications of these properties on the vulnerability or resilience of marine life to climate change and pollution.

____

____

____

B. Reflecting on the role of water's insulation in maintaining warmer temperatures underneath frozen surfaces, how could this knowledge be harnessed to benefit both ecosystems and human activities in cold regions? Explore innovative strategies that leverage this property to promote sustainable practices and enhance local resilience to changing climates.

____

____

____

17 Forests: Our Lifeline

Curricular Goals

- Explore the living world in scientific terms **(CG-3)**
- Explore the nature and processes of science through engaging with the evolution of scientific knowledge and conducting scientific inquiry **(CG-6)**
- Communicate questions, observations and conclusions related to science **(CG-7)**

Competencies

- Describe the diversity of living things observed in the natural surroundings, including at a smaller scale **(C-3.1)**
- Analyse patterns of relationships between living organisms and their environments in terms of dependence on and response to each other **(C-3.3)**
- Illustrate how scientific knowledge and ideas have changed over time and identify the scientific values that are inherent and common across the evolution of scientific knowledge **(C-6.1)**
- Use scientific vocabulary to communicate science accurately in oral and written form, and through visual representation **(C-7.1)**

Let's Get Started

Identify the source of the products shown below.

Wooden chair

Source: __________

Firewood

Source: __________

Herbal tooth powder

Source: __________

Honey

Source: __________

Forests are our lifeline. We all depend upon forests in some way or the other for our survival. Forests help us in many ways to meet our daily requirements. The word *forest* comes from the Latin word *foris*, which means 'outdoors' or 'away from civilization'.

Forests are home to diverse plants and animals, sustaining herbivores and providing resources such as timber, fruits and medicines. They impact climate, air quality and rainfall, serving as reservoirs for greenhouse gases. Beyond their aesthetic value, forests offer habitats, promoting biodiversity and supporting various life forms.

FOREST PROFILE

There are different kinds of plants of varied heights and sizes in forests. Parts of a tree above the stem, including the branches and leaves are collectively known as the **crown**. Depending on the type of trees, there are different shapes of crowns. Trees belonging to the genus *Pinus* have tapering crowns, while a neem tree has a crown that looks like a globe (Fig. 17.1).

Fig. 17.1: Different shapes of crowns

The ground of the forests is covered with leaves and shrubs. Various kinds of animals dwell on trees in forests but at different heights. For example, birds live on the top branches of the trees, while monkeys use the lower branches as their homes. Depending on the height of the trees and the types of animals that live there, forests are divided into layers. They are shown in figure 17.2.

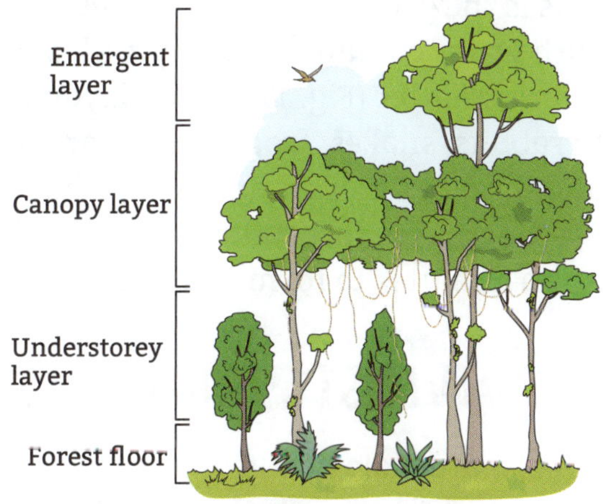

Fig. 17.2: Forest profile

Emergent Layer

The branches on the topmost layer of the tallest trees are known as the emergent layer. This layer is at a height of 40 metres from the ground and receives sunlight in abundance. Preying birds such as hawks and eagles live on this layer as it is easier for them to spot their prey.

Canopy Layer

This layer is formed when trees growing close to each other appear as a roof over the rest of the two floors below (Fig. 17.3). The canopy measures from about 20 metres to 40 metres above the ground. It has abundance of food; hence, it is a dwelling place for many birds, insects and monkeys.

Fig. 17.3: Canopy of a forest

Understorey Layer

Fig. 17.4: The understorey of forests

This layer of a forest starts from the foot of trees and goes up to 20 metres from the ground. The canopy blocks the sunlight, so this layer has shade (Fig. 17.4).

All the lower branches of the canopy trees, shrubs, bushes and smaller trees are a part of the understorey. Many birds, insects and a few animals such as leopards and sloth bears live here. Animals such as deer, bison, elephants, etc. eat the herbs, shrubs and dwell in the understorey.

Forest Floor

Fig. 17.5: Forest floor

This is the ground layer of a forest. The soil is moist with water containing decaying leaves, fruits and animal matter (Fig. 17.5). This layer of forests is home to rabbits, snakes, frogs, earthworms, fungi, termites and insects. The decomposers (microorganisms) present on the forest floor decompose dead plant and animal matter to form fertile soil known as **humus**.

BIODIVERSITY IN FORESTS

Forests are biologically diverse systems representing the richest biological areas on the Earth. They cover almost a third of the global land area and harbour most of the Earth's terrestrial biodiversity.

Forests offer a variety of habitats for plants, animals and microorganisms. Forests act as a habitat to 80% of the world's plant and animal species. They contain about 60,000 different tree species, 80% of amphibian species, 75% of bird species and 68% of the world's mammal species. Animal and plant species exist in every layer of the forest. All of them have a significant impact on preserving the planet's healthy ecosystem.

INTERDEPENDENCE OF PLANTS AND ANIMALS

Plants and animals depend on each other. You have studied that plants (autotrophs) produce their own food by photosynthesis. Plants are called **producers**. Animals (heterotrophs) such as deer, bison, zebra, elephants, etc., known as herbivores, depend on plants for their food.

Carnivores are the animals that feed on herbivores, for example, tiger, lion, wolf, etc. Thus, both herbivores and carnivores depend on plants for food and they are known as **consumers**.

> **Science in Context**
>
> The sun is the ultimate source of energy on our planet. Plants use the energy from the sun during photosynthesis to prepare food. Animals eat plants. So, the flow of energy is from producers to consumers, where producers are always at the start of a food chain.

Food Chain

a

*A **food chain** is formed when one organism eats another organism for food.* For example, grasshoppers depend on grass and plants for food. Frogs eat the grasshoppers. Snakes eat frogs as their food (Fig. 17.6). This dependence of organisms on one another for food forms a food chain. There is a flow of energy in the form of food from one organism to another.

Fig. 17.6: Food chain

Here, grass produces its own food. It is a **producer**. The grasshopper depends directly on grass. So, it is known as a **primary consumer.** The frog then feeds on the grasshopper. It is, therefore, indirectly dependent on the producers and is called a **secondary consumer**. The snake then feeds on the frog. The organisms that eat the secondary consumers are called **tertiary consumers**. Forests are home to many such food chains.

There is another group of animals that depends on both plants and animals for their food. They are called **omnivores**. For example, bear, wild boar, wild dogs, etc. are omnivores. When animals die, their bodies are eaten by crows, vultures and hyenas. This group of animals is called **scavengers**. The bodies of dead plants and animals get broken down into simple substances or are decomposed by **decomposers** such as fungi and bacteria present in the soil. The fertility of the soil is increased by these decomposers. Plants and trees grow better if the soil is fertile. The herbivores depend on these plants and trees, carnivores depend on the herbivores and the chain continues.

The energy from the plants enters the consumers in the form of food. This eventually ends up at the decomposers and is released into the soil. This is again used by the plants forming a cycle known as the **cycle of nutrients** (Fig. 17.7).

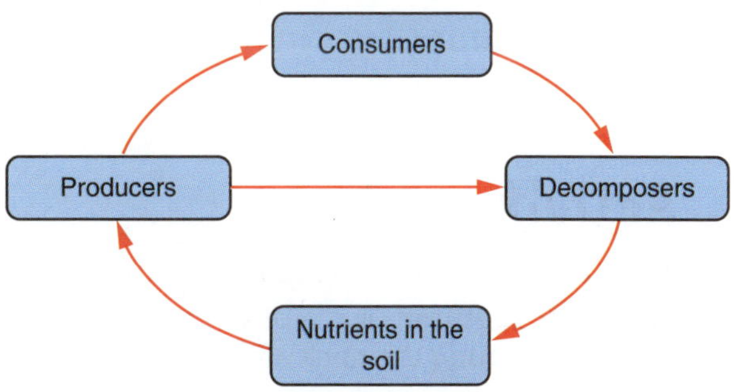

Fig. 17.7: The cycle of nutrients

Food Web

Multiple food chains are interlinked together to form a ***food web***. This happens because secondary consumers depend on different types of animals (primary consumers). In the food web given alongside, rats are eaten by snakes and also by eagles, and snakes that eat rats are eaten by the eagles. This shows the interlinkage between different food chains, which together forms the food web (Fig. 17.8).

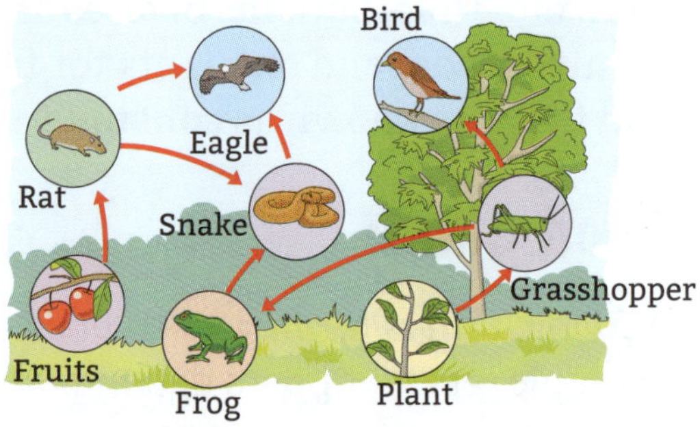

Fig. 17.8: A food web

Dependence of Plants on Animals

Not only do animals depend on plants, but plants also depend on animals in many ways. Insects and birds feed on the nectar found in the flowers of plants. This helps in the process of **pollination** of flowers, which leads to the reproduction of plants.

Fruits and seeds are produced after pollination. These are then eaten by animals and some seeds may stick to the fur or skin of animals.

When these animals move from one place to another, the seeds sticking to them may fall off or some seeds may be let out in animal droppings, giving rise to new plants. This process is known as the **dispersal** of seeds by animals.

Revise and Recall

Fill in the blanks.

1. The second layer from the top of a forest profile is ________________ layer. (canopy/emergent)
2. Multiple food chains are interlinked together to form a ________________. (food chain/food web)
3. ________________ of flowers leads to the reproduction of plants. (Pollination/Plucking)

Activity

Aim: To understand the food chain and food web

Materials required: A roll of string, picture cards of plants and animals (with a string to hang the cards around the neck of the students)

Procedure:

1. Ask the students to assemble in a circle.
2. One animal card is given to each student.
3. Students should wear the card around their necks.
4. Start the activity (from a plant) with the help of a volunteer.
5. The volunteer has to hold one end of the string roll and then pass the roll on to another student who represents his/her dependent to form a food chain.
6. Continue the same process until a web of strings is formed.

Conclusion: Each and every organism in an ecosystem is important and has a role to play. Every organism is dependent on another organism for food. If one organism is eliminated from the ecosystem, then there is an imbalance created due to which there is a probability of many other organisms getting eliminated.

USES OF FORESTS

Purification of Air

Photosynthesis takes place in all kinds of plants, trees and algae in a forest. We know that the process of photosynthesis releases oxygen used by plants and animals for breathing. After breathing in oxygen, plants and animals breathe out carbon dioxide. This is used by the plants during photosynthesis as it is required as a source of carbon for plants. In this way, a balance is formed between the amount of oxygen and carbon dioxide in the air.

Forests are also called the green lungs of nature. However, due to the exhaust gases from vehicles and fumes from factories, the level of carbon dioxide in the air is increasing. This increase in the level of carbon dioxide in the atmosphere has led to an increase in the temperature of the planet Earth. This is called **global warming**. If more and more trees are planted, they can keep the level of air pollution and global warming in check.

Plants and trees in a forest absorb water from the soil. Some of the absorbed water is lost by the plant through the stomata present on the underside of the leaves. This process is called **transpiration**. This water goes to the atmosphere in the form of water vapour, which helps in the water cycle and keeps the atmosphere cool.

Rainfall Due to Forests

Rainfall is dependent on forests. *Excess of water from the trees is released into the atmosphere in the form of water vapour by the process of* ***transpiration***. The water released in the form of water vapour from the forests helps in the formation of clouds by a process of **condensation**. Clouds undergo **precipitation** to form rain. The water vapour transpired from the forests keep the forests cool.

Water evaporates at a faster rate if there are no trees, thereby making the Earth devoid of water. The dead leaves that fall from the trees on the ground help retain water. The canopy of the trees prevents the rain from hitting the ground directly. The roots of the trees hold the soil and rainwater seeps into it, which helps to maintain the water table. The absence of forests and trees may lead to floods, soil erosion, depletion in the water table and poor rainfall.

Prevention of Soil Erosion

Soil erosion is the removal of the top layer of soil. This layer is fertile and the removal of this layer makes the land barren. The roots of the trees hold the soil together and help the water to infiltrate into the soil. In this way, soil erosion due to the runoff water and wind is prevented by the forests. Hence, trees act as windbreakers.

Uses of Forests in Our Daily Life

We completely depend on forests for our needs. Forests provide us with food, medicinal plants, honey, firewood, timber, rubber, spices, perfumes, oils, resins, natural dyes, etc. Forests are homes to many animals and provide food and shelter to them.

Ecotourism and jungle safaris are very popular these days. People like to spend their holidays in the lap of nature. This can be done by hiking, camping, going on safaris, etc.

This creates awareness about forests and animals and educates people about the importance of forests.

DESTRUCTION OF FORESTS

Deforestation *is the destruction of large amount of trees in a forest and overuse of forest resources*. The following are the reasons for deforestation:

- Construction of dams, highways and clearing of forests to convert them into cultivable land and residential areas
- The need for timber and medicinal plants, resulting in illegal logging and smuggling of the precious forest products
- Construction of resorts in and around forests, leading to their destruction
- Lack of awareness in people about the importance of forests
- Overgrazing in forests by cattle from nearby villages
- Forest fires during dry summer months and also due to human negligence
- Poaching or hunting of animals for their meat, skin and bones, causing a decrease in the number of animals and disturbance in the food chain

Science in Context

Smokejumpers are specially trained wildland firefighters who provide an initial attack response on wildfires. They are dropped to fire-infested areas from planes using parachutes to put off a forest fire. Smokejumpers are employed where vast forestlands are present. Russia and the United States of America have teams of smokejumpers.

Consequences of Deforestation

- With no plants and trees to hold the soil together, the soil gets washed away by strong winds and flowing water.
- Things such as wood, medicine and various other products, which we obtain from forests, would no longer be available if deforestation carries on indiscriminately.
- The most important consequence of deforestation is the change in climate. Without a forest cover, the amount of carbon dioxide will increase in the atmosphere. Being a greenhouse gas, it will aid in global warming, increasing the temperature on the Earth.
- Animals will lose their natural habitat and they might even die. This will eventually lead to extinction of different species.

CONSERVATION OF FORESTS

Forest conservation is the need of the hour. Even though forests are being destroyed due to human activity, forests should be conserved from further depletion for our own good.

So, steps must be taken to create awareness about the hazards of deforestation and preserving the rich resources of forests.

- Trees should be planted in wastelands where the forest cover is disappearing. *The plantation of trees in large numbers is called* ***afforestation***.
- People should be encouraged to plant more trees through programmes such as 'Vanamahotsava'.
- Awareness and education regarding the importance of forests should be given to people.
- Overgrazing by cattle should be prevented by providing sufficient pastures in the areas near forests.
- Illegal logging of trees for timber must be prevented.
- Conversion of forestland for the purpose of industrialization must be stopped.
- People who go on trekking and camping should be cautioned about the hazards of forest fires due to human negligence.
- Personnel in forest departments must be trained and equipped to control forest fires.
- Farmers must be educated to plan cultivation in their lands without cutting down trees.
- Every city should have a green patch reserved for developing parks.

Go Green

We should conserve our forests. One of the best ways through which we can contribute towards it is by limiting the use of forest products such as paper, timber, firewood, etc. and not wasting them. We should make wise use of paper, which is made by cutting trees, and not waste it. We should use both the sides of a paper.

Case Study: Joint Forest Management in Haryana

Many people living close to forests depend on them for firewood, medicinal plants and grazing their animals. Forests have become their only way to live and earn money, but excessive usage of forest products has a drastic effect on the forests.

So many plans have been implemented by government and non-governmental organizations to help these people and at the same time, conserve the forests for the future. One of the models that has been successfully implemented in Haryana is known as Joint Forest Management by the involvement of the Haryana Forest Department and the local communities by forming cooperatives. Training programmes are conducted to educate the people about the products of the forests and to conserve them for the future. Water harvesting methods are implemented for the growth of plants and trees. Different cooperatives depend on various products such as fodder, grasses, bamboo and other products to prepare ropes and bamboo products and for their animals to graze. Permits are issued for the cooperatives and also to keep a check on the activities inside the forests.

Keywords

Crown: The part of the tree above the stem that includes branches and leaves
Canopy: The uppermost tree branches of tall trees
Understorey: The layer below the canopy made up of branches at the lower level of the tree
Producers: Plants that can prepare their own food
Consumers: Animals that depend on plants for food
Decomposers: The microorganisms that convert the dead matter of plants and animals into simple substances
Food chain: A chain formed when one organism is eaten by another organism as food
Food web: Multiple food chains interlinked together
Deforestation: Large-scale destruction of forests
Afforestation: Planting trees to increase the forest areas
Flora: The plants of a particular region, habitat or geological period
Fauna: The animals of a particular region, habitat or geological period

Summary

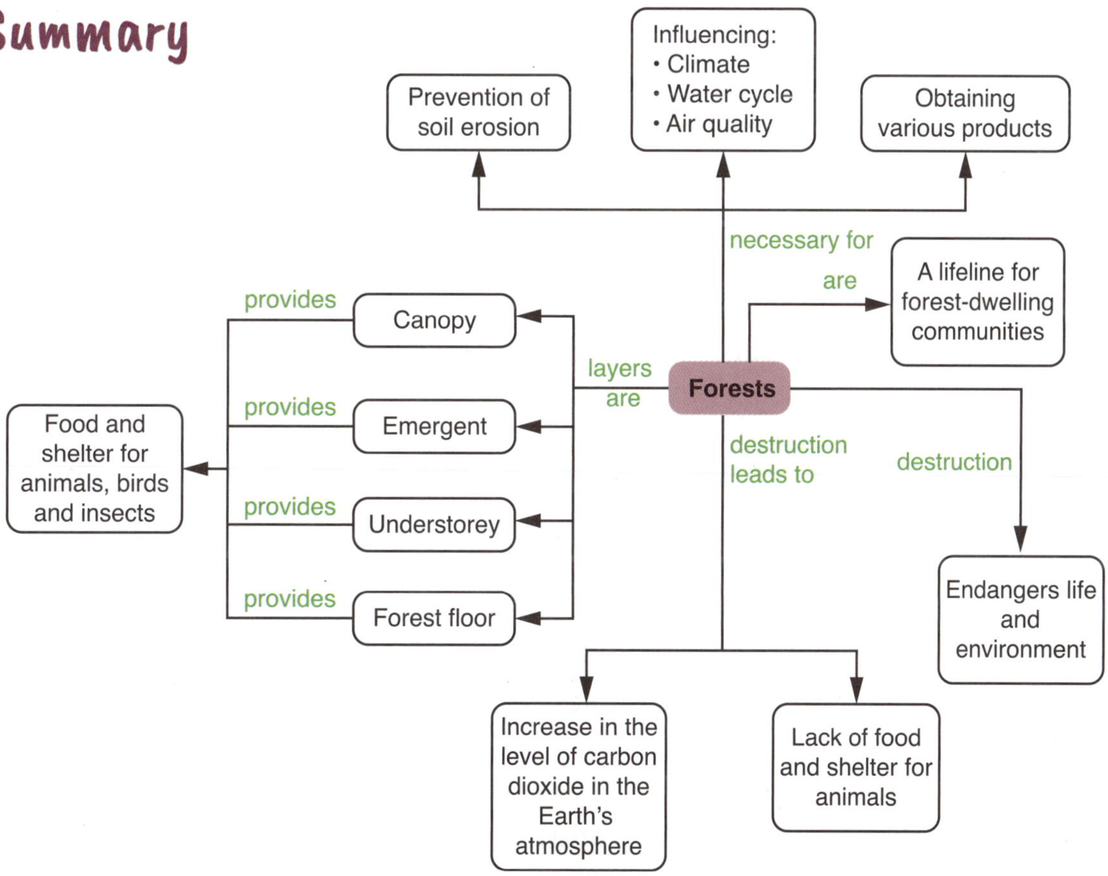

EXERCISE

A. Choose the correct option.

1. The layer of a forest that has dead and decaying material is the ___________.
   (a) forest floor (b) understorey (c) canopy (d) emergent layer
2. As a part of the water cycle, the trees in a forest absorb water through the roots and release it into the atmosphere in the form of ___________.
   (a) water vapour (b) oxygen (c) carbon dioxide (d) nitrogen
3. The canopy layer of a forest is formed by one of the following:
   (a) the trunks of trees (b) the crowns of trees
   (c) the roots of trees (d) All of the above
4. Which of the following can form food chains?
   (a) Rice grains, farmer, elephant (b) Rice grains, sparrow, eagle
   (c) Rice grains, mouse, cat (d) Both (b) and (c)
5. Which of the following acts as windbreakers?
   (a) Soil (b) Trees (c) Water (d) Light

B. Fill in the blanks.

1. In forests, all the kinds of animals ultimately depend for their food on the ___________________. (plants/air)
2. The topmost layer in a forest profile is called ___________________. (understorey/emergent)
3. An increase in the number of herbivores is kept in control by the ___________________. (carnivores/producers)
4. A forest floor has microorganisms that depend on dead matter the help in the cycle of ___________________. (nutrients/water)
5. In the layers of a forest, herbs are a part of the ___________________. (understorey/canopy)

C. State whether the following statements are true (T) or false (F).

1. Eagles and vultures decompose dead bodies of animals. ☐
2. Deforestation can lead to the extinction of animal species. ☐
3. Herbivores will have enough food if there is an increased number of carnivores in forests. ☐
4. Food chains can be linked together. ☐
5. A food chain includes both producers and consumers. ☐

D. Define the following terms.

1. Primary consumer
2. Secondary consumer
3. Scavengers
4. Dispersal of seeds
5. Global warming

E. Give reasons for the following.

1. We should worry about the issues related to forests far from us.
2. Deforestation may lead to floods.
3. Human negligence causes forest fire.
4. Forests help in maintaining the oxygen-carbon dioxide cycle.
5. Deforestation can increase the temperature of the Earth.

F. Answer the following questions briefly.

1. What is special about a forest floor?
2. How is a food chain formed? Give an example.
3. Write a note on the different types of consumers.
4. How do cattle destroy forests?
5. Why are forests called the green lungs of nature?

G. Answer the following questions in detail.

1. Explain food web with a suitable example.
2. Explain the uses of forests.
3. What are the effects of deforestation?
4. Suggest some ways to conserve forests.
5. Write a note on the cycle of nutrients.

COGNITIVE CORNER

Critical Thinking

1. Is growing only one type of fast-growing trees to regain a forest a better option than growing different types of trees?
2. Cycling of paper helps in conservation of forests. Justify.
3. What would happen if forests disappear?

Picture Study

Look at the diagram and name the layers of a forest in the space provided.

Project

Imagine a forest with depleting conditions of pollution and deforestation. Draw or paint the status of such a forest 50 years from now. **(C-7.1)**

Life Skills

1. Form a nature club in your school to know more about plants, animals and their interrelationships. Organize field trips to experience the beautiful nature and the benefits that we get from it. Organize tree-planting programmes on the World Environment Day. Look after these trees by regularly watering them. **(C-6.1)**
2. Make a list of all the products you use in your day-to-day life, which you think are products from the forests. Discuss the ways in which you can use these products more economically. **(C-6.1)**

15 LIFE ON LAND

Worksheet

13 CLIMATE ACTION

Wildfires release carbon dioxide (CO_2) and other greenhouse gases into the atmosphere and contribute to global heating. Particles and gases from burning biomass can be carried over long distances, affecting air quality in regions far away.

2 ZERO HUNGER

Many people's livelihoods, especially in developing countries, depend on intact forest resources. Therefore, an abnormally large wildfire can be disastrous.

1 NO POVERTY

The poor are often hit hardest by global heating caused by forest fires. They tend to be more heavily reliant on natural resources, such as firewood, forest-based plant food and medicines.

FOREST FIRES

12 RESPONSIBLE CONSUMPTION AND PRODUCTION

Unsustainable consumption of natural resources in many countries, and associated pollution, are contributing to global heating which in turn makes wildfires more likely.

3 GOOD HEALTH AND WELL-BEING

Smoke from wildfires causes air pollution and is bad for your health no matter where you live. Wildfires release harmful pollutants including particulate matter and toxic gases into the atmosphere.

6 CLEAN WATER AND SANITATION

Harmful particulates and black carbon from forest fires are carried in the air and enter water courses.

5 GENDER EQUALITY

Women and girls, especially in developing countries, tend to be more at risk during disasters such as forest fires. Studies have shown that disaster fatality rates are much higher for women than for men.

A. What can you do to prevent wildfires?

____

____

B. How does the interplay between different Sustainable Development Goals (SDGs) exemplify the interconnectedness of global challenges and solutions, demonstrating how progress in one goal can positively or negatively influence the advancement of others? Explain with an example.

____

____

____

18 Wastewater Management

Curricular Goals

- Understand the interface of science, technology and society **(CG-5)**
- Communicate questions, observations and conclusions related to science **(CG-7)**

Competencies

- Illustrate how science and technology can help to improve the quality of human life **(C-5.1)**
- Use scientific vocabulary to communicate science accurately in oral and written form, and through visual representation **(C-7.1)**
- Design and build simple models to demonstrate scientific concepts **(C-7.2)**

Let's Get Started

Water is an essential resource for the functioning of all life forms on our planet. A human body needs water for survival and growth. Our body itself comprises 70% water. Further, we also need water for all our household activities on a daily basis. In this way, water acts as a lifeline to us.

In the images given below, identify the activities that require water and write them in the space provided. Also, mention an alternative method of carrying out these activities such that water is conserved.

All the above activities need water. The water becomes dirty after it is used for such activities. This used water which becomes dirty and unfit for further use is called **wastewater**. Where does this water go after being used? It needs to be safely disposed off to avoid the stench from spreading and to prevent the pollution of our surroundings. Let us learn about wastewater, its sources, where it goes, its treatment, etc. in this chapter.

SOURCES OF WASTEWATER (SEWAGE)

Wastewater or sewage is produced due to human activities and natural causes such as the rain. The main contribution to sewage is from activities such as bathing, sanitary needs, cooking, farming, and washing utensils, clothes and vehicles.

This sewage water contains detergents, toxic chemicals, food wastes, paper, human faeces, plastics, metal objects, microorganisms, blood, human/animal tissues, etc. These kinds of materials present in wastewater are called **contaminants**.

Water is very important for plants. In agricultural practices, pesticides are used to protect crops from pests and weeds, and fertilizers are added to the soil for the better yield of crops. During rains or floods, water from agricultural fields mixed with pesticides may enter into the freshwater sources, thereby contaminating rivers and ponds.

As per the reports, industries are a major cause behind water pollution. They let off untreated wastewater into the nearby streams, rivers and seas. The wastewater from the industries may contain lubricant oil, paints, dye, chemicals and metals. These are also called **industrial effluents**. This act of letting the industrial effluents into the water is illegal. There is a Pollution Control Board that checks these kinds of activities.

Construction of buildings, mining for iron, gold, etc. leads to the generation of wastewater that contains cement, paints, metals and chemicals.

Due to an ever-increasing growth in population, large number of houses, hospitals, offices, industries, etc. are being constructed. This leads to the formation of sewage. Sewage contains sullage (kitchen) wastewater from hotels with huge amount of fats and oils. Blood and other tissues from patients in hospitals also contribute to the disease-causing microorganisms in sewage.

Abattoirs (slaughterhouses), animal farms and veterinary hospitals too contaminate water and contribute to sewage.

Nuclear plants use a lot of water as coolant. Hot water emerging from these plants is let off into seas and oceans, polluting these water sources.

One of the major sources of wastewater is domestic sewage from homes (Fig. 18.1).

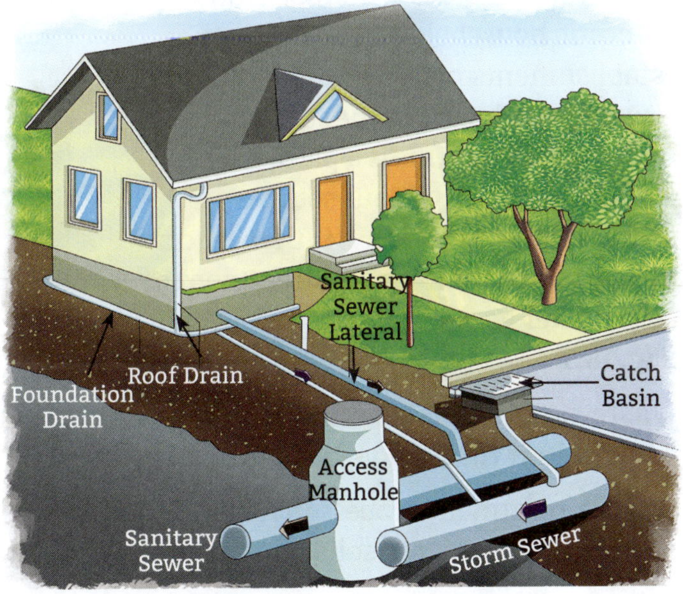

Fig. 18.1: Sewer system at homes

DISPOSAL OF WASTEWATER

Let us study how the wastewater is disposed off:

1. Wastewater from kitchen sink flows into the drainpipe and moves into the sewage pipeline.
2. The sewage pipeline forms a network of pipelines.
3. The wastewater that travels through these pipes and then joins the main sewer lines or the sewerage.
4. The junction of the sewerage from different homes of the street or lane has an opening, which can be used for the maintenance of the sewerage by the personnel from the city corporation. This opening is called a **manhole** (Fig. 18.2).
5. Further, wastewater flows to the main sewerage pipeline and goes to the wastewater treatment plant.
6. Rainwater from the roads flows into a separate pipeline called the **storm drain** (Fig. 18.3), which can be treated before letting it into the nearby water resources.

Fig. 18.2: A manhole

Fig. 18.3: A storm drain

TREATMENT OF SEWAGE IN CITIES AND TOWNS

Cities and towns have sewerage systems in place to carry the wastewater (Fig. 18.4). Sewage from domestic households, hotels and other establishments moves through the sewerage and reaches the sewage treatment plant. This is a place where wastewater from various sources is collected and treated. It is then let off to other water sources. The treatment of wastewater goes through different stages (Fig. 18.5).

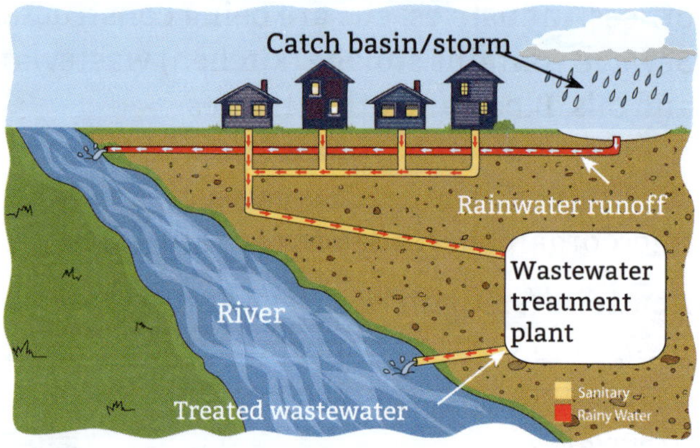

Fig. 18.4: Sewer system in cities

Wastewater is treated to remove the physical, chemical and biological contaminants present in it through various processes.

The pre-treatment process involves the sewage being sent through grids or vertical bars that can remove large solid substances such as metal cans, paper and plastic materials.

Primary treatment process: In this process, the sewage flows through the grit chamber very slowly so that the sand, pebbles and soil settle down at the bottom.

It is a mechanical process; the sewage flows into the settling tank or sedimentation tank where solid wastes such as faeces are allowed to settle down. Wastes such as soaps, oils and grease rise to the top of the wastewater. The waste material that settles down at the bottom is called the **sludge** and the floatable material is called the **scum**. The scum is then removed from the top using a skimmer. The sludge at the bottom is removed with a scraper every few days and treated further. The water that is left out is called the **clarified water**.

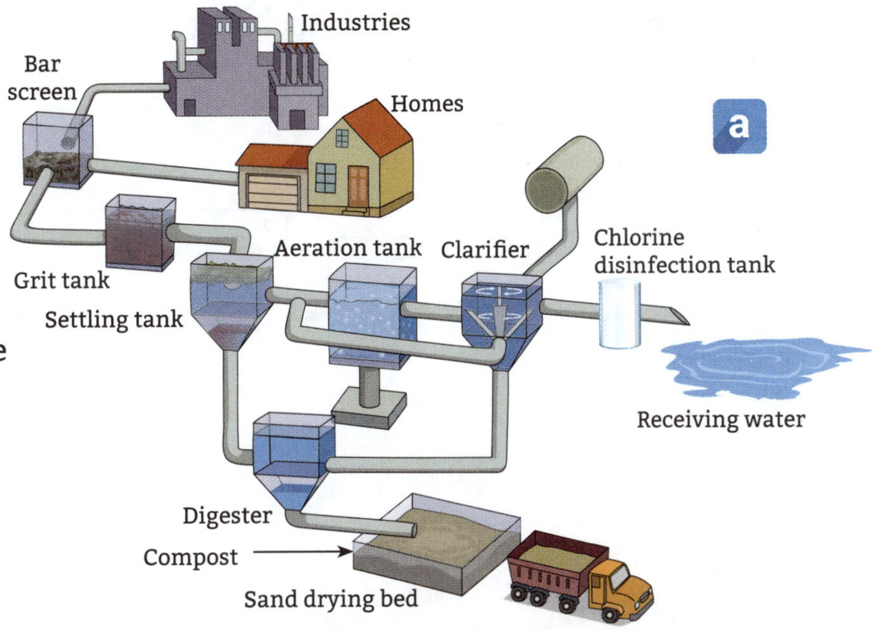

Fig. 18.5: Different stages of sewage treatment

Secondary treatment process: In the next process, biological or organic wastes that are still there in the clarified water are removed. It is a biological process. This is done by transferring the clarified water into an aeration tank where air blowers bubble air, which helps the aerobic bacteria to grow and feed on the organic contaminants such as food waste, faeces and other organisms. The microscopic organisms in this process produce **biogas**. Treated wastewater is then pumped into clarifier to allow any remaining organic sediment to settle out of the treated water flow. The leftover liquid waste is allowed to remain in tanks so that microscopic organisms settle down at the bottom. This is called the **activated sludge**.

The activated sludge contains 2% solids and 98% water. A part of the activated sludge is returned to the aeration tank to increase the bacterial concentration and accelerate the breakdown of the organic material. The remaining activated sludge is then left in sand-drying beds. When water evaporates, we get the dried sludge which can be used for making fertilizers or compost.

Tertiary treatment process: This is the last process of wastewater treatment in which the leftover liquid waste is treated with chlorine to remove the phosphorus compounds, nitrogen compounds and bacteria. It is a chemical process. Chlorine tablets are added to kill the germs. Chlorine acts as a disinfectant. The addition of chlorine to wastewater to kill the germs is called **chlorination**. Then, this water is let off into the water bodies.

The following flow chart shows the various stages in wastewater or sewage treatment (Fig. 18.6).

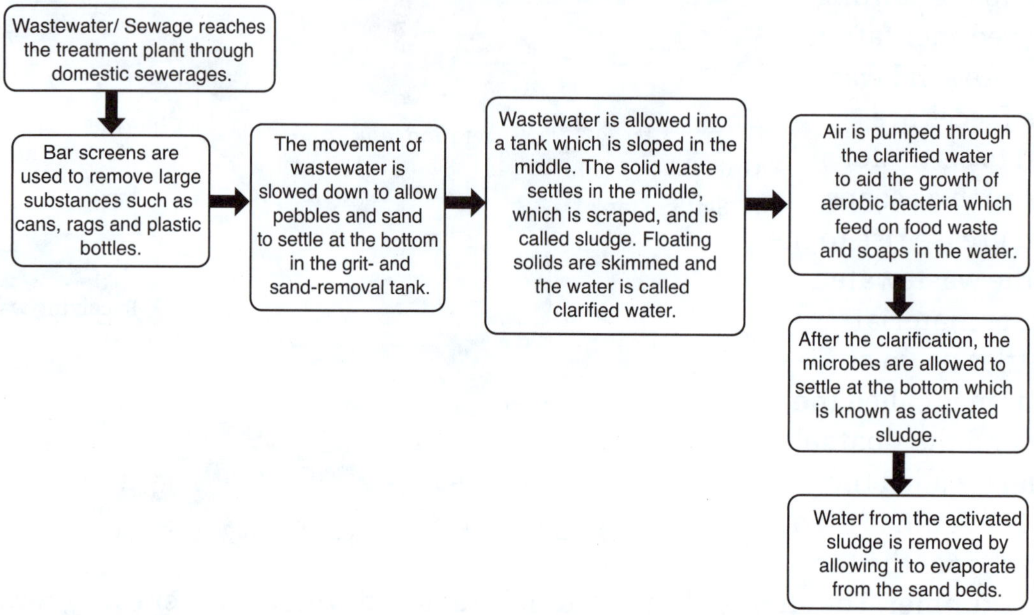

Fig. 18.6: A flow chart on the various stages involved in sewage treatment

Revise and Recall

Fill in the blanks.

1. The kinds of materials present in the wastewater are called ______________.
2. ____________________ are the major cause of water pollution.
3. Water is used as a coolant in the ____________________.
4. The main sewer pipelines are called ____________________.
5. Aerobic bacteria feed on organic matter and produce __________________.

EFFECTS OF IMPROPER SEWAGE MANAGEMENT

- Many places in our country have open drains in the streets. These serve as breeding places for mosquitoes. When mosquitoes multiply, they cause diseases such as malaria and *chikungunya*.
- Drains also attract a lot of flies and insects which feed on the refuse and spread diseases.

- Open drains get easily blocked by plastic bags and garbage dumped into them especially during monsoons. Blockage leads to overflow of the drains, growth of microorganisms and pests. All this causes unbearable stench too.
- Untreated wastewater or sewage contains nutrients which are beneficial for the growth of algae. If this untreated wastewater is released into the water bodies then it leads to an increase in the algal growth called **algal blooms**. This causes the depletion of oxygen in the water bodies, making them unable to support aquatic life. Such a condition is called **eutrophication**.
- Overflowing drains can contaminate wells and streams too.
- Defecation in the open becomes a breeding place for flies that feed on the excreta and spread diseases such as diarrhoea, dysentery, cholera, typhoid and hepatitis.

SANITATION AT PUBLIC PLACES

Sanitation is the hygienic practice of ensuring cleanliness of our surroundings to maintain good health. Sanitation can be maintained by the proper disposal of refuse or the waste produced due to human activities. This can be done by ensuring the proper usage of toilets, sewer systems, treatment of wastewater, safe disposal of garbage and implementing personal hygiene practices.

A few steps that can be taken for better sanitation are given below:

- People in rural and urban areas should be educated about sanitation.
- The government should provide monetary aid for the construction of proper sewerages.
- Sufficient toilets should be constructed in public places. If sanitation in such places is poor, diseases can spread fast as people travelling from one place to another can act as the carriers of diseases.
- Washbasins with clean water supply and soap should be provided.
- Proper dustbins should be provided for the disposal of refuse.
- Surroundings must be kept clean by not allowing water to stagnate because stagnated water can be a breeding place for mosquitoes and other insects.
- Garbage cans and public dustbins must be cleared every day in order to prevent diseases.
- Wastewater from various sources should be treated before it is let off into the water bodies for use.
- All the open drains should be covered.
- Precautions should be taken to prevent pollution of surface water and groundwater due to the leakages into the sewer systems.

METHODS OF SLUDGE MANAGEMENT

Some methods of sludge management are discussed below:

- Sludge can be incinerated[1] in sludge incinerators to convert it into ashes, which can be used for construction purposes or to supplement the nutrients in the soil (Fig. 18.7).
- Dewatering of the sludge can be done with the help of sludge-drying machines or it can be allowed to dry on sand beds where the water evaporates and percolates into the sand (Fig. 18.8). The leftover solid waste is used in the manufacture of fertilizers.

Word Web

[1]**Incineration:** The process of burning of organic waste materials found in the wastewater

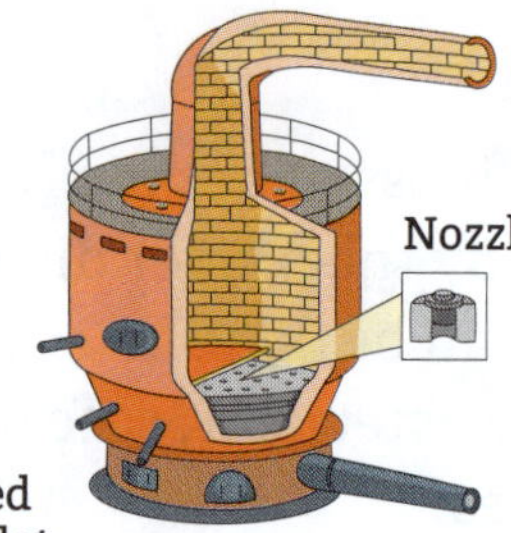

Fig. 18.7: Sludge incinerator

Fig. 18.8: Equipment for drying of sludge

- The gas produced by aerobic bacteria acting on the sludge in the aeration tank is used as a biogas, which is a source of energy for cooking and electricity.

ALTERNATE METHODS OF WASTEWATER MANAGEMENT

Some alternate methods of wastewater management are discussed below:

Septic Tank

Houses in the villages are far away and too few, so it is uneconomical to build a sewage system in such areas. One of the alternate methods is to build septic tanks (Fig. 18.9). In this system, sewage from houses flows through drains and into underground tanks made of cement and stones.

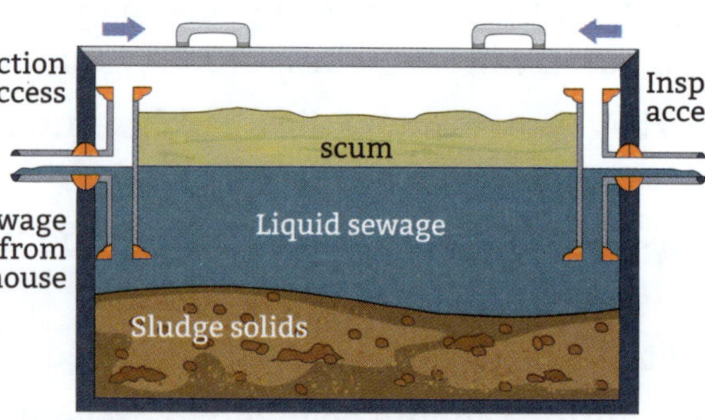

Fig. 18.9: A septic tank

The solid waste in the sewage settles down at the bottom. Anaerobic bacteria in the tank decompose the solid waste. Wastewater then moves out of the perforated pipes into the soil and percolates into the soil. It then gets filtered through the pores of the soil and joins the groundwater.

Production of Biogas from Wastewater

Animal excreta and plant wastes are made into a slurry by mixing with water in a biogas plant (Fig. 18.10). This flows into an underground tank where anaerobic bacteria act on the slurry to produce biogas. This is then used for cooking and lighting purposes.

Fig. 18.10: A domestic biogas plant

Chemical Toilets

A chemical toilet is a portable toilet facility which can be used as a temporary toilet in aeroplanes and at places where a sewage system is not available (Fig. 18.11). In such toilets, dilute chemicals are used instead of water to act on human waste. The waste from toilets is dumped out at regular intervals.

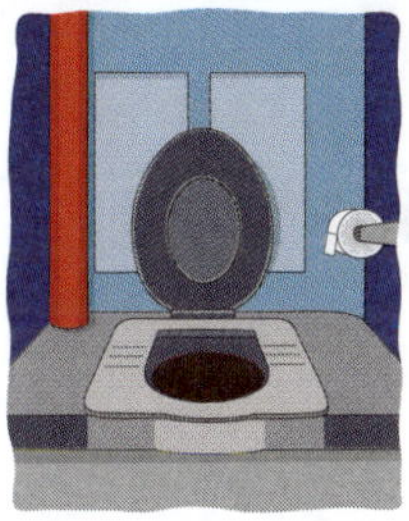

Fig. 18.11: A chemical toilet

CONTROL OF SEWAGE AT HOMES

- Sewage generation can be minimized by monitoring what is thrown in the drain.
- The disposal of cooking oil and fats down the drain leads to blockage. Fats and oils harden and block pipes which is hazardous. Oils and fats must always be disposed off in dustbins.
- Chemicals such as paints, solvents, insecticides, motor oil and medicines may kill decomposer microbes that help purify water. So, these must never be thrown down the drain.
- Used tea leaves, solid food remains, soft toys, cotton, napkins, etc. should also be thrown into the dustbin. These wastes choke the drains. They do not allow free flow of oxygen. This hampers the degradation process of the garbage with the help of microorganisms.

Freshwater is a finite and irreplaceable resource. It is renewable only if managed well. As responsible citizens, we must be sensitive towards our water sources and the different ways in which we consume water. We must take initiatives to conserve water sources and prevent wastage and pollution of water.

Keywords

Wastewater: The used water that enters drains from bathrooms, toilets and kitchens

Contaminants: The kinds of materials present in the wastewater

Sanitation: The hygienic practices that help us maintain good health and cleanliness in our surroundings

Sewers: The network of pipes that carries the wastewater from homes

Sewerage: The pipes that carry the wastewater from homes to wastewater treatment plants

Manhole: An opening at the junction of a sewerage

Sludge: The waste material that settles down at the bottom of the settling tank

Scum: The waste material which floats in the settling tank

Clarified water: The water that is left after the removal of sludge and scum

Summary

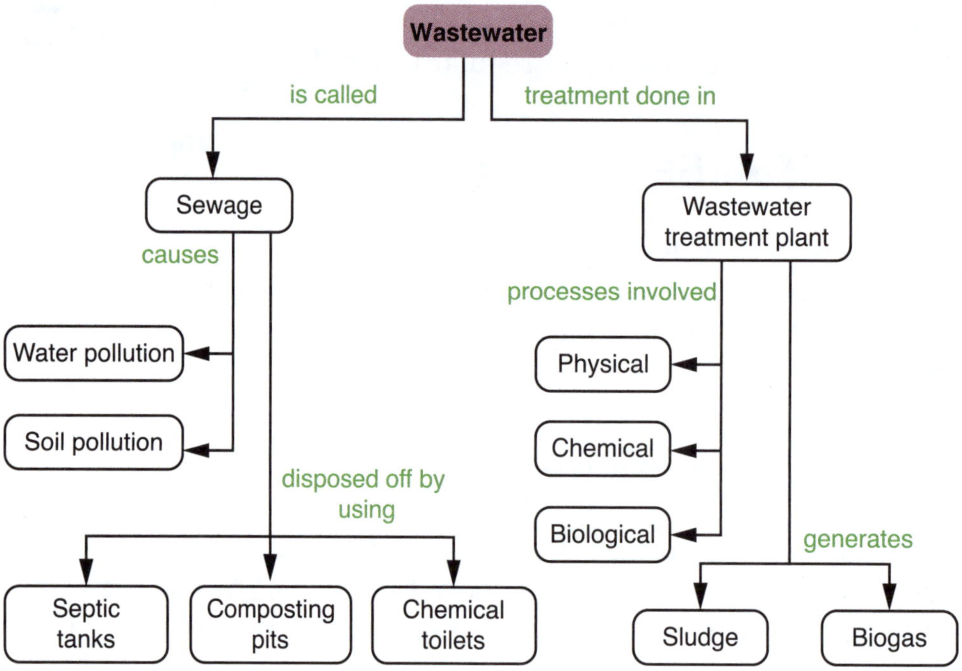

EXERCISE

W

ia

A. Choose the correct option.

1. In the second step of the wastewater treatment plant, the speed of the incoming wastewater is decreased to
   (a) allow the sand, grit and pebbles to settle.
   (b) allow large objects to settle.
   (c) allow rags, plastic packets and cans to settle.
   (d) All of the above
2. Which one of the following is not a method of sewage disposal?
   (a) Septic tanks (b) Composting pits
   (c) Chemical toilets (d) Aerator
3. Which of the following can be used in the production of biogas?
   (a) Activated sludge (b) Sludge
   (c) Clarified water (d) All of the above
4. Which one of the following is used for the disinfection of wastewater?
   (a) Chlorine (b) Pumping of air
   (c) Oxygen (d) Biogas
5. Which of the following is an organic contaminant?
   (a) Polythene covers (b) Chemicals
   (c) Glass bottles (d) Food waste

B. Fill in the blanks.

1. The junction of sewers from homes is called ____________________. (manhole/sewerage)
2. The microorganisms which help in wastewater treatment settle at the bottom of the tank to form ____________________. (activated sludge/sludge)
3. The treatment of wastewater basically includes the removal of ____________________. (contaminants/water)
4. Large objects and garbage in the wastewater are removed by passing them through the ____________________. (bar screen/incinerator)
5. The activity of bacteria on the sludge causes ____________________. (decomposition/contamination)

C. State whether the following statements are true (T) or false (F).

1. Treated wastewater can be let off into the sea and oceans. ☐
2. Sewage is made up of solid waste suspended in water. ☐
3. Activated sludge is decomposed by bacteria to produce biogas that can be used in the production of electricity. ☐
4. In an open drain, fats can clog the pores in the soil, affecting the filtering of water through it. ☐
5. Plastic covers should be disposed down the drains; it is the safest disposal method. ☐

D. Define the following terms.

1. Sewage
2. Scum
3. Sludge
4. Industrial effluents
5. Clarified water
6. Contaminants

E. Give reasons for the following.

1. Clarified water is not fit for drinking.
2. Treated water does not harm aquatic life.
3. Sewage causes soil pollution.
4. Incinerated sludge residue can be used as plant nutrients.
5. Industrial effluents must be removed before releasing it to drains.

F. Answer the following questions briefly.

1. What is wastewater?
2. What happens in the secondary stage of wastewater treatment?
3. Explain the different types of contaminants with examples.
4. How is sludge disposed?
5. Draw a septic tank and explain how it works.
6. Explain the sewage system at homes in cities.
7. Write a note on the sources of contamination.

G. Answer the following questions in detail.

1. Mrs Mathur disposes of all the waste into the drain. How would you educate her about the effects of her negligence on the sewage treatment?
2. Schematically represent the process of wastewater treatment.
3. How can you control the generation of sewage at homes?
4. Explain the importance of sanitation.

COGNITIVE CORNER

Critical Thinking

1. You might have seen the air vents from a sewer line in your homes. What is the purpose of that?
2. Why is sanitation important? Mention two ways by which awareness for the need of sanitation in public places can be created.

Picture Study

Identify the following structures that help in the disposal of wastewater.

____

____

Project

1. Visit your city or town sewage treatment plant. Have a guided tour for better understanding of the sewage treatment and prepare a report. **(C-7.1)**
2. What is '*Sulabh* International' and how have they tackled the problem of environment sanitation? **(C-7.1)**
3. As a part of Eco Club activity, make a miniature sewage water plant. Explain the processes involved in its functioning and create awareness among people. **(C-7.2)**

Life Skills

Rainfall is the source of freshwater for all of us. In cities, there is higher amount of concrete due to houses, buildings, shopping malls, etc. There is less amount of soil receiving rainfall, which leads to very little rainwater percolating into the soil or reaching the water table. The rainwater that falls on buildings goes through the pipes from the roofs into a storm drain. So, the rainwater goes waste and this wastage of water can be avoided. Through the method of rainwater harvesting, water can be saved for the times of water scarcity. Talk to your neighbours, friends and parents to create awareness in them about rainwater harvesting. **(C-5.1)**

Worksheet

In India, heavy rainfall often causes urban flooding due to overwhelmed drainage systems. Urbanization, such as concrete roads and buildings, leaves little ground for rain absorption, causing surface runoff and water wastage. Remarkably, ancient Indian urban planning included sophisticated water drainage systems, such as the Great Bath of the Indus Valley Civilization (2600 BCE), which managed water flow and flooding, showcasing historical inventiveness and skills in addressing similar challenges.

A waterlogged area

Rainwater being discharged into rivers by drains

Handpump using groundwater

A. Using the Internet, learn more about the water drainage system used in the Indus Valley civilization and write a short note on it.

____

____

B. How can governments solve the issue of waterlogging during monsoon by combining the ancient indigenous knowledge and the modern technology?

____

____

____

____